EDUCATIONAL DEVELOPMENT OF SLUM WOMEN

EDUCATIONAL DEVELOPMENT OF SLUM WOMEN

Dr. Kishori Dash
M.A., M.Ed., M.Phil., Ph.D.
Sr. Lecturer, RCET, Rourkela (Orissa)

Commonwealth

Educational Development of Slum Women

Edition **2027**

ISBN 81-311-0099-5

Published by :
COMMONWEALTH PUBLISHERS (P) LTD.
4831/24, Govind Lane,
Ansari Road, Darya Ganj,
New Delhi - 110002
Ph. : 23272541, 23242541
e-mail : commonwealthpublishers2016@gmail.com

Distributed by :
ARJUN PUBLISHING HOUSE
4831/24, Govind Lane,
Ansari Road, Darya Ganj,
New Delhi - 110002
Ph. : 23272541, 23242541
e-mail : arjunbooks2001@gmail.com

Laser Typesetting by :
Dimple Computers
Delhi

Printed at :
Milan Enterprises
Delhi

DEDICATED
TO
THE DIVINE MOTHER
AND
THE DEPRIVED

ACKNOWLEDGEMENTS

In the course of my research work and publication of this volume I am indebted to several persons of various capacities. Without whom this endeavour of mine would not have seen the light of the day. And now it is time to talk of heart and express a few words of gratitude. I shall forever be indebted to my mother, who, despite being illiterate and ailing brought me up without allowing the sense of gender discrimination to creep into my psyche. With her pain staking efforts and support even in her eighties, her role has been seminal in keeping my spirit high. It is with venerable sentiments that I wish to express my heart felt gratitude to my beloved father Late Jayalal Dash and dearest friendly brother Late Basant Dash, who had been the source of inspiration for this research endeavour. Although they are not here to see their dreams coming true, I am sure they are with me in their ethereal forms.

I expatiate my unfathomable feelings of gratitude to my guide Dr. N. Pradhan, Reader and Head, Department of Ednal. Admn., Faculty of Edn. & Psy., The M.S. University of Baroda, for his insightful and sustained guidance, critical comments and expert suggestions during my research work and encouragement to publish of this Doctoral Thesis. I sincerely acknowledge his support, which has been instrumental in my efforts to reach the goal.

My sincere thanks also hold for the entire RSS family and the family of SVP, Rourkela, for their help, co-operation and prompt services in providing me with the relevant data for my research, without which my study would not have been completed successfully.

I owe a word of thanks with an abysmal sense of gratitude to the dedicated volunteers of RSS, the Rourkelites, and above all the deprived slum-dwellers, who helped me in multiple ways during my study in the field for years together. They have provided me incredible and insightful learning experiences for a meaningful living along with research knowledge and have invoked within me a sense of enormous generosity and goodwill. The slum-dwellers and the selfless volunteers have taught me the joy of commitment and voluntarism, and essence of prioritising the larger collective intent over individual ego.

I am very much grateful to Government of Orissa for enabling me to avail study leave in order to complete my research work. I am also thankful to my principal, colleagues and students for their support and best wishes for this academic endeavour.

I would further like to extend my gratefulness to Prof. R.G. Kothari, Head, CASE & Dean, Faculty of Edn. & Psy., Prof. S.M. Joshi, Ex-Dean, Faculty of Edn. & Psy., Prof. D.R. Goel, Ex-Head, CASE, and other staff members and fellow scholars of the faculty of Edn. & Psy., The M.S.University of Baroda for their academic support and encouragement at different points of time during my research work.

I am thankful to the librarians of both CASE and Hansa Mehta Library, and also the librarians of some other parts of the country for extending a helping hand and allowing me to make use of

their libraries. I also acknowledge my indebtedness to the authors of different works I have referred to, for my research work to make it bonafide.

My sisterly Banaja and her lovely daughter Anvesha provided me a home away from home during my study at Baroda. I am thankful to them for their caring and sharing. I am equally thankful to Smt. Maya Vyas, Warden, S.D. Hall of M.S. University, Baroda and her entire family for their generosity in completion of my research study in time.

The timely help and encouragement of Dr. Ashutosh Biswal, Lecturer in CASE, counted immensely in completion of my thesis in time. To him, I owe more than the customary acknowledgement.

The enlightening discussions held with the organisers of National and State (ORISSA) BGVS like M.P. Parameswaran, K. Krishnakumar, Vinod Raina, Dr. Madan Pradhan, Dr. S. Mudali, B.N. Dash, S.K. Biswas and many others at different points of time have provided an impetus to my research and encouragement me to get this volume published. I acknowledge their intellectual support with thanks.

I am very much thankful to Sri Asit Tripathy, IAS, Sri D.N. Das, Director, S.V.P., Rourkela and Late Dr. Usha Kiran Sharma who shared their insight and guided me in various ways during the conceptualisation of this academic endeavour.

My sincere thanks are also due to Gopal, Prasanna, Chitra Madam, Bichitra, Sabita, Anu and many others for their willing help and co-operation during data collection for this study.

I am thankful to Sri Aurobindo Behara, IAS and Dr. Aurobindo Padhi, IAS, for their generosity and brotherly disposition during the tenure of my study.

I also owe a word of thanks to various Government, Non-Government and Voluntary Organisations of the City, State as well as the Nation for their overwhelming co-operation and help in providing me with the valuable data and resources for my research work.

Stuti didi, Bina nani and Reena who have kept their unshaken faith in me and have taken a great pride in my research work as well as publication of this volume. I find words deficient to express my feelings towards them for their support and inspiration for which I am thankful.

I would sincerely like to thank Bhuban Pradhan for employing his typing skills with patience and care, and my nephew Ajit and his friend Ranjit for their moral and technical support to complete this endeavour.

I also take this opportunity to express with a sense of pride and humility, my profound gratitude to my reverend teacher Late, Prof. G.K. Samantaray for his aura of inspirations and blessings which count a lot in my academic growth and research endeavour in this field unto his death.

I am very much thankful to the Commonwealth Publishers, New Delhi (India) for venturing this piece of Doctoral Research.

Finally, my thanks also hold for those who have gone unacknowledged over here.

Kishori Dash

CONTENTS

List of Tables

List of Maps

ABBREVIATIONS

AD	—	Anno Domini (in the year of our Lord)
ADM	—	Additional District Magistrate
AEC	—	Adult Education Centre
BC	—	Before Christ
BCG	—	Bacillus Calmette Guerin (Anti T.B. Vaccine)
BCS	—	Basti Chetana Samiti
BDO	—	Block Development Officer
BGVS	—	Bharat Gyan Vigyan Samiti
BFW	—	Breast-Feeding Week
BPL	—	Below Poverty Line
CASE	—	Centre of Advanced Study in Education
CDPO	—	Child Development Programme Officer
CE	—	Continuing Education
CEC	—	Continuing Education Centre
CSWI	—	Committee on Status of Women in India
DAE	—	Directorate of Adult Education
DI	—	District Inspector
DIG	—	Deputy Inspector General
DME	—	Directorate of Mass Education
DOE	—	Department of Education
DPEP	—	District Primary Education Programme
DPI	—	Director, Public Instruction
DWCRA	—	Development of Women and Children in Rural Area
EB	—	Environment-Building
EE	—	External Evaluation
EER	—	External Evaluation Report
EOIO	—	Each one Teach one
FGD	—	Focused Group Discussion
FICAE	—	Fourth International Conference on Adult Education

FLAW	—	Functional Literacy For Adult Women
GC	—	General Caste
GIDSL	—	Giri Institute of Developmental Study, Lucknow
GNP	—	Gross National Product
GOI	—	Government of India
HDR	—	Human Development Report
HSL	—	Hindustan Steel Limited
HRD	—	Human Resource Development
IAEA	—	Indian Adult Education Association
ICDS	—	Integrated Child Development Scheme
ICMR	—	Indian Council for Medical Research
ID	—	Independence Day
IDS	—	International Development Strategy
IGH	—	Ispat General Hospital
IIPS	—	International Institute of Population Science
IJAE	—	Indian Journal of Adult Education
ILD	—	International Literacy Day
ILS	—	Inspat Lower Secondary
IMR	—	Infant Mortality Rate
IPCL	—	Improved Pace and Content of Learning
IRDP	—	Integrated Rural Development Programme
ITDA	—	Integrated Tribal Development Agency
IWD	—	International Women's Day
JSS	—	Jana Siksha Sansthan
KCEDT	—	Karnataka Cultural and Educational Development Trust
KRP	—	Key Resource Person
KSSP	—	Kerala Shastra Sahitya Parisad
MHRD	—	Ministry of Human Resource Development
MIDS	—	Madras Institute of Development Studies
MIS	—	Monitoring Information System
MP	—	Madhya Pradesh
MPFL	—	Mass Programme for Functional Literacy
MT	—	Master Trainer
NA	—	Not Applicable
NAC	—	Notified Area Council
NAEP	—	National Adult Education Programme
NCAER	—	National Council of Applied Economic Research

NCERT — National Council of Educational Research & Training
NCW — National Committee for Women
NCWE — National Committee on Women's Education
NCWE — National Council for Women's Education
NFE — Non-Formal Education
NGO — Non-Governmental Organisation
NHP — National Health Policy
NIEPA — National Institute of Educational Planning and Administration
NLM — National Literacy Mission
NLMA — National Literacy Mission Authority
NPE — National Policy on Education
NSS — National Service Scheme
NSSO — National Sample Survey Organisation
NYK — Nehru Yuvak Kendra
OBC — Other Backward Caste
ORG — Operation Research Group
PHC — Primary Health Centre
PL — Post Literacy
PLP — Post Literacy Programme
PTG — Primitive Tribal Group
RD — Republic Day
RDA — Rourkela Development Authority
RFLP — Rural Functional Literacy Programme
RGH — Rourkela Government Hospital
RMS — Rourkela Majdoor Sabha
RP — Resource Person
RSP — Rourkela Steel Plant
RSS — Rourkela Saksharata Samiti
SAIL — Steel Authority of India Limited
SAMU — Sakshar Muzaffarpur
SC — Scheduled Caste
SDMO — Sub-Divisional Medical Officer
SLMA — State Literacy Mission Authority
SM — Sishu Mela
SMPTB — Special Multi Purpose Tribal Block
SPIESR — Sardar Patel Institute of Economic and Social Research
SRC — State Resource Centre

SSA	—	Sarva Siksha Abhiyan
ST	—	Scheduled Tribe
SVP	—	Shramik Vidya Peeth
SUPW	—	Socially Useful and Productive Work
THRTIB	—	Tribal & Harijan Research-Cum-Training Institute, Bhubaneswar
THSE	—	Teacher's Handbook of Social Education
TLC	—	Total Literacy Campaign
UA	—	Urban Agglomeration
UBS	—	Urban Basic Service
UD	—	Utkal Divas
UEE	—	Universalisation of Elementary Education
UGC	—	University Grant Commission
UN	—	United Nations
UNDP	—	United Nations Development Programme
UNESCO	—	United Nations, Educational Scientific and Cultural Organisation
UNPC	—	United Nations Population Commission
UP	—	Uttar Pradesh
UPE	—	Universalisation of Primary Education
URS	—	Urban Revamping Scheme
VI	—	Volunter Instructor
WAD	—	World Aids Day
WDR	—	World Development Report
WPD	—	World Population Day
ZSS	—	Zilla Saksharata Samiti

GLOSSARY

Adivasi — Scheduled Tribe
Ahuti — Sacrifice
Alpana — Hand Painting on the ground made of liquid rice paste
Anganwadi — Child Care Centre run in the court yard of the volunteer
Badi — Unfried dry food articles made of different types of pulses
Bal-mela — Children's fair
Bal-sabha — Children's Meeting
Balwadi — Child Care Centre
Bapa Maa-nka-payen — For Father and Mother
Basti Chetana Samiti — Slum Awareness Society
Basti Safai Karyakram — Cleaning Programme of Slum
Biradari — Family
Bhobi — Sister-in-law
Chetana Kendra — Centre for awareness
Danda Nachha — Dance with Wooden Sticks (a typical folk dance of Orissa)
Dasi — Slave Girl
Didi — Elder Sister
Dubni — Small Pot (Bowl)
Ghasaphoola — Flower of grass
Guru — Teacher
Gyan Vigyan Samiti — Society for Knowledge and Science
Handia — Country Liquor made of rice
Hita Katha — Healthy Talk
Janma Mati — Mother Land
Khawuish — Will
Khandani Family — Royal Family
Maa — Mother
Mahila Kala Yatha — Procession on foot by Women
Mahila Jagruti Talim — Women's Awareness and Leadership Training

Muduku	—	**Salty fried food articles made of the power of rice and pulses**
Murhi	—	**Puffed rice**
Naba Taranga	—	**New Wave**
Nai Talim	—	**Basic Education**
Nani	—	**Elder Sister**
Paon Ki Juti	—	**Foot Wear**
Police Abom Apana	—	**Police and you**
Prabhat Pheri	—	**Morning Circumambulation for a cause**
Pudupulaxmi	—	**Thrift Group**
Purdah	—	**Veil**
Rangoli	—	**Floral pattern made of rice flour and other couloured power on festive occasions**
Reja	—	**Women Labourer**
Saheli	—	**Friend**
Saksharata	—	**Literacy**
Saksharata Mela	—	**Literacy Fair**
Sakshara Sahara, Bikasita Sahara	—	**Literate City, Developed City**
Samachar	—	**News**
Samata	—	**Equality**
Sambhab	—	**Possible (Name of a Cultural Troop)**
Sankalp	—	**Oath (Name of a cultural organisation)**
Sati	—	**Practice of widow immolating herself on husband's funeral pyre**
Sevak	—	**Servant (Male)**
Sevika	—	**Servant (Female)**
Seva Sadan	—	**House of Service**
Shakti	—	**Power**
Spandan	—	**Heart Beating (Name of a Socio-Cultural Organisation)**
Tola	—	**Hamlet with in a village or even in a town**
Uttara Saksharata	—	**Post Literacy**
Zenana	—	**Women**

1

INTRODUCTION

INTRODUCTION

India, the greatest democracy of the world is a land of great variety in terrain, race, language, religion and culture. A very large country, the seventh largest in the world, India sprawls about 3,219 Km. from the icy heights of the Himalayas in north to the tip of Kanyakumari (Cape Comorin), washed by the waves of the Indian ocean in south. It spreads 2,977 Km from east to west. The country's 5,689 km. of coastline, 15,168 Km. of area encompasses geographical conditions, climate, scenery, and people as diverse as those in Europe or America. India ranks second in the world with respect to population. According to the 2001 Census, population of India is 102,70,15,247 (Female—49,57,38,169 and Male—53,12,77,078). The density of population is 324 per square kilometer. (Census, 2001).

Efficiency of a democratic government depends on its educated citizens as because education brings individual and social maturity. The acculturating role of education brings a change in human behaviour, and refines sensitivities and perceptions that contribute towards national cohesion, a scientific temper and independence of mind and spirit. Education has to cater to the goals of socialism, secularism and democracy that are enshrined in our Constitution.

Education serves as an instrument of social change, and is a unique investment in the present and the future as it develops man-power for different levels of economy. "Education is not a profit-making, business, but a costly one; nay, even the best attainments of it are always unprofitable, in any terms of coin. No nation ever made its manufactures by its practical knowledge, yes; but its noble scholarship, its noble philosophy and its noble art, are always to be bought as a treasure, not sold for a livelihood."(Ruskin, 1926).

Education is also the substratum on which development flourishes, and provides guarantee of the principle of national self-reliance and self-efforts that aims at elimination of poverty and creation of conditions for active and greater political, economic and social participation of the poor, the downtrodden and the under-privileged.

If India is to progress, our core task lies in developing the under-developed and the downtrodden, remote, tribal and rural areas and urban slums into effective unit of modern economy, and the integrated development of women, especially the neglected and the backward women of the society. Integrated development attempts to solve problems in a comprehensive manner covering every aspect of life, like production, health and nutrition, co-operation, communication, skilled and trained manpower, because "knowledge, information and skills are increasingly being regarded as the major weapons in the crusade for supremacy on the Economic Front". (Rajput, 1998).

The University Education Commission (1948) has rightly remarked : "There cannot be an educated people without educated women. If general education had to be limited to men or to women, that opportunity should be given to women for then it would definitely be passed onto the next generation." Because, women education is considered to be more important than men and the key to modernisation and economic development of the society.

PROVISION FOR EDUCATIONAL DEVELOPMENT OF WOMEN

Educational Development of a nation is the key to its prosperity and welfare. It has been proved in many countries that no investment is likely to yield greater returns than investment in human resources, of which the most important is education. Strictly speaking, it is the foundation on which the edifice of a nation is erected.

Realising the essence of educational development among women as one of the important indicator of national development, provisions have been made accordingly at different points of time in history throughout the globe.

PROVISION ABROAD

The role of American and British Women's Right Movement during 1820's is remarkable with regards to enhance and develop educational status of women all over the world.

Till about 1825 education of women in America as well as in England was a thing of "Shreds and Patches". The conception of the women's rights movement is often traced to the first Women's Rights Convention held in Seneca Falls, New York in 1848. However, the origin of the American Women's movement can be traced to the involvement of middle-class women in the moral reform, educational development, temperance and abolition movements between1820–1850.

These age-long ideas also dominated minds of the Japanese in the days of feudalism under the Tokugawa regime. Very few women in Japan were allowed to go to Terakoya to receive the elementary knowledge of reading and writing. This condition continued till the early seventies of the last century after which they abandoned the feudalistic idea of considering women as inferior by nature to men (Black and Cottrell, 1981). But during the past two decades due to many developments and efforts to involve women in Education, women's educational level has improved substantially in higher education. (Hara, 1984)

In Phillippine, opportunism plays an important role in the policies of Philipino Government towards women's education and the development of their families (Beers, 1994). Bautists (1994) has mentioned the causes of non-schooling of Philippine girls in her article "Philipina Girl" that `the interaction between political, educational and economic policies that were not supportive of the majority of Philipino families who live in poverty combined with deeply entrenched social and cultural factors complicate the situation of Philipina girls, who already live a difficult and burdened life. She also points to the parents and the society at large as having an ambivalent attitude towards childhood and girlhood. (Beers, 1994)

Despite non-uniformity in status among the Philipino women, they have improved by having taken advantage of educational opportunities which the law and the society have made available to them. As a result they have been able to raise their literacy rate, as high as primitive and medieval Christianity enlarged 90 per cent women education after the renaissance. The objectives and method of women education were also changed. While renaissance changed the curriculum of education, the reformation changed its nature for women's development. A women's movement also developed in Britain about the same time as that of American Women's movement by the middle-class women. This movement was directed towards employment, charity, moral, educational, legal (electoral) reform between 1840 and 1870 (Everett, 1981). Prior to this women's movement Martin Luther was the first to advocate Universal Compulsory Education for both the sexes during the fifteen century, while John Khox advocated the same thing in Scotland at the end of fifteen century. Before the beginning of the Seventh Century there was not a single separate school in England for girls. A very few convents admitted girls here and there. The girls were not admitted either to the elementary school or to the grammar school. People showed much astonishment when Red Maid's school was started at Bristol in 1627. Though Luther had advocated Universal Elementary Education long back in 1500, it was only after passing of the Education Act of 1870 that universal education for both the sexes specially girls was enforced in England which is accredited to the sincere efforts of the Women's Movement in Britain.

In the continent of Europe, the stage of women education was still worse. The ideal of housewifeliness and submission to the male or the husband was very much encrusted in the minds of the Germans to make it easy for them to provide openings for education of their women. Rousseau's teaching in France retarded progress and it was only after 1848 as an impact of French Revolution that opportunities were given to women in Europe for their educational development. (Evertt, 1981)

Kenya formed no exception to this rule. Gender-role and status of the women, division of labour within the home, the home environment itself as well as the physical and psychological security of a girl child within a school environment are other factors which act as depressants to girls, education. In spite of a considerable decline in disparity and socio-cultural constraints of the women, education in Kenya has become a National Concern (Munyakho, 1994). As a result a considerable decline in the disparity in the status of boys and girls could be seen, and the country has almost achieved a 50-50 enrolment rate among girls and boys in primary education and in over all educational attainment.

The status of women in Nigeria is almost same as the women of Kenya. The literacy rate among adult women is still over 50 per cent in Nigeria. Although there are a number of constraints faced by the Women of Nigeria with regards to their educational development, their government is concerned about their development by making provisions in the educational programmes like *(i)* basic education programme supporting the family, *(ii)* expansion of initial education services for the educated women, and *(iii)* existence of three educational models side by side traditional, formal and religious for the masses through education department. As a result, there has been a conspicuous development in women in the field of education.

In Bangladesh, although the women are eligible to vote as well as to contest and hold office in any publicly elected body, the voting rights are seldom exercised properly by the women due to their low level of literacy, deficient political awareness, and social restrictions. The social motivation for participation of girls in education is extremely poor (Rao, 2000), which has become a major constraint for the government to get success in any of the development programme in Bangladesh. Despite social non-cooperation to the government, there was an increase in the number of female teachers through out the education system and increase in the literacy rate from 17% in 1971 to 60% in 2000. This was possible because of the provisions made for the education of women like *(i)* infant feeding programme, *(ii)* special attention to marginalised women, *(iii)* mass adult literacy programme, *(iv)* programme of integral development for rural women, *(v)* school attraction programme, and *(vi)* policy of keeping 10% of the job reserved for women. (Rao, 2000)

The educational development among women in China is much better than many of the Asian and even European countries of the world. They have a high level of literacy rate *i.e.* more than 90% among the women. The educational attainment of Chinese women has helped them towards the rapid decline of fertility in China. The Chinese government and various organisations have made effective networking for the education of women in China, *viz.*, *(i)* Development of personal education networking; *(ii)* Special recruitment programmes for rural girls to work as teachers; *(iii)* Building of housing for young teachers (women) in rural areas, *(iv)* Providing high level of schooling to the girls in the whole country, despite a 70% approximate rural population.

PROVISION IN INDIA

Before Independence

Educational development of women is not a new concept in India. India had a rich tradition of women education during Vedic Period and Buddhist epoch. The parents and well-wishers of the Vedic and Buddhist women took special care to provide facilities for their spiritual progress and intellectual development in the form of moral and religious education. During Vedic period there were provisions to become two types of women students : *(i)* Brahmavadinis: These were life long students of theology, and *(ii)* Sadyodvahas : Those who studied upto the age of 16 or 18 years and learnt Vedic hymns by heart. There was provision for women even to become specialists in theological work and were considered Kasa Kritshi (Srivastava, 2000). There was provision for their higher education including Vedic studies in Gurukulas, which was regarded as a necessary accomplishment for being well placed in life. Provisions were also made for Vedic discourses open equally to men and women and many ladies distinguished themselves not only as Vedic scholars but also as great philosopher, debaters and teachers.

It may, therefore, be stated that the overall status of women in the Vedic ages was much higher than in any other ancient society that we know today, *viz.* those of Greece and Rome.

In the Buddhist epoch women enjoyed greater freedom to develop their intellect. In spite of centre and social status, their education was properly taken care off and they were given much scope for religious discussion before the gathering. Further, widowhood of women was not considered inauspicious, and they were allowed everywhere even in the learning centers. But in the later period (Brahmanic Period and Puranic Age) educational as well as social status of women was degraded and lots of restrictions came to be imposed on them by the Brahmins and the writers of the Puranas in the name of Pervasive Brahmanic Code and conspiracy.

Since Brahmins were regarded as Guru (teacher) and were the most powerful in those days, the common people especially from the power middle strata of the society didn't dare to go against them in taking initiation or making efforts for the education of the girls in a formal setting.

During the medieval period this trend with regard to the educational development of women continued, and no specific efforts were made by the people or even by the parents of the girls. Girls were only given the informal household training from the near and dear.

During the period of Mughal rule, the position of women deteriorated further and no identical efforts were made for the education of women.

Gradually, the rights of women (educational and social) were taken away from them. Such great women of Vedic and Buddhist periods have gone into legends, mythology and history that even today they are heard in the beautiful talk songs of the women labourers in the village, grinding corn or working in the field at harvest time or drawing water at the common well. They are also recognised as "Shakti" in many places. These famous women would be found here and there at different points of time in history. On the contrary, for the women who have always made a very significant contribution to their societies in various ways, a particular conspiracy prevented their contribution from receiving their due recognition. The reason is that, society's legitimating myths, creation of written historical records, and the production of authoritative self-knowledge have all been enterprised and controlled by the male.

Today in Modern India the birth of a girl is unwelcome as she is considered to be an economic burden. As a result, female infanticide, which was very common in Rajasthan and in many other parts of India, is still continuing as a practice.

In many tradition-ridden Indian Society, women is treated as Dasi (slave girl) or "Paon Ki Juti" (Shoe). Till date her position has been no better than a pair of shoes which may be laid aside, discarded or changed at the sweet will of the master. This inferior status of women is established right at the birth. From the very childhood she is taught to remain a salve to the man, father, brother or the husband, supposedly to be her protector. The confusion created in her life brought her to the crossroads where the proverbial "Shakti" appears to be helpless and needs support of others to keep herself going. "This help has come now through the parliamentary legislation approving the 20-point programme proposed in 1986 and finally launched on 1st April, 1987." (Ashok Kumar, 1993)

Indian women in general, suffer on numerous counts due to gender bias and have to face a high degree of social insecurity. By and large, their occupational skills are low except in rare cases, where matrilineal system is prevalent. They are seldom involved in decision-making. "Strong socio-cultural taboos, practices of value systems, illiteracy and privation of poverty status of women and discrimination against girls hinder to their progress" (Vaidyanathan, 1996).

Therefore, till the beginning of the present century, women's education in India was not countenanced with much favour. The progress of other nations, especially western countries and the involvement of women in freedom movement of India has acted as an eye-opener in India during last part of nineteenth century. As a consequence, various provincial government and the native states have passed legislations enforcing universal elementary education both for boys and girls, and have also made provisions for higher studies of women in spite of public censure and reproach.

Although there was effect of Western Countries on educational development of Indian People during 19th Century, the progress of women education was very slow for several reasons. Indigenous schools for girls have ceased to function. The initiative taken by Christian missionaries, made intelligent later by British Government, saw a gradual growth of educational institutions promoting educational development of women. There were three agencies through which the Christian Missionaries worked for promoting women education, *viz.* *(i)* Girls Day Schools, *(ii)* Orphanages and Boarding establishments, and *(iii)* Domestic teaching of women in Middle and Higher-class families popularly termed as "Zenana teaching".

During 1819-20, Devid Hare, a Christian missionary took special interest in establishing a Girls School in Calcutta. Later on people especially of missionary mind took initiative in starting girl schools. In the close of 1850's the various missionary efforts for female education in whole India embraced 354 days schools with 11,549 girls; boarding schools with 2,346 girls, taught mostly in vernacular languages in Bengal (N.W. Provinces, Madras Presidency, Bombay Presidency and Ceylon). (Srivastava, 2000)

In 1954, the Education Dispatch (Wood Dispatch approved the order of Lord Dalhousie) was given to the council for the development of female education and thus, the responsibilities of education was taken up by the Government directly. Also, there was a positive increase of government's expenditure on women's education.

In the year 1854 there were 2,875 schools for the education of men all over India, with 1,06,040 pupils, but at the same time girls' schools numbered only 65 with an enrolment of about 3,500 pupils (Srivastava, 2000) following the Wood Educational Dispatch of 1854. Government offered in 1857, small annual rewards to those primary teachers who could form girls classes in their schools. But the progress of this scheme was slow and even in 1864-65 the government schools contained only 639 girls. In that year, the proceeds of the local funds also became available and it was possible to start more girl schools in all the presidencies. In 1870-71, there were as many as 218 girls schools (against 23 in 1865-66) with 9,190 pupils and the government expenditure on the education of women which was Rs. 341 in 1964-65 increased to Rs. 39,337 in 1870-71.

The Indian social reformers who in their individual capacities encouraged women's education picked-up the work begun and steps taken by the Christian missionaries. Reformers like Raja Rammohan Roy, Ishwar Chandra Vidyasagar, played important roles by lending support to the opening of girls' schools. Through the efforts and activities of the leaders of Brahma Samaj, Ved Samaj, Arya Samaj, Khalsa Diwan, Dev Samaj, Ram Krishna Mission, and other organisations a number of girl's schools were established. Iswar Chandra Vidya Sagar took up the cause of women education by establishing 36 schools for girls (Srivastava, 2000). Government in British India too gave its coordial support to the cause of women education.

The period 1857—1921 also intensed the introduction of special courses in Primary schools for girls. The prevailing opinion in the 19th century was to have an absolutely separate system of education for girls with separate schools, separate syllabus and even separate textbooks, not to speak of women teachers and women inspectors. Separate Schools for and women teachers had already become a reality by 1875. The Principle of appointing women inspecting officers was also recognised. Need for separate courses and textbook for girls was also felt during 1877-78, but they were introduced only as late as 1906.

During the period 1857—1921, some more significant efforts were made by the communities like Europeans, Anglo-Indians, Indian Christians and Parsis and even the government for establishment of girl's high schools, training colleges for women primary school teachers, and colleges for women. As a result, high school for Indian girls in Poona was established in 1884 and the expansion of the secondary education of girls was followed by their entry into colleges.

An important step was taken for the development of medical education on of women with the establishment of the Countess of Lady Dufferin Fund in 1885. The main objective of this fund was to establish hospital, maternity homes for women, to train women as nurses and midwives, to give scholarships to such women who desired professional education in medicine, and to promote child welfare and anti-natal care etc. A large amount was collected and it was utilised to give scholarship to women undergoing some type of education in medicine (Srivastava. 2000)

By the year 1901-1902 there were 76 women in medical colleges and 166 women candidates in medical schools as students. (Nayar, 1997). The period between the appointment of University Commissions in 1902 and the transfer of education to Indian control (introduction to the System of Dyarchy) in 1921 witnessed the sincere efforts of government and other organisations for the progress of women education due to public awakening. With the encouragement and inspiration of Mrs. Annie Besant, and the members of Women's Organisations for the first time in Indian history in 1917 made a clear demand before the Secretary for state for women's struggle and asked for adequate educational facilities. Since that time there has been, practically speaking a unanimity between all sections of public opinions in Indian Political Life that women should be given their due share in all walks of life. Establishment of S.N.D.T. Indian Women's University in Bombay by D.K. Karve in 1916 is another remarkable effort for the educational development of women of this period. As a result by 1921-22 the numbers of colleges for women from only 2 in 1891-92 increased to 15 and similarly the number of women scholars increased from 45 in 1891-92 to 1263 in 1921-22 (Srivastava, 2000). The number of high schools and primary schools for girls were also increased to 675 and 21,956 respectively. (Nayar, 1997).

The efforts of Mahatma Gandhi to organise night schools and literacy classes for illiterate adults (men and women) during 1920's, the phenomenal awakening of Indian womenhood, introduction of Provincial Autonomy in 1937, and the mass mobilisation for freedom struggle not only inducted women into political process but made them came into their own as a constituency with the birth of women's Indian Association on May, 1917 and All India Women's Conference in 1924. Later on, Mass Literacy Programmes were launched in 1937-38 in many provinces like Assam, Bengal, Bihar, Bombay and Punjab. Provisions were also made for the education of women in all the literacy programmes.

The early demand for compulsory Universal Primary Education was sort down in 1911, but re-appeared more strongly in the Nai-Talim (Basic Education). The report on post-war Educational Development (1940) was the last important educational document before the independence struck as new note by observing that it was no longer necessary to treat the education of women as a special problem requiring special measures for its advancement. It assumed that all education which was good enough for boys would be equally beneficial to girls (Report of NCWE, 1959).

With the advent of Independence of our country in 1947, a new era has begun for educational development of women. Though the efforts were rooted from pre-independence period it concretised after independence through various plans and programmes, especially the Five-Years plan. At the time of Independence there were 59 arts and science colleges for women, 2,370 Secondary Schools and 81,479 Primary Schools for girls. There were also 4,288 institutions for professional, technical and special education for women. This period shows an increase in the trend towards co-education. From this time education was no longer confined to only schooling or literacy, health, handicraft, along with reading, writing and numeracy.

Provision in Orissa

The Orissian tale of women educational development of women is not much different from that of other part in the country. In ancient times, education was imparted through religious teachings by Priests and Saints and education was persued not for its own sake, but as a part of religion; and, the priests and saints tried, mostly, to impart moral and social education to both male and female. Education was imparted orally and literacy was not considered as so much an important factor of education. In exceptional cases, *i.e.* for the girls and women of royal families, special cares were taken to provide education in specific areas as like philosophy, religion and administration etc. There was also impact of Vedic culture and Buddhist education on the people (both men and women) in Orissa.

It is evident from the history of Orissa that there was provision for persuing religious education among the people of all sectors (including women) in an organised way on Buddhist philosophy.

Lakshmikara, the sister of king Indrabhuti of Sambal State (Modern name is Sambalpur), and the daughter-in-law of Jalendra, the king of Lanka Puri (modern name Subarnapur district), was a famous luminary of Tantrik Buddhism during 8th Century A.D. She is also revealed as one of the 84 Siddhas and composer of Buddhist literature "Advaya Siddha". She was the initiator of "Sahajayan" Dharma which come out as a reaction against strict and artificial principles of sex and human desires of "Bajrayan" wing of Buddhism, and encourages to lay great emphasis on physical satisfaction (Sahu, 1958). The Principles of Sahajayan, and the activities of Lakshmikara have influenced a lot to the people of Western Orissa in changing their attitude towards life and it helps in giving impetus to the cause of women freedom and development especially in Western part of Orissa.

During the medieval period, when Maths, Ashrams, Pathsalas, Maktabs and Madrassas came into existence, some provisions were made for the education of the people. But no specific provisions or efforts were made to educate the girls and women of the common strata.

Overall, women of Orissa were illiterate. Leaving aside the women of the Royal Zamindar class and the rich section of the society who though were given education of an extremely elementary and informal kind at home, the other remain totally illiterate. Although there were schools in the villages and towns, women were not allowed to go to schools owing to customs such as Purdah and child marriage. Women of upper strata of the society were informally taught the art of house decoration, about the observance of religious rituals, festivals and the like. A medieval outlook then prevalent in the Oriya society assigned only domestic duties to the women. In short, women all most all of them, were forced to remain illiterate and ignorant.

At the turn of the 19th century, the earlier opposition to women's education fizzled out. However, a number of obstacles remained in the way of women's education and their attaining better status. Government laws or even the personal efforts of social reformers like Fakirmohan Senapati, Madhusudan Rao, Pyari Mohan Acharya, Gourishankar Acharya, Gopalbandhu Das, Madhusudan Das, Radhanath Ray, etc. are rendered ineffective by the painfully slow process of change in traditions during the first part of 19th century. The result of such social and traditional prejudices and beliefs at the turn of the century in Orissa was that only upper-middle-class women of the elitist society had some sort of schooling.

Owing to the noble deeds of these pioneers, quite a few lady social workers, writers and social reformers came out of the confines of their homes, when Purdah was prevalent, to set an example to the women folk that education was a stepping stone for their upliftment (Mohanty and Nayak, 1998). Some of the pioneers in the field were Smt. Reba Ray, Smt. Sailabala Das, Smt. Rama Devi, Smt. Malati Choudhary, etc. They spearheaded the women's education movement in Orissa. This movement opened the door to educational development of women thereafter.

In 1942, the Utkal University was established. A special provision was made for women to take the matriculation final examination without appearing at the text examination at school, which was a screening test for promotion. This system encouraged a lot many women to take the matriculation examination privately. Further, after independence in 1947, the National Government as per the constitutional provisions took special measures for the education of women. As a result, several women availed the opportunity to get educated. Later on adult education and mass literacy programme were also introduced for the educational development of the illiterate adults (both male and female) in 1949 by setting up a special wing in the State Directorate of Education to organise adult literacy programme. The programme got momentum during 1950 when the social education programme was launched at the initiation of the then national government. During 1952 three urban and rural development projects were allocated to Orissa. Two voluntary organisations namely Ford Foundation and American Friends Society came forward for the educational development of people through social education. Three compact areas namely Bhadrak, Bhanjanagar and Dharamgarh were selected by the government for the operation of the three projects, while the two voluntary organisations selected Kendrapara and Barpali respectively as field of activity. The Education Department, Government of Orissa, selected three more areas such as Baripada, Hindol and Nayagarh to concentrate their activities to make the people literate.

The need for educated women was very much felt at the time of implementation of the First Five-Year Plan in 1951. Hence, educational development of women became an important agenda in national level through Five-Year Plans and provisions were also made accordingly.

After Independence at National Level

After Independence, the conceptual frameworks and concerns about women's education have emerged from other sources. The work of the committees and commissions headed by eminent persons have guided actions and given a thrust to education as a part of socio-economic development. Since then, educational development of women has become an area of major policy concern and is seen as an element seminal to national development. In the developmental efforts, Government of India has laid stress on rapid speed of education among women through reservation of seats for women students in different educational institutions, and opening of educational institutions mainly of residential types at different levels. The Secondary Education Commission (1952-53) in line with Sergeant Report did not include a separate chapter on women education 'as it felt that all the prestige of our social evolution there is no special justification for dealing with women's education separately. Every type of education, open to men should also be open to women' (Siddiqui, 1993). Provision of free tuition for girls in general education was also made. Special attentions was given to the ST, SC and socially backward centre people (both male and female) by providing stipend at Pre-secondary Stage, Post-metric scholarship etc. Different types of educational institutions like Girls' school (both residential and non-residential type), Women's college, women's polytechnic, etc., have been opened for providing professional educational facilities to girls of both general and other reserved categories. The details of provision made and steps taken in the field of educational development of the girls during different plans, committees and commissions are presented below:

Indian Constitution

The constitution of India, in the year 1950, made provision for women with a set of fundamental rights whereby they enjoy equal opportunity relating to employment [Article-16(1)], free and compulsory education up to the age of 14 years (Article 45), equal rights for education for women [Article 29(2)], and education and other developmental activities for weaker section of the society like ST, SC and others (including women) in (Articles 46 and 275).

Five-Year Plans

Successive five year plans have consistently emphasised the acceleration of women's education, and steps were taken accordingly with a number of special programmes for their development.

The First Five-Year Plan (1951—56) provided due importance to women's education, and stated that the general purpose and objective of women's education cannot of course, be different from the purpose and objectives of men's education. There are, however, vital differences in the way in which this purpose has to be realised. Girls are forced to suspend their studies in the early teens due to variety of reasons. Realising the magnitude of the problems of girls, education provisions were made to facilitate resumption of studies by women at a time when they have leisure.

The Second Five-Year Plan (1956-61) describes the importance of girls' education under its head "Secondary Education (Girls Education)." At the secondary stage, the education of girls lags seriously behind. During this period the Central Welfare Board was set-up to supervise the developmental and welfare activities in the country. Further, the Central Board of Workers Education was set-up for organising Trade Union Oriental Education to both male and female workers.

The National Committee of Women's Education was set-up in 1959 under the Chairmanship of Durgabhai Deshmukh during the period of Second Five-year Plan to examine the problems of women education very comprehensively. This committee took a very forward-looking stance by suggesting among others, home science as a compulsory subject both for boys and girls for classes VI, VII and VIII. As a result of the recommendation of this committee, State Councils for Education of Girls have been set-up in the states and the Union Territories.

During the Third Five-Year Plan (1961–66) efforts were made to start a mass movement for literacy in the name of Gram Shikshan Mohim in 1961. It was started by several state government, functionaries, voluntary organisations in different parts of the country. This mass movement made a deep impact on the general mass, especially on the women to eradicate illiteracy and develop education (Siddiqui, 1989).

In the same period, Smt. Hansa Mehta Committee on Differentiation of curricula for Boys and Girls (National Council for Women's Education) was set-up in 1961 to examine comprehensively the problem of curricula for girls at all stages of education. The committee observes : "In the ultimate democratic and socialistic pattern of society, education will be related to individual capacities, aptitude and interests which are not related to sex. There would therefore, be no need in such a society to differentiate curricula on the basis of sex" (Biswas and Agrawal, 1971).

In 1963, the Bhaktavatsalam Committee was appointed to look into the causes of lack of public support particularly in rural areas for girls education and to enlist public co-operation. This committee recommended that the state should create public opinion in favour of girls education, and direct co-operation of the public should be encouraged in this matter, *i.e.* women education (Siddiqui, 1993).

The Education Commission (1964-66) headed by Dr. D.S. Kothari made valuable recommendation regarding the status of Indian women and their education. The national Commission for Women (1998) also supported for equal educational opportunities of women in all fields of education. The commission observed : "In the modern world the role of women goes much beyond the home and the bringing up of children. She is now adopting a career of her own and sharing equally with her male counterpart the responsibility for the development of society in all its aspects."

The recommendations of Kothari Commission formed the basis for the First National Policy on Education, 1968. The resolutions on the national Policy on Education also laid special emphasis on Women Education. The Policy stated : "The education of girls should receive special emphasis and funds required for its advancement particularly for the implementation of its special programmes should be provided on a priority basis. The funds of girls education and its special programmes should be earmarked so that there is no possibility of their being diverted into other uses." (NPE, 1968)

After independence, there has been a very wide gap between the avowed goal of equality to access to education and its realisation. Though education has been considered crucial for development, the empirical reality is not very encouraging (Desai, 1987), for which not only the recommendations of the National Policy on Women Education (1968), but also the other committees and commissions appointed for the purpose since independence, have remained unimplemented or not fully implemented.

During the Fourth Five-Year Plan (1969–74) : A depressing picture of women's development was found in the report of 1971 Census. In 1971 Census Report, there was observed : *(i)* a constant decline of sex ratio and work participation rates of women, *(ii)* higher mobility and mortality, *(iii)* higher unemployment and, (iv) lower literacy and educational participation among them. Based on the observation of 1971 census, a report was submitted by the Committee on Status of Women in India (CSWI) entitled "Towards Equality" in 1974, (GOI, 1974) in preparation for the International Women's Conference at Mexico, 1975. The report highlighted for the first time the shocking state of affairs *vis-a-vis* the position of women at all levels and in all spheres in the country (Haldar, 1997).

The report of CSWI stated that in 1971, about 68% of the total number of women in the age group of 15–25 years and nearly 87% in the age group 25 years and above were illiterate (Pandey, 1987). As a result, all national and international networks of women activists and scholars, the national government and the international organisations began viewing women's education and development as integral to human growth and development during this period. (Nayar, 1997)

During the Fifth Five-Year Plan Period (1975–80) The central and state governments have taken a number of steps to stimulate the education of girls and women which includes separate cells in the state "Directorate of Education" to look after the programmes of girl education, establishment of Polytechnics for girls, construction of staff quarters for women teachers in rural areas, and girls hostels, introduction of condensed educational courses, assistance to voluntary educational organisations working in the field of women's education, and holding of seminars in different states to discuss problems and programmes of girls education.

Further, the National Education Policy (1979) which was set-up during the plan period also emphasised that women education is of top most requirement and women instructors should be appointed for implementation of such programmes of family planning, health and nutrition, child and mother care etc.

During the Sixth Five-Year Plan (1980–85) : For the first time in the history of planning in India, provision was made to open a separate chapter on Women and Development. Provisions were also made on three important sectors for Indian Women, *viz.*, Education, Employment and Health. Sincere efforts were also made through special drives for higher enrolment and retention for girls under the programme of UEE. As a result, the enrolment of girls increased from 272.78 lakhs (64.9 per cent) in 1979-80 to 301.58 lakhs (72.4 per cent) in 1982-83 in classes I–V. The target for 1983-84 was 319.60 lakhs (76.3 per cent). Similarly for classes VI–VIII the enrolment of girls improved from 61.53 lakhs (26.0 per cent) in 1979-80 to 73.83 lakhs (3.10 per cent) in 1982-83. The target for 1983-84 was 87.41 lakhs (35.8 per cent).

Further, financial assistance to ST, SC and OBC students (both male and female), scholarships for meritorious students and cash reward for teachers of schools showing outstanding results in the school certificate examinations were provided. Special coaching to SC and ST girls student in order to enable them to take the entrance examination for admission to medical and engineering colleges, book-bank in technical institutions for the benefit of SC/ST students (both male and female), pre-examination coaching for different competitive services including I.A.S. and other competitive examination like, Bank Services etc. were organised.

During the Seventh Five-Year Plan (1985–90) : period made serious efforts on 100 per cent coverage of girls' education up to the age of 14 years. Modifications were made of educational content of adult education programme to incorporate a new value system regarding the role of women, open learning system including correspondence course for women, promotion of technical and vocational education. Special provision of additional facilities for women of weaker sections under the "Development of Backward Caste", provision of scholarship for female participants in games and sports, priority for women in teacher's training programme etc. were also made to increase the availability of trained women teachers.

During this period, the National Policy on Education, 1986 (NPE, 86) was made as a landmark in the mandate of bringing about women's equality and empowerment through revised curricula, reorientation of educational personnel and making women's studies the drive arm for generating, studying and supporting action. On education for women's equality the policy states : "Education for equality has been incorporated, whose preamble reads, 'new policy will lay special emphasis on the removal of disparities and to equalise educational opportunity by attending to the specific needs of those who have been denied so far (NPE, 1986).'" POA, 1990, in the context of women's education made various recommendations with regard to the following :

The Review Committee on National Policy on Education, 1986, and its Programme of Action: *(a)* Access to education and quality of learning, *(b)* Content of Education and gender bias, *(c)* Vocational education, *(d)* Training of teachers and other educational personnel, *(e)* Research and development of women studies *(f)* Representation of women in the educational hierarchy *(g)* Empowerment of women, *(h)* Adult education, *(i)* Resources, and *(j)* Management.

The NPE (1986) and its revised Programme of Action (POA, 1991) adopted by the Government of India gives education the mandate to become an effective tool of women's equality and empowerment. The parameters of which are :

(a) Enhancing the self-esteem and self-confidence of women,

(b) Building a positive image of women by recognising their contribution to the society, policy and the economy, and developing ability to think critically.

(c) Fostering decision-making and action through collective processes.

(d) Enabling women to make informed choices in area like education, employment and health (especially reproductive health).

(e) Ensuring equal participation in development process, and providing information, knowledge and skill for economic independence.

(f) Enhancing access to legal literacy and information relating to their rightsand entitlement in society with a view to enhancing their participation on an equal footing in all areas. (Revised POA, 1991, p. 2)

During the Eighth Five-Year Plan (1992–97) period, emphasis was reiterated mainly on human development. Woman as a human being was also considered as the core of all development efforts like men (Siddiqui, 1993). A number of Literacy programmes were launched in the districts or regions which are educationally backward or have high concentration of ST and SC population or have low female literacy. Cent per cent literacy in the age group 15–35 years was envisaged as target of this plan. Based on the report and recommendations of CABE committee on NPE-1992 and with a view to bring out an improvement in the access to women education, various government and non-government organisations, departments, voluntary organisations, societies etc. were involved in those activities and educational endeavour. The participation of the women in different educational programmes were also closely monitored, supervised and taken care off.

Non-Formal Education (NFE)

Efforts were also sincerely made on provision of special NFE centres for girls who are unable to attend female schools due to socio-economic or personal problems. Although focus of the NFE scheme is for the 10 backward states it also covers urban slums, hilly, tribal and desert areas. The NFE system is being extended to meet the needs particularly of the girls. NFE centres running exclusively for girls are getting 90% assistance from the central government (Agrawal, 1999). Mention may be made here that in the mid-term appraisal of Ninth Five-Year Plan importance has been given to NFE for the educational development of dropouts, working children and girl (MHRD, GOI, 2000). Out of 3 lakhs currently running NFE Centres (Catching about 75 lakhs children) about 1.18 lakhs centres are exclusively for girls. (India, 2000, GOI).

Further, under this plan highest priority was given to universalisation of Elementary Education and more importance was given to the education of girls. The suggestions were given by NPE, 1986 and its programme of Action, 1992. The National Commission on self-employed women in informal sector (1987-88) was to provide special facilities like provision of shifts in schools for girls at suitable times, honourarium for women helper for accompanying the children from house, free uniform, mid-day meals and free text-books, etc., and for the need based content in the primer women have to be taken care off. The suggestion for mid-day meal has been properly taken care off by the Govt. of India for record states.

It is also important to mention here that under the scheme of operation Black-Board, of the 1.47 lakhs teachers appointed, 47 per cent, *i.e.* 69,090 were women. In future at least half of the teachers appointed are expected to be women.

Under the Ninth Five-Year Plan (1997–2002) : The thrust area of educational development is UEE and literacy programme for all. Greater importance in the plan is further given for the upliftment of the educational status of women through its various educational endeavours like condensed courses of education and vocational training, continuing education, Non-Formal and Alternative Education, Promotion of Primary Education through 100% enrolment etc.

District Primary Education Programme (DPEP)

It focuses on an improving girls' access to and participation in school. The programme is now operational in 52 districts spread over eleven states : Assam, Haryana, Karnataka, Kerala, Maharashtra, Madhya Pradesh, Tamil Nadu, Andhra Pradesh, Gujarat, Himachal Pradesh and Orissa. It is proposed to cover another 61 districts by the end of the 8th plan. The attempt is to build in an equity focus from early formal schooling. DPEP district focus is a conscious attempt to decentralise the planning process as a strategy to universalise elementary education. Educationally backward districts that have a female literacy rate below the national average have been selected for the programme. "As DPEP has a well defined gender focus which ensures that all interventions and activities are gender aware, this effort to integrate a gender perspective begins with the planning process." (Agrawal,1999)

Navodaya Vidyalaya : At the end of the spectrum are the Navodaya Vidyalayas, centres for excellence, where at least one third of the students would be girls. In both the Kendriya Vidyalaya and Navodaya Vidyalaya education for girls is made free up to standard XII.

Sarva Shiksha Abhiyan (SSA) : Gaining from the experiences of the scheme of operation black board, non-formal education, national programme of nutritional support to primary education, and DPEP, and to looking toward to accomplish the target of UEE, the government has launched sarvashiksa abhiyan—a holistic and convergent approach towards achieving UEE through a time bound-integrated approach in close collaboration with the state governments. It is a collective progress of nation, a non-violent war against inequalities based on gender, religion and ethnicity, a process of human enrichment that empower and transform people and a goal-directed intensive action as well as high level commitment for universalisation of elementary education. (MHRD, 2000).

SSA was evolved as a national resolution in 1998 in the education minister's conference, and a national committee of education ministers' was set-up under the chairmanship of Minister of HRD to examine the modalities of adopting holistic and convergent approach to achieve UEE in mission mode.

The national committee submitted the report in 1999 with a vision to provide a relent elementary education of satisfactory quality for all by 2010 bridging social and gender gaps. The main characteristics of SSA are : *(a)* all children in school, education guarantee centres, alternative schools, and back to school camp by 2003, *(b)* all children complete five-years of schooling by 2007, *(c)* all children complete eight years of schooling by 2010, *(d)* focus on elementary education of satisfactory quality with emphasis on education for life, *(e)* universal retention by 2010 and *(f)* bridging social and gender gap.

The National Policy for Women in India (1996)

It seems to be the outcome of Fourth International Women's Conference at Beijing in 1995. There has been insistent and consistent pressure on the Government of India to formulate a National Policy for Women since the late 70's that went unheeded for two decades. Finally in 1996, the Government has been sufficiently motivated to take action, though it seems only under pressure from International Commission of Women and to keep its image untarnished therein, as has been its regular practice, and a final draft of the National Policy for Women has been released. The draft of National Policy for Women gives stress on gender equality and women empowerment through development of education. Because the Government of India has never been sensitive, sufficiently concerned, or far-sighted enough to take unproved initiatives on its own, independently, to devise its self-inspired policies and plans of action, where the women question as it came to be known in the nineteenth century in the country is concerned. (Haldar, 1997)

According to the draft report, education of the women should be given priority and different plans and programmes should be implemented so that they will achieve equality in all the other spheres by enhancing productive capabilities in them and their knowledge about rights and responsibilities and how to fight for them.

Mahila Samakshya

One of the most successful efforts for education development is Mahila Samakhya. The programme is operational in 17 districts spread over the four states of Andhra Pradesh, Gujarat, Karnatak and Uttar Pradesh. This programme begins with the understanding that the problems of women can be identified and solved by the development of women especially educational and location at their own place. (Agrawal, 2001)

Women's Studies Centres

The University Grants Commission has been encouraging institutions/centres to take up research projects in the area of women's studies by providing necessary funds. The researches that are emerged from the women's study centres have had a definite influence in shaping not only educational policies, plans and programmes but also in giving a direction to the national effort in the area of women's development as equal partners in a secular democracy, and in bringing home the centrality of women's education to women's empowerment as a non-negotiable area of social progress and enhancement of women's status. The initiative work of NCERT in this regard is remarkable. UGC has also assisted 22 Universities and 11 colleges to set-up Women's Studies Centre. This is in addition to the 40 positions of part-time research associateships for women.

It is true that despite strong linkages between women's education and their equality and empowerment, educational development among women remains very low in India. This is especially the case in rural areas and urban slums, where only about 30 per cent of the adult women are literate (Mittal, 1996); and, due to their illiteracy development programmes become handicapped for implementation because education and training are highly essential for achieving quality and replication. Philosophically, an educational training programme should necessarily address six major objective *i.e.* *(i)* behaviour, *(ii)* self- awareness, *(iii)* technical knowledge base, *(iv)* skills, *(v)* motivation, and *(vi)* orientation. Illiteracy of people especially among women is handicapped in training programme due to lack of down to earth resource personnel and need based training materials. In a poor and developing country like ours, where educational programme should have a multiple effect, illiterate trainees, are unable to transfer knowledge and skill effectively (Seth, 1997)

The National Perspective Plan for Women's Education (1998-2000) formulated some important and specific objectives for women education, so that women may also participate in the area of social, cultural, economic and political activities etc. The objectives were to be obtained by 2000 AD in regard to women's education. Some of the objectives are :

(a) Elimination of illiteracy, universalisation of elementary education and minimisation of the dropout rate in the age group 6–14 years and stagnation to negligible proportions.

(b) Ensuring opportunities to all women for access to appropriate level, nature, quality of education and also the where withhold for success comparable with men.

(c) Substantial vocationalisation and diversification of secondary education.

(d) Making education an effective means for women's equality.

(e) Providing non-formal and part time courses to women to enable them to acquire knowledge and skills for their social, cultural and economic advancement.

To achieve these objectives for women education the plan includes the following strategies :

- Involvement of local leaders, Voluntary Agencies and Women's group.

- Learning is to be made more attractive by providing adequate teaching materials in schools.
- Multi-entry system for girls who cannot attend schools continuously should be adopted.
- Wherever necessary, school meant exclusively for girls, may be set-up.
- Non-formal education, correspondence course, self-study programme, open school system and condenses courses should be organised.

The International Commission on Education for the 21st Century Constituted by UNESCO to reflect on education and learning for the 21st Century in January, 1996, at New Delhi. The Commission framed a number of recommendations concerning different aspects of education. Regarding women-education, the commission strongly recommended a policy of strong encouragement for the education of girls and women following the same line of recommendations of the Beijing Conference held in September, 1995 (Yadav, 1999).

Unless women are given access to education they will not have equal access to opportunities and the benefits of development. The returns from educational development of girls and women have few parallels in any other type of social investment.

PROVISION OF EDUCATION FOR THE DISADVANTAGED

The educational problems of the people in the country appear to have close relationship with the ethos of the society. Most of the socially and economically disadvantaged and deprived groups of the society are found to be educationally backward. Therefore, it is necessary to examine the status of these groups, understand their socio-economic setting and resolve the problem at hand, like illiteracy and ignorance. It is reported that the 'culture of silence and the legitimation' and exploitation have been co-habiting in the Indian conditions of peculiar historical circumstances. Disadvantaged individuals and groups are there in all the countries of the world and are struggling hard for their survival and development.

Provision of Education in the Past

Education that has been acclaimed as the prime mover of development opens the door to modernisation. The educational process, however, does not benefit the disadvantaged groups evenly, regulating a differential development. The educational inputs like provision of education in the form of opening of schools, providing tuition without payment of fees and of scholarships and stipends for the upkeep of scholars, supply of textbooks and other teaching materials, enrolment drives, measures of students retention, etc., are expected to facilitate the educational process and attract the disadvantaged people. It also affects the formation of personality and mould their attitudes in society. "Although education is primarily the responsibility of the state, in India a number of voluntary organisations are also contributing their mite. The foremost among them are the Christian Missionary organisations. In many parts of India, their role in educational field has been crucial as it preceded government effort in this field. The Arya Samaj movement, Ram Krishna Mission and Theosophical Society have taken pains to establish institutions both for the general public and for the disadvantaged". (Sachidanand, 1983)

Provision of Education at Present

India started the momentum of progress after independence among scheduled castes and scheduled tribes and other disadvantaged group of the society with a constitutional agenda of securing to all its citizens justice, liberty and equality. Moreover, right to education was also envisaged. Article 41 states in this regard that 'the state shall, within the limits of its economic capacity and development make effective provision for securing the right to education'. The Constitution of India states, "We the people of India solemnly resolve to secure for all our citizens, justice - social, economic equality of status and opportunity and also to promote among them all fraternity assuring the dignity of the individual and unit of the nation." In fact, provision for free and compulsory elementary education for all in the country in spite of caste, colour, sex and religion was made. Article 45 of the Constitution states that, "The state shall endeavour to provide within a period of ten years from the commencement of this constitution, *i.e.* 1950, for free, and compulsory education for all children until they complete the age of fourteen years".

Article 46 of the Constitution provides for the promotion of the educational and economic interest of the weaker sections of people and in particular of scheduled castes and scheduled tribes people and for their protection against social injustice and exploitation. Education provides a shield against such injustice and exploitation. Since then provisions have been pursued vigorously and steps are undertaken to speed up the educational progress of the disadvantaged and weaker sections.

In 1935, Government of India passed the Scheduled Caste Act in which certain Castes, race and tribes were put together. The Government provided some incentives for improving the conditions of scheduled castes, but desired result could not be achieved. After independence the list of the scheduled castes were revised in 1950 and some more avenues were provided for minimising the gap between scheduled caste and general castes.

Substantial funds were also allocated in the National Five-Years plans for ameliorating the condition of the scheduled caste and scheduled tribes. After that the government took various steps and made provisions to promote through various projects and welfare schemes, which were operated from central and state levels. In 1947, the congress redeemed its pledge to the Harijan's by declaring that, "untouchability in any form is abolished and imposition of any disability on that account shall be an offence". As a result, in 1955, the Untouchability Offence Act 1955 was passed. It must be noted here that, the provision *viz.* Articles 41, 45 and 46 are placed under the Directive Principle of State Policy of the Constitution. "These are not enforceable by court but regarded as fundamentals in the Governance of the country". It is made the duty of the state to apply in making laws.

A number of acts were enforced for development of the backwards from time to time, and certain territories were declared "Backward Tracts" under the Government of India Act, 1935. On the whole, the provision of such areas largely left the situation as it was in 1874, barring only certain areas on the then Frontiers. "The Constitution of India contains exhaustive provisions for protection and promotion of the interest of scheduled caste and scheduled tribes. These could be broadly classified into three categories, namely : (1) Political (reservation of seats in Legislative Assemblies and House of the People) *e.g.* Articles 330, 332 and 334, (2) Protective e.g. Articles 15(4), 19(5), 36,335, 5th and 6th schedules and, (3) Developmental (e.g. Articles 46 and 275). These provisions are not isolated directives, but part of a well-knit arrangement. The special constitutional provisional for scheduled tribes bear testimony to the statesmanship of the Indian Leadership. Commenting on the adequacy of the constitutional provisions, the Dhebar Commission (1961) has to state : 'The Constitution arranged for the provision of resources and provided the required institutional apparatus. We fee, so far as the basic framework is concerned, it cannot be considered inadequate'.

For the development of these disadvantaged and backward group, the constitution of India specially provides for appointment of certain commissions, *e.g.* Finance Commission (Article 280),

Commission on Administration of Scheduled Areas and Welfare of the Scheduled Tribes (Article 339), and Commission to investigate the condition of Backward classes (Article 340).

The idea of Nehru's Panchsheel for Tribes (1952), formed the basis for designing suitable programmes for tribal development in India. Keeping in view the tribal problems specially educational and economic, Ministry of Home Affairs, the Government of India invited special schemes for the development of tribal people to supplement the benefits accruing from community development programme during 2nd Five-Year Plan. The first attempt was made in 1959 by opening Forty-three Special Multipurpose Tribal Blocks (SMPTB) in most underdeveloped tribal concentrated areas. The priority areas for development in SMPT blocks were education, communication, economy, health, culture, housing and water supply. But the efforts did not achieve the desired goal and success (Verma, 1990, Patnaik and Bose, 1976).

The Kothari Commission of 1964 advised to the Government on the national pattern of education and on the general principles and policies for the development of education at all states and in all aspects.

It recommended that (1) one of the important social objectives of education is to equalise educational opportunities, enabling the backward or underprivileged classes and individuals to use education as a lever for the improvement of their condition. Every society that values social justice and anxious to improve the lot of the common man and cultivate all available talent, must ensure progressive equality of opportunity to all sections for an egalitarian and human society in which the exploitation of the weak will be minimised, and (2) the other forms of educational inequalities which are peculiar to Indian situation need attention. The wide disparity in educational development between the advanced classes and backward ones, the scheduled caste and the scheduled tribes .On the ground of social justice as well as for the furtherance of democracy, it is essential to make special efforts to equalize educational opportunities between these groups.

The Report of Smt. Renuka Ray, M.P. on the Committee on Plan Project, Planning Commission, constituted in May, 1958 (a study team on Social Welfare on Backward Classes) recommended for the educational provision and development. (1) The general pattern of education prevalent in the country should be extended to tribal and other backward classes so as to evolve one common pattern of education in the country. (2) The accepted principles of imparting instructions at the primary level in the mother tongue of the child should be extended to tribal children as well. (3) Text-books of the tribal schools specially in primary level may have to be based, based on the materials related to tribal life without substantially deviating from the general outline of the common syllabus—lessons on national heroes, common festivals, interest, and the like should also include selection from tribal life and conditions. (4) The school hours, as also holidays and vacations in the tribal areas should be so adjusted as to synchronize with their occupational seasons and social festivals.

The Report of the Study Team on Tribal Development Programmes, 1966

The study team constituted by Planning Commission recommended in 1969 that, to accelerate the progress of education, primary school should be established within one or two miles of the home of every child and the problem of education of tribal girls should be given special attention. The medium of education for the first two years in the school should be tribal language (using the script of regional language). The programme of opening Balwadis or Pre-Primary Schools should be intensified. Single-teacher schools whose performance has been unsatisfactory, should be abolished and if possible they should be replaced by Ashram Schools.

Working Groups on Tribal Development during the Sixth Plan (1980–85) and the Seventh Plan (1985–90)

This working group constituted three sub-groups, such as on S.T., S.C. and on weaker sections stated that : *(i)* While core economic sectors might hold primary in planning, education is the key to tribal development. It is an input not only for economic development, but also for inner strength of the tribal and other disadvantaged communities, so that they can meet the new challenges in terms of some degree of equality; *(ii)* Education has to be tackled on both the non-formal and formal levels; *(iii)* Low literacy pockets, backward communities and areas where intensive economic programmes have been or are being taken up should be identified and special educational efforts mounted, *(iv)* The state should be asked to consider and take action for instruction at the Primary State in the mother tongue of tribal children, *(v)* Norms establishment of educational institutions at the primary, middle and secondary levels should be scrutinised once again with a view to ensure their relevance for tribal and underdeveloped areas in the context of the low density of population and scattered habitations. The structural balance among the primary, middle and secondary institutions should be properly struck and maintained; *(vi)* Greater efforts in promoting Adult Education including women's education in tribal areas, particularly with association of voluntary organisations and traditional tribal social institutions, should be taken up levels. Also Grant-in-aid should be given to voluntary organisations to promote education among S.T. and S.Cs. And these programmes have been launched by the state in addition to the special thrust given to the weaker sections in the general programme for educational development such as opening of schools, running of NFE and adult education centres and scheme of operation black board.

Challenges to Education (1985) states, "To the scheduled castes, scheduled tribes and other backward candidates, access has been provided through reservation of seats. This however is not enough. Arrangements have to be made to provide special coaching before and after admission to undergraduate courses" (GOI, 1985). The National Policy on Education (1986) mentioned this, as the central focus in the education development of scheduled tribes, scheduled caste and other disadvantaged group at all levels and stages of education. By 1990, 100% enrolmentin 6 to 11 age group had to be achieved. To ensure timely payment of scholarship, a single nodal agency will be identified for disbursement. Rates and amount of schemes will be raised. Constant monitoring, planning and verification will be done to ensure that enrolment retention and successful completion of course by SC, ST and disadvantaged students do not fall at any stage. NPE (1986) also mentioned that crash programme for recruitment of teachers from ST and SC communities will be undertaken to remove existing gaps and to equip all single teacher schools. Adequate provision will be made for continuing education of teachers recruited and to ensure their professional up gradation. Preparation of primers for classes having more than one lakh students would be undertaken. The Ninth Five-Year Plan (1997–2002) also commits to empower the Socially Disadvantaged Groups by making provision of Construction of Hostels for ST/SC Boys and Girls, Ashram Schools for STs, Coaching and Allied Scheme, Book-Banks; upgradation of merit of SC/ST students, special Educational Development Programme to SC/ST girls belonging to low literacy areas, special assistance for the education of girls belonging Primitive Tribal Groups (PTGs); national scholarship to meritorious SC/ST students to pursue higher studies abroad etc. For the educational development amongst OBCs, schemes were introduced to provide scholarships for post matric/pre-matric courses as well as other higher education supported by hostel facilities. They are also allowed to enjoy the existing facilities meant for SC and ST boys and girls. The centre and state government would constitute committee at appropriate levels to review contents of existing curricula to ensure that caste and other prejudice do not come in the way of integration, leading to establishment of an egalitarian society constitute committees at appropriate levels to review contents of existing curricula to ensure that caste and other prejudice do not come in the way of integration, leading to establishment of an egalitarian society.

EDUCATIONAL PROVISION FOR THE SLUM- DWELLERS AND DOWNTRODDEN

Education, health and social welfare assume greater importance in programmes of slum improvement than housing and other public services (Seetharamu, 1983). Education is the foremost single factor in the economic development of slum-dwellers. Because it is observed and discovered that lack of education binds a slum-dweller to the horrifying conditions of slum life. (Seetharamu, 1983).

Realising the transparency of the situation, and essence of education for the upliftment of the downtrodden people like slum-dwellers and other disadvantaged group, the Indian Constitution has given the right to its citizens accordingly. The Constitution has made equality before law (Article 14), equality of opportunity in matters of public employment (Article 16), abolition of untouchability (Article 17), prohibition of discrimination on grounds of religion, race, caste, sex or plaçe of birth (Article 15) and prohibition of traffic in human being and forced labour (Article 23) as fundamental rights. The Directive Principle of State Policy further recognises the rights to work, to education, and to public assistance in cases of undeserved social want (Article 47); promises improvement in levels of nutrition, public health and standards of living (Article 47); directs the state to secure just and humane conditions of work and maternity relief (Article 42) to guarantee a living wage, full employment, and social and cultural opportunities to all workers (Article 43), and to promote welfare of the people. With regard to education, Article 45 of the Directive Principles of State Policy has enjoined upon the state the duty of providing universal, free, and compulsory primary education to all. Other constitutional provisions with regard to education are : "No individual shall be denied admission to educational institution maintained by the state or receiving aid out of state funds on grounds of religion, race, caste, language or place of birth (Article 29). Article 46 has been amended to give protection from social injustice and all forms of exploitation to the weaker section of people. Lastly Article 15 and Article 16 have been amended to lay down that 'nothing in these articles shall prevent the state from making any special provisions for the advancement of any socially and educationally backward classes of citizens, or for the scheduled caste and scheduled tribes (Article 15-iv; Article 16-iv)'.

Various committees, commissions have been appointed and plans and policies have also been made by Government of India, after independence, for the educational development of the disadvantaged people. They are National Adult Education Programme of 1978, Kothari Commission of 1964, National Policy of Education 1986 and the Five-Year Plans.

The documents of these policies and programme show that Government has no specific policies or programmes of education targeted at the large number of adults living in the innumerable slums in the country. "Rather government has adopted policies and programmes for adults in general. Obviously, there is no realisation of the specificity of the conditions of slum-dwellers' (Choudhary, 1997). So, the general policies and programmes of adult education and literacy programmes of National Literacy Mission apply to the urban slum-dwellers as to the adult illiterates living in the rural and tribal areas.

National Adult Education Programme (1978) was launched to eradicate illiteracy in the age group 15 to 35 all over the country. This NAEP brought to the limelight the problems of illiteracy and its magnitude, and proposed for life long education as a cherished goal in the village and urban centres where learning was imparted through adult centres in the group of all sections of people those who are illiterate. The Sixth Five-Year Plan (1980–85) gave emphasis on education to all citizens irrespective of their age, sex and residence. It adopted technology as the major instrument for the spread of literacy, numeracy and practical skills relevant to the economic activities of the people concerned. The plan gave priority to non-formal education for adults particularly in the age group 13–35 years due to its potential for immediate impact on raising the level of productivity in the economy. The programmes aimed at extending appropriate educational support to the concerned group of individuals through carefully designed group specific and work-based curricula which could be integrated as part of development activities. Slum-dwellers formed under the scheme a priority group besides women, scheduled castes, scheduled tribes and agricultural labourers. (Choudhary, 1997)

Under the Seventh Five-Year Plan (1985–90), eradication of adult illiteracy and the development of a programme of continuing adult education formed a major thrust area. The task identified in this connection was to cover all the illiterates in the age group 15–35 years by 1990. The strategy envisaged to achieve the goal was 'through a mass movement involving social institution, voluntary organisation, students, teachers, employers, and the community' (Seventh Five-Year Plan; 1985 : 258). This programme was to be linked with various development programmes particularly the IRDP, 1985.

The programmes of Nehru Yuvak Kendra (NYK) and National Service Scheme (NSS) also had to give focus on eradication of illiteracy special for the disadvantaged people like slum-dwellers, schedule tribes and schedule castes, etc. Like the Sixth Plan, training on functional skills relevant to specific economic activities formed another important aspect of adult education under the Seventh Plan Programmes for this purpose had to be strengthened, and sufficient resource support provided for organising technical and vocational skill-based courses for the advantage of adult learners through Shramik Vidyapeeths and other similar institutions.

The Government of India came out with its National Policy on Education in 1986. Adult Education constitutes a part of the policy. The NPE considers the ability to read and write as the main instrument of learning. "Hence the crucial importance of adult education, including adult literacy (NPE, 1992 : 15) the documents affirm the pledge of the whole nation under the National Literacy Mission (NLM) to the eradication of illiteracy, particularly in the 15–35 age group in spite of caste, colour, creed, sex and social status through various means with special emphasis on Total Literacy Campaign (TLC). Mass Literacy Campaigns under NPE-86 include as the past programmes of literacy and functional knowledge and skills. The new and radical element however is generating awareness among learners about those socio-economic realities and the possibilities to change it. (NPE, 1992)

No doubt, the disadvantaged people like scheduled tribes, scheduled caste, slum-dwellers and others have now become conscious about their own educational progress to a certain extent and also are trying to utilise the provisions offered to them. Of late they have realised the very essence of education for their development. Still the level of progress they have made is not satisfactory. In a democratic set-up, the dream of an "Egalitarian Society" would not be realised with out

Universalisation of Education. But if we analyse the situation minutely, it reveals that we still have a long way to go. The statistics available on enrolment and literacy rates for STs, SCs and other backward population like slum-dwellers indicates this very well. Thus, educational provision for the masses has to be a cultural action of freedom, and what is needed is an educational programme initiating cultural action for freedom of the oppressed and disadvantaged minorities like STs, SCs and slum-dwellers. Equality of educational opportunity cannot be established overnight. This has to be pursued till the condition of the family, language, etc., are equated among the competing group. This requires protective discrimination.

The Slum Women and their Development

Women play a very critical role in the growing industrialisation and urbanisation as pilots, doctors, engineers, lawyers, professors, journalists, judges, actresses, architects, politicians, administrators, social workers, etc. But they are very limited in numbers and they mainly belong either to the middle-class or the upper-class.

If we observe their percentage in other fields of work, definitely it will be shocking to us. It is studied that, most of the women from the lower-class work in the factories, or in the quarry sides or in the field as contract labourers. They even accept the job of iron and rag picker, maidservant, sweepers etc., especially in the city or urban areas. They also accept prostitution as a means of their livelihood in some of the slum areas of the metropolitan or cosmopolitan cities of the country.

India is predominantly a rural country. But its urban population can only be ranked among the largest countries of the world. The inadequacy of income, wretched poverty and social oppression in rural areas get transformed into slums, and the rapid growth of industrialisation has caused for rapid urbanisation with increasing slums. Urbanisation provides job opportunities thereby allowing immigration both to the male and female from the neighbouring areas. The poor immigrants gravitate towards a wretched housing and living with extreme poverty, casual employment, lowest paid jobs, illiteracy, serious deprivation, social insecurity and instability, mental and physical disease, alcoholism, higher rate of infant and general mortality, group violence, illegal activities and crime, juvenile delinquency, isolation, frustration and a perpetual struggle for sheer existence.

There is no general agreement among researchers and scholars on the definition of a slum. In general parlance, slum is defined as 'foul-back street of a city, especially one with a slovenly and often vicious population; a low squalid neighbourhood' (Webster, 1931 : 19). According to Newman (1959 : 93), it can note the worst structural sanitary conditions and most degraded occupancy usually by the lowest income groups of any given period. In the opinion of Gist and Halbert (1950 : 162), "Slum is a special type of disorganised area with dirty and crowded house". Desai and Pillai (1971) note that "Slum have become the inevitable by products of the process of urbanisation. They grow over years defying all attempts at planned urban development. They are basically the area of darkness, despair and poverty."

It may be noted that, slums are of different types and according to Charlse (1970), "Types of slums vary from place to place as does the definition". There are metropolitan and rural slums, new slums and hand-me-down, handmade and fabricated slums. Some are in shack towns, other are found in the back all eyes of mansions. Some are made of scrap; other one built with mud, adobe, thatch or wood finding. Many are one-storied, but there are also six-storied slums (Desai and Pillai, 1971).

In India, a slum denotes a conglomerate of dilapidated physical structures, built with the cheapest, readily available, and easily perishable materials, needing repair more often, but receiving rarely, if any. Observing the ecology of the Indian Slum, Bharat Sevak Samaj, (1958 : 9) defines, "The term 'slum' should be applied to those part of the city which may be considered unfit for human habitation either because of structure therein are old, dilapidated, grossly congested and out of repairs; or because it is impossible to preserve sanitation for want of sanitary facilities including ventilation, drainage, water supply etc. or because the sites, by themselves are unhealthy (Bharat Sevak Samaj, 1958)". The Baroda Municipal Corporation (1976) states : "Slum applies to all those dwellings, that do not provide the basic minimum facilities for human subsistence. The very lack of infrastructure facilities, high infant mortality, utter negligence of personal health and hygiene, all these together characterise what may be termed as slums. A Slum or Basti is defined according to Calcutta Municipal Act as "An area of land occupied by any collection of huts on a plot of land, not less than ten cottahs (1/6th acre), (Gill, 1994)". Although it is a worldwide phenomenon, the magnitude of slum population in India is very large and has emerged as an ugly but integral part of the modern industrial and urban space in our country. The urban slums are the hotbeds of social problems. Very low levels of literacy, high dropouts from schools, wretched poverty. Drunkenness, bootlegging, drug addiction, prostitution, smuggling, social tension, juvenile delinquency, high rate of criminal and violence, high growth rate of population, higher rate of general and child mortality, chronic and infectious diseases, a more than average calamity rate due to storms, rains, fires and accidents are to be found abundance in the Indian urban slums. Sex ratio here is generally in favour of males. Mostly, rural migrants come to urban areas in search of livelihood rather than improvement in job status. "All-pervasive feature of slums everywhere is the poverty of its inhabitants (Patel, 1978 and Gill, 1994)". Majumdar (1983 : 6) observed, "The high proportion among them (Slum Dwellers) engaged in the 'organised sector' which hardly offers them any protection against irregularity of income and economic exploitation". As a result, they constitute the highly disadvantaged, deprived and exploited lot. They suffer from wretched poverty both economic and cultural, though studies focus mainly on the former (Desai and Pillai, 1971), rightly told in this connection that the problem of slums is linked with the types of socio-economic structure within which urbanisation and industrialisation have taken place. The problem of "slum clearance" has eluded the solution offered so far, so much so that now planners have given up the phrase in favour of 'Slum improvement' or "urban renewal" (Desai and Pillai, 1971).

Among the slum-dwellers women and girls are the worst suffers. Commenting on the living condition of women and children in Indian Slums, Bijlani (1991) stated that 'women in the slums are the greatest suffers. They slog and sweat for the whole day. They are ignorant of many things including how to guide their children to remain clean, keep way from diseases; their children suffer from many handicaps. The environment of the slum itself is one handicap from which the child suffers. Hence, slum is a social soil'.

The boys are encouraged to attend school, the slum girls are forced to sweep, wash clothes, clean utensils, fetch water, collect fire wood, and mind younger siblings. It is also observed that they are engaged with income generation activities from the very childhood. Department of Social Welfare, Government of India, adopted in 1974, a Resolution of National Policy on children in which it is clearly stated that no child under 14 years shall be permitted to be engaged in any hazardous occupation or to be made to undertake heavy work. This desire is still a distant dream because in spite of this policy implementation quite a good number of girl children in urban slums as well as rural areas are cheap source of labour in variety of jobs along with the male children. The girls are mainly employed in factories, cottage industries, middle and super class houses as maid servants for as long as fifteen hours a day in sub-human conditions and for a pittance as wage. In match industries, fireworks. Many of them are even before attending their puberty subjected to sexual exploitation by their employers, adult co-workers and others. Some times these illiterate, ignorant and unprotected slum girls lured on to or sold into prostitution (Devasia and Devasia, 1991).

The poor, abused and powerless slum-women cannot raise their voice against exploitation or harassment, and even for social justice and equality in an organised way due to their low level of educational achievement, wretched poverty, lack of self-confidence, strong faith in superstitions and old tradition and deep ignorance towards their social and basic human rights. As a result they swallow their pain and suffering voicelessly for years together.

The weaker section of the society specially poor women, who live in a pathetic condition of life due to lack of minimum infrastructure and amenities, can never exist and develop properly without special attention and care. Any development for the women, especially urban poor therefore, must aim at transforming society's attitudes towards women and also their own attitude towards themselves. Development of the level of education among the women is the main strategy through which their exploitation can be avoided and the process of social, economic and political change in their status enhanced. (Sharma, 1994)

Development which may be multifaceted in nature can be defined to mean 'Process of efforts to attain specific standard of life to have fulness in life especially for the women of the weaker section of society (Devasia, 1995)'. It also points out individual and collective responsibility to meet the basic needs of the under privileged, *i.e.* the weaker sections and of the slum women. Hence, it includes all types of educational, social and economic interventions that have a primary and direct concerned with promoting both the progress of the individual and of the society as a whole. Human being is the central concern and human dignity is the supreme value. Without having human equality and freedom, sustainable development of women is not possible. In other words, the values of social justice and dignity must be inherent in the philosophy of development, especially in its application in relation to the underprivileged in a society, such as women of the most neglected area, *i.e.* the slum. To humanise Indian society, we need more meaningful expression of these values. (Devasia and Devasia, 1994)

In our country, development had its origin in efforts to deal with illiteracy, poverty and unfortunately, there are still the priority concern; although our efforts must be for freedom from exploitation, oppression, elimination of corruption and nefarious political opportunism, of promotion of self-help and environmental protection. Such efforts reflect our conflict between self-help and environmental protection. Such efforts reflect our conflict between self-help and societies priorities in promoting human progress. Development of women in all areas of life is absolutely essential for sustainable development.

"The total development of women is imperative for the development of a society, such a development is inclusive of educational development, but also emphasises in terms of economic, political, social, cultural and environmental aspects". In a society there are various hurdles in ensuring the participation of women who are highly stratified and are culturally and economically divided into small groups. "The challenge of development in the society is not only the problem of education and finance but also the problem of motivation and mobilisation of women who belong to various castes and classes is inextricably intertwined with the developmental programmes in a society." (Devasia and Devasia, 1991)

Developmental policies and programmes for women specially the downtrodden like slum women, motivating and mobilising them for participating in such activities and helping them to enjoy the fruits of their labour, define the holistic human perspective of a community. To seek educational freedom is the most important priority for the development of self-confidence and inner potentialities of women, because educational development provides self-respect and independence to a woman.

So, there is a need for implementation of programmes based on equality and social justice and recognition of aspirations of poor women based on social security and social insurance. Poor women can develop only when they are given protection, education and special treatment. Hence, social development of women in India must be considered as a corrective measure, because social justice is the backbone of such development perspectives.

Keeping in view the transparency of the problems of women development and recognising its urgency for the need of sustainable educational development of the poor women and the underprivileged, various developmental plans and programmes in government as well as non-government level have already been set-up. Most of the plans and programmes have already been implemented from national level to grass-root level. In this background National Literacy Mission as an indispensable part of the Ministry of Human Resource Development was launched for the development and upliftment of the downtrodden people.

LITERACY PROGRAMME IN INDIA

Illiteracy is a worldwide problem eating into the fabric of the society. In many of the developing countries illiteracy remains a social problem even today. "On an average fifty per cent of the world's adult population does not know how to read and write. In some areas of Africa, Asia and Latin America, the illiteracy rate is as high as almost 70 to 80 per cent". (UNESCO, E/3771-1963)

It is disturbing to learn that, India is one of the largest contributors to world illiteracy. Though India has been making progress in literacy from 16.7% in 1951 (Census Report, 1951) to 52.21% in 1991 (Census Report, 1991), 62% in 1997 (53rd round NSSO report, 1997) and at the beginning of the millennium, the literacy rate for a population of over one billion is estimated 65.38% (Census Report, 2001). According to the NLM (Report of NLM, 1988), the number of illiterates in the age group 15–35 increased from 91 million in 1951 to 110 million in 1981. On the basis of trend analysis, the number of illiterates in the age group was likely to go up to 116 millions by 1991 and decline to 110 by 2001 AD. It is estimated that, with the intervention of National Literacy Mission (NLM) in addition to the efforts of Universalisation of Elementary Education (Formal and Non-formal streams), the number of illiterates in 15–35 age group would reduce to 12 million by 2001 AD (NLM, 1988).

It is presumed that formal schooling promotes literacy. But adult literacy remains a matter at great social concern since long. Efforts have constantly been made to fight against illiteracy among adults through social education programme, community development programme, adult education programme and similar other programmes.

During pre-independence period, adult literacy and education were taken up on voluntary efforts by some agencies, philanthropists and social workers. Their efforts were sporadic, and therefore the demonstrability of its impact was limited (Singh, 1996). In the year 1936, adult education was adopted for the first time as a definite responsibility of the Government, and adult literacy was organised as a movement. In the year 1938 Central Advisory Board of Education (CABE) acted as an Adult Education Committee, which recommended that no government can make an appreciable headway with its schemes for promoting socio-economic welfare of its people unless the people are prepared to make proper use of the facilities provided to them. Subsequently, in the year 1944 a scheme for adult education identifying the target age group 10–40 years was prepared. Accordingly, within one year of time span, training to the adult education instructors, involvement of voluntary agencies, and other necessary pre-arrangements for imparting adult education among the illiterate adults were made. In the year 1948, a sub-committee was formed by the Central Advisory Board of Education (CABE) to report on the achievements of adult education. In their report the committee opined that, literacy and general education form a part of adult education to enable every Indian to participate effectively in the new social order. The concept of general education was further developed to Social Education in the year 1949 as the goal for the education to the adults. This concept of social education included Literacy, Extension work, General Education, and Leadership Training. After Independence, Adult Literacy became an important activity of the Community Development Programme launched in 1952. Social awareness, spirit of social solidarity and importance of planned development were inculcated in the minds of people. In the year 1963, a project was submitted on social education in which clearly mentioned that 'adult literacy is largely a matter of leadership. The function of leadership in literacy is to provide literacy movement integrating literacy ideologically and harnessing people's energy to fight out illiteracy'. The Education Commission of 1964-66 acknowledged the achievement of adult education as a voluntary activity; the basic driving force of which was individual motivation of adults. The basic integral motivation for literacy was the result of slow growing environmental pressure and rising personal aspirations.

By early 1970's two significant events—Paulo Freire's writings on Concientisation Approach and the deliberations of International Symposium on Literacy held in Persepolis in 1975—seem to have influenced the concept of adult education. Viewing education as an element in the process of human liberation, Freire considered that the main task of adult education is to bring about a process of critical reflection that leads to action and change. According to him, dialogue and participation are key elements of liberating education and the role of adult educator is to enter into dialogue with illiterates about concrete situations and offer them the instrument with which they can teach themselves to read and write (Lind and Johnston, 1990). Freire's ideology was reaffirmed in the declaration of Persepolis, which considered literacy to be not just the process of learning the skills of reading, writing and arithmetic, but a contribution to the liberation of man and to his full development. Further, the declaration clarified that the concept of functionality must be extended to include all its dimensions political, economic, social and cultural. Just as development is not only economic growth so literacy must aim above all to grouse in the individual a critical awareness of social reality and to enable him or her to understand, master and transform his or her destiny. (Bataille, 1976)

These overseas ideas had their impact on Indian Adult Education and literacy programme. The scope and significance of combining the twin components of functionality and liberation was realised then in 1978 to alleviate poverty and liquidate illiteracy. It became an historic event, when the Government of India gave top priority to adult education by issuing a policy statement on Adult Education and formulated the National Adult Education Programme (NAEP) on 2nd

October, 1978. The conceptual framework of NAEP laid equal emphasis on literacy, functionality and social awareness, and visualised adult education as a means to bring about a fundamental change in the process of socio-economic development. The NAEP brought to limelight the problems of illiteracy, its magnitude, and it proposed for life long education as a cherished goal. The NAEP was mainly based on the establishment of adult education centres in villages and urban slums where the learning was imparted in groups. But in comparison with the magnitude of the problem of illiteracy, the endeavour was quite meagre. Thereby, the national adult education programme, the torch-bearer for more viable alternative for the eradication of illiteracy in the country received the boost.

The Fourth International Conference on Adult Education, held in Paris in March 1985, also took efforts at the eradication of illiteracy from among the adults of the world by declaring that 'the right to learn is now more than over a major challenge for humanity'. Elaborating its meaning the conference states, "The right to learn is the right to read and write; the right to question and analyse; the right to imagine and create; the right to read one's own world and write history; the right to have access to educational resources'; the right to develop individual and collective skills." (FICAE-Paris : 1985)

The 1980s also witnessed the expansion of University Adult Education in India when the University Grants Commission under the dynamic leadership of Dr. Madhuri Shah provided hundred per cent grants to 93 Universities to take up adult continuing education and extension activities with the active participation of Universities (UGC Report, 1987). Realising the severity of the problem of illiteracy, Government of India launched Mass Programme for Functional Literacy (MPFL) on 1st May, 1986, with a view to eradicate illiteracy from the country as early as possible. According to this programme, it is anticipated that educated persons would teach at least one illiterate adult voluntarily taking it up as his/her moral duty. As a result, participation of students both in colleges and schools increased tremendously. This programme was also termed as "Each One Teach One" (EOTO) Programme. The expansion of Nehru Yuvak Kendras provided an opportunity to non-student youth to participate in this literacy programme and other developmental activities all over the country.

Upholding literacy as an important component of human resource development, the Seventh Five-Year Plan (1985–90) stated the need for strengthening the programme for training in functional skills relevant to economic activities, and adopting the strategy of mass movement to cover the huge target of illiterates. (GOI, 1985–90)

The importance of eradication of illiteracy was reiterated by National Policy on Education in the year 1986, which envisaged that education 'provides the instruments for liberation from ignorance and oppression. Since the ability to read and write is the main instrument in the modern world, it will naturally include in Education to develop the skills for further development of the individual. Hence, there is crucial importance adult education including adult literacy'. Adult education including adult literacy would be a means for reducing economic, social and gender disparities. The nation as a whole would assume the responsibility for providing resource support to the eradication of illiteracy particularly, in the 15–35 age group through campaigns of National Literacy Mission. Since the involvement of the participants of the literacy campaigns in the development programme is of crucial importance, the National Literacy Mission will be geared to the national goals such as alleviation of poverty, national integration, environmental conservation, observance of the small family norm, promotion of women's equality, universalisation of primary education, basic healthcare, etc. It will also facilitate energisation of the cultural creativity of the people and their active participation in development process". The National Policy on Education (NPE, 86) further states : "Comprehensive Programme of post-literacy and continuing education will be provided for neoliterates and youth who have received primary education with a view to enabling them to retain and upgrade their literacy skills, and to harness it for the improvement of their living and working condition."

NATIONAL LITERACY MISSION (NLM)

Concept and Function : National Literacy Mission is one of the seven National Technology Missions under the Ministry of Human Resource Development, Government of India, (the other six National Missions are ; Immunisation, Literacy, Drinking Water, Oil Seed Production, Tele ommunication and Dairy). The National Literacy Mission (NLM) was launched on 5th May, 1988 by the then Prime Minister Late Shri Rajeev Gandhi to impart functional literacy to 100 million neo-literate persons in the age group 15–35 in a time bound manner. The then Prime Minister appealed to all citizens of the country in general and educated mass in particular to extend their active co-operation for undertaking literacy work as a National Service with Missionary spirit and to make it a People's Mission in true sense.

Therefore, NLM, the mission for all, is concerned and totally concerned with the issues of literacy and total literacy.

NLM embodies an urgency. The 1991 census indicated that 332.9 million citizens (of age group 7 and above) remained still illiterate as compared to 305.31 millions as per 1981 census. NLM therefore, signifies a resounding commitment to tackling this problem, which actually affects national, productivity, and social harmony. The NLM thus is an effort on a national scale. NLM is not an exclusive club for a few pedagogues and administrators. The NLM depends upon every individual citizen and organised groups of citizens to respond to the adverse situation of illiteracy, and to volunteer their co-operation to eradicate illiteracy of this dimension over an agreed deadline. (Rajan, 1994)

In operational terms, the contribution expected of the citizens is just a little of their time for a limited period, whereas this little contribution would account for an enormous achievement for the national plan.

On its very inception, the NLM studied the previous programmes implemented for literacy, and also examined the models available elsewhere in the world. As for the earlier literacy programmes there was a consensus that, India needed a more comprehensive programme which would close in on the deadline much more rapidly, effectively, credibly.

As for international models, it was found that India could not readily import a model in toto. The numbers involved were much higher than elsewhere, the felt urgency to liquidate illiteracy keen and the operational modalities had to accommodate many more of diversities of geographic terrain, national subcultures and administrative mechanisms. What was therefore required was not that a few people get together, and fabricate a die-cast model of a literacy programme to be enforced all over the country. In order that the programme remained viable, it had to evolve organically through initiative at the grass-root level, enlisting the people's movement, and be cost effective and time bound and be adequately tented for its acceptability.

A happy and fortuitous discovery consisted in the mass literacy campaign initiated in 1989 and successfully completed in 1990 in the district of Ernakulam in Kerala. Instead of launching a pre-determined government sponsored programme, the district administration thought of campaigning for literacy, with people's participation in all stages of planning and implementation. Ernakulam had sparked off a truly people's movement for literacy. The campaign was eventually adopted all over the state of Kerala and many more districts in different parts of the country. Since then, such literacy campaigns have been launched with full or partial coverage in as many as 442 districts in the country located in 22 states and 4 Union Territories. The literacy campaigns of NLM are funded both by the Central and State Governments in the ratio of 2:1 ensuring a statutory Centre-State partnership.

The achievement under Total Literacy Campaign (in terms of coverage of learners and literacy competency) could vary from district to district for various causes. The TLC nevertheless represents a studied, disciplined and well-planned thrust of campaigning for literacy and achieving it by a deadline on a massive scale as "Never Before." (Rajan, 1994)

"Literacy" as the learner's achievement and Total Literacy as the intended coverage of the target group are sensitive terminology. In popular perception "Literacy" remains all things for all men. "It is important that this basic terminology be properly understood in the TLC context, not only by the public at large, but also by the TLC functionaries themselves". (NLM Report, 1994).

Concept of Functional Literacy in Terms of NLM

The literacy campaigns in India are being spoken and written about with some interest since the 1990s, after the successful experiment of Ernakulam Total Literacy Campaign. Once again, there was concern and renewed national interest when promotion of literacy was identified as one of the National Missions in the Seventh Five-Year Plan. As a result, NLM was launched in 1988 with the objective to impart functional literacy to 80 millions illiterate person in 15–35 age group, 30 million by 1990, and 50 million by the year 1995. Subsequently, changes were made in the target which now stands at 100 million people to be made literate in the same age group by the year 1999, and full literacy to be achieved by 2005, through a variety of means, and with the active involvement of all sections of society (NLM, 1998).

The concept of functional literacy envisaged under NLM was much broader than that envisaged earlier and included the following four aspects :

(i) Achieving self-reliance in literacy and numeracy.

(ii) Becoming aware of the causes of one's deprivation and moving towards its amelioration of one's conditions of life through organisation and participation in the process of development.

(iii) Acquiring skills to improve the economic status and general well being.

(iv) Imbibing the values of national integration, conservation of the environment, women's equality, observance of small family norms etc.

The NLM further had defined the desired level of competencies in 3 R's.

Reading : Reading aloud with normal accent and at a speed of 30 words-a-minute a simple passage on topic of interest to the learner.

- Silent reading, at 35 words-a-minute, a small paragraph in simple language.
- Reading with understanding the road-signs, posters, simple instructions and newspapers/ broadsheets designed for neo-literates.
- Ability to follow simple written passages relating to one's working and living environment.

Writing : Copying with understanding at 7 words-a-minute.

- Taking dictation at 5 words-a-minute.
- Writing with proper spacing and alignment.
- Writing independently short letters and applications, and filling in forms of day-to-day use to the learner.

Numercy : Reading and Writing numbers from 1 to 100.

- Doing simple calculations (without fractions), involving addition and subtraction up to 3 digits, and multiplication and division by 2 digits.
- Working knowledge of metric units of weights, measures, currency, distance, area, and units of time.
- Broad idea of proportion and interest (not involving fractions) and their use in practical situations, *i.e.* in working and living conditions.

The campaign approach adopted as a dominant strategy of NLM proved itself to be the most appropriate strategy, because the goal goes beyond the simple achievement of self-reliance in the 3 R's. to functional literacy and other spin off. It also includes skill development, which enables people to improve their economic status.

Concept of Post-Literacy and Continuing Education

It is a well-recognised fact that neo-literates who acquire basic literacy skills through the literacy campaigns, may face a great difficulty in retaining them, and unless timely follow-up measures are taken most of them may regress to partial or total illiteracy. Thus, it is absolutely essential that those who acquire basic literacy skills make them permanent by reinforcing them through post-literacy programmes. (NLM, 1991)

One of the major objectives of post-literacy campaign taken up of a Total Literacy Campaign of NLM is therefore to enable neo-literates to learn the application of literacy skills as problem solving tools, so that learning becomes relevant to living and working. Within a limited period of time available during TLC's, it is usually not possible to dwell adequately on the functionality and awareness aspects of the literacy programme. Therefore, in the post-literacy phase the objectives take centre stage. The NLM has visualised the post-literacy programme as an extension of the TLC in the continuum of life long education.

Continuing education programmes under the specific scheme of NLM are taken up only in the districts that have completed both the TLC and PLC phases, and the external evaluation of the TLC has been conducted. (NLM Report, 1991)

The scheme of NLM aims at providing an institutionalised mechanism for continuing education through Continuing Education Centres (CEC's) to enable the neo-literates to retain, improve and apply their basic knowledge and skills in fulfilling their needs and aspirations (NLM Report, 1991)

The literacy campaigns taken up in most of the parts of the country today have not merely been campaigns for literacy, but also the campaigns for family welfare, immunisation, maternal and child-healthcare, conservation of environment, communal harmony, cohesion, national integration and women's development. Because, the aim of literacy mission is not just to enable people to read, write, compute in mother tongue, or in a national language, but also to acquaint them with their rights and duties, to make them realise about the causes of their poverty and deprivation, and to improve their characters, habits, scientific ideas and values etc., which are essential for development of their personalities, communities and nation. Thus, there have been several exciting, interesting and positive spin-offs beneficial to the individual and to the community at large. (NLM Report, 98-99)

LITERACY PROGRAMME FOR WOMEN

In the modern world that is characterised by a vast array of human achievement in diverse fields of knowledge and action, the instrumentality of literacy as the prime mover of change and development has been obvious. "The most critical challenge of the new vision is to reduce gender gaps in learning, especially in countries where female illiteracy rates are higher than those of males. India is a classic example where the literacy status of a majority of women is particularly groom." (Vanka, 1995)

Though there has been a steady increase in the female literacy rate since independence, the fact that the female literacy rate stood at 39.29 per cent as compared to 64.1 per cent for males (Census of India, 1991) explained the gravity of the problem. Of course, the report of the 53 round Survey of National Sample Survey Organisation (NSSO, 1997) is definitely a hopeful one for the increase of literacy rate in general and women in particular. As per the survey report of NSSO, 1997, the literacy rate of India has increased to 62 per cent in 1997 from 52.21 in 1991 with male and female literacy rates being 73 per cent and 50 per cent respectively. (*Source* : Ministry of Information and Broadcasting GOI, 2000).

The NSSO figures although show an optimistic increase in female literacy of India with in a period of six years *i.e.* from 1991–1997, but the number of illiterate women is higher than that of men and their illiteracy needs to be arrested very soon for active participation in community development services. "While it is recognised by policy planners that the problem of illiteracy is grave amongst women, women literacy has never received the priority attention it deserves. Despite the magnitude of the problems of illiteracy among women, their educational needs are not systematically addressed in National Educational Policies and Plans." (Dighe and Patel, 1992)

The major thrust of Government of India is the educational strategy in development plans. The major thrust has been on making women literate through an expansion of formal educational system. The assumption has been that access to formal education would solve the problem of illiteracy among women. In spite of the policy initiatives to improve women's education since independence, problems of access, quality, quality and relevance have exacerbated over the years.

The significance of female literacy did not receive due priority during post-independence period. The problem of women literacy has in recent years been examined by a number of committees like National Committee on Education of Women under the chairmanship of Smt. Durgabai Deshmukh (1959), the Committee on Differentiation of Curricula under the chairmanship of Smt. Hansa Mehta (1961), and the committee of Shri M. Bhaktawatsalam (1963) which studied the problem in the six states where the education of girls is less developed or illiteracy rate among women is high. But, there was no solid groundwork for the eradication of women's illiteracy by 1950s (Dighe, 1993). It is also a point to note that adult literacy has been a national concern by fits and starts for more than 60 years. Some of the important programmes implemented for eradication of illiteracy among adults (both for male and female) in post-independence period in India includes Social Education Programme (1951), Maharashtra Gram Shikhan Mohim (1959),

Farmers Functional Literacy Programme (1967), Non-formal Education (1974), Polyvalent Adult Education Centres (1978) and Functional Literacy for Adult Women (1977). National-wise efforts in the field of Adult Literacy were started in 1978 under National Adult Education Programme (NAEP) in terms of Rural Functional Literacy Projects (RELP), and Mass Programme of Functional Literacy (MPFL). A massive campaigning for Adult Literacy and Learning was launched by National Literacy Mission in 1988, to impart functional literacy to the mass non-literates.

The Adult Literacy Programmes mentioned above were mainly participated by the male members of the society, although one of the programme was meant for both the sexes. There was only one specific literacy programme implemented for the development of female literacy in rural areas and its development was rather very slow. It was the year 1950's with the exception of condensed courses for adult women started by central social welfare Board, where the women literacy remained as an integral part of community development programme.

During 1960s when a direct correlation emerged between education and economic growth, the emphasis of literacy programme shifted from civic to functional literacy. It was felt that literacy, if it is worthwhile, must be functional and the participation of people from each and every sector specially the women and the downtrodden, is essential. (Shah, 1995)

Realising the essence of literacy and education of the women in the country, the Education Commission of 1964-66 recommended that 'for the full development of human resources, the improvement of homes and for molding character of children during the most impressionable years of infancy, the education of women is of greater importance than that of men. In the modern world the role of women goes much beyond the home and the bringing up of children'. (Report of Kothari Commission, 1964-66)

As a result, during the 1970's Functional Literacy for Adult Women Project was implemented with a view to accelerating the participation of Adult Women in developmental efforts of local communities and bring about attitudinal changes among them. This project also proved the efficiency of functional literacy as a tool for accelerating the pace of women's development.

But this literacy programme was tentatively to be ad hoc, short-term and limited in scope. The gravity of the problem of illiteracy among women received proper attention by the Government of India during the late 1970s, and early 1980s when it was noted that 'Literacy itself is not a solution to the basic problems of the poor women, and any attempt to eradicate poverty should lead the women to deal with the question of equality, social justice and development'. (Shram Shakti, 1988)

It was on 2nd October, 1978, "The National Adult Education Programme" was launched by Government of India to enable men and women to play an active role in socio-cultural sphere. The programme gave a new thrust to the overall development of human resources to meet the changing demand of the country. Literacy was recognised as an integral part of the NAEP. It also aimed at upgrading functional skills and in creating social awareness among the illiterates. The problem of illiteracy among women was given special attention and a special committee was set-up by Ministry of Education to study the problems of women literacy in 1977-78. The Committee identified the urgent necessity of recognising the productive and economic roles, which the large majority of adult illiterate women played in society, particularly in case of rural women. The committee opined that adult education programme should aim at : *(i)* making women and men more conscious of their rights and responsibilities, and laws governing women's status, *(ii)* assisting women to improve their economic conditions through literacy and other skills, *(iii)* providing women access to knowledge in other areas including health, childcare, family planning etc., and *(iv)* assisting women to form their own groups for learning and productive activity and to strengthen their participation and voice in the development process. (GOI, 1985)

Based on the literacy activities of NAEP, 1978, the Review Committee on National Adult Education programme reported in 1980 that only 35 per cent of the population covered up to 31st January, 1980 were women. The committee identified certain special problems for this slow progress in women's access to this programme. These were *viz.* resistance among men and the community, lack of time and energy among poor women, difficulties in finding common time for men and women to attend classes, inadequate number of women instructors and supervisors and absence of childcare facilities. The committee recommended more meaningful efforts to relate educational content to the characteristics and need of the women's groups, provision of childcare facilities with each adult education centre for women, and organising classes during and as a part of women's working time by reorganising work schedules of Government, developmental agencies and other employers in the organised and semi-organised sectors. The committee also advised stronger effort to involve women and women's institutions (Schools, Colleges etc.) in the programme and the promotion of grass-root level women's organisations (Mahila mandals) along with education centres (GOI, 1985).

During 1984-85 (up to December, 1984) total enrolment under Adult Education was 55.34 lakhs, out of which 26.44 lakhs were men and 28.90 lakhs were women, coverage of women being 52.33 of the total. In addition, 3.52 lakhs were covered under the Functional Literacy for Adult Women (FLAW) programme. For literacy learning which was introduced in 1975-76 and covered in 23 States and Union Territories by 1977. This programme was exclusively meant for the rural women. (GOI, 1985)

The aims of FLAW programme was to impart non-formal education using functional literacy as the means accelerating participation of adult women in the developmental efforts in the community so as to bring about attitudinal changes among them which would enable women to play their role as citizens. The scheme was conceived as a package of services to adult women in 15–45 age group and was implemented jointly by the department of education and social welfare in the experimental ICDS project areas. The functional literacy classes were organised by the Anganwadi workers of ICDS projects, who were given an additional honorarium of Rs. 50 per month. The contents of the programme included elements of health and hygiene, food and nutrition, home management and childcare, civic and vocational education (Shah, 1995).

To promote adult literacy among women, Government of India has made provision to liberalise grant-in-aid rules for the voluntary organisations working in the field of adult education to run adult education centres exclusively for women. Also a scheme of special award has been introduced by GOI to promote adult literacy especially among women in the 15–35 age group. There are three categories of awards for adult education centres: District, State and Union Territory level. To encourage completion among equals for the state level awards, the states have been grouped into four categories :

(a) Those with a female literacy rate up to 16 per cent.

(b) Those between 20 to 26 per cent.

(c) Those between 27 to 37 per cent.

(d) Those above 32 per cent.

In each of these categories the state, which has shown the best performance in raising female literacy has been awarded a prize of Rs. 25 lakhs during the current year. In spite of these special attention and introduction of special award scheme, the participation of women in Adult Education Programme during late 1980s is far from satisfactory. (Laso, 1997)

The New Education Policy on Education, 1986, emphasised elimination of disparities in educational system and provision of facilities through qualitative programme interventions for women empowerment. The NPE (1986) revised in 1992, and the Programme of Action (1992) reflect an unqualified priority to Total Literacy, Elementary Education and the ending of Gender Differentials (GOI, 1997).

With the emergence of National Literacy Mission (1988) there has been an increased emphasis on the aims, as laid down in NAEP, for women's development. NLM, set-up in 1988, is one of the most concerted efforts put so far to promote functional literacy in the country. It is based on the promise that literacy is an indispensable component of human resource development aimed to harness the advances in science and technological science for the benefit of the people specially the disadvantaged, the women, ST, SC and backward classes (Jena, 1999). The level of literacy of the women is acknowledged by NLM as one of the most significant indicators of human development, and makes this all more alarming. With one-third of the seats in Panchayats and Nagarpalikas reserved for women the need for them to become literate is visual (NLM, 1997).

NLM's approach of campaigning and environment building mechanism of Kala Jattha, in local folk form, street plays, padayatras, public meeting cum interaction programmes, people's platform on concurrent social issues, etc., in generating consciousness for National Integration, Environment Protection, Maintaining Small Family Norms, and the Women Issues and their solutions have been able to motivate the mass, mostly women, to join the campaign enthusiastically. It's clear, objective, time-bound, centre-based teaching at the interest and convenience of the learners, mainly women (both housewives and working), linkages of literacy with other developmental activities like skill development and income generation activities, child and maternity care, small savings and co-operatives, etc., and scope for grass-root leadership have generated awareness among the people to join the literacy programme actively. As a matter of fact, women's literacy for equality and development became one of the most important components within the literacy programme of ongoing Total Literacy Campaigns since 1988, and the mission has established important milestones by bringing 448 districts under the folds of literacy campaigns. By 1998, 965.76 lakhs people were enrolled in the TLC out of which 586.69 lakhs (60.75%) are women, and out of the total achievement *i.e.* 524.73 lakhs neo-literates 310.12 (59.10%) are of women. (NLM Report, 1998)

The literacy movement has to its credit several achievements it can be proud of. Apart from achieving the required level of literacy they experience a tremendous increase in self-worth, and go on to form groups, co-operatives and small business. Women's empowerment has resulted in their getting organised to protest against social evils such as alcoholism, abuse, etc. (NLM–A People's Movement 1997).

Jena (1999) has observed and stated : "Literacy campaigns in India have already been successful in imparting skills to the people specially to women." With the success of the campaign approach for literacy, the traditional roles are breaking down and women have started accepting non-traditional roles in some places *e.g.* The neo-literate women of Baroda district have learnt how to repair handpumps. Where as neo-literate women of Solan (Himachal Pradesh) have launched a environmental pollution drive by launching a crusade against polythene bags. And district like Dumka (Bihar) and Pudukottai (Tamil Nadu) have accelerated the process of women's empowerment by allowing women to take up non-traditional vocations. In Nallore, Andhra Pradesh, thrift groups called 'Pudupu Laxmi' were formed where each women contributed at least one rupee every day from her meagre earning and there were no defaulters and today such thrift groups generate lakhs of rupees.

The neo-literate women of Nallore District of Andhra Pradesh have formed 'thrift groups' called "Pudupu Laxmi" by contributing one rupee each every day from her meagre earnings. These habits of savings have enabled them to get away from the clutches of the traditional money lenders who charged them exorbitant rates of interest. Perhaps, it was peer pressure or perhaps it was their knowledge that such soft loans would only be possible if there was repayment, but the fact is that there were no defaulters, and today such thrift groups generate lakhs of rupees (Jena, 1999).

The anti-arrack agitation which started in Nallore District of Andhra Pradesh, and which finally resulted in total prohibition being enforced throughout the state was an outcome of the active participation of women in literacy movement of NLM. (BGVS, 1997)

Bharat Gyan Vigyan Samiti (BGVS) is a nationwide NGO working in close association with the National Literacy Mission, Government of India since 1989 and it has been contributing its level best to achieve the goal of NLM in a successful direction. To energise the people specially the disadvantaged lot like women and downtrodden of the society and to make literacy an issue before them, BGVS has so far organised 3 Jatthas in 1990, 1992 and 1993 covering 412 districts (nearly 4000 villages) in the country (excluding Arunachal Pradesh, Goa, Jammu and Kashmir, Meghalaya, Mizoram and Sikkim). The third Jattha *i.e.* 'SAMATA' (8th March and 19th April, 1993) was organised by the women wing of BGVS. It was exclusively addressed to the theme of education, equality and empowerment of women. The explicit aim of the Jattha was to draw women and women's organisation into the literacy campaign and to highlight the need of educating the girl child. The event was marked by nearly 130 young women and men taking out 8 women's Kala Jatthas from different parts of the country and closing at Jhansi (UP) on 8th April, 1993. (Rajan, 1994).

As a result of this 'SAMATA' Jattha 1993, the literacy campaigns and their activities took a new shape in the country. Women from different sectors of social life and living came out to join the campaign spontaneously as learners and volunteers. A number of voluntary women organisation also came forward to take up the programme of NLM for the development of women literacy and equality (BGVS, 1994).

The Mahila Samakshya programme is a direct outcome of the commitment of affirmative action in support of women's education mandated in the National Policy of Education (1986). It is a Indo-Duch Project launched in April, 1989. It seeks to mobilise rural women for literacy development and empowerment through Mahila Sanghas. It is an endeavour towards creating a learning environment where women can collectively affirm their potentials, gain strength to demand information and knowledge, and move forward to change and take charge of their lives. Mahila Samakshya has been related with National Literacy Mission to link women's empowerment with literacy development and education. By 1999 this programme has been implemented in 17 districts spread over the four states of Andhra Pradesh, Gujarat, Karnataka and Uttar Pradesh.

The Mahila Samakshya approach begins with the understanding that women must identify their problems and evolve solution at their own pace by means of literacy and educational development (Agrawal, 1999). This programme has been able to lay the foundation for literacy development of the women and empowerment at grass-root levels and make strategic interventions to support education of girls and adult women. Also it has met with success in raising the demand for education especially among women. (INDIA, 2000)

LITERACY PROGRAMME FOR THE SLUM WOMEN

Adult Literacy emerged as a distinct field of activity in India during 1937 when provincial governments organised mass literacy programmes. Since then, a variety of adult literacy programmes have been undertaken in the country and can be classified under three types of agencies *viz.* government, non-government and international. The adult literacy programmes in India thus have seen more changes than any other development programmes in such a span of time. Some of the important programmes implemented for eradication of illiteracy among adults in post-independence period have already been mentioned earlier.

The adult learners appear to have been perceived in all those adult literacy programmes as large categories differentiated in terms of sex (Male and Female) to a large extent and place of residence (rural, urban and tribal) to a lesser extent. In fact, except the polyvalent adult education centre (Shramik Vidyapith), all major adult literacy programmes implemented so far primarily focused on eradication of illiteracy from rural areas (Ahmad, 1999).

Thus, the situation in the slum combined with numerous complex socio-cultural and economic factors have made the slum women the most deprived group as far as education and literacy development is concerned. Despite facilities for education equally available for boys and girls, there is a significantly lower level of utilisation of facilities by the girls and women, and these facilities are almost absent in case of slum women. Women who form a pivotal point around whom family life, living and the community development resolve constitute the bulk of illiterates in general and slum setting in particular. "The problem of illiteracy among slum women is not an isolated phenomenon. It is inextricably linked to the socio-economic conditions and rapid growth of urbanisation that prevails in different parts of the country" (Dighe, 1993). While it is realised by the policy planners, administrators and implementators that the problems of illiteracy is serious among the disadvantaged women of urban slums, ST, SC and other disadvantaged backward categories, literacy development has never received serious attention it deserves.

It is true that, steps have been taken for the eradication of illiteracy among the rural people in general and women in particular since 1937, and some satisfactory results have also been achieved through these programmes. But it can be seen that almost all the programmes are implemented only for the rural people. Only programmes like functional literacy for adult women (FLAW, 1977) and Mahila Samakshya (1989) programme have been implemented so far for the literacy development of women in urban slums. "There is no adequate programme in our country to guide the women and youth in the slum about opportunities of literacy development, training and employment are available to them." (Bijlani, 1991)

The major education policy documents of the Government of India pertaining to the last two decades are the National Policy on Education, 1986 and the Five-Year Plans. A glance at these documents shows that, the Government has no specific policies and programmes of education targeted on the large number of adults (both male and female) living in the innumerable slum in the country. Rather, the government has adopted policies and programmes for adults in general.

Obviously, there is no realisation of the specificity of the condition of slum-dwellers including the slum women. So, the general policies and programmes of adult literacy development apply to the slumdwellers as to the adult illiterates living in rural and tribal areas (Choudhary, 1997).

The Polyvalent Adult Education centre in the form of 'Shramik Vidyapith' however, provides non-formal and continuing education to the urban workers. It is meant to provide the individual (both male and female not only the skills to enhance his/her productive potential, but also the knowledge necessary to improve the quality of his/her life. This institution speaks for its concern for the economically and educationally deprived sections of the urban society. The Mass Programme for Functional Literacy (MPFL) up to a certain extent has had urban coverage. It was implemented in the urban areas mainly through the Shramik Vidyapiths (Agrawal, 1999). However, the programmes of Shramik Vidyapeeth and MPFL were implemented for all men and women. Some provisions were also made for the education of slum children of urban areas through NFE Centres under 8th Five-Year Plan. No specification was made for the slum women for literacy development, although some of the activities/items of 'Shramik Vidyapeeth' were meant for the women viz. mehendi application, food preservation, safe motherhood course etc. (SVP, 1998).

Further, the scheme of Shramik Vidyapith (SVP) is an unconventional programme—Non-Formal, Adult and Continuing 'Education implemented primarily in urban and industrial areas'. The basic objective of this scheme is to improve the occupational skill and technical knowledge of workers (both men and women) for enhancing their efficiency and increasing productive ability. It is proposed to be continued with a new nomenclature, *i.e.* Jan Sikshan Sansthan (JSS).

The impact of policy planning of education in general and adult education programme in particular during the last two decades shows that the decadal increase in rural literacy rate is higher than that of urban literacy rate. The increase in rural literacy rate during 1971-1981 was 6.15 per cent as against the urban literacy rate of 4.63 per cent, while the decadal increase in rural literacy rate during 1981-91 was recorded as 8.69 per cent as against the urban literacy rate of 5.88 per cent (Ahmad, 1999). The literacy rate among the urban people (both male and female) was 73.08 per cent in 1991 whereas among rural people (both male and female) was 44.69 per cent, and the literacy rate of male in rural areas was 59.87 per cent and female 30.62 per cent. The male literacy rate in urban areas was 81.09 per cent whereas the female literacy was 64.05 per cent in urban set-up (Census Report, 1991).

Even the programme implementation process of the campaign mode of mass literacy programmes adopted by National Literacy Mission (NLM) since 1990s also indicated the success of the programme in rural areas. This effort of NLM is however most appreciable and invitable (Ahmad, 1999). The idea of launching a literacy campaign for the illiterate mass of the country was revived in 1985, when the Government of India initiated the process of "re-shaping the education system" and circulated the document : "Challenge for Education" (Kidd and Timus, 1992). Importance given to Literacy in National Literacy Mission in May 1988 by the Prime Minister of India had given considerable boost to literacy programme for the upliftment and development of the people. In the light of the 73rd and 74th constitutional amendments, literacy has assumed even greater significance. If power for local self-governance is to evolve, to the panchayat in rural sector and Nagarpalikas in Urban areas, literacy is an essential pre-requisite for these institutions to be effective (NLM-A People's Movement, 97).

It was for the first time in Indian history that a serious thought was given to the human resource development in a true spirit by recognising the participation of people from each and every sector of the society in spite of their sex, level of education, socio-economic background and cultural identity. The NLM had a target of making 100 million people in the 15–35 age group functionally literate by 1999. This age group was selected, because they are both in productive as well as reproductive period of life. If they missed the opportunity or were denied access to mainstream formal education, TLCs offered them a second chance. Unlike the FLAW (1977), and Mahila Samakshya (1989) programme for the rural women no such specific programme was implemented by NLM for the literacy development of slum women in Urban India. (Choudhary, 1997)

However, special care is being taken to bring disadvantaged group like women urban poor, scheduled caste and tribes and the backward classes into the programme. The basic objective is to create a generation, which will ensure that their children are educated to realise the dream of "Education for All" (NLM, 1997).

The first breakthrough of NLM came in Kerala in Kottayam city followed by Ernakulam District, where the campaign was initiated in 1989 and successfully completed a year later. Here for the first time, an area specific, time bound campaign was used in a totally urban set-up, and the community became responsible for running its own development programme and consequently for determining its own future. The participation of women especially from the slum areas of Kottayam city as learners and volunteers in the campaign was encouraging. Active function of literacy campaign in urban area is a challenge to the mission because the heterogeneity in the social profile of urban situations restricts the process of mass mobilisation, which is a key component of the campaign mode of adult literacy programme (Ahmad, 1999). In urban areas campaigns have by and large met with little success so far. Continuous rural migration and the large 'floating' population that it has brought in its wake, has made sustaining any campaign extremely difficult (NLM, 1997). In spite of the urban challenge, the high literacy rate of 96.58 per cent was recorded in Kottayam Urban Agglomeration of Kerala in 1991. Since then the Nagarpalikas and District Administration of different states dare to accept the challenge of implementing literacy programme in their respective urban areas in the districts.

Shramik Vidyapeeths (Jana Siksha Sansthan) as implementing agencies of National Literacy Mission, extend their services to provide integrated education and training courses for different categories of urban workers mainly neo-literate men and women with a view to improving their professional competency and also enriching their views (Shah, 1999). In some places Shramik Vidyapiths have taken the initiatives in launching the literacy programme in the town/city. They are also giving priority to the sustainable development of the slum women basically to neo-literate women by imparting different types of training on vocational skills for increasing productivity and to make them self-sufficient in all respect for improving their quality of life. (SVP, 1998)

The efforts made by Shramik Vidyapith as implementing agency of NLM is no doubt effective and appreciable, but is not sufficient enough to bring equality and raise the social standard of the slum women in urban India. It needs a specific programme based on the magnitude of the problem of slum development for implementation because the basic philosophy and objectives of literacy programme revolves around the education of the masses (especially the disadvantaged group like slum-dwellers, SC, ST, Women etc.) through the propagation of scientific ideas, values and awareness among them, that they develop competence and confidence to counteract, realise the causes of their downfall, deprivation and discrimination, and even exterminate the orthodox and obscurant ideas and practices prevalent in the society.

It is clear that 'Women are the most deprived sections of society, especially among the poor and the destitute : Any development must ameliorate their misery if it is to be meaningful'. Literacy and Universal Elementary Education Programmes, especially for the females, can help to modify the ante-diluvian attitudes and bias against women. Literacy as well as focused adult education, both for men and women in the backward areas of the country, can help women face the challenges of life and to help their families. Such literacy programmes could be the least costly schemes to reach the disadvantaged women. Finally, it may be said that, what is needed in our country today is to implement specific literacy programmes for the disadvantaged group based on the magnitude of their problem of development, which is an exercise in maintaining culture of silence with the conscientisation of the slum and disadvantaged women for their liberation from oppression and exploitation, and for creation of a new egalitarian and just social order.

LITERACY AND DEVELOPMENT

Development in a country of India's size and diversity depends on the participation and is possible only in a democracy, when all the people will be literate.

Concept and Meaning of Development

The concept of development is not a new phenomenon , nor are the concerns of its sustainability. Development is a loaded word, which has been looked at differently by individuals based on their varying perception. To the extent, it is a changed strategy, directed towards achieving a better fit between needs, problems and community resources. The development debate of last fifty years has thrown-up several new formulations regarding alternative designs for living, and has brought into sharp focus a number of new concerns. The accent now is on human-centred development, and not on growth-rooted indication of GNP and national income. Nehru (1961) stated : "By development we mean development of consciousness; progressive change in our knowledge, understanding, attitudes, perceptions, aspirations, intensions, opinions, motives and values in the skills, technologies, systems, institutions, laws and organisational mechanisms constitute the foundation, a driving force for the process of development."

Development is nothing but a dynamic process of increasing the capacity and the potential of a human being; to identify the opportunities and skills; to tackle the problems of the humanity to increase the quality of life (Palanithurai, 1996). This concept of development emphasises the quality of life, not the pursuit of wealth, it takes note of deeply held cultural values and seeks to promote endogeneous creativity. The new concerns among others are focused on environment, energy and food security, and all three being interconnected and inter-dependent.

The meaning of the term development is so elusive that frequently varied interpretations are coming out in different human history. This is perhaps best illustrated by Dudly Sheers (1969), who conceived development as involving not only economic growth, but also conditions in which people in a country have adequate food and jobs and the income inequality among them, is greatly reduced. Furthermore, Sheers (1977) adding one more dimension of self-reliance to his earlier definition writes that the addition of this new element entails that the main emphasis on development would no longer be an overall growth rate or on patterns of distribution. The crucial targets from now onwards would be ownership as well as output in the leading economic sectors, consumption patterns that economise foreign exchange, institutional capacity for research and negotiation and cultural goals of the country.

A similar idea with different interpretation stressing more on the power structure is given by Abdul Mayeed (1982) that 'Development is no longer' considered a politically neutral process based on social science theories as applied to the autonomic integration of various socio-economic forces. It is largely the result of the political will of the power structure that the initiate a desired changes. It really means distributing the *status quo*, aiming at the amelioration of the conditions of the poor, but at the same time maintaining harmony and a spirit of co-operation within the community. Mayeed's statement points specifically to the fact that certain forms of development are a direct result of the wishes of the power structure. The implications of Mayeed's statement are that for social change for development depends on the will of the upper classes, and he suggests that they might undertake the altruistic exercise of ameliorating the conditions of the poor. Might not such social change be initiated by the poor themselves, provided that they are given the opportunity? If they do seek to improve their conditions, it might actually bring them into conflict with the state. Dutta (1979) suggests that the change only occurs through struggle between haves and have-nots, and that the distribution of wealth in a society occurs through class struggle so that development might occur only as a result of class struggle.

Modern Concept of Development

The use of the term development in its current sense began with the emergence of the nations of Third World. Though development is not infrequently identified with economic growth, and the tendency to interpret it so still persists, it is recognised as a multidimensional concept by developing nations and the developed nations. To overcome the controversies over the meaning of the term development, the U.N. General Assembly in 1971 has clearly spelt out seven principal objectives of development *viz.* *(a)* a minimum standard of living, consistent with human dignity, *(b)* sustained improvement in the well-being of an individual, *(c)* sharing of benefits by all, *(d)* more equitable distribution of income and wealth, *(e)* a greater degree of income security, **(f)** expansion and improvement of education, health, nutrition, housing and social welfare, and *(g)* the safe guarding of the environment (IDS, 1971).

These objectives of development embrace the whole gamut of a nation's economic, social and cultural life, and progress towards their realisation, which cannot be measured entirely by the rate of economic growth or by any other single indicator. In this connection the concept of UNDP (1981) on development is as follows : *(i)* Development is increasingly seen as a process that should be geared to the human factors, both as the agent and the beneficiary of development. *(ii)* It should be indigenous involving the autonomous definition by each society of its own values and goals. *(iii)* It should rely primarily on the strength and resources of each country. *(iv)* It should encompass the transformation of obstructive structures both national and international. *(v)* It should be in harmony with environment and should respect ecological constraints (UNDP, 1981). The purpose of development as stated by UNDP (1993) is to enlarge human choices-not just income-so the human development concept focusses on the entire society and not just the economy. Policy-makers are searching not only for development models that are people centred. They also want development to be more sustainable to project the options of future generation. This means that the conventional definition of capital must be broadened beyond the physical capital to include human capital.

Mishra (1981) in this connection states : "Development refers to a relatively stable long range increase in real national income that is accompanied by a change in the attitudes of the people, their motivations, institutional set-up, production, technique etc. Development from another angle may refer to production and utilisation of material resources or to the enrichment of human resources. The current indicators of development include both the economic and non-economic factors."

At the entrance of 21st century, all nations of the world face the challenge of properly integrating economic growth with human development. Links between economic growth and human development need to be explored. According to the Human Development Report (1995), human development is erected on four pillars—Productivity, Equity, Sustainability and Power. It regards economic growth as essential but emphasises the need to pay attention to its quality and distribution and analyses at length its link with human lives (UNDP, 1995). Recognition of human development concerns and the global commitment to human development issues emerged prominently at the United Nations Conference on environment at Rio (1992), the World Conference on Human Rights at Vienna (1993), the International Conference on Population and Development at Cairo (1994), and the World Summit for Social Development at Copenhagen. (1995)

Development is at any cost meant for man and mankind. The purpose of development is liberation of man. The same is also true of literacy and education. Education provides the instruments for human liberation from ignorance and oppression. Education as an organic entity changes and grows with the time, responds to the needs of the society and adopts to the environment. It was mostly an ornament in the agricultural civilisation, a tool for economic development in the industrial era and has become today all-pervasive resource that can find substitutes for other resources but has no substitute for itself. In the present scheme of things 'the onward march of a nation will stop if education system ceases to be dynamic and fails to respond adequately to the emerging challenges of a developing society'. (Kulundiswamy, 1997)

In a developing society, literacy is virtually the precondition for an individual's evolution and national development. With little access to information, modernisation and communication and virtually no access to survival tools the non-literate remain helpless, victims of poverty, deprivation and exploitation (Jena, 1999). According to Mahatma Gandhi, "Literacy was not the end of education, nor even the beginning. It was only one of the means where by men and women can be educated and developed." (Harijan, 1937)

Role of Literacy for Development

Role of literacy for development has been much discussed and debated in India and abroad. Whether literacy precedes development or follows it, literacy cannot be separated from the development process. In fact 'they are intrinsically related and there is a dynamic interplay between the two at various levels of society.' (Shah, 1999)

Literacy has been historically thought of as agent of individual and social development. Development is strictly human phenomenon. Development is basically about the people. There is no development without people. Development according to Nyerere (1988) is for the man, by the man, and of the man. The basic unit human factor is of utmost value. It is not agriculture or technology or industry that develops the humanity. It is humanity that develops agriculture, technology or industry—individually or collectivity, which is the centre of activity responsible for change and development. Literacy as an indispensable and indisputable component of human resource development is an essential tool for communication and learning for information and experience for national development. Literacy is not an end in itself but a means for better understanding of the surrounding world. It makes the individual largely autonomous for further learning.

Literacy, which involves more than the technical skills of reading and writing, is also about learning a language. Language, however, is not simply a tool or a medium of communication; it is packed with ideology and reproduces the oppressors world. What is needed in Adult Literacy

Process is initiating cultural action for freedom of oppressed illiterate masses. It would involve campaigns for what Freire (1975) calls conscientisation of the masses.

Over the last fifty years, numerous operational and philosophical definitions of literacy and development have emerged. The United Nations Population Commission (1948) has recommended that 'Literacy should be defined for census purposes at the ability both to read and to write a simple message in any language.' (GOI, 1955)

The World Congress of Ministers on the Eradication of Illiteracy, convened by UNESCO in Teheran (1965) concluded that "Literacy should be regarded as a way of preparing man for a social, civic and economic role that goes far beyond the rudiments of literacy training. The process of learning to read and write should be made an opportunity for acquiring information that can immediately be used to improve living standards. Reading and writing should lead not only to elementary general knowledge but to training for work, increased productivity, a greater participation in civic life, a better understanding of the surrounding world and should ultimately open the way to human culture."(UNESCO, 1966)

UNESCO's Revised Recommendation (1978) concerning the International Standardisation of Educational Statistics distinguishes the difference between literacy and functional literacy. A person is literate 'who can with understanding, both read and write a simple statement on his every day life', whereas an individual who is functionally literate is able to 'engage in all those activities in which literacy is required for effective functioning of his group and community, and also for enabling him to continue to use reading, writing and calculation for his own and the community's development'.

On the development of community and nation building perspective UNESCO observes and emphasises the following :

- Illiterates grounded deep in oral tradition and literates having acquired technologically advanced skill as literacy live in two kinds of socio-economic world.
- Illiteracy hinders the economic and social development.
- Orality is incompatible with what is required by the advances in scientific and technical evolution that mankind is witnessing.

It has also been recognised that literacy cannot alone deterministically engineer development, though it is almost possible to conceive of development without literacy, which is an "enabling or accelerating factor".

Keeping in view the changing priorities of India's development goals and influences of international bodies like United Nations, UNDP, World Bank, etc., the concepts of literacy and development have undergone tremendous transformation. Although, the significance of literacy as an instrument of galvanising and mobilising the masses and thus arousing community consciousness and participation for bringing about social change was highlighted by our national leaders, educationists etc., literacy did not receive due priority during the 1950's, when it remained as an integral part of community development programme. While the concept of development revolved around building factories, industries and dams, the focus of literacy was on enabling the common man to live a better of qualitative life in all aspects and instilling civic consciousness among masses. During the 1960's when a direct correlation emerged between education and economic growth, the emphasis of literacy programme shifted from civic to functional literacy. It was felt that literacy is worthwhile, and must be functional and should lead to development in all respect.

It is universally accepted that developmental efforts like family welfare, health and sanitation, agriculture, etc., are bound to fail if the population is not literate and that literacy is, a pre-requisite for successful development. That is why India's most literate state Kerala is also one with the lowest fertility rates and low female mortality.

A man develops himself through literacy and education, which broadens his mental horizon, widens his choices and capacity to take decisions. Since decision decides direction and direction decides destiny, 'literacy enables the men to take control of their destiny'. When the adult acquire the ability to shape their lives, it not only enables them to bring about desired changes in their own lives but also enable them to provide proper guidance to the younger generation. It becomes a vehicle for them through which they can fulfill their aspirations, convictions and commitments for self and social development. This 'literacy enables adults to read the world by reading the word which opens the roads to development'.

Aspects of Development

The preceding discussion so far, indicates that, development always remains the constant goal for society and thus, it has to continuously renew some criteria through which the goals can be achieved in certain specific aspects of the society. Owing to heterogeneity in all spheres of life, goals differ to a large extent from one society to another. But, development remains the main goal while its connotation changes across time and across society. Having attained these periodic goals further goals are set for development, and periodic goals are sought in every aspect of human life.

While individual development and social progress become the target for development, it becomes necessary to operationalise these targets with regard to specific functional areas such as economic, social, cultural, political, environmental etc. This would mean specifying the indicators for development in each of these aspects. Since the nature of each aspect of development is different, the specific indicators sought to be achieved will also be varied.

In the field of economy which leads to productivity, development would refer to the exploitation of all productive resources by a country in order to expand real income and continuous progress of capital accumulation to increase the productive equipment available to it, possession of technical skills, opportunity for improvement in real income and purchasing power, increasing in life expectancy, a civilisation assigning high priority to its scale of values to material well-being and possession etc. Thus, all these indicators of economic development imply both qualitative and quantitative aspects. While the specific expected behavioural changes are qualitative in nature and cannot be measured in terms of quantitative indicators to increase in the national real income *i.e. per capita*, GNP etc. which indicate quantifiable measures. So, economic development can be best measured in terms of quantifiable things, However, qualitative aspect also determine the tangible products. Therefore, both the aspects are closely interwoven and we cannot put them in watertight compartments.

On the contrary, the other aspects of development like social, cultural and political, determine the set of indicators would be in terms of human attributes and characteristics of both of which are entirely qualitative. It means development in these fields are not in terms of quantity, i.e. "how many" but in terms of quality *i.e.* "how well". Such qualitative changes will have to become perceptible with respect to some social, cultural and political characteristics. That the socio-political developmental indicators in the developing society would be with respect to the following attributes: *(i)* the ideology of society holds such as democratic, autocratic etc., *(ii)* the social structure that obtains there from reflecting the social stratification and nature and extent of social mobility, *(iii)* nature and direction of role specification within and across social sub-system, *(iv)* the system of social values evolved through time, *(v)* attitude towards change, motivation for social action and social awareness and such other attributes. That's motivation for social action and social awareness and such other attributes. That's why it can be said, development is possible in an ideal limit of co-ordination in various aspects of qualitative indicators, that is, changes in anyone indicator do not necessarily and automatically bring in changes in other aspects. In India, the socio-political ideology is democracy, which implies that it accepts fraternity, etc. Making them a reality is essential for development. To be able to attend these broad based goals, such goals are stated on the tolerance for different castes and religions, high social mobility which would mean, there is scope for every person to have his own aspirations, active participation of the individuals in social and political affairs with awareness and responsibilities and so on. The democratic ideology does not seem to have brought about perceptible changes in respect of all these indicators.

The above discussion of development in terms of its indicators in the functional areas emphasises that development is concerned not only with material needs but also the social conditions of life like environmental pollution, superstition, poverty, population explosion, dowry, purdah, malnutrition, child labour, unemployment, casteism, gender discrimination and so on. Development is therefore, not only concerned with economic growth but growth and change, i.e. social, political, cultural, environmental and institutional etc. A society like ours wherein casual interactions between and among various aspects of life are yet unclear, it becomes difficult to set some uniform development goals for all, because what may be the development for one may not be so for others. Moreover, the scientific and technological advancement and the speed of changes that are taking place in the society are greatly influencing the needs of the people in various ways. It only means that in order to realise economic development there is a need for evolving the necessary socio-cultural and political conditions. So, while planning strategy of development for the developing countries like ours, much care should be taken and equilibrium must be maintained between the demands of the people for social change and the resources available therein.

In this context it is seriously felt that, the planned goals are to be achieved for development through community support, *i.e.* active participation of the people and provision of the government and political will. These goals cannot be achieved by and large unless and until people develop social awareness to realise their individual and social responsibilities. Literacy and education as the process of social transformation is expected to develop such awareness, make individual responsible to their developmental needs, to equip them with necessary knowledge and skills.

Integration of Literacy with Different Aspects of Development

Economic Aspect : Integration of literacy with economic aspect of development of that society has been strongly argued by many. Education, the most critical development ingredient has been considered as the engine of economic growth, *i.e.* productivity and social transformation. Rao (1966) feels that, education is a potent agent not only for the social and psychological changes, but it may influence the productivity and economic development also, and that is the reason why in the recent years, there has been much talk about the relationship between education and economic development, and about education as investment.

Literacy influences the people in their economic and social development by inducing change in technology through the systematic application of scientific and other knowledge for specialised tasks as a consequence of their division and differentiation, and in values and attitudes, to provide the necessary incentives for increasing productive efficiency.

Social Aspect : Based on the celebrated human capital theory, literacy and education have been characterised as the power house of knowledge, skill, efficiency and productivity which act as catalytic agents of individual and social transformation. The integration of literacy and education with social development has been emphasised by Jones (1992), who said, "Education is seen not only in terms of its potential to produce and distribute knowledge and skills, it is also seen as a powerful allocator of economic and social roles, not always distributed equality on the basis of merit".

Productive Aspect : The World Development Report (1988) issued by World Bank makes the following observation of the economic and productive aspects of development accelerated through literacy : "Studied based on wage, employment data show that the social rate of return to education as calculated by comparing by the higher life time productivity of the literate workers with the social cost literacy generally exceeds that of most alternative investments." These findings are corroborated by evidence that literate workers with the social cost literacy generally exceed that of most alternative investments. These findings are corroborated by evidence that literate farmers are considerably more productive; the crop yields of farmers with four years of education are up to nine per cent higher than those of farmers who are non-literate (WDR, 1988). Because, literacy is integrated with the occupation of the learners and directly related to the development (GOI, 1972). The same logic also explains the fact that, literate workers in the shop floor industry perform much better than their counterparts. Industrial safety record of literate workers shows that production of literates is invariably higher than that of the non-literates. It goes without saying that quality control industry is greatly facilitated by the level of literacy of the workers.

Technological Aspect : The strong influence of literacy and development has also been noted in Japan. Japanese development during the post Maiji restoration was speeded by aggressive accumulation of skilled and technical manpower built through commitment and consistent efforts to increase literacy and technical development (WDR, 1991).

Through its commitment to literacy and training, South Korea has emerged as a first growing, technologically developed and one of the industrialised country of the world (WRD, 1991). The Research Reports of World Bank has also indicated that there is a strong and identical relationship between literacy, growth of GNP and per capita income, and output. "A one-year-increase in schooling can augment wages by more than ten per cent after allowing for other factors." An additional year of schooling has raised output by nearly two per cent in the Republic of Korea and five per cent in Malaysia (WDR, 1991). Therefore, there is essence of integration between literacy and development process in our country; because, the net change in growth which is observed by World Bank is nothing but the result of productivity of skills and technology assisted by changes in values and attitudes of the people through functional literacy.

Health Aspect : The need for integrating the components of literacy and health has been emphasised by National Health Policy (1982), and National Policy on Education (1986). The National Health Policy states :" "The Public Health Education Programmes' should be supplemented by health, nutrition and population education programmes at various levels. Simultaneously efforts would require to be made to promote universal education, specially adult and female education, without which various efforts to organise preventive and promotive health activities, family planning, material and child healthcare, cannot be achieved."

World Bank studies in 29 developing countries have shown that infant and child mortality rates are in reverse proportion to the level of literacy of mothers, and that each year of schooling for girls and women's literacy means further reduction of IMP and the lower birth rate. The study conducted by ICMR in 1990-91 on immunisation programme and maternal and child health in the state Bihar, M.P., Rajasthan and Uttar Pradesh has shown that the immunisation status of children of literate mothers is better than that of non-literate mothers both in urban and rural areas.

Primary Education : Universal literacy *i.e.* development of education in all stages cannot be achieved without the integration of adult literacy and universalisation of primary education. The report of the Survey of India, 1990-91 indicates that, literate parents would not only enroll their children in schools but also ensure their retention. Educational statistics since 1950s show that, highly literate states and districts have a higher enrolment ratio for 6-14 age group and lower dropout rates. While highly literate states like Kerala, West Bengal, Pondicherry have had an enrolment ratio of 102.45, 149.79 and 125.31 for classes I–V, in Bihar and Uttar Pradesh, which had lower literacy rates the enrolment ratio was also lower *i.e.* 81.70 and 81.39 respectively, (MHRD, 1990-91).

While literacy is a great leveller and provides opportunities even to the vulnerable in a society to improve their conditions of life in various ways *i.e.* economic, health, education etc., it also creates an environment of cultural progress. A nation cannot exist and develop with health and bread alone, it needs cultural support for its mobility and social development.

Cultural Aspect : A well defined, socially acceptable, composite culture is needed for sustaining economic development. Socio-cultural development can play the role of supporting factor in economic and other development. Literacy increases the information level and understanding of one's own culture and induces the individual to contribute to its enrichment. It also enables one to rise above conservation and parochialism and to imbibe cherished human values.

While integrating literacy with development, two points are to be taken into the consideration as pre-requisites *viz.*, the human resources and life long adaptation. While formal literacy is the main tool available in a society for developing its human resources and that through literacy the kind of human understanding and human skills that are highly essential for progress are brought into existence. The later approach refers to the provision by which institutions, programmes and activities of various types are able to, despite the rapidity of social change, maintain participation of people of all ages and for all personality types. Active participation of people from each and every sector of the society needs importance. Because peoples participation has been recognised as the process of people's empowerment (Seth, 1996) and in the view of changing scenario at global, national and regional levels, old concepts and prevalent paradigm of development must now be radically reviewed. "Development must be women around people, not people around development" (Jena, 1999). So no section of the population should be excluded by prejudice, oversight, or lack of foresight nor should they be neglected or forgotten in participating activities for development.

RATIONALE OF THE STUDY

It has been observed that India has accorded a lot of importance to education after independence. This is because education is a means to awaken people's self-awareness and selfesteem, and hence the capacity to improve their economic condition. In a democratic set-up like ours, the role of education is crucial, because democracy can work effectively only if there is an intelligent and active participation by the people. The responsibility of providing the people with necessary understanding of the problems of daily life rests with the provision of education through various educational programmes and institutions. Such education and educational programmes are specially needed for the backward and disadvantaged classes to help them become intelligent citizens to train them to be observers, thinkers, creators and critic in whatsoever humble manner it may be.

India as a democratic, socialistic republic is wedded to the principle of equality of opportunity in all field including education. Moreover, equal educational opportunity is considered to be the basic instrument to ensure opportunity of every type. Again the country is committed to providing universal primary education to all children in the age group 6 to 14 (Article 45 of Indian Constitution) and to protect with special care the educational and other interest of the weaker section of the people (Article 46).

Prior to the implementation of Indian Constitution (1950). Article 25 and Article 26 of the universal declaration of Human Rights adopted by General Assembly of United Nations on 10th December, 1948, has proclaimed rights to a standard of living with social protection and right to education of each and every members of our society.

In keeping with the provisions of the constitution and universal declaration of Human Rights, there has been a fantastic proliferation of educational institutions and programmes in the country at all levels. Recognising the rights of free access to education of the people, adequate provisions have also been made accordingly. The provision of ancillary services and students support in the form of mid-day meals, free supply of textbook, and reading material, school uniform, scholarship, stipends and hostel facilities etc. have also been attached with the free access to education. Special facilities have also been given in order to spread education among the socially and educationally backward and discriminated classes like ST, SC and women etc.

Despite this conscious effort at equalising educational opportunities in the country the overall picture remains unfortunately that of pervasive inequality, and till date the rights of man specially the disadvantaged and women are not yet protected and respected properly.

Active participation of women in National Development is not possible as long as majority of our women are illiterate and ignorant. Half of our population comprises of women, and the grim reality is that not joint their problems, but their very existence has been ignored, despite the fact that majority of our labour force consists of women, who produce a little less than 50% of our food. In general the position of women in our country is not a happy one, as they are illiterate and ignorant about political, legal, social and economic issues.

Orissa, one of the economically backward state of India had a population of 3,67,06,920 as per the 2001 census. Out of the total population, 1,80,580 are female. The literacy rate of the state was 49.09 per cent in 1991, which was lower than the national average of 52.21 per cent. The male and female literacy rate was 63.09 and 34.68 per cent respectively. As per the census report of March, 2001, the literacy rate of Orissa has been improved to 63.61 per cent and the male and female literacy rate has been dismal with a growth of 12.86 and 14.29 per cent respectively in 2001 from 1991. Although the female literacy rate of Orissa has been improved to 50.97 per cent but it still is lower than the national literacy rate of the female *i.e.* 54.16 per cent. While different approaches have been attempted since independence we have been unable to significantly increase the total numbers of literate women, who evidently are the strong pillars of the society, have been neglected, discriminated and exploited a lot in all strata of education, employment, empowerment and even for their sheer existence.

The Rourkela City of Orissa is not free from the aforesaid problems related to women. Rourkela, which is famous for steel plant is one of the cosmopolitan cities of India. Fifty years back it was a very small place surrounded with beautiful hills, forests, mines and tribal villages. But now, due to the advancement of science and technology the steel plant and many other industries have sprung up around the city. As a result, unskilled and semi-skilled, poverty-stricken villagers from different parts of the state as well as the country (neighbouring states) have flocked nearby the steel plant areas and to the other industries in order to earn their livelihood. Women who constitute about the half of the total population have also sprung up around the city in the slums with their family members to struggle for their existence.

It is seen that the educated women of Rourkela also work in different fields to improve economic condition of their families. They do work in professions like teaching, medical, engineering, law, administration, banking and management etc. Even they are found in trade, industry, journalism, architecture etc. But they are only a few in number.

In the rural settings majority of the women are generally found as housewives. Very few women normally from working class or from poverty-stricken families have to fight for their livelihood. But in urban set-up especially in urban slums it is just the reverse. Women in urban slums are the worst sufferers and more disadvantaged than the men. Due to wretched poverty and social discrimination in urban slums majority of the women have to earn and struggle for their families like the male members. As a result they work as contract labourers on daily wages, maidservants, sweepers, rag-pickers, iron pickers in the dumping yards of steel plant and so on. Some of them even accept prostitution and sell rice beer as their source of income.

In spite of their day-long hard labourer both in the family and work field, they have to swallow the mental and physical torture of their husbands. Also they have to tolerate the economic exploitation and social and gender discrimination by the family members and bosses. Because most of them are poor, illiterates, and their superstition is deep-rooted, and because they are not organised and are lacking in self-confidence, they do not dare to go against their family members and even to the bosses for ill treatment and exploitation.

The most neglected and discriminated section of the urban set-up *i.e.* slum-dweller in general and women in particular can never develop properly without bridging the gulf of discrimination through proper implementation of equalisation of educational facilities, guideline, protection and serious attention. Realising the above things and keeping in view the magnitude and transparency of the problems based on the guidelines and objectives of the National Literacy Mission (NLM) the Literacy campaign of Rourkela Saksharata Samiti started functioning with the downtrodden and people residing in slums in general, and women in particular for their educational development and upliftment since 1991.

Keeping in view the above situations and the programme in operation, certain questions that come into the focus at this stage are :

(1) How far the activities of the literacy programme of Rourkela Saksharata Samiti have been able to develop the skills of reading, writing and numeracy of the women in slums?

(2) Whether the women in slums have become aware of family welfare and small-family norms, evils of dowry, drugs, alcoholism, castesm and superstition?

(3) Whether they have become conscious of their own and family health status and health issues, child and maternity care, regular immunisation to their children, need for nutrition, sanitation and cleanliness?

(4) Whether they have become conscious about the schooling of their children and sending them to the formal schools regularly?

(5) Whether they have become conscious to avail of their voting rights, public distribution system, urban basic services, medical facilities, different loan facilities and other basic rights?

(6) Whether they have developed a positive attitude towards women life and have developed self-confidence and a self-image and are taking an active participation in various social, political and cultural activities ?

(7) Whether they have modified their pattern of behaviour and life style in adopting small family norms, maintaining friendly relationship with others in the basti, doing plantation for environment protection, cleaning basti with others, taking interest and initiation for basti welfare activities like motivating people to stop the practice of gambling, taking drugs and alcohol, organising basti meetings, etc.?

(8) What are the problems faced by the activists and organisers in motivating and bringing the women learners to the campaigns ?

(9) How the material resources are mobilised tapped and utilised ?

(10) Whether the activities of the literacy programme executed are well planned and executed properly?

(11) Whether the literacy campaign of the samiti has been able to make it a people's movement?

(12) If the result of the campaign is not effective what model or strategy can be adopted to make it fruitful?

The research scenario in adult education reflects reveals that Agnihotri (1974), Bastia (1982), Mohanty (1988), Tantry (1990), Thakra (1991), Saldhana (1992 A,B), Sachchidanand (1992), Rao (1992), Parikh (1994), Patel and Dighe (1993) and others have conducted some studies on impact of adult education and literacy programme in on learners in the form of evaluation study of some campaigns. Except for the studies of Rao (1992) and Patel and Dighe (1993) all the studies have been conducted on urban people in general. They have not focused their studies on the poor urban women. Rao (1992) conducted the study on rural women of Madhya Pradesh, where as Patel and Dighe (1993) conducted a small project on the slum women of Delhi. From the review of the research literature on adult education it was found that sincere and critical research studies on impact of literacy programme on women, particularly urban slums have been neglected.

The research work conducted till now indicates that limited studies have been carried out with regard to the slum-dwellers in general and there is an absence of researches on slum women and their educational development both in India and abroad. The studies carried out by Clinard (1962), Chatterjee (1962), Hams (1973), Child (1975), Shah (1978), Mohishin (1979), Saikh (1983), Aikara (1984) and others reveal the different aspects of life of the people in slums in general whereas the small-scale research conducted by Shridhonkar (1993) in Indore slums and the study of Devasia and Devasia (1994) carried out in Nagpur slums focused on the participation of slum women in different developmental programme for income generation and other activities. But not even a single study has been carried out on educational development of the women in slums.

The work carried out till now as evaluation studies of the literacy programmes have not taken into consideration the educational and social parameters, the historical and contextual differences, but mainly followed a standard quantitative format. Very few researchers like Tantry (1990), Seetharamu (1991), Saldhana (1992 A and B) and Sachchidanand (1992) did present both qualitative and quantitative analysis. But except for Saldhana (1992 A and B) and Sachidananda (1992) the major thrust of these studies was of quantitative and limited in their scope and suffers methodological limitations.

So far as the methodology is concerned it is observed that great importance has been given to research of normative survey and descriptive method by the above mentioned researchers. Very few researchers like Rao (1992) and others have followed experimental methods for their studies. But methods like case study and historical research are highly neglected by the researchers.

Regarding research tools much importance is given to questionnaire, interview, schedule of structure type and record study. Very few researchers like Seetharamu (1991), Saldhana (1992), Rao (1992) have adopted observation schedule, group discussion and field visit of very short duration along with other tools for their studies. Sachchidanand (1992) has adopted discussion, meetings and participatory observation along with questionnaire and interview schedule for his study. Here mention may be made that none of the researchers have adopted case study and brain storming techniques for their studies to collect relevant data from the respondents. Due to this methodological short coming co-satisfactory answers to the above stated questions could not be found from the related researches.

If systematic researches on impact of different education programmes are conducted especially on disadvantaged people they would be quite useful to present a Gestalt's view. Further, it would also be useful in understanding the feelings, behaviour and experiences of the people. Their educational and social needs could be better identified, which is urgently needed.

The investigator therefore embarked upon this study where it was decided to study the impact of literacy programme on educational development of slum women. It was also decided that the activities and efforts of Rourkela Saksharata Samiti and the problems and constraints faced by the organizers and functionaries should be examined. Further, the investigator also thought of finding out causes for the underdevelopment of those two slum women who, despite their participation in the Literacy Programme, have not achieved either the NLM expected proficiency level in literacy skills or even developed the desired level of awareness, were purposively selected from two different slum for case studies. After finding out their causes of under-development suggestions were made by the investigator as remedial measures.

Since this piece of research work is taken up to study the educational development of slum women through literacy programme of Rourkela, the findings will be helpful to the organisers of the programme in understanding the changing interests, attitudes, behaviour and experiences of slum women as well as their educational and social needs which are highly essential to chalk out need-based and effective programmes and activities for their further development. As educational development of slum women is a continuous process and it cannot be the end, there cannot be prescriptive ways of achieving the targets.

OBJECTIVES OF THE STUDY

(1) To study the activities and efforts made by Rourkela Saksharata Samiti for the development of education in Rourkela slums with special reference to women.

(2) To study the problems and constraints faced by the organisers and functionaries in organising, mobilising and monitoring the activities of the literacy programmes for slum women.

(3) To study the impact of literacy programme on slum women in terms of *(a)* their level of literacy *i.e.* reading, writing and arithmetic, *(b)* level of awareness developed pertaining to family welfare, small family norms and various concerning issues related to health and sanitation, child and maternity care, environment protection, etc., *(c)* changing attitudes towards evils of dowry, early marriage, alcoholism, superstition, etc., raising voice against exploitation and taking interest for social welfare, and *(d)* enrolment of their children in formal schools and other systems of education like Anganwadi and NFE centres etc.

(4) To find out the causes for the underdevelopment of the slum women who are not developed.

(5) To make suggestions for the suitable modifications in the programme for its future course of action.

OPERATIONAL DEFINITION OF THE TERMS USED

Impact : In the present study impact has been referred to the desired change resulted from the activities of literacy programme. The desired changes found in the slum women were as per the parameters laid down for their educational development.

Slum : Slum is basically the area of darkness, despair and poverty in an urban set-up which may be considered unfit for human habitation because of its sub-standard and dilapidated houses, high density of population, lack of minimum infrastructure and amenities like electricity, drinking water, sanitation, medical services and education, poor physical and mental health condition of the people, social tension, criminal activities and wretched poverty etc.

Slum Women : The most neglected resident of the slum area living in a miserable condition of life due to lack of minimum infrastructure facilities and social exploitation.

Educational Development of the Slum Women : It refers to the level of attainment of the slum women on the basis of the following parameters.

Level of literacy (*i.e.* reading, writing and arithmetic), earning and saving, awareness about the environment, health, sanitation, nutrition, child and maternity care, small family norms and family welfare, knowledge about different rights and responsibilities of women and women issues, knowledge about the evils of alcoholism, dowry, superstitions etc., and educational facilities provided to their children etc.

2

REVIEW OF RELATED LITERATURE

INTRODUCTION

This chapter is a review of the related literature in the area of Women's literacy and its impact. During the past few years several trends of developmental activities have affected the education of the downtrodden and weaker sections of the society. They include an increasing emphasis on the educational development of the socially, economically and culturally disadvantaged people for social growth and human race and a more thorough research for the definition of their active participation in the nation's development process.

The review of related literature has been presented here to take a stock of research conducted in the above mentioned area, *i.e.* educational development of the disadvantaged and weaker sections of the society and to highlight the gaps of researches. They have been categorised and presented here under three headings as follows :

(1) Educational Development of the Weaker Sections.

(2) Impact of Adult Education and Literacy Programme.

(3) Education of the Downtrodden Women.

EDUCATIONAL DEVELOPMENT OF THE WEAKER SECTIONS

Mathew (1979) reviewed the studies of a few researchers in his paper on "Research Trends in Education of the Deprived" and it is found that it is not education only but also other factors, including the economic factor being the most significant, that are responsible for keeping the people deprived from other facilities that educated classes take the advantage. These studies tried to find out the causes of educational backwardness of the weaker sections of the society. The main findings of the studies reviewed were in tune with the following conclusions : (i) Children cannot continue with studies due to poverty. (ii) Excessive involvement of the children to domestic and other kinds of work to supplement the family income. (iii) Inadequate financial facilities. However, by educating all the children of deprived communities and the slum-dwellers in India, we can attend one of the social objectives of education to equalise opportunity enabling the under privileged classes and individuals to use education as a lever for improvement of their condition.

In India, studies on the relationship between socio-economic status and educational achievement have been conducted in good numbers. Such studies have been reviewed extensively in "A Survey of Research in Education" (Buch, ed. 1972, 1977), and Educational Research in Rajasthan (Khanna and Verma,1976).

Most of these studies have found strong relationship between socio-economic status and academic performance in general and specific subject.

Among the studies reviewed in "Survey of Research in Education" (1972), Mathur (1963) and Chopra (1964) found that the socio-economic and family background of the pupils influence even their intelligence and conduct which are essential for overall development. Few studies conducted in the area of educational rights of the child of Lioyd (1972), Sharma (1973), Hams (1973), Child (1975), Maitra (1975), Armstrong (1975), Patel (1978), Aikara (1979), Shah (1979), Sujatha (1980), Seetharamu (1980), Maitra (1981), Shaikh (1983), Joshi (1985) and Sabina (1991) highlighted that, educational rights of the people of weaker sections are not properly respected and protected. And due to this an imbalance was found between the weaker and vulnerable section and elite class. Dasgupta (1980) has specifically stated that the policy makers at the top level have failed to realise the importance of the relative level of education and the "factor market". The educational programme and facilities which are intended for the weaker and the downtrodden people were deficient in proper co-ordination, and the status of the educational programme maintained was low.

He has further stated regarding the quality of education in the disadvantaged area that the chance for a person belonging to a vulnerable class crossing the threshold level is very poor owing to the long gestation period involved, and the poor quality of education that they receive compared to the children of elite class due to the caste factor.

Devasia and Devasia (1994) have also highlighted findings from their studies conducted on Nagpur slums to know about the plans and programmes, implemented for the sustainable development of women since 1985 that there is a lot of communication from outside the government both Central and State level, but very poor feedback from the grass-roots.

From the studies conducted at grass-roots Chawla (1972), Khatu (1973), Bharadwaj (1974), Bijlani (1977), Prajapati (1979) and Mani (1980), it can be said that illiteracy is exceptionally high in urban slums. The high degree of illiteracy among the slum adults and children is due to lack of proper educational facilities in the slum areas. They are not conscious about the education of their children. Problem of education is serious among the slum-dwellers, especially among the women. Those few, who had been to school, have not crossed the primary level due to their seclusion from the society. Therefore, the rate of dropouts among the slum and deprived children has been found high. Clinard (1962) has highlighted that there is a general lack of social and cultural heritage among the slum-dwellers and they do have lack of community consciousness. The Operation Research Group (1973) has opined that 'particularly the illiterate and jobless youth have taken shabby activities like running illicit distilleries and gambling.

The investigation of Clinard and Chatterjee (1962) and Mohishin (1979) have further stated that disease and rates of infant mortality are high in slums as there is little knowledge of health and sanitation, nutrition and childcare among the people of slum children of Patna, Calcutta and Bangalore (where the studies were conducted) suffer from nutritional anemia and calorie-protein malnutrition due to lack of knowledge among the mothers of the slum children. A contradictory finding is stated by Shah (1979) in connection with the knowledge and practice in health and nutrition in the growing slums of Baroda city. Shah conducted a study to find the impact of NFE programme related to personal and community health and food and nutrition of the slum-dwellers and found that the impact of knowledge and practice in health and nutrition was average.

Resenkranz (1975) highlighted that in a developed country like America there exist weaker sections that need special attention in the overall social, educational and economic planning. Resenkranz has recorded that more than a million of American are said to be unable to read any language. Millions more cannot perform well enough on reading task to complete form or read highway directions.

Nayar and Singh (1975) as reviewed by a "Survey of Research in Education in India" (1977), have concluded that the teachers of the children coming from adverse family circumstances were of the view that they were not inherently low in calibre, but their participation in extra-curricular activities was low. However, their educational and occupational aspirations were quite high. The studies by Pande (1974) Rajgopalan, Desai, Nayar, Singh, Adiseshiah Nayar and Sachchidananda above highlight the high educational and occupational aspiration of the disadvantaged children, but Rath (1976) reported that a low self-concept and occupational aspiration has been cited as one of the major characteristics of the disadvantaged children. A poor self-image and aspirations are surely the result of a life of imprisonment, negligence and insignificance and leads to inferior academic achievement or failure and retention. Also these lead to dropouts in maximum cases.

A number of studies have been conducted on "Wastage and Stagnation" in India. But limited studies have tried to know about the causes of drop out among the disadvantaged and weaker sections of the children. From the studies of Naik (1941), Gadgil and Dandekar (1955), Choudhary (1965), NCERT (1967), Patel (1978), Aikara (1979), Seetharamu (1980), Shaikh (1983) and Rangrej (1998) it can be said that poverty or economic status has been found to be the predominant cause of failure and dropout of disadvantaged slum children. In the studies of Gadgil, Dandekar, NCERT and Patel it is categorically focused that maximum dropouts were found to be the children of low education and low income people, labourers and artisans from lower castes and backward classes whose families needed a helping hand in running the home, looking after younger children or earning a living. The study of Rath (1976) is also important in this connection that low self-image and low educational and occupational aspiration among the disadvantaged groups also lead to academic failure and increase in dropout rates. The studies of Patel (1979), Shaikh (1983) and Rangrej (1998) have highlighted that there is a high percentage of female dropouts among the children from weaker sections as compared to their male counterparts. Shaikh's finding in this regard is very pertinent. She found that since many slum-dwellers move from place to place in search of better opportunities, this does not allow their children to pursue education in one particular place. As a result their children, if at all join schools, have to give up their studies in order to accompany their parents and thus suffer educational loss. The state of girls' education at the age of 8 or 9 years to a co-educational institution is not favoured by majority of the parents. Some of the parents even opine that sending the girls to school is not essential. The finding of Seetharamu is also very important. He states that majority of dropouts come from homes where parents are either in skilled or unskilled jobs. After a follow-up study on the mothers of dropouts and regular children, who were either housewives or unskilled labourers, it was observed that the size of the family was an interesting factor. The study of Aikara (1979) highlights on two major points on the needs of the out-of-school children in Bombay slums. Twenty per cent random sample of the out-of-school children and five per cent random sample of the in-school children was drawn for the purpose of interviewing parents and guardians for the study of Aikara. The study revealed that parents of these out-of-school children were eager to send them to an educational programme that combined literacy and vocational training and they wanted the classes to be conducted during the evening hours in their mother-tongue.

Shaikh (1983) has observed a slight contradictory point in her study at Baroda slums. She has noted that some people living in slums compare their earning with that of educated people and they find that they earn more than the educated people. Hence, education cannot help them to earn more, instead they earn more, by doing physical labour and manual work. As a result they give less importance to education and training. This type of attitude has perhaps developed in them due to their family background and socio-economic status which has also been observed to some extent in the studies by Mathur (1963) and Chopra (1964).

Desai and Pillai (1970), Hams (1973), Bijlani (1977), Dasgupta (1980), Desai and Raj (1987) and Devasia and Devasia (1994); have observed in their studies that the main reason for equating slums with wretched poverty lies not only due to the high concentration of poor therein, but also in terms of the lack of infrastructure, educational welfare and development facilities to the slum-dwellers. As a result, slum-dwellers constitute the highly disadvantaged, deprived and exploited lot and suffer from poverty both economic and cultural and lead a miserable life. Bijlani (1977) has specifically stated : "Children in the slum area grow and attend youth without any preparedness for work and employment. There is no adequate (educational or vocational) programme in our country to guide the youth in the slums about opportunities of training and employment available to him."

The observations and findings made by Devasia and Devasia (1994) in Nagpur slums have supplemented further to the findings of Bijlani that there are not approved and recognised forum where the grievances from grass-root level could be voiced, through which their voice could be reached to the planners, so that the process of setting targets and scrapping of unproductive and outdated schemes.

From the studies reviewed about the following conclusions can be derived :

(1) Weaker and disadvantaged sections of the society are present everywhere in the world (even in the highest developed country like America) and are in need of adequate educational facilities for their development.

(2) Educational development or failure is highly related with the socio-economic status and family background.

(3) There is serious lack of infrastructure facilities and developmental programmes for the slum-dwellers.

(4) Poverty generates poverty and illiteracy breeds' illiteracy. (Patel, 1979)

(5) Although majority of the people from weaker and disadvantaged sections of the society are interested in their development specially in education and vocation during the evening hours through mother-tongue, their interests, aptitudes and basic rights (to live, to work, to education, to information and friendship) are not respected properly and protected seriously.

Therefore, they remain illiterate, abused and poverty stricken and contribute towards the highest number of diseased and illiterate or dropout children as child labourers.

Regarding methodological implication most of the researchers in this area have adopted stratified sampling procedure. However, very few of them have also adopted both the random sampling and purposive sampling procedure.

The tools used for data collection are mostly achievement tests, questionnaires, interview schedules, checklists and observation schedules. However, few investigators have used checklists. Only one study could be found which is of a case-study type.

Three researchers have adopted the in-depth discussion technique along with questionnaires and interview schedules and only one investigator has adopted the participant observation technique along with other interview schedules.

Based on the nature and objectives of the studies most of the investigators have followed descriptive survey method for their studies. However, only one investigator has followed both evaluative and descriptive type of survey method for her study by using statistical techniques like percentage, intensity indices, and descriptive statistics for data analysis.

Further the data of the studies reviewed above have been analysed by the investigators both quantitatively and qualitatively.

IMPACT OF ADULT EDUCATION AND LITERACY PROGRAMME

Researches in different areas of Adult Education and Literacy Programme have been conducted by many researchers and the researches in this thrust area, *i.e.* impacts of adult education and literacy programme have been reviewed below :

Chaturvedi (1969) in his study on the life of the participants of Gorakhpur, Jhansi, Lucknow and Mathura districts of Uttar Pradesh found that, the social education programme under the community development scheme has a positive impact in changing the overall life style of people in the rural areas in spite of the many limitations like inadequate resources and training facilities of the programme. Sahni (1971) investigated the impact of agricultural extension programme on the farmers in terms of knowledge and practice of new methods of agriculture as well as attitudinal changes towards new practices and found that the programme was helpful in changing the attitudes of the farmers, and most of them knew about the uses of manure including chemical manure. Venkataiah (1977) at Andhra Pradesh and Prakash (1978) at Delhi and Haryana also studied the impact of the farmers functional literacy programme on the participants. Laxminarayan (1982) and Ganguli (1985) studies the impact of Adult Education in tribal and they found that the programme had made a significant impact on the adoption of behaviour of the farmers, and the experimental groups had significantly higher knowledge of modern agricultural practice and adult literacy than their counterparts in the control group. In spite of a favourable impact of the programme on the experimental group, it was also observed in Prakash's study that gain in knowledge was higher among men than women. But Vankataiah in his study did not differentiate the gain of knowledge in terms of sex. Rather, he investigated that there was a significant increase in the literacy achievement and acquisition of modern agricultural knowledge with the increase in the socio-economic status of the participants. The findings of the studies of Mathur (1989), Kaur (1992), Bhagria (1992), Rao (1992), Chopra (1993), Pati (1996), and Singh (1996) have also revealed similar findings. Mathur (1989) studied the development of a set of values among the adult education learners and observed that there was a significant effect of adult education programme in development of values among the participants and, the programme helped in developing reasonable attitudes towards social mobility, position of women and family planning etc. The programme has been successful in developing awareness for better social participation and a healthy scientific outlook.

Chopra (1993) developed packages for adult learners and found that the packages were not only a better learning material but also involved the learners in teaching learning situations. She explored that adult learners had attained literacy, numeracy and social awareness after their exposure to modules of the adult education programme. However, the female and male adults showed variations in different aspects of the package.

Kaur (1992) also developed three similar types of learning packages for the illiterate adults of Punjab and highlighted the findings that the packages of literacy, numeracy and social awareness were equally effective on both male and female groups of learners.

Rao (1992) studied the impact of the programme on the uplift of women in the rural areas of Madhya Pradesh and noticed that there was an overall improvement in all the fields, *viz.* social, economic, hygiene etc. in women in experimental group due to the adult education programme. Attitudinal changes towards living conditions were also noticed in them. The experimental group women became aware of the legal rights of women and the social welfare programmes of government. They have also realised the importance of education and started educating their children. Bhagia (1992) stated a similar type of finding in his study that Shramik Vidyapiths have played a major role in raising the quality of life, improving the thinking process and life pattern of the industrial workers. The employers were reportedly happy with these programmes as these were found to be useful in terms of cost benefit production, quality, resource expertise formulation and implementation of the programme as per their requirements.

Pati (1996) revealed in his study that neo-literates were in favour of small family norm secularism and equality of sex. Pati has also analysed the leisure time activities of adult illiterates. Dash (1987), Manavalane (1990) and Swami (1991) stated that adult learners in general have developed a favourable attitude towards the activities of adult and literacy programme. But while comparing the attitudes of urban learners with the rural, urban learners have shown more favourable attitudes than rural learners in the study of Swami, and the non-tribals of Sundargarh district of Orissa have shown more favourable attitude towards adult education than the tribals in the study of Dash (1987). But in Malanvalane's investigation, the participation of S.C. learners were more in numbers than the general people. Also the SC learners had shown more favourable attitudes and had secured better learning achievements like literacy outcome and level of awareness than the people of other centers.

The External Evaluation Reports of the Literacy Campaigns conducted by MIDS (1992 and 1993), Menon (1993), THRTI (1993), Behera (1993), Parikh (1993, 1994, 1995), KCEDT (1994). GIDSL (2000) stated that the programmes of the ongoing literacy campaigns of the country have undoubtedly helped in improving the life style of the participants. While evaluating the total literacy campaign of Rourkela city, Behera (1993) observed that the activities of the campaign have influenced the slum-dwellers in general and brought about a many far reaching changes in their life. Also he stated : "It has gone a long way in raising the level of aspiration and awareness among the girl child and women." A similar type of result has also been observed by Parikh (1994) while evaluating the literacy campaigns of Surat, Baroda, Valsad and Surendranagar districts of Gujarat. Parikh observed a marvellous change among the people and their level of attitudes towards social mobilisation in the TLC districts. Parikh also noticed matchless performances of the neo-literates of Surendranagar district. A little similar type of impact in the development of the awareness level and literacy achievement was also found in Surat, Amreli and Sabarkantha literacy campaigns. The literacy campaign of Baroda district had also been able to influence the learners and neo-literates in general. But when the comparison was made between the success of Baroda city (urban area) and the rural areas of Baroda district, literacy programme of Baroda city was found to be more successful than the district literacy programme in the rural areas. The literacy campaign of Baroda city was able to generate different aspects of awareness among the people along with literacy outcome.

THRTI (1993), reported that Total literacy campaign of Sundargarh district of Orissa has brought the literates into the mainstream. Through this programme women and tribals have become more aware of their rights along with the development of their reading, writing and numeracy skills.

Menon (1993) observed in Ernakulum district of Kerala that the programme had created among the neo-literates a noticeable change, and there was an improvement in their level of awareness in health and hygiene with an increased interest in electronic media with a view to update themselves with the day-to-day affairs. There was a marked improvement in the level of self-confidence as a feeling of "I/we" should also know something like others was generated. MIDS (1992 and 1993) reported that the literacy outcome of Kamraj, Kanyakumari, Madurai and Puddukotai literacy campaigns were successful both qualitatively and quantitatively. Kamraj district progressed with a success of 87.2 per cent of literacy outcome whereas Kanyakumari district was having a percentage of 88.2 per cent, urban areas of Madurai was 97.55 per cent and rural holds 92.85 per cent. In comparison to the literacy outcome and level of awareness of the above stated districts with functionality, it was observed that the programme was not much influential like other aspects of the programme. But it will be worthwhile to mention here that participation of women as volunteers and learners was highly appreciable in all the literacy districts as stated by the report of MIDS.

GIDSL (2000) reported that there was a remarkable impact of the post-literacy programme of Rourkela city on the neo-literate in particular and community in general. They also stated that original awareness about legal rights was evident to have increased.

The Report of the External Evaluation Team of Bharathiar University, Coimbatore (1993) on Pondicherry (1993) stated that Literacy Campaign TLC has brought various kinds of changes in self and families of the learners in maximum cases (except only 64 learners). Impact has been registered both in literacy and awareness and functionality. Socio-political awareness among the people was found high. All cross-sections of the society especially women and women organisations participated actively. The campaign has made them self-confident, and liberated the poor from fatalism. Economic self-dependency has developed in them. They have started thinking for the education of their children.

KCEDT (1994) evaluated the literacy campaign of Bidar district of Karnataka and stated that the overall achievement of the sample learners accessed as 75.19 per cent on NLM norms. About 75 per cent of the sample learners have viewed that they have benefited by the literacy programme. Both male and female have shown favourable effect of the programme in different aspects of life. In spite of non-cooperation from the village leaders and government officers, the campaign was successful in influencing people.

On the contrary to the findings of KCEDT (1994) the studies of Chandra (1970), Agnihotri (1974), Snyder (1974), Brahma Prakash (1976), Kumar (1981), Singh (1982), Tantray (1990) and Mishra (1999) have stated that there was a very low level of (not at all significant) impact of adult education and literacy programme on the adult learners and neo-literates.

Bastia (1982) examined the impact of NAEP on tribals, and Patel (1981) evaluated the NAEP programme. They found that NAEP had helped in raising the socio-political consciousness among tribals to some extent. Agnihotri (1974) attempted to evaluate the adult education programme in

Wardha district and found that rural people had started realising the importance of modern farming methods. Also a good percentage of them had understood the necessity of personal hygiene and cleanliness. People were mostly conservative and fatalists. They spent their leisure time in praying to God than in doing any constructive and income generating work. As a result there was no improvement in their standard of living. Kudesia (1972) in his study noticed that the level of achievement in the health and recreation aspect of the participant was the highest as compared to the other areas. People remained conservative with respect to caste system, poverty and social injustices. Political awareness remained at a very low level. Brahma Prakash (1983) found a positive and overall effect of farmer's literacy programme on the experimental groups with regard to knowledge attitude and adoption except on male farmers who are above 35 years. Female respondents proved themselves better in reading and writing skills but were more conservative than their male counterparts to change the traditional practice and adopt new techniques.

Scth, Malhotra and Roy (1983) assessed the impact of Functional Literacy Programme in Delhi and revealed that while the overall rate of learning was very slow, the learning pattern with regard to reading, writing and numeracy varied considerably. Women who were wage earners or were required to do calculations in their day-to-day life did better in numeracy than in reading and writing. Incorporation of vocational activities and literacy programme, they further observed a method of motivating illiterates but then there is every possibility in such case is neglected altogether.

Tantray (1990) undertook an appraisal of adult education in Jammu and Kashmir and noticed that most of the learners could read the alphabets hesitatingly and could write them, though not correctly and some could scribble their names, again indirectly. Awareness had been found to exist but functionality was totally absent.

Siddiqui (1989) studied the impact of Rural Functional Literacy programme (RFL) on rural women of Jorhat district of Assam and found no significant impact of the programme on the respondents. The study further revealed that impact of the programme was lower on Muslim respondents than that of the Hindu respondents. It was negligible in the numeracy and family planning aspects of the literacy programme.

The study of Chugani (1987) on RFLP in North Arcot district in Tamil Nadu also revealed the results in the same line that age, caste and family income of the participants were significantly correlated with their literacy achievement.

The impact assessment by Thakre (1991) on adult education programme of Nagpur University revealed that there was no significant impact; the criteria for selection of supervisors and instructors were disregarded and no valid evaluation of learners achievement was adopted. Mohanty (1988) evaluated the Functional Literacy Programme in the Puri district of Orissa and noticed that more emphasis was laid on literacy than functionality; actual skill development on functionality was observed in only 40 per cent. Similar type of findings have also been observed by the studies of Naik (1994), NIRD (1992), Parikh (1995) and Mishra (1999).

The External Evaluation Report of NIRD Hyderabad (1992) on Kurnool, Medak and Vishakhapattanam literacy campaigns of Andhra Pradesh State the following :

(i) The impact of the campaign on the participants was positive only, although it was not highly significant.

(ii) Number of female dropouts were more than male, and dropouts among ST and SC were more than the general category.

(iii) More than 50 per cent of the learners' achievement was below average,

(iv) The level of awareness was just positive.

(v) Co-operation of the public was also favourable.

(vi) Frequent migration and daily wages were the marked causes of high dropout rate.

A similar type of finding was also stated in the External Evaluation Report of East Godavari Literacy Campaign conducted by SRC (1995) of Hyderabad for Adult Education, Andhra Mahila Sabha. It was found that the co-operation of villagers and Government was healthy for the campaign and the achievement of the learners in literacy outcomes, level of awareness and functionality was also favourable. The literacy achievement of female was more than the males and dropout rate was also less among the female than in the male which was contradictory to the findings of NIRD of Hyderabad. The causes for high dropouts among males were migration, lack of time due to agricultural season, illness, daily wages, and that the launching timing of the campaign was not suitable to the participants since it started in the month of November.

Parikh evaluated the literacy campaigns of Bhavnagar City (1994), Rajkot (1995) and Banaskantha Districts (1995). He observed that the campaigns in general were able to arouse awareness among the neo-literates with regard to health and hygiene and socio-political aspect. To some extent it was even able to make them conscious about their occupation and source of earning. But no significant impact was observed in terms of the participation of women as learners or volunteers. Even the participation of socio-economically backward people was also not favourable. But in Bhavnagar city impact of the literacy programme was found to be simply positive. Women learners did better than the men and general people did better than the ST, SC and slum-dwellers with regard to literacy and awareness. People of slum areas of the city secured only about 50 and 56 per cent in literacy skills respectively, whereas the suburbs and elite did much better and achieved 88 per cent in literacy skills. The literacy programme of Bhavnagar city as stated by Parikh and his associates 'appeared to have been by and large unsuccessful in generating the desirable impact on both (a) literacy outcomes as also on, (b) different aspects of functional literacy like social awareness, environmental awareness etc.'

Naik (1994) evaluated the literacy activities of Betul district of Madhya Pradesh on behalf of MHRD, Govt. of India, and stated that the overall result of male learners was better than the female folk. The result amongst younger age group (15–25) was found to be better than the older age group of (25–45). Learners of general category secured comparatively better in literacy outcome awareness and functionality than the SC and ST people. The results of ST people were found to be very poor. It was further observed that people who are economically stratified only showed mere interest in learning. The overall result (literacy outcome, level of awareness and functionality) of females and people earning less were found to be very poor. The study of Mishra (1999) on the neo-literates of four districts of Orissa such as Angul, Dhenkanal, Keonjhar and Sundargarh (two tribal and two non-tribal) revealed that the literacy programme has been able to generate awareness among the people in some aspects like awareness in health and hygiene aspect and against social evils from among the women. But in general, quality of life has not been improved and the community involvement was not significant. The campaign modality was not suitable to their needs and desires.

Saldhana (1992) studied two literacy campaigns in Wardha and Sindhudurg districts and found two different types of result. That, in Wardha district the literacy campaign created a pro-literacy atmosphere which was favourable to formal primary education to some extent. Men performed marginally better than women and women with no jobs performed better than women with job. Workers of urban sector performed better and instructors especially men influenced the learners of same sex. Involvement of school teachers, students and unemployed youth got more involved in the teaching process of literacy campaign. Whereas, in Sindhudurg literacy campaign the findings were little different. Saldhana came to the conclusion that learners, variables, *e.g.* sex, higher age and Buddhist community influenced literacy rates negatively; female instructors had negative influence on male learners. But at the same time like Wardha campaign, school teachers and young enthusiastic people make good teachers, and village literacy committee played a vital role in TLC. In spite of number of limitations in both the districts, a positive impact of the programme on the people was observed.

Ahmed (1999) studied the effects of Functional Education Programme learners in three districts of Bangladesh and found that there were overall positive effects of the programme on the learners. She found that reading skills of the learners (both male and female) were not satisfactory. Only 34.4 per cent were assessed to be good in reading skill test. But they were satisfactory in writing skills numeracy and level of awareness. In terms of writing skills, males performed better than females and in awareness aspect females were more aware in health and personal hygiene than their male counterparts. She has further noticed a favourable attitude of local people towards the Functional Education Programme. The locals opined that school attendance has registered an increase due to the realisation of people through the FE programme by sending their children.

On the contrary, the studies of Gupta (1988), Khatun (1991), Pathak (1991), Ramesh (1991) and Sachchidanand (1992) revealed that adult education and literacy programmes have failed to influence the people in improving their life style.

The evaluation study of Adult Education Centres in relation to their programme objectives by Gupta (1988) in Himachal Pradesh State that people of age group 15–35 years were mainly the participants of adult education centres and the interesting thing noticed was that most of them stayed in the centres for about a month to learn to write their names (signatures). Due to lack of physical and infrastructure facilities, lack of occupational training courses, inadequate training and supervision of the volunteers, a large number of people dropout from the centers, and a favourable impact was not observed from the study. Khatun (1991) studied the problems of adult education in Jagatsinghpur of Orissa, and Pathak (1991) studied the relation of adult education with socio-economic development in Azamgarh. The findings of both the researchers had similarities in certain points. Unlike Gupta (1988), both of them observed that due to lack of infrastructure and other learning material in the adult education centres and ineffective teaching of the instructor, the participants did not show eagerness to come to the centre regularly. More than 50 per cent dropout was a regular phenomenon in Khatun's observation. Also she noticed that the illiterate women do not get status equal to literate women in the society. But Pathak after a careful observation of his study came to the conclusion that the NAEP had lost its effectiveness due to various factors. Some of the factors are similar to the findings of Khatun and have already been mentioned and others are lack of proper publicity, motivation, supervision, departmental coordination meager honorarium to the volunteers and low achievement in functionality and awareness of the learners. He also noticed an important point that 81.4 per cent participants of Adult Education Centres could not learn copying language or writing of letter or applications.

The study of Ramesh (1991) revealed that adult education programme failed in respect of imparting political knowledge into the minds of adult learners. Since illiteracy is the result of poverty, the adult education programmes are attended by poverty ridden and culturally deprived sections of the society. Adult education programmes are making literate the illiterate masses without touching the roots of the problem. As it is not an important objective of adult education programme and since most of the participants are agricultural labourers engaged in agriculture, they don't take interest to find time for political discussions or politics. They are only well acquainted with the knowledge pertaining to electoral political parties and their symbols. It will be relevant to mention here that Kudesia (1973) although found a positive impact of adult education programme on the participants, has also noted a similar type of result in relation to political consciousness which remained at a very low level in the learners.

From the studies of Gupta, Khatum, Pathak, Ramesh and Sachchidanand it can be stated that, impact of adult literacy programme depends on various factors like method of teaching, need-based activities, motivation, publicity, mobilisation and community involvement, adequate learning material and infrastructure facilities, proper monitoring and supervision etc. Due to lack of these factors adult literacy programme has failed to influence people in improving their standard of living.

Sachchidananda (1992) evaluated the Literacy Programme of Muzaffarpur (SAMU Saksharata Muzaffarpur) and found that the school teachers and students played a crucial role in environment building, survey, organising literacy centres and performing teaching activities by themselves and monitoring and co-ordination of the SAMU programme. In spite of their sincere efforts the concept of earning while learning did not prove effective due to lack of income generating activities in the literacy classes. Furthermore, the monitoring system (MIS) did not work effectively and there was no means of knowing if the MLL were achieved. It was also noticed that the programme lacked support from the government, and the political will needed a conspicuous demonstration. The functionality and awareness components of the programme have suffered at the cost of the 3R's. The only positive side noted was that SAMU had successfully involved the women particularly from the backward communities for teaching learning activities and participation in cultural programmes. The researcher saw the possibility of greater co-operation from the people if its management was toned up and the loopholes were plugged.

Bikaner Adult Education Association (1973), Muthayya and Hemlatha (1982), Desai (1982), Singh (1982), Parikh (1985), Chugani (1987), Mohanty (1988), Tantray (1990), Sharma (1990), Sivapalan (1991), Thakre (1991), Seetharamu (1991) and Soundrapondian (1997) found favourable impact of adult literacy programme on learners, and intimated about the factors responsible for high dropouts of the learners from the centre and less impact of the programme. They found lack of awareness concerning the developmental scheme among the learners and volunteers, inadequate training of the volunteers and resource persons, lack of infrastructure facilities and learning materials as per the learners choice and need, lack of planned community participation in programme implementations, lack of significant mobilisation, effort, co-ordination and monitoring and supervision of the activities of the campaigns to be the factors responsible for the ineffectiveness of the programme. Gupta, Khatun, Pathak, Ramesh and Sachchidananda have also revealed similar findings.

Muthayya and Hemlatha (1982) have analysed the efforts of adult education in the rural development programme whereas, Desai (1982), Parikh (1985) and Mohanty (1988) have emphasised on community involvement in programme implementation which is essential for the success of the programme. Sharma (1990), Soundrapondian (1997) Sivapalan (1991) and Tantry (1991), having laid stress on the teaching-learning materials which were neither adequate nor need-based or if at all supplied were not in time. The findings of Gupta (1988), Mohanty (1988), Khatun (1991), Pathak (1991) and Sachchidanand (1992) can also be supplemented to this result. Tantry (1990) and Seetharamu (1991) have recorded a very poor monitoring information system and lack of mobilisation and co-ordination of the programme. Gupta (1988), Pathak (1991) and Sachchidanand (1992) have also found similar result in their studies with regard to monitoring and co-ordination. Pathak (1991) has specifically noted in his study that there was lack of proper publicity, facility and knowledge of NAEP among the trainers, occupational training course to the participants, departmental co-ordination and insufficient honorarium to the volunteers, for which NAEP lost its effectiveness. Findings of Sivapalan (1991) had some similarities with Pathak's findings with regard to honorarium Sivapalan (1991) noted dissatisfaction among the worker teacher due to lack of rewards, incentives, recognitions etc. He further identified that modern methods and techniques were not used in the teaching-learning programme of Kerala. As a result, both learners and volunteers did not take keen interest for the success of the programme. Desai (1982), Shankar (1982), Pati (1985), Jacob (1990), Malhotra (1991), Sivapalan (1991) and Mohan and Usha (1992) stated the findings of their studies with regard to reading materials of neo-literates and adult learners that the readers of adult literacy programme preferred religious and story books ànd technical reading on local dialect. The scale of their reading interest indicates a preference for religious, functional and recreation oriented reading materials in the observation of Shankar's study (1982), whereas, male readers preferred to read newspaper in addition to stories and religious books as highlighted by Pati (1985).

Mit Chell (1977) studied the Development of Curriculum Guide for Adult Basic Programme for Teachers in Arkansas and found that *(a)* the teachers wanted to become more aware of needs and goals of adult learners. *(b)* They needed more assistance in the selection of materials as well as techniques and methods to be used in working with adults. *(c)* Some of the teachers recognised inadequacy of training and wanted to improve themselves by attending adequate workshops.

Malhotra (1991) studied the learning needs for adult education among rural and tribal youth in Bihar and found that the tribal youth felt the need for the primer in mother-tongue, whereas rural youth had accepted the existing medium of instruction. Mohan and Usha (1992) in their evaluation studies of the TLC in Bijapur and Dakshina Kannada districts of Karnataka probed that the content of the primers was found to be comprehensive and gender issues were given priority and yet the latter lacked perspective.

With a view to suggesting improvement on the reading materials of worker's education programme in Kerala, Sivapalan (1991) enquired into the reading materials and stated that the topics dealt within the unit level class were generally limited to trade unionism, industry and labour legislation and related literature was not sufficient to the participants.

Jacob (1990) studied the curricular areas in functional science and developed models for adult education. He noted that the functional science areas are inadequately covered in the primers of adult education and irrelevant. The emphasis on science subject was also inadequate. For which the learners did not have adequate awareness of the science of health, home, agriculture and veterinary aspect. There was resemblance of the observations of Das (1990) and Desai (1990) with the findings of Jacob (1990) that adult literacy programme was not need based for the participants. For which they did not take keen interest for the programme.

Ann (1993) undertook a case study of Non-Formal Functional Education Programme with a view to ascertain the elements contributed to successful acquisition and retention of literacy skills. This was conducted with a savings group development project in the Fani and Noakhali districts of Bangladesh. The important conclusion of the study was that literacy programmes need to be relevant to the social context of the learners which was conspicuously deficient in the programme.

S. Rao (1980) and Singh (1996) studied adult education and its relation to modernisation. Rao studied the impact of adult education on individual modernity in rural and tribal development. Whereas, Singh assessed the programme on modernisation of rural learners. Rao's study shows that there is a meaningful link between adult education and modernity particularly among the tribal groups as a counter force to earlier beliefs. Rao's study could have been based on a clearer enunciation of the constituents of modernity, social awareness and functionality. But in case of Singh's study he stated that learners of modern villages are more empathetic as compared to those of traditional villages. Learners were trying to imitate the life style of modern living in respect of food practice, clothing, education of children and mode of working. Change of attitude and knowledge taken place to a significant degree. However, it was also observed that they were traditional in majority of social customs due to cultural barriers of the society, *e.g.* in case of marriage, existence of a son in the family, authority of women in family and liberty to women folk etc. On the whole the investigator found that the learners were semi-modern of semi-traditional, their degree of modernity or traditionalism differing from individual to individual.

Thus, it can be concluded that, adult education programme is effective enough in modernising the people of rural as well as tribal areas and their level or degree of modernity varying from person to person and place to place.

In terms of research techniques most of the researchers have adopted stratified random sampling and purposive sampling method in their studies. These sample were drawn from restricted areas, districts, zones and states. Mishra (1999) has drawn sample from a zone consisting of four districts (two tribal and two non-tribals) in Orissa. NIRD of Hyderabad has evaluated a cluster consisting of three districts of Andhra Pradesh, whereas Parikh of SPIESR, Ahmedabad evaluated the TLC districts separately with different objectives. MIDS of Madras, Behera (1993), Menon (1993), Naik (1994), and others also have drawn their samples accordingly. For the purpose of data collection questionnaires, interview schedules, observations schedules, attitude scales have been invariably used by many researchers. However, Bastia (1974), Agnihotri (1974), Parikh (1994), Behera (1993), Naik (1994), GIDSL (2000) have adopted open ended interview along with their questionnaires and interview schedules. Whereas, Shankar (1982) adopted structured interview for his study and Dash (1987) applied five point attitude scale of Likert to determine the intensity of learner's feelings.

Methods of different types have also been followed by the investigators according to the nature and necessity of their studies. But it is a general observation from the studies that most of the evaluation studies have been conducted by following normative survey and descriptive analysis. Chopra (1993) and THRTI (1993) had studied the qualitative aspect of effectiveness of adult literacy programme with the help of case study approach along with experimental design and normative survey for their studies respectively.

Venkataih (1977), Prakash (1978), Muthayya and Hemlatha (1982) and Singh (1996) have employed experimental method, whereas Panwar (1978) employed quasi-experimental method for their studies. But in case of Sahani (1971), Kudesia (1973), Agnihotri (1974), Kumar (1982), Parikh (1985), Dash (1987) and others, they have followed normative survey and descriptive

method for their research work. The review shows that there is dearth of in-depth research in adult education and literacy programme. Further, the data of the studies have been analysed both qualitatively and quantitatively by the investigators.

The researchers of the above stated studies have not only highlighted on the findings but also have presented their ideas as suggestions to make the adult education and literacy programme more effective and comprehensive.

Some of the pertinent suggestions are as follows :

(1) Strengthening the post literacy programme of literacy campaigns by Mohanand and Usha (1992), Parikh (1994, 1995), Behera (1993), Menon (1993), Naik (1994).

(2) Second stage of literacy campaign to sustain the results of the first stage and make literacy and enduring experience in the lives of the neo-literates (Menon, 1993).

(3) Thorough reorientation of the partly successful literacy campaign like Bhavnagar city, its approach, strategy and contents—a further streamlining of the administration and execution machinery and methods as also the need for a more careful planning for the post literacy efforts in the city (Parikh, 1994).

(4) In the II Phase, the dropout learners of the II Phase should again be identified and reached (Naik, 1994).

(5) Sivpalan (1990) on revising the Adult Education Curriculum and Shankar (1982), Pati (1985) and Malhotra (1991) have suggested to develop need based reading materials and supplementary literature for the neo-literates in local dialect.

(6) Sachchidanand (1992) in the light of shortage of manpower in Muzaffarpur literacy campaign suggested, to take up areas in smaller segments like blocks and consolidate rather than spread to large areas. Further, it might be worthwhile to have a uniform test to assess the learners' achievement in 3R's awareness and skills.

(7) It has been suggested that the neo-literates should be given adequate opportunities to participate actively in post-literacy programme and in various decision-making process (Behera, 1993).

From all these studies it can be concluded that,

(1) There was impact of both adult education and literacy programme on the participants. But the degree of impact differs from person to person and campaign to campaign.

(2) Development of awareness in various aspect of life among the participants was found in all most all the studies. But awareness in terms of health and hygiene aspect was found to be more prominent in both adult education and literacy programme.

(3) Literacy outcome was favourable in maximum cases. Even in some cases it was highly significant.

(4) Functional aspect was not significant.

(5) Male participants did much better than female in maximum cases.

(6) Dropout rate among women/ST/SC were found to be higher than others.

(7) Community participation in both the programme was positive, not highly favourable. But the community involvement in literacy programme was noticeable and better than adult education programme.

(8) Supply of infrastructure facilities and need based learning materials in local dialect for the participants were neither adequate nor supplied in time in various adult education programme and in some literacy campaigns.

(9) Lack of proper environment building and motivation, significant mobilisation, monitoring and co-ordination, adequate training to the teaching volunteers were found in various programmes and campaigns.

(10) Lack of need based activities like income generation etc. for the participants were also noticed.

(11) Lack of reward or honorarium to the volunteers was found to be one of the main causes for demotivation among the volunteers was found to be one of the main cause for demotivation among the volunteers. As a whole adult education programme had a little impact on the people. Whereas in literacy campaign the impact is much better to change the life style of the neo-literates.

EDUCATION OF THE DOWNTRODDEN WOMEN

The analysis of Census Data (1981), Advance Report on Marriage Differentials in India (1984), Census of India, Occasional Paper No. 2 (1981), Child Marriage, Age at Marriage and Fertility in India (1989), Mohapatra (1987), Nuna (1986, 1990), Sharma and Ruetherford (1987), Lockhead and Verspoor (1990) corroborate the findings that the educational level of women is strongly correlated with quality of life expectancy, infant mortality, nutrition and school enrolment. Advance Report on Age at marriage Differentials in India (1988) presented a comprehensive findings of the studies related to marriage age. It states that age of marriage is positively related with the levels of education of the women both for urban and rural areas. For a gradual increase is seen in mean age at marriage with the increase of women's educational levels. The occasional paper No. 2 of Child Marriage, Age at Marriage and Fertility in India (1989) analysed the educational level of mothers by various fertility indicators and showed a positive correlation between women's level of education with their fertility. In order to understand to what extent literacy is a basic concomitant of development, female literacy rate of women aged 15 and above were correlated with the socio-economic and demographic indicators for 14 major states by using interview schedule and questionnaires. The study showed that female literacy is strongly and positively related to infant mortality rate, crude birth rate and total fertility rate. Studies conducted by Nuna (1986, 1990) corroborate similar findings that female literacy is strongly related with the quality of life indicators as mentioned by Sharma and Ruetherford (1987). Likewise, Lockhead and Verspoor (1990) studied to understand the correlation between mother's education with infant and child mortality rate and came to a conclusion that the relation was highly significant. Mohapatra (1987) compared the attitudes of adult literates and illiterates towards early marriage and family size to know the literacy factor on population control and to identify the accepted age range of marriage of girls. The study revealed that almost all the literates like doctors, teachers, officers, officials and non-working literates were in favour of small family norms and delayed marriage. The illiterate women were in favour of having five to six children because of the fear of infantile mortality, and almost 30 per cent of illiterate housewives were for delayed marriage and 25 per cent of the respondents were not in favour of delayed marriage. However, the educational qualification of women had significant effect on their attitude towards family size and marriage. In the study of Mohapatra the title is misleading in the sense that literates include professionals, which is a very high category, consequently the comparison appears to be unfair. A similar type of result was also found by Choudhary (1988) in his study that educated girls are aware of minimum age for marriage and favour small family norms, use of contraceptives and spacing. The study of Devi (1991) revealed similar findings about the relationship between the education and socio-economic background of women and adoption of the family planning method. The report on the state of World Children (UNESCO, 1989) established the link between the female illiteracy and all other basic indicators of under-development such as *per capita* gross national product, life expectancy, infant mortality, school enrolment and nutrition. It would therefore not to be a truism to state that the map of female illiteracy, on the whole, coincides with the map of under-development.

The studies of Upadhyaya (1983), Bhasin (1985), Chitra (1969) and Nayar (1991, 1992) revealed injustice and inequality on the development of women education. Chitra (1969) tried to determine the relationship between social origins, inequalities in educational opportunities and social mobility. It was identified that individual from the upper strata of Mysore Society had greater opportunities for higher education than those from the middle and lower strata. Accordingly, women from upper strata of the society had the opportunity to receive education. Upadhyaya (1983) identified the causes of educational backwardness of girls and found that girls from large family had to help their mothers and the parental attitude towards girls' education was negative. Girls were considered to be the weaker members of the society. The village community had also negative attitude towards girls' education. Likewise Bhasin (1985) also found injustice and inequality prevailing in women education and thus stated that the strategy for eradicating illiteracy has to be part of and related to the strategy for removal of inequality, injustice and political subjugation of the people.

Nayar made a situational analysis of the education of the girl child in India with the focus on girls from a gender equity perspective and found that the learning opportunities available to the Indian girl child in real life situation throughout the life cycle are very low. On the heels of this study Nayar (1992) further conducted a national study on a sample of 3,000 households located in the urban slums and rural areas of Delhi, Bombay, Orissa and Rajasthan, and identified factors of continuance and discontinuance of girls in elementary schooling. She observed in her study that the dropout rate is extremely heavy after the primary stage at the places where the middle school is located outside the village. Gender discrimination was found evident in intra-household distribution of food, healthcare, education, play and recreation. The girls expressed their feelings of being discriminated compared to their brothers. Parents have substantially lower academic and occupational aspirations for girls and are unwilling to spend money on non-tuition costs for items such as books, uniforms, stationery, shoes, etc. because they consider girls as temporary members of the household and a poor investment. The study brings out the need for disaggregated analysis and differential planning inputs at the micro level for improving the educational situation of girls. It will be pertinent here to present the suggestion given by the researchers like Singh and Saxena (1995), Jain and Arora (1995), Jangira and Ahuja, (1995) in terms of academic achievement that girls especially those from the poverty group.

Very few researchers have studied the status of Indian women and their education in a historical perspective and have stated that the evils of social customs and traditions are deeply rooted in the society. Therefore the question of their education was hardly thought of during early post-independence period. The causes for the slow progress of girls' education were also typical in most of the states of India. Efforts made by Christian Missionaries in spreading girls education in India was worthwhile, *i.e.* Rai (1995) made the objectives of his study to present a comprehensive and coherent picture of social life in India during 1813–1957 and focused on the efforts made by

Christian missionaries for the development of women education. He informed that the first war of independence in 1857 caused a set back to the movement but the enthusiasm of the people made it possible to spread girls education afterwards.

Mishra (1961) traced the history of women education in India in the context of their status and education. His study revealed that there has been a rapid progress in women education in all the sphere as along with the existing evils of wastage and stagnation. He further found that women education at primary and higher stages is still on imitation of boys' education. The special courses like home science, drawing, painting, music, nursing etc. still need improvement. Funds for women education are available but proper utilisation is needed.

Das (1973) in his in depth study about the progress of secondary education in Assam from 1874—1947 stated that the condition of secondary education was far from satisfaction due to low standard of education. It happened due to low standard of the teachers and poor management. The study of Das further stated that the missionaries were responsible for the spread of education among girls and started a network of female school all over the state and maintains a high standard of efficiency in their institutions.

Dane (1971), Desai (1976) and Thakkar (1976) investigated the development of women education and growth of girls' school in Gujarat in their studies. Dane (1971) made an incidental inquiry into the position of women in the society during the period 1854–1947. He identified the factors responsible for the growth as well as those hindering the education of women and concluded that girls were neglected in the family and considered as a burden on their parents until they were married. There was no right to property by girls or women in the family. Child marriage was a deep-rooted cause for the non-schooling of girls. Desai (1976) while examining the growth of girls school education in Gujarat from ancient to modern times found that there was an impact of caste system, child marriage, social values, administrative policy, political climate etc. on the spread of girls education. The overall sense of insecurity and social unsafe condition put the girls within the four walls of home up to 1818 A.D. The advent of the British in early nineteenth century brought a change in educational progress of Gujarati girls. The Christians and Zoroastrians did promote girl's education in their community and its impact was found in later state in Gujarati society. As a result in 1950-51 the progress of girls education came to a level of satisfaction. Thakkar (1976) observed in his study that problem of wastage and stagnation in case of girl students both at primary and secondary stage was persistently typical in Gujarat. Economic factor had played a tremendous role along with social customs, values and beliefs in the progress of female education. For which, the position of women education in Gujarat which was third in the country in 1961 dropped to the fifth position in 1971, although female literacy was higher as compared to 1951.

Gandhi (1977) in his study found that although there was a progress of higher education of women in greater Bombay as compared to other states of India, but still there was a significant difference between the education of female with education of male. He found that 55.7 per cent of women and 69.7 per cent of men were literate in 1973-74 and the percentage of wastage in case of girls had increased from 59.0 per cent to 70.0 per cent in the said period.

Rajlaxmi (1984) examined a similar study in Madras Presidency and found different result that there was a tremendous expansion of higher education of women during 1921-47 with 180 per cent increase in terms of number of institutions. Private initiatives especially on the part of Christian missionaries yielded more results than that of the government in starting colleges for

women. Because the expenditure on higher education for women was not an important segment of provincial government.

The study of NIEPA (1986) to identifying the backward districts in terms of female education stated that only 9 districts had a high level and 137 had a medium level of female education in the country. There were 59 districts in the country with a very low level of female education.

From the above study it can be concluded that people had favourable attitude towards female education. But due to various factors like economic condition of family, administrative policy and political climate in the country. Evils of social customs and traditions, values and belief of society for women education got a set back. But the private efforts made by the Christian missionaries in spreading women education by starting girl schools and colleges in different parts of the country was worthwhile as compared to the government during pre-independence period.

Leela Kumari (1984) studied the development of education of women in India in general and U.P. in particular up to independence and noticed favourable attitude of people in general towards women education. But the girls showed more favorable attitude than the boys. A similar result in terms of attitude towards women education was found in the study of Santha (1986). Santha studied the status of women in its historical perspectives, the changing role of women in different spheres of life and found that women had a more positive attitude towards their own role in the cultural sphere than men. Man had a more positive attitude towards the role of women in the economic, political and social sphere than women. Men and women in Indian society had similar attitudes towards women's role in religious sphere. Women had a more positive attitude towards woman's role in religious sphere. Women had a more positive attitude towards their role in the educational field than man. Women did not differ in their attitude irrespective of their age and attitude in the economic sphere. Education and age did not influence the attitude of women in the cultural and religious sphere.

From the above studies of Leela Kumari and Santha it can be said that people in general have a favourable attitude towards women education. There is a little difference of attitudes between the male and female in different spheres of life. But specifically towards women education female do have a more favourable attitudes than the males.

Some of the researchers have studied the problems of women education and found that various factors were responsible for the girls' non-enrolment in school and dropping out of girl children from their studies.

Naik (1949) undertook a study to investigate into the problem of the education in the province of Bombay and found that both the social status of Indian women and their educational position were at the lowest ebb in the beginning of the nineteenth century. Education of women lags behind the education of men in almost every branch of educational activity.

The study of Avinashingam (1970) revealed that parents of high income, small family structure and higher occupational levels favoured their daughters going to school. Socio-economic conditions were more conclusive to school going girls than to dropout girls. Parents of both school going and dropout girls were not satisfied with the prevailing school conditions. Bokil (1987) studied the factors that had adversely effected the completion of primary education of girls and observed that the girls of lower income strata of the society remained outside the schools and they either helped their parents in work at home, in farms or earn their own livelihood. However, education of their brothers continued. Girls from families having better socio-economic status were better enrolled and better retained in schools. It was also observed that distance of school from the home also caused for dropping out of girls. But their percentage was low.

Upadhyaya (1983) found a very poor attitude of parents and community towards women education in his study. Other than poor attitude, lack of trained lady teachers and socio-economic conditions of the family were also responsible for low enrolment of girls in the school.

Basu (1975) found a little similar result in his study as found by that the major handicaps for the progress of girl's education in Bihar were inadequate fund, dearth of trained teachers and attitudes of the parents of middle and lower classes to girls' education.

Likewise, Dutta (1982) investigated the causes of dropouts among girls from schools and found that caste discrimination, poverty, helping parents in their work and looking after younger children, apathy of parents towards girls education, early marriage, inadequate school facilities, teachers' behaviour and lack of separate girls schools were the factors responsible for drop- out of the girls from school. It is important here to mention that Dutta has found two most important factors such teachers behaviour and lack of separate girls school in his study. Other factors found in his study were almost common to the study of Basu, Upadhyaya, Bokil and Avinashingam. Patel (1984) studied the rate of enrolment and educational attainment of tribal girls and their problems of education in Gujarat. Her study revealed that spread of education among tribal was insignificant up to the end of 19th century. But after independence with the sincere efforts of "Thakkar Bapa" the eminent follower of Gandhiji, there had been a rapid expansion of educational institutions and enrolment of tribal students in different levels of education. Inspite of high enrolment of tribal girls in standard I, about sixty per cent of school going girls did not ever attend the school due to poor economic condition of their families and indifferent and apathetic attitudes of their parents towards girls education. It was also observed that there had not been many special programmes to motivate the tribal girls to persue education.

Sarkar (1981) studied the development of education among the females of different social groups in rural areas of Murshidabad, Nadia and Birbhum districts of West Bengal. The study revealed that ten per cent of the wives in family life were educated above the primary school standard. Among them only three per cent were Muslim. The yearly growth rate was one per cent in education among the women in rural areas which ever far from Calcutta. The growth of education among higher-caste Hindus was the higher and among the Muslim lowest. Higher-caste Hindu wives were more motivated to accept educational development due to urban influence but Schedule Caste women were found unmotivated. Educational disparities were found among the three Hindu social groups.

Pathan (1986) studied the position of Muslim women and factors responsible for their educational backwardness. The study stated that giving less education to the girls was the common attitudes in the parents both in rural and urban areas. The practice of early marriage was seen especially among the rural illiterate Muslims. In urban areas main factor for educational backwardness was economic, whereas in case of rural Muslim women there was a wide diversity of causes. Women were quite aloof from the concept of small family and it was also observed that the number of children in the family was seven or more. Lack of social stimulation and opposition of the family members and relatives contributed heavily to Muslim women's educational backwardness.

Karlekar (1983) Desai and Raj (1987) studied the factors affecting the goals for education of women and noticed that formal schooling has a marginal role in slum areas. The girls are needed to help in household work and sending daughters to the school is a waste of money and time to some mothers. Therefore, while interviewing for the research study one mother said, "Why should

I waste my time and money on sending my daughter to school, where she will learn nothing useful? What does the Hindi alphabet mean to her? (Karlekar, 1983). On the other hand, it was also observed by Desai and Raj (1987) that the demonstrative effect of education providing opportunities of better jobs creates a feeling among poor people that if education were given to girls they would be able to improve their status. Maidservants particularly, aspire for their daughters to have jobs other than domestic work. The social roles of girls define their educational needs and goals and the possibility of girls getting education is determined by factors like looking after siblings, to help in household chores etc. which are non-pedagogic considerations that effects the goals of education for women.

From these studies it can be stated that factors like poor economic condition of the family, negative attitudes of parents and other members of the community towards girls education, evils of social custom like child marriage, caste discrimination, gender inequality in the family and society, lack of separate schools for girls and trained lady-teachers, apathetic behaviour of the teachers and inadequate school syllabus, lack of motivational programmes and activities and domestic problems had adversely affected girls enrolment in school and girls education in the country.

Lind (1989), Stromquist (1987) and Vanka (1995) examined the problems of dropouts among women in adult education centres and found that lack of easy access to reading material, need-based and interesting activities like income generating and feminine activities for women, household drudgery causing fatigue and a discouraging environment in the family were the major causes for the withdrawal of women learners from the Adult Education Centres. Vanka (1995) has further observed in her study that since the majority of the sampled dropouts were women mainly from backward communities and were engaged either as casual labour or had petty trades, they didn't have time for educational activity. As a result they withdraw themselves from the Adult Education Centre.

Lind (1989) noticed that due to lack of adequate reading and writing material in the center, women learners didn't take a keen interest for learning and were prone to relapse into illiteracy. On the other hand, while studying the problems of enrolling rural women in AEC it was found that majority of women learners belong to S.C. group with low income strata and faced social barriers like casteism, untouchability and conservative attitudes of upper class people in the communities which gave them a sense of inferiority and resulted in demotivation among the learners. Also the study showed that inadequate planning, poor delivery systems of learning materials and lack of interests and motivation among the women learners were the factors of acute problems of mass illiteracy. It will be pertinent to mention here that although the objectives of Vanka (1995) and Dash (1991) were almost same, the findings were a little different. Social barriers played a major role for illiteracy in their study of Das, whereas in Vanka's study economic crisis, family background and lack of adequate centre activities played major role for the withdrawal of women learners.

Sardamma (1992) and Trivedi (1992) analysed the learning needs of rural women and found contradictory results. Sardamma (1992) investigated the learning needs of women in Kerala with a view to evolving a suitable curricula. The study revealed that the women were very much concerned with their needs, and their learning needs were found to be linked to their occupation. Most of them were interested in tailoring, embroidery and chair-making. As a part of the study, the investigator prepared a need-based draft-curriculum for these women. On the other hand, Trivedi (1992) found in his study that the physical, social and cultural milieu and women's activities and roles revealed that all these have a significant influence on shaping women's needs, perceptions and attitudes towards formal and non-formal education. Social and cultural norms and constraints often determine women's access to programmes, information about services and programmes, and their participation. Women were not aware of many of their needs, which were complex. In general, high interest was shown in learning income-generation skills.

It is important to mention here that although the nature of studies in both the cases were almost same but the findings were different and contradictory. The factors responsible for the contradictory result of similar studies have yet to be investigated through further research.

The studies of Bhasin (1984), Patel (1986), Ekstrand (1989), and Grewal (1991) have stated on the content of the primers used in various literacy/adult/non-formal education programmes for women. Bhasin (1984) on a study of seven primers used in North India by Government agencies and non-governmental organisations revealed that the main contents of these primers were related to housework, childcare and family planning. Patel (1986) in her study noticed that the content of a literacy primer for women in the adult education programme of Gujarat ignored women's roles as productive workers and focused exclusively on their roles as wives and mothers. Though the primer imparted some information about various Government schemes dealing with the domestic sphere of women's lives such as minimum age for marriage restraint act, and family planning, still was inadequate and not systematic in its presentation.

Analysis of content of some of the literacy programmes were conducted by Ekstrand (1989) showed similar emphasis on immunisation, kitchen gardening and breast feeding.

Grewal (1991) while studying both adult education and non-formal education programme stated that almost every participant was satisfied with the content and timing of the programme, about three-fourth of the participants were regular. Non-attendance in the centres was attributed to the role of learners in improving the family income not due to timing of the centre or content of the primers. The findings of Grewal (1991) thus present a contradictory notation on the findings of Bhasin, Patel and Ekstrand and call for a systematic and rigorous research work in terms of the content of the primers. Ramdas (1990) thus suggested for a drastic revision of content and materials so as to make them consciously emancipatory as opposed to promoting a "*status quoist*" approach.

Observations of Srivastava and Sharma (1990), Patel (1990), Dighe (1992), Rao (1992), Dighe and Patel (1993) and Shirdhankar (1993) state the active participation of women in collective process of learning and group activities reduce their isolation and contribute to building self-confidence in them.

Srivastava and Sharma (1990) while capturing the texture of one "Literacy camp at Udaipur observed that learning was woven into the daily living experience of the learners. Though learning basically is an individual activity, the learning situation allowed collective process of learning to come into play. Group affirmation enhanced the learning process." It is important here to mention that women who were unable to spend long stretches of time away from their village during a period of intense agricultural activity seem to opt for such intensive residential camps. They expressed their views to learn in a camp for four to five days instead of learning in the centre for one or two hours a day after being tried with household work.

A similar type of result was observed in a descriptive case study of residential training camp for sathins of Women Development Programme in Ajmer district conducted by Patel (1991). She stated that supportive environment, collective mode of learning, participatory approach to literacy material play important role in developing self-confidence in women learners who otherwise had low self-image as learners. Likewise, Rao (1992) in his study observed that active participation of women in adult education programme have brought in them attitudinal changes towards living conditions and developed in them a self-confidence and started solving social problems of the community.

Patel and Dighe (1993) reported an evaluation study of literacy programme in Delhi slum that women learners of the slum areas have reduced their isolation and gained self-confidence through active participation in literacy programme. The strength of literacy programme for them clearly was, that it ended their isolation, their feelings of being alone and of not being able to relate to others.

Shirdhonkar (1993) studied the level of women's participation in developmental activities of slum development programme in Indore. Although, her study was not directly connected with the participation in educational activities but her findings were almost similar and effective to the findings like Patel and Dighe (1993). Her study showed that participation of women in different programme was satisfactory. The participants had expressed their feelings that their effective participation had greatly helped them in developing their self-confidence and status in the family and society. It was noticed that 48.9% acquired better status than before due to the collective activities of the programmes. 39.5 % of the respondents acquired better status by participating as per the need of the programme. Those who never participated had found no change in themselves.

Dighe (1992) conducted an in-depth study of Bharat Gyan Vigyan Jattha (cultural group) in six states of the country, and stated that the participation of women in pre-campaign activities was encouraging. They also gained self-confidence through the group activities of the Jattha. However, their involvement in decision-making process has remained marginal.

From these studies it can be concluded that active participation in-group activity programme and collective learning reduce isolation among women and develop in them self-confidence and their self-status in the family and society. Thus women should be given proper scope to participate in different types of developmental activities, so that they can realise the need for their active participation in development and decision-making process and start solving their own and social problems confidently.

Participation of women in social, education, economic and cultural spheres of life have been studied by researchers like Santha (1986) and others and their observations have already been mentioned earlier that their level of participation was found to be satisfactory. But it is important here to state that the level of political participation among women especially in the rural and neglected areas is yet to be developed. Because the only investigation made by Mahesh (1991) in the field of political participation of women in rural Tamil Nadu presents a very poor picture irrespective of their marital status, religion, caste and occupation. It was observed that participation in politics by women was higher in nuclear families than in joint families, and among the women of high educational level in rural areas. It was also observed that around 89% respondents have a lower level of obligatory and spectacular political participation and all of them have low level of voting and campaign participation.

Ramdas (1989) in her study related to the various problems of women made an important point and stated that women are discouraged by the attitudes of men in their families. Husbands, fathers, brothers at times even completely forbid their women-folk to participate in literacy/ education programmes. This is because men are afraid that if their women learnt more than they themselves did, it might expose their own ignorance and subsequently even challenge the power relation within the families. Ramdas therefore, suggested that women should demand for literacy on their own and literacy must be practical and relevant to the lives and needs of women.

From the above reviewed researches, it can be stated that various factors are responsible for the educational development of women. Among them a very strong relationship has been observed among the education of women with the attitude and effort of the family and level of social development, although they are discouraged by people in many ways.

Therefore, they should not wait for the consideration of others and generate self-confidence in them to demand for education of their own as their basic human right.

With regards to the research techniques, most of the researchers have followed survey method of different types and have used the secondary sources of data. Limited number of investigators have followed the historical method and investigated their studies. Whereas, four investigators have followed survey-cum-historical method and have collected data by using the tools like interview schedule and questionnaire. Rest of the researchers stated above in this section have followed survey method of various types.

Some of the investigators have followed descriptive survey method for their studies, whereas three investigators have followed evaluative survey and only one investigator has followed cross-sectional method of survey for his study by using questionnaires of both open and fixed type as his research tool for data collection.

Most of the researchers have adopted stratified sampling and random sampling procedure to draw samples from their restricted areas. Very few of them have adopted purposive sampling procedure to draw sample.

For the purpose of data collection most of the researchers have used questionnaires and interview schedules of both structured and unstructured type. Some of them have also adopted achievement tests along with questionnaires and interview schedules for their studies. Two investigators have used attitude scales for their studies. Whereas only one investigator has collected data by using money problem checklist along with Vyaktiva Prakash Prashnavati and Socio-Economic Status Scale of Verma and Sexena for his study.

Two investigators have investigated the field and collected their data by in-depth discussions, field visits, observations and informal interviews for their studies along with questionnaires. In addition to these tools one of the investigator has conducted case studies for her research.

Regarding the analysis of data both quantitative and qualitative methods have been followed by the researchers to analyse the data and to interpret the facts. But much importance is given to the quantitative form of data analysis by the researchers.

Implication of the Related Literature for the Present Study

The main purpose of the present investigation is to study the impact of literacy programme on educational development of slum women in Rourkela with respect to their levels of literacy, *i.e.* reading, writing and arithmetic level of awareness developed in terms of their family welfare, small family norms and various issues related to health and sanitation, child and maternity care, environment protection, etc., changing attitude towards evils of dowry, early marriage, alcoholism, superstitions, etc., raising voice against exploitation, taking interest for family and social welfare to estimate their levels of aspiration and self-confidence, enrolment of their children in formal schools and other systems of education, and to find out the causes for their under-development.

The studies that have been reviewed under three sections in this chapter throw a very dim light on the theme. But no significant evaluative study has been conducted as a venture of scholarly endeavour either to assess systematically the educational development of the slum women in terms of their levels of literacy, *i.e.* reading, writing and numeracy and awareness in different aspects of life concerning with various issues, level of self-confidence and aspiration, their power of decision-making and leadership qualities, techniques of solving problems both in the family and society, or to analyse seriously their causes of underdevelopment in education, low socio-economic, cultural and political status etc. Most of the existing studies have only described how things are, but there is an overall lack of studies attempting to rigorously examine why things are as they are among the disadvantaged slum women.

Furthermore, in the recent years literacy programme has been launched for the overall development mainly educational, of the disadvantaged illiterate people like ST, SC, slum-dwellers and women etc. Research in this area has shown that there is a differential rate of responsiveness to literacy programme by the disadvantaged people specially the ST, SC and slum women. The argument put forward by the research scholars that it is due to inter socio-economic and cultural variation in the educational attainment of these sections of the society that lead to negligible responsiveness to literacy programme. But the researchers have mostly neglected careful researches in this area. Only a few number of evaluation studies are available which are limited in their scope and suffer from certain methodological limitations. Hence, it is necessary to examine the literacy programme as well as its impact and responsiveness systematically and carefully.

So far as the methodology of research in concerned it has been observed from the studies reviewed in this Chapter under three different headings and dimensions, great importance has been given to research of survey type. Some researchers have also conducted their research work by following the historical method. Some of the researchers have even preferred to follow survey-cum-historical method for their research work. But very limited research works have been conducted in experimental design by the researchers. Even in the field of qualitative method of research no satisfactory studies have been found from the above reviewed studies.

Regarding the research tools much importance is given to the use of questionnaire and interview schedule of structured type by most of the researchers. Some of the researchers have also used checklists, attitude scales, observation schedules along with their questionnaires and interview schedules. Case studies, in depth discussion, unstructured interviews and field visit of short duration have also been adopted by a few researchers along with their other research tools.

Participant observations and field analysis techniques have been made by a very few researchers for their studies.

The description of facts and information have been analysed and presented by the researchers in quantitative as well as qualitative form. But the major thrusts of their presentation were of quantitative type.

Hence, it has been thought of to undertake a systematic research work on the impact of literacy programme on slum women focusing on their educational development and to take guidelines to an appropriate methodological stands as has been discussed in the Chapter 4.

3

THE SETTING

INTRODUCTION

In a developing country like ours, the level of development especially educational is determined by the socio-ecological setting, which consists of a number of factors like the economic condition, the geographical condition, the political and ideological ambience, education and socio-cultural patterns. These factors effect directly or indirectly in the immediate and distant educational development of that society. Thus, it is pertinent to be familiar with the setting of the area under investigation. That's why any picture of educational development emerging from the study will necessarily have a direct bearing on the above stated factors affecting educational development.

The study was conducted by taking Rourkela city as a part of the Sundargarh district of Orissa. Incidentally this city is one of the growing urban agglomerations not only in the state but also in the country. This is due to the "Steel Plant" and other sister plants as well as industries located in the city. This chapter clearly describes the setting against the background of the city and the state. The details about the city and the state is presented below.

THE STATE OF ORISSA

Location and Population

With an area of 1,55,707 square kilometer, Orissa is the 10th biggest and 11th populated state of the country having a population of 3,67,06,920. The number of males and females are 1,86,12,340 and 1,80,94,580 respectively. According to the 2001 census, the state has a population density of 236 per sq. km. and a population growth rate of 15.9 per cent.

Past Glory

Orissa, one of the most interesting states of India, was known by many names in the past like Udra, Kalinga, Utkal etc., probably, signifying different parts and is known as political Orissa today.

The State of Orissa has had a glorious past and its people "the Oriyas" seem to be determined to revive its ancient traditions. As seen, Ashok, the emperor of Maurya dynasty waged a bloody war with the people of Kalinga at Dhauli near Bhubaneswar in the 261 B.C. causing great devastation and untold miseries to the people. The devastation of the war compelled Ashok to repent and embrace Buddhism. Afterwards Kharavela emerged as a ruler of great eminence and the 'Oriyas' even today are proud of the name as his rule lead the state to prominence, peace and prosperity. Then the imperial Guptas held sway over Orissa for many years and even Harshavardhana had extended his kingdom to the state.

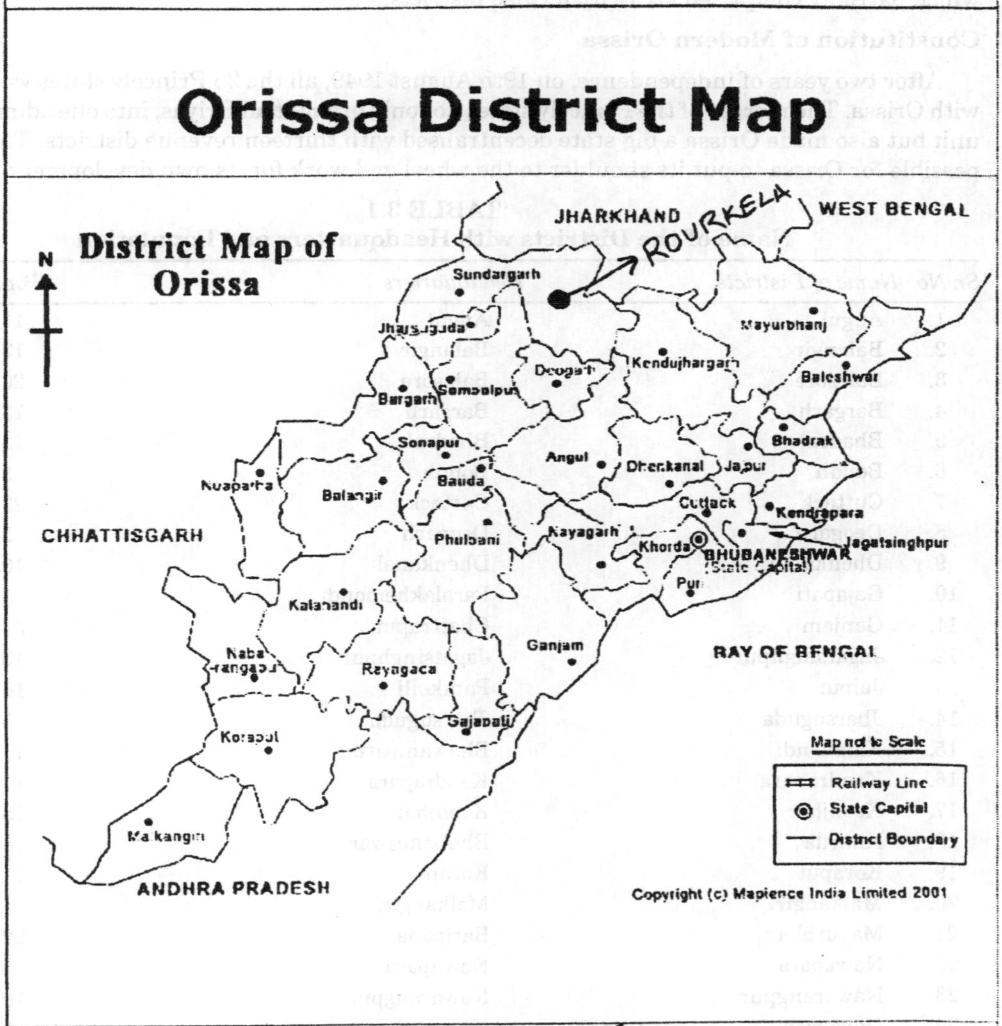

Map 3.1 : Districts of Orissa.

A number of Oriya dynasties came up one after the other and ultimately, the British took over the state from the Marathas although as many as 26 indigenous princely states continued to function in some parts of Orissa. On 1st April, 1936 the British rulers of India created Orissa as a separate province giving it a geo-political entity and the name as "Swatantra Orissa Pradesh" which partially comprised six British ruled districts.

Constitution of Modern Orissa

After two years of independence, on 19th August 1949, all the 26 Princely states were merged with Orissa. The merger of the Princely states not only brought all Oriyas, into one administrative unit but also made Orissa a big state decentralised with thirteen revenue districts. This made it possible for Orissa to put its shoulder to the wheel and work for its own development.

TABLE 3.1
Name of the Districts with Headquarters and Population

Sr. No.	*Name of Districts*	*Headquarters*	*Population*
1.	Angul	Angul	11,39,341
2.	Balangir	Balangir	13,35,760
3.	Balesore	Balesore	20,23,056
4.	Bargarh	Bargarh	13,45,601
5.	Bhadrak	Bhadrak	13,32,249
6.	Boudh	Boudh	3,73,038
7.	Cuttack	Cuttack	23,40,686
8.	Deogarh	Deogarh	2,79,095
9.	Dhenkanal	Dhenkanal	10,65,983
10.	Gajapati	Paralakhemondi	5,18,448
11.	Ganjam	Chattrapur	31,36,937
12.	Jagatsinghpur	Jagatsinghpur	10,56,556
13.	Jaipur	Panikoili	16,22,868
14.	Jharsuguda	Jharsuguda	5,09,056
15.	Kalahandi	Bhawanipatna	13,34,372
16.	Kendrapara	Kendrapara	13,01,856
17.	Keonjhar	Keonjhar	15,61,521
18.	Khurda	Bhubaneswar	18,79,405
19.	Koraput	Koraput	11,77,959
20.	Malkangiri	Malkangiri	4,80,232
21.	Mayurbhanj	Baripada	22,21,782
22.	Nawapara	Nawapara	5,30,524
23.	Nawarangpur	Nawarangpur	10,18,171
24.	Nayagarh	Nayagarh	8,63,934
25.	Phulbani (Kandhamal)	Phulbani	6,47,912
26.	Puri	Puri	14,98,604
27.	Rayagada	Rayagada	8,23,019
28.	Sambalpur	Sambalpur	9,28,889
29.	Sonepur	Sonepur	5,40,659
30.	Sundargarh	Sundargarh	18,29,412

Source : Census 2001.

Districts, Tahasils and Towns of Orissa

At present the thirteen districts have been extended to thirty revenue districts. The name of the districts with their headquarters and population are given below.

These thirty districts consist of 58 sub-divisions, 143 Tahasils, 315 Community Development Blocks, 2482 Gram Panchayats, 123 Towns and Urban Agglomerations (UAs) (114 Towns + 9 UAs) with 46,989 inhabited and 5,941 uninhabited villages. Out of these 123 towns and UAs, 7 are of class I category (No of UAs : 4; Towns: 3) 10 are of class II category (No. of UAs: 2; Towns: 8), 26 are of class III category (No. of UAs : 3; Towns : 23) and rest of the 90 towns have a population of less than 20,000 (Bhatt, 1997).

Orissa and Its Natural Division

The tropical state of Orissa lies along the eastern sea coast of India, South of Bengal. The state is bounded by the sea the Bay of Bengal on the east, Madhya Pradesh on the West, Andhra Pradesh on its South, West Bengal on the north-east, and Bihar on the north. The state is generally divided into four natural parts the table lands of the Eastern Ghats in the west, part of the central plateau and in their midst are the green valleys of live big rivers.

Natural Resources

Though Orissa is one of the poorest states in the country still it is rich in natural resources like, water and electricity, forests and minerals etc.

Rivers and Electricity

The state is full of big rivers like Mahanadi, Brahmani, Kathajodi, Subarna Rekha, and Budhabalanga which flow into the Bay of Bengal through coastal plains. The rivers are advantageous to the farmer because they add to the fertility of the soil and is a source of hydroelectricity.

Forests

In the upland region and on the upper slopes, which is about 30.3 per cent of its total area, are lush green forests abounding in wild elephants, Bengal tigers and rare species and are enriched with forest products like sal, teak asan, kangada, sandal wood, rose wood, lac, tussar, silk, kendu leave and medicinal plants like, nux vomica raw wolfia serpentina etc.

Minerals Resources

The state is rich in minerals and there are as many as twenty different types of minerals in the state and twelve of them are commercially exploited. The state of Orissa exports iron ore in large quantities to Japan and other countries through the Paradeep Port. It has a large steel plant in Rourkela.

Climate

Situated between 17,490 north to 22,340 North parallel, Orissa is well within the tropical belt and hence has tropical climate. The monsoons, both south-west and north-east effectively control the climate conditions with a specific period of summer rains (from June to September with about 72 rainy days in a year) and a prolonged dry season from the autumn through winter to the spring. Its location in the eastern coast of India restricts it from receiving sufficient rainfall from the south-east monsoon unlike the Bengal region. There is more rain in the hilly region of Eastern Ghats than in the coastal and river plains. The variation is about 181 cms in some area to a moderate 101 cms in some parts. The inadequate rainfall due to its location, coupled with the lack of better irrigation facilities has seriously affected the agricultural sector.

PEOPLE OF ORISSA

Economic Condition

Despite the bounties of nature, Orissa is one of the India's poorest states and as many as 52 per cent of people live below the poverty line (NCEAR, 1999). The per capita income of the state was also much below the national average, *i.e.* Rs. 1851.7 against the all India per capita income Rs. 3146.8 in the year 1997 (World Bank, 2000).

Although there is a burst of energy among the middle classes that manifests in diverse fields from high attainments in the all India services to literature and other creative activities, the average Oriya is considerably behind his counterpart in several states. The fact that the growth rate of population of the state was quite high, *i.e.* 15.9 per cent during the year 1991—2000 (Census, 2001) is one of the major obstacle for the economic development of the state. The state has also occupied a fairly high position among the Indian states for her indigenous tribal concentration of as many as 62 distinctive tribal groups, 22.2 per cent against the all India average of 7.76 per cent and a fairly large population of scheduled caste population of 93 types, 16.2 per cent against the national figure of 15.75 (Census Report, 1991). These adds to the burden of the state, because the economic, the educational and the social level of the disadvantaged has to be raised. Besides the problems stated above, Orissa's economy is often destabilised by natural calamities like flood, drought, cyclone or tornado. Cyclone has in recent years become a regular feature. The Super Cyclone of 1999 had broken down the total structure of Orissa and Oriyas. However, flooding in Mahanadi Delta, which used to occur regularly, has been reduced greatly by the Hirakud Dam constructed in 1958.

Agriculture

Orissa is, predominantly, a rural state. So the level of urbanization in the state is low in comparison to some other states of the country, *i.e.* 14.97 per cent against the all India figure of 27.78 per cent of the population (Census Report, 2001). The bulk of the population i.e. about 85 per cent of the state live in rural Orissa and their dependence on agriculture is greater.

The grass cropped area of the state is about 92.70 lakh hectares, slightly more than one fifth. Rice is the principal crop and the staple diet of the Oriyas. Due to inadequate irrigation facilities, its cultivation or output per hectare is below the national average. Thereby, the Central Rice Research Institute is established in Cuttack for better output and development. Sugarcane is the main cash crop and the production is of a substantial level. Besides rice and sugarcane, the other food crops are pulses and oilseeds of which as many as nine varieties are sown, including groundnuts, mustard, seasamum, rapeseeds and limeseeds.

Language

The state of Orissa gives shelter to a number of communities. They can broadly be divided into several linguistic groups. Out of the 58 languages spoken in the state, Oriya tops the list as mother– tongue or state language and as many as 2,61,99,346 persons (82.75 per cent) speak in Oriya (1991, Census Report). Among the other recognised languages are Hindi (2.40 per cent), Telugu (2.10 per cent), Urdu (1.59 per cent), Bengali (1.40 per cent) and other languages like Assamese, Gujarati, Kannada, Kashmiri, Malayalam, Marathi, Punjabi, Sindhi, Tamil etc. (9.79 per cent).

Religion

Orissa is basically a Hindu state and its position is the 11th in the Country. Some other religions, such as Christianity and Islam are also found to be in a considerable proportion. The minor religious groups include the "Sikhs", the "Buddhist", and the "Jain". Religion wise, the percentage of Orissa's population is Hindus : 94.7 per cent (2, 99,71,257 persons), Christians : 2.1 per cent, Muslims; 1.8 per cent, Sikhs : 0.05 per cent, Buddhists: 0.03 per cent, Jains : 0.02 per cent and other religions : 1.3 per cent (Census, 1991).

Festivals

Orissa is a land of fairs and festivals. Some of the more famous of the Orissan festivals and fairs are the Makaramela, Rajaparba, Dolapurnima, Dasahara, Nabanna Parba (Nuakhai), Baliyatra, the Car Festival of Lord Lingaraj of Bhubaneswar and the most important and popular of all, the Ratha Yatra of Lord Jagannath in Puri. The Ratha Yatra of Puri has a special significance. During this period many pilgrims from India and overseas throng Orissa. There are not many things comparable to Ratha Yatra as the chariot in which the idols of Lord Jagannath, his brother Balaram and sister Subhadra are placed is drawn, not by horses or other animals, but by the devotees themselves.

Tourism

Orissa is a tourist's dream. There are so many places to see here like the Sun Temple at Konark, the seabeach and Jagannath temple of Puri, the beautiful Chilika lake, the Gopalpur and Chandbali sea beaches, the Siva temple of Kapilash, the Nandan Kanna Zoo and the Lingaraj temple of Bhubaneswar, the immense Buddhist monastic complexes of Ratnagiri, Lalitgiri, Khandagri and Udaigiri near Bhubaneswar, the Khandadhar water fall of Sundargarh District, the Ushakothi wildlife centuary and the Hirakud dam of Sambalpur.

Handloom, Art and Handicraft

Orissa has a wide distinctive range of handloom fabrics and handicrafts. The best known handloom fabrics are Sambalpuri silk, tusser and cotton handwoven tie and dye sarees and ikat fabrics, Berhampuri handloom silk saree, Nuapatna silk saree, Barpali tusser shawl etc. The famous among handicrafts are applique work of Pipili, silver filigree jewellery of Cuttack, pattachitra of Rashurajpur, wooden and stone carving work of Puri district and coir work of Sakhigopal etc.

Nature and Behaviour of the Oriyas

The Oriyas, nearly 40 per cent of whom are indigenous tribals and scheduled castes are simple, friendly, hospitable and co-operative, which made it possible for the launching of the test purposes of missiles for the use of the Indian Defence Forces. The test of the long distance missiles are conducted near the site at Balasore and has hit the world head lines for the successful test of missiles like Prithvi, Akash and Agni for the past several years.

Performing Art

The mention of Orissa and its people would be incomplete without mentioning the classical Odissi dance and other vigorous forms like Paik (Warrior) dance, Chhau dance, Karma and so on. Orissa has its supreme offering in the form of Odissi dance to the world of performing art and culture.

Literacy

In Orissa, while higher education has made strides in all directions, the general level of literacy among the mass is still below the national average. The challenges before the state are enormous. Still in the last few decades, there has been a significant increase of literacy rate (from 15.8 per cent in the year 1951 to 63.61 per cent in the year 2001). But, despite a 47.81 per cent increase in the level of literacy of the state between 1951 and 2001, the literacy rate of 63.61 per cent of Orissa is still below the national average of 65.38 per cent.

This average picture of the state, however, hides the vide radiance prevailing in different areas. Out of thirty districts, thirteen districts had the literacy rate above the national average of 65.38 per cent in 2001. Khurda district tops the list with 80.19 per cent followed by Jagatsinghpur (79.61 per cent), Puri (78.40 per cent), Kendrapara (73.33 per cent), Cuttack (73.13 per cent), Bhadrak (79.64 per cent), Jaipur (72.19 per cent), Jharsuguda (71.47 per cent), Nayagarh (71.02 per cent), Balasore (70.94 per cent), Dhenkanal (70.11 per cent), Augul (69.40 per cent) and Sambalpur (67.01 per cent). Seven districts were in the range of 55 to more than 65 per cent, namely, Sundargarh (65.22 per cent), Bargarh (64.13 per cent), Sonepur (64.07 per cent). Ganjam (62.94 per cent). Deograh (60.78 per cent), Keonjhar (59.75 per cent) and Boudh (58.43 per cent). Four districts were in the range of 45.55 per cent, namely Kalahandi (46.20 per cent), Mayurbhanj (52.43 per cent), Kandhamal (52.95 per cent) and Balangir (54.93 per cent). Four more districts were in the range of 35-45 per cent, namely, Rayagada (35.61 per cent), Koraput (36.20 per cent), Gajapati (41.73 per cent) and Nawapara (42.29 per cent). Two districts were recorded below 35 per cent of literacy rate namely Nawarangpur (34.26 per cent) and Malkangiri (31.26 per cent). The lowest literacy rate was recorded in Malkangiri (31.26 per cent) (Census, 2001).

Education of Women in Orissa

Orissa, recognised as one of the economically and educationally backward states of India ever since Independence, has a female population of 80, 94,580 according to the census of 2001. Although, there are instances such as the involvement of Christian missionaries in promoting education among women and disadvantaged people (like, STs and SCs) and the significant recommendations of Kothari Commission of 1964, National Policy on Education, 1968, National Policy on Educational, 1986, and its Review Committee Report, 1990, and almost all the Five Year Plans report (like 1st, 2nd, 3rd, 4th, 5th, 8th and 9th five year plans) level of literacy still low. No serious efforts were made by the Government to promote education among the women for their development. After independence some concerted efforts has been under way for the development of women on the basis of the provision made in the constitution of India under Articles 15(1), 15(3), 39(a), 39(d), 45 and 46. Programmes related to women's welfare and development have been taken up and priority has been given to educational programmes as a pre-requisite to an overall development of women who are also the responsible citizens of the country.

After independence, the first census was conducted in the year 1951. During that period Orissa had a literacy rate of 15.8 per cent (male 27.30 and female 4.50 per cent). It rose to 21.70 per cent (male 34.70 and female 8.60 per cent in 1961); 26.18 per cent (male 38.29 and female 26.18 per cent) in 1971; 34.12 per cent (male 46.90 and female 21.11) in 1981; 49.09 per cent (male 63.09 and female 34.68) in 1991; 51.00 per cent (male 64.50 and female 38.00) in the year 1997 (NSSO, 98) and 63.61 per cent (male 75.95 and female 50.97) in 2001. Although the figures of female literacy rate show an increasing trend like male literacy rate, it may not be out of place to mention here that female literacy rate of Orissa has been below in all the census years against not only their male counterpart in the state, but also against the female literacy rate of national average. This is evident from the table given below :

TABLE 3.2
Growth Rate of Literacy in India and Orissa

Year	*India*			*Orissa*		
	Total	*Male*	*Female*	*Total*	*Male*	*Female*
1951	16.67%	24.95%	7.93%	15.8%	27.30%	4.50%
1961	24.02%	34.44%	12.95%	21.70%	34.70%	8.60%
1971	29.45%	39.45%	18.89%	26.18%	38.29%	19.92%
1981	43.67%	56.50%	29.85%	34.12%	46.90%	21.11%
1991	52.21%	64.13%	39.29%	49.09%	63.09%	34.68%
1997	62.00%	73.00%	50.00%	51.00%	64.00%	38.00%
2001	65.38%	75.85%	54.16%	63.61%	75.95%	50.97%

Source : Report of SRC, Orissa (1995), NSSO (1997), Census 1971, 1991 and 2001.

According to the Census Report of 2001, the female literacy rate of Orissa was the highest in Khurda district *i.e.* 71.06% which was much higher than the national female literacy rate and followed by six districts who were in the range of 60-70 per cent, namely, Jagatsinghpur (69.92%), Puri (67.80%), Kendrapara (67.29%), Cuttack (66.19%), Bhadrak (63.62%) and Jaipur (61.45%). Eight districts were in the range of 50–60 per cent, namely, Balasore (59.57%), Jharasuguda (59.23%), Dhenkanal (58.55%), Nayagarh (58.10%), Angul (56.01%), Sambalpur (54.79%), Sundargarh (54.25%) and Bargarh (50.03%). Four districts were in the range of 40-50 per cent, namely, Ganjam (45.70%), Deogarh (47.56%), Sonepur (47.28%) and Keonjhar (46.71%). Five districts were in the range of 30-40 per cent namely, Bondh (39.78%), Bolangir (39.27%), Mayurbhanj (38.28%), Kandhamal (36.19%), Nawapada (36.01%) and six districts are in the range of 20-30 per cent namely, Kalahandi (29.56%), Gajapati (28.91%), Koraput (24.81%), Rayagada (29.3%), Malkangiri (21.28%) and Nabarangpur (21.02%) recorded the lowest female literacy rate in the state (Census, 2001).

Two major concerns at hand are to fulfill the constitutional commitment of Universalisation of Elementary Education by achieving cent per cent of enrolment (100%) and educational development and empowerment of women and socially disadvantaged groups. For this, the Government has been persistently trying with various alternative strategies, but still a large chunk of school going girls are out of school, and female adults remain illiterates. This is evident from the table given below :

TABLE 3.3
Enrolment Figure by Stages of Sex

	Primary School (Classes I to V)			Middle School (Classes VI to VIII)			High School (Classes IX to X)		
Year	Boys	Girls	Total	Boys	Girls	Total	Boys	Girls	Total
1980-81	1667186	1083171	2750357	395295	190123	585418	231679	877994	319473
1990-91	2376276	1643968	4020244	700191	420426	1120617	387593	177643	565236
1997-98	1632000	2313000	3945000	830000	466000	1296000	561000	305000	866000

Source : Directorate of Elementary Education, Orissa, Bhubaneshwar (1998-99) and DOE, MHRD, GOI, Planning, Monitoring and Statistical Division, New Delhi,1998.

TABLE 3.4
Gross Enrolment Ratio at Different Levels

Year	Primary School (Classes I to V) (6-11 Yrs)			Middle School (Classes VI toVIII) (12-14 Yrs)			High School (Classes IX to X) (15-17 Yrs)		
	Boys	Girls	Total	Boys	Girls	Total	Boys	Girls	Total
1980-81	93.0	60.3	76.6	41.1	20.0	30.6	31.6	12.3	22.2
1990-91	131.48	95.36	113.85	67.72	41.21	54.55	27.77	12.70	20.23

Source : DOE, MHRD, GOI, Planning, Monitoring and Statistical Division, New Delhi, 1996.

It can be seen from the tables that the enrolments of boys are increasing almost satisfactorily both at the primary and high school levels but the girls' enrolment is still poor. It means much effort is needed in this direction. Further, it has been observed that there is around 46% of dropout rate among girls' students in primary, 68% in middle and 81% in high school level demanding an urgent attention to motivate these girls to come to school.

ROURKELA CITY

Steel city Rourkela is an urban agglomeration, situated in the tribal district of Sundargarh, Orissa state, India (for location see Map 3). This industrial cosmopolitan complex gives shelter to the people of the different corners of the country including the original tribal inhabitants of the area. In historical perspective, the Primary State of Gangpur and Bonai constituted the Sundargarh district. The present Sundargarh district came into existence on the 1st January, 1948 and merged into the state of Orissa as one of its districts covering an area of 9812.49 sq. km. It has a total population of 18,29,412 comprising about 934902 males and 894510 females, and occupies the 6th place among the districts of Orissa. The district has a population density of 188 per Sq. Km. and the decadal growth (1991–2001) was 16.26 per cent.

Sundargarh is one of the northern most districts of the state of Orissa. Placed in the midst of the most stunningly beautiful hills and forests, this district is not a compact one. Rather, it consists of indently dissimilar tracts of extensive and fairly open country, dotted with tree clad isolated peaks, vast impregnated forests, winding rivers like the Ib and the Brahmani and extensive river valleys, sparsely populated villages and mountainous terrains. About 38.6 per cent of the geographical area of the district is covered with virgin forests (NLM, 1993). The east and west of Brahmani valley is filled with high range of mountains, of which are Mankarnacha (3664 ft.), Chheliatoka (3331 ft) and Bichakani (2964 ft) in the east. The last hill has acquired importance as it contains million of tons of iron-ore, manganese ore, limestone, dolomite, bauxite etc. (Bhatt, 1997).

The economy of the district is essentially agricultural, with nearly 56.05% of the population depending on it. There are pockets of industrial growth around Rajgangpur, Rourkela and Biramitrapur emanating from a more developed industrial infrastructure.

The district at present comprises of 3 sub-divisions, 7 tahasils and 17 community development blocks. It has 9 towns and 1744 villages (1688 inhabited villages and 56 uninhabited villages). The present city of Rourkela is the outcome of a tribal "Rourkela" which means "your home" in Sadri language. People from the 'Roulia' tribal community had been living in the "Rourkela" village since time immemorial. This tribal village was once under the jurisdiction of the Nagraestate. Later on, it came under the feudal state of Gangpur which was kept under the jurisdiction of the

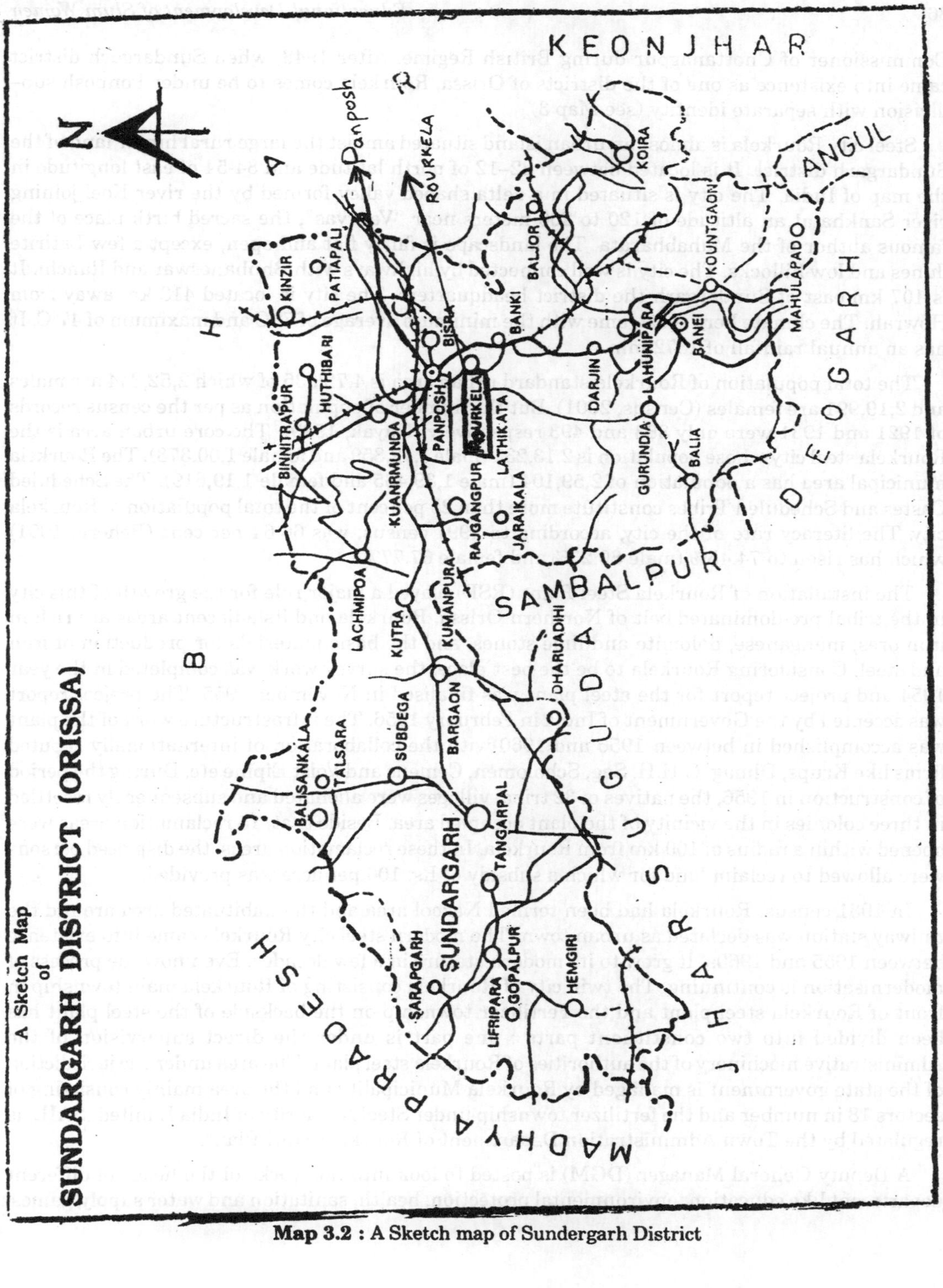

Map 3.2 : A Sketch map of Sundergarh District

Commissioner of Chottanagpur during British Regime. After 1948, when Sundargarh district came into existence as one of the districts of Orissa, Rourkela comes to be under Ponposh sub-division with separate identity (see Map 3).

Steel city Rourkela is almost an urban island situated amidst the large rural hinter land of the Sundargarh district. It is located between 22–12 of north latitude and 84-54 of east longitude in the map of India. The city is situated in a delta shaped valley formed by the river Koel joining river Sankha at an altitude of 120 to 200 meters near "Vedvyas", the sacred birth place of the famous author of the Mahabharata. The landscape is fairly flat and open, except a few Latirite dunes and low hillocks. The city is well connected by highways with Bhubaneswar and Ranchi. It is 107 km east of Sundargarh the district headquarters. The city is located 413 km away from Howrah. The climate here is extreme with the minimum average of 7° C and maximum of 47°C. It has an annual rainfall of 1372 mm.

The total population of Rourkela standard urban area is 4,72,335 of which 2,52,344 are males and 2,19,991 are females (Census, 2001). But the number of population as per the census records of 1921 and 1931 were only 383 and 493 respectively (Nayak, 1999). The core urban area is the Rourkela steel city whose population is 2,13,231 (male 1,12,859 and female 1,00,373). The Rourkela municipal area has a population of 2,59,104 (male 1,39,485 and female 1,19,619). The Scheduled Castes and Scheduled Tribes constitute more than 25 per cent of the total population of Rourkela city. The literacy rate of the city, according to 1991 census, was 66.64 per cent (Behera, 1991) which has risen to 74.45% (male 80.27% and female 67.77%).

The installation of Rourkela Steel Plant (RSP) played a major role for the growth of this city in the tribal pre-dominated belt of Northern Orissa. Rourkela and its adjacent areas are rich in iron ores, manganese, dolomite and lime stones, and the basic materials for production of iron and steel. Considering Rourkela to be the best place, the survey work was completed in the year 1954 and project report for the steel plant was finalised in November 1955. The project report was accepted by the Government of India in February 1956. The infrastructure work of the plant was accomplished in between 1956 and 1960 with the collaboration of internationally reputed firms like Krups, Dimag, G.H.H. Sag, Scholomen, Cemens and Voist Eipine etc. During the period of construction in 1956, the natives of 32 tribal villages were alienated and subsequently resettled in three colonies in the vicinity of the plant occupied area. Beside that, 15 reclamation areas were opened within a radius of 100 km from Rourkela. In these reclamation areas, the displaced persons were allowed to reclaim land for which a subsidy of Rs. 100 per acre was provided.

In 1931 census, Rourkela had been termed Nazool area and the habituated area around the railway station was declared as urban town. The modern steel city Rourkela came into existence between 1955 and 1960s. It grew to its modern stature in a few decades. Even now the process of modernisation is continuing. The twin city of Rourkela consisting of Rourkela main township in front of Rourkela steel plant and the Fertilizer township on the backside of the steel plant has been divided into two constituent parts : one part is under the direct supervision of the administrative machinery of the authorities of Rourkela steel plant. The area under the jurisdiction of the state government is managed by Rourkela Municipality and the area mainly consisting of sectors 18 in number and the fertilizer township under Steel Authority of India Limited (SAIL) is regulated by the Town Administration Department of Rourkela Steel Plant.

A Deputy General Manager (DGM) is posted to look into the works of the heads of different department like education, environmental protection, health, sanitation and water supply, games, sports and recreational facilities, construction of roads and staff quarters and their allotment, commercial centers and market management etc. The town administration department provides different facilities like education, culture and civic amenities for the all round development mainly for the steel plant employees and their children. The town administration has also undertaken developmental works for the welfare of the area that lie on the periphery like building schools, health centres, pucca roads for communications, organisations of games and sports and different schemes.

The administrative head of Rourkela city is the Additional District Magistrate, Rourkela, assisted by other Government Officials like P.A. ITDA (Project Administrator, Integrated Tribal Development Agency), Sub-Collector, Panposh, S.D.M.O. for medical services, a Superintending Engineer for the Department of GRIDCO, D.I. of schools, for the Department of School Education, Executive Officer, Rourkela Municipality and Officers of other departments. The Government of Orissa has fixed-up the, headquarters of the D.I.G. of Police (Northern Range) at Rourkela and have also posted an S.P. to lookafter the law and order of the city.

Rourkela Development Authority (RDA) started functioning for the people of Rourkela city since 1976. It has to shoulder the responsibility of providing different development schemes like establishing housing colonies, ensuring residential plots etc. to beautify the city which is surrounded by hills, rivers and trees.

The present city of Rourkela is not only a planned and beautiful city in the physical aspect, but also developed in many respects. There is no denying the fact that Rourkela is one of the educationally and economically developed city not only in the district of Sundargarh, but also in the state of Orissa. After independence and just before the merger in 1948, there was a rapid progress all over the country. But it did not happen simultaneously in Rourkela. The available archive material indicates that after independence and prior to the installation of Rourkela Steel Plant, education and modern civilization could not get momentum in this area as it was surrounded by hills and dense forest. Before R.S.P was commissioned, there was one primary school in each village of Rourkela, Tarkera, Panposh and Tumkela and there was a mission managed high school at Hamirpur.

Provisions were not made for education during the pre-installation period. As a result a number of private colleges, English medium schools and charitable hospitals have been started by their own efforts.

By the year 1998-99 the number of primary schools in Rourkela have risen to 112 with a total number of 27,336 (14,563 boys and 12,773 girls). The numbers of upper primary schools (class I to class VII and class VI and class VII) have risen to 79 with a total number of 17,515 students (9,079 boys and 8,436 girls). The numbers of high schools and english medium schools have also risen to 58 and 27 respectively (Source : Office of the D.I. of Schools, Rourkela). Similarly, a number of 39 different types of colleges and training centres have been developed in the city. Inspite of Pharmaceutical Science, etc. special institutions like Regional Engineering College, have also been functioning for the progress of the local people as well as outsider.

Inspite of a very large number of schools and colleges functioning in the city, the literacy rate of Rourkela was only 66.64 per cent according to 1991 census. A number of 1,22,214 persons (male 56,832 and female 75,382) remained illiterate (Census Report, 1991). Out of the total illiterates, 26,050 were from Scheduled Castes and 38,573 were from Scheduled Tribes.

The reason is that, the Rourkela steel plant its ancillaries and other small industries employ a large number of workers. The expansion of the steel plant had assimilated many linguistic and religious groups from various states of the country. The demographic nature of the present city is characterized by a high degree of pluralism, multi-ethnic, multi-linguistic and multi-religious communities. Though Oriya is the most common language, yet Hindi finds an important place as a language of communication.

In the recent years, as many as 196 slums have come up in the Government lands of civil and Steel Township of Rourkela. A population of more than one lakh live in those slums of unauthorized lands in extreme poverty and lacking minimum infrastructure facilities and amenities like housing, ration card, sanitation and medical facilities, education, water, electricity etc.

SLUM WOMEN OF ROURKELA AND THEIR STATUS

Women have been regarded as the nuclei of a nation and the builder and moulder of its destiny. Position and status of women in any society is an index of its civilization. So, the best way to understand the spirit of a civilization and to realise its limitation is to study the status of women in it.

The constitution of India and the legal codes bestowed upon women, the privilege of equal rights with men, like the facilities of education, the same opportunities of profession and employment and even right to property from the parents. Despite the constitutional safeguard and progressive legislative measures, the bulk of Indian women are deprived of this boon of raised status and suffer under the shadow of our orthodox and conservative society, whether it is rural, tribal, urban or the slum. One of the root cause of their low status and subjugated position in the society is due to the high level of illiteracy and educational backwardness compelled with ignorance, orthodox beliefs, taboos and rigid social customs and traditions. That is why we found more cases of suicides among women than men, lower facilities for girls and women with in the household, sexual exploitation of girls and women by the employers, close relatives and even the father and uncle in some cases, (Giladia, 1992) the increasing number of rape and kidnapping, prostitution, inequality of wages between female and male labourers. Also the burden of the domestic work is unshared by male members even when women are working outside all the day long.

Slum women of Rourkela city are not free from the aforesaid problems with regard to their status and position in the society. Before highlighting their status in the society, a comprehensive picture of the Rourkela slums and about their dwellers, need to be mentioned for better understanding.

Rourkela, as mentioned earlier, is an industrial city with cosmopolitan characteristics. Due to the Rourkela Steel Plant and other sister industries, there is a constant flow of people to the city from outside. For which the city has the most rapid increase in the number of slums in unauthorised land of the steel plant and the state government. As mentioned earlier, more than one lakh people of the city (which constitute 25 per cent of the total population) live in the slum areas in a wretched condition of life, due to the lack of minimum infrastructure facilities and amenities. The typical nature and characteristics of any urban slum in India is found in Rourkela. The characteristics are tremendous problems regarding housing and substandard condition of living, poverty, lack of proper schooling for the children, lighting, public distribution system, ration cards, medical facilities, sanitation etc. Most of the inhabitants of these slums are the displaced tribals and the rural migrants of the neighbouring districts and the states. They are the most disintegrated, disorganised people with great diverse and heterogenic characteristics. They primarily depend on wages from physical and odd jobs of public and private undertaking like contract labour, rag and iron picking in the dumping yards of Rourkela steel plant, and picking roadside garbage, working as kuli in railway station, market places, and different type of cottage industries and factories. Some of them work as both full time and part time maid servants in higher and middle class families. Also they work as sweepers, gardeners, watchman and caretakers of newly constructed buildings and apartments. It is also seen in Rourkela slums that a good number of people use to make handia (a type of country liquor made of rice) and sell it to earn their livelihood which is very common in Rourkela slums where the tribal concentrations are high. There slum-dwellers are highly illiterate, ignorant about their rights, culturally deprived and the most disadvantaged sections in the city of Rourkela.

In addition to these common characteristics some peculiar nature of slum composition in Rourkela city is its cosmopolitan nature and the activities of the native tribals those who have already got their compensation from RSP Authority against their land and not yet vacated the place. Also some of the families have left their native place, gone to the resettlement areas, settled there for some time and once again came back to the city to earn their livelihood as they didn't have better scope in the stated resettlement camps. Although these native tribals are staying over the city slums, they have not yet fully adopted to the urban slum culture. Up till now they were leading a typical tribal life composed with the rhythms of drum, dance, music and handia-daru (country liquor). They are innocent, simple and sometimes wild. They are ignorant of their basic rights and schemes meant for their upliftment. They are not even able to obtain their ration cards and other essential amenities from the Government Offices. As a result, they lead a miserable life being exploited by the upper classes, politicians, government officers and others.

It is seen that women and girls are the worst sufferers in the slums. Their status is much inferior in the families as well as in the society. Unlike other slum women and girls, majority of them have to struggle very hard at every point of their lives for livelihood and sheer existence. Thus, they have to perform dual role in the family and in the society, *i.e.* the productive and reproductive. Inspite of their day long hard labour as a strong earning member of the family along with the total household chores, they are tortured physically and mentally by their drunk husbands and other members of the family. They don't have rights to take any decision of their own or in family matters, even if they are the main contributor to the family's survival. Since they are illiterates and educationally backwards, abused, superstitious, ignorant to their basic and legal rights, disorganised and lack self-confidence, they face a lot of problems. They are being harassed, discriminated and exploited economically, culturally, morally, socially and even sexually. They don't even raise their voice strongly against any of the exploitation and tolerate everything silently.

These are very common to the majority of women in Rourkela slums. In general, they are underestimated, discriminated and have a very low level of status in the family as well as in the society. But there are certain communities in the slums setting where women do have a peculiar and contradictory status both in the family and in the society as compared to others. But they are few in numbers.

Rourkela, as mentioned earlier, is an industrial urban agglomeration developed in a tribal district. So the native of the district as well as the city are basically local tribes. They are concentrated in different parts of the city after being displaced from their original area and have formed slums, which are like the "urban villages". Unlike other slum women, the women and girl children of the tribal communities in the slums are also abused. They are illiterates, wretched, poverty stricken, ignorant of their basic social rights, innocents, sick and superstitious. But the difference is that they enjoy full freedom and equal status at most of the social and cultural institution with the male counter- parts as compared to the non-tribal and urban migrants in the slum. Their birth or arrival in the family is welcome. In fact, it gives an opportunity to increase the numbers in the tribes as every girl child is conceived as a potential mother (Deogaonkar and Deonkar, 1991).

The mother earth and the girl child command equal respect in the tribal community whether it is a typical tribal village in the dense forest or in Rourkela slums. This is highly contradictory to the status of women from those families who have migrated from the interior rural areas of eastern Orissa, Bihar, Madhya Pradesh and other places. Even the migrants of the drought areas of Western part of Orissa provide some equal facilities and status to their girls and women. They consider "girls" as their "Laxmi". But in cases of the rural migrants especially from the coastal belt and the states like Bihar and Madhya Pradesh, girls are burdens to the families. They are discriminated and exploited at every stage of their life. They are even deprived of nutritious food and other needs required for growth and development. They are forced to do the household chores, mind younger siblings and do other activities. Their vocational responsibilities start when they are quite young. Instead of learning alphabets, they have to struggle in dumping yards, railway platform, factories and other places.

Almost all the tribal slum girls and women in Rourkela work hard like the other slum girls and women and the male members of their families, both inside and outside the household. They work extensively in the field, in the quarry sides, in the dumping yards, inside the steel plant for more than 10 to 12 hours as contract labourers. Also they prepare and sale "handia" (country liquor made of rice) and tackle the drunk and unsocial customers quite boldly. Their existence and hard labour both are recognized as important in most of the tribal families and of the society. Hence, they enjoy a better status in socio-cultural sphere. But this recognition of womanhood is not found among the maximum women and girls of non-tribal slum families. Rather they are highly neglected, ignored at the time of decision-making and exploited in various ways by the family members.

It is quite peculiar to mention here that young tribal girls and women in Rourkela slum enjoy the freedom of drinking handia, dancing and singing with the young male members of their communities. During their festivals like Ratha Yatra, Nuakhai, Karma, Dasahara, Tusu, Makara, Pushpunai etc. the girls dominate the scene. Many a times, they outwit the boys. They are free and display uninhibited exuberance.

In case of other non-tribal slum girls and women, they can not even think of drinking handia or to sing and dance with any male member. Slum people from the typical rural background have not yet changed their attitudes. They are conservative, orthodox, and rigid to their thought regarding the freedom of girl and women. In case the girls try to be free like others and deviate from the so-called family tradition and the norms, the situation becomes worse and horrible.

More important among the tribal slum girls are their economic worth for the families and their superiorities during marriage and is recognized through bride price (even during divorce). They are free to choose their boy friends and life partners for marriage. Parents are secondary in decision-making with regard to their marriage. Also divorce is easy on the part of women and they can initiate the process and exercise their will.

This is just opposite and contradictory to the marriage of other slum girls and women of Rourkela. Inspite of their hard labour for the survival of the families, the girls and women do not have rights to think for their future. Their fates are determined by their fathers, brothers and other male members of the families. They cannot even express their views or choice regarding their own marriage. Women in general cannot go for divorce from their own side. Whatever the circumstances may be, they have to tolerate it. In the worst cases, they even commit suicide. Divorce is initiated and made mainly from male side.

Giving dowry to the bridegroom on the bases of their demand is very common in Rourkela slums. Inspite of the wretched financial conditions of the families, the fathers of the girls give dowry to the bridegrooms and they also demand dowry from the bride's family at the time of their son's marriage. It is very common in the areas where the migrated people of Bihar, Eastern Orissa, (like coastal belt of Jaipur, Jagatsinghpur, Kendrapada, Berhampur and other districts) and other people are concentrated. But dowry system is very rare in case of the migrated people of some of the districts of western Orissa like Sambalpur, Bargara, Jharsuguda, Bolangir, Kalahandi, Nawapara and even of Sundargarh district. Although the marriage of the girls are fixed by the fathers and elder members, but the opinions of the mothers are also invited at the time of the marriage of their daughters. The prestige of the girls is also kept by not giving dowry on demand basis to the bridegrooms. Rather, girls are to be offered some gifts from the in-laws in the form of ornaments, clothes (Sambalpuri sarees) and even bride price in some cases. The parents of the girls offer some presentations to their daughters and son-in-laws at the time of marriage according to their own wish, choice and financial condition. But it is not compulsory.

It has been observed in most of the Indian slums that women are ill treated. They tolerate the physical violence and men's brutality. They don't raise their voice against the violence. Still, in some cases especially with the tribal and semi-tribal slum women, when it happens, they don't tolerate it quite silently. They oppose their husbands strongly and sometimes the tribal women reply to them in the same manner boldly, which is quite impossible in case of other types of slum women. If at all they oppose their husbands by raising their voice against violence, no body would come for support. Rather they will be discouraged and blamed in many ways.

It is a fact that tribal girls and women of Rourkela slums are exploited and discriminated a lot. But generally they are not exploited and harassed by their family members or the members of their own community. Rather, they are discriminated and exploited a lot economically, morally, emotionally and even sexually by the other people like shopkeepers, steel plants contractors and supervisors, Government Officials and other personnels due to their educational backwardness, ignorance, simplicity, innocence and traditional style of living. Though the percentage of tribal slum women are not much higher (it is only about 13 per cent of the total slum population of Rourkela) like other people of the slum, they also face many health hazards due to malnutrition and disease, wretched poverty and problems related to alcohol, socio-economic exploitation by non-tribal and other people. It can be observed that the social position of average tribal girls and women in Rourkela slums have been better and promising than any other type of slum women in Rourkela.

In fact, status if seen as a derivative, is the result of a pattern of relationships between men and women a pattern composed of images they have of themselves and each other. Status lies in the eyes of the beholders.

In a developing country like India, and specially in its slums of urban agglomerations like Rourkela, where majority of the people are socio-economically and culturally deprived, educationally backward, morally, mentally and physically sick and diseased, abused, biased and superstitious, whose attitudes and reactions towards women's education, equality of rights and freedom are still deep rooted with rigid and discriminatory age old social traditions, cannot be altered so easily. Rather, the centuries old bias against women and womanhood can perhaps at best be removed only by changing the attitude of the community or the society as a whole, which sees the female child as an expense, a waste and a burden. This change can only be brought about to a great extent by the educational development of women themselves, whether they belong to remote rural areas, tribal villages or urban slums.

Slum women in Rourkela industrial city brings the setting in focusing their socio-economic and educational status, analysing and interpreting their problems with regard to education (as perceived by them) and also comprehending the extent of impact exerted by literacy programme. A brief account is presented below.

ROURKELA SAKSHARATA SAMITI (RSS)

Inspired by the success of Ernakulum Total Literacy Campaign, the Literacy Campaign of Rourkela was visualized, planned and promptly taken-up as a challenge by the Rourkelites in December, 1990. As an independent urban based project, Rourkela Literacy Campaign was the first of its kind in the state of Orissa along with that of Sundargarh District. Even before the Planning of Literacy Campaign, the Shramik Vidyapith, which is presently known as Jana Siksha Sansthan (JSS), Bethel Charitable Trust, Community Welfare Society, *i.e.* Sevasadan, Deepika Mahila Samiti, and few other organisations were engaged in the literacy and other developmental activities in few slum pockets of Rourkela. As an implementing agency of NLM, the Shramik Vidyapith (SVP) imparted literacy activities along with vocational training to the socio-economically weaker sections of Rourkela.

With hardly any progressive movement in the recent part, a mass movement like total Literacy Campaign becomes instrumental in this industrial cosmopolitan city to bind the people socially and perhaps culturally too. The Rourkela Saksharata Samiti was formed and registered accordingly under the Society Registration Act as an independent Saksharata Samiti. Based on the Philosophy of National Literacy Mission, the project proposal submitted in December, 1990 and was finally sanctioned by the Government of India in March, 1991 with the following objectives :

(1) Impact functional literacy to one lakh illiterates in the age group 10–60 years.

(2) Motivate the parents of the children below 10 years of age for enrolment in formal schools.

(3) Create awareness among the people regarding health, environment, sanitation, family welfare, developmental activities etc. and help them to improve their quality of life.

(4) Concentrate on literacy of women.

(5) Promote post-literacy and continuing education for the neo-literates.

Preparation for the mass movement of Literacy Programme of Rourkela was started in December, 1990 with environment building and motivational activities, preliminary survey of illiterates, identification of literacy volunteers and resource persons, agencies and institutions, training and preparation of reading and other related materials. The teaching-learning programmes, supply of reading materials, monitoring and supervision of the literacy centres and other activities of the samiti was started from April, 1991, where people from various walks of life and organisations participated actively. As a result, the programme is still going on in the form of post literacy and Continuing Education Programme. The Post Literacy Programme of the Saksharata Samiti was launched on June, 1992 with the following objectives :

(1) To retain the basic literacy skill achieved by the neo-literates and to introduce self-learning in place of guided learning.

(2) To enable the neo-literates to use their literacy skills in their occupation and daily life and make them to question the basic issues relevant to their life.

(3) To motivate children (above 10 years) to join school or Non-Formal Education Centres.

(4) To cover the illiterates who are left out, or dropped out in the campaign.

(5) To involve the masses in the developmental process of the nation.

(6) To develop skills for better generation of income specially among the neo-literate slum women.

(7) To develop awareness for improving their quality of life.

ORGANISATIONAL STRUCTURE OF ROURKELA SAKSHARATA SAMITI

For the effective launching of the literacy programme,"Rourkela Saksharata Samiti" a broad based organisation was formed involving government and non-government departments, institutions, voluntary agencies and activists. The RSS was registered in February, 1991 with the Additional District Magistrate (ADM) Rourkela as its Chairman for the implementation of the programme. Next to Chairman there is a Secretary in the Samiti. Then there is an Advisory Board (Governing Body) which constitutes of 6 members (excluding Chairman and Secretary) at the apex. There is a working group consisting of 21 activists from different sectors of life that coordinates and monitors the campaigns at various levels to strengthen the programme. For the smooth functioning and operational convenience, the whole area covered under the campaign was divided into 12 literacy zones. No fixed criteria was followed for the division of the various zones. Each zone consists of a number of areas and each zone was managed by three zone coordinators. Each area had at least one coordinator who was organising the activities of the literacy programme at the grass-root level and supervising the activities of the literacy volunteers who were managing the teaching-learning activities of the literacy centres of the concerned slum areas, whereas the zone coordinators were mobilizing the people and organising the programme at zonal level, supervising the activities of the area coordinators and monitoring the teaching-learning centres.

Two control rooms were set-up by the Samiti for the smooth functioning of the organisations, like quick delivery of the teaching-learning materials, monitoring and mobilization of the resources etc. The main control room is located at the old RTO building, annex of the ADM Office, Udit Nagar, Rourkela, coordinated the activities of all the seven zones under civil township, zones i.e.1, 3, 4, 6, 8, 9 and 12. The another control room being located at the Social Welfare Department of RSP, Sector 4, regulated the activities of rest of the five zones under steel township, i.e. zones 2, 5,7,10 and 11. Both the control rooms were headed by two controllers respectively. But both the control rooms have merged into one in 1996 and now functions as the main control room, at the annex of the ADM Office, Rourkela.

After launching the Post-Literacy Programme in June, 1992 the designation of the zone coordinators have changed. A new council (post literacy) has been formed in place of the working group with the same Governing Body, Secretary and Chairman. A number of "Chetana Kendras" were formed in each area. At the grass-root levels where there was the formation of "Basti Chetana Samiti". The Basti Chetana Samities were constituted mainly with the basti people (slum-dwellers) and neo-literates. It is important to mention here that the Chetana Samities had made provision for at least fifty per cent women member in the Samities. Hence they will be involved more actively with the developmental activities and decision-making process of the Samities. The Chetana Kendras of the slum areas were managed by the Basti Chetana Samities (Slum Awareness Committees). And the BCS (Basti Chetana Samiti) were monitored and supervised by the RSS. The Chetana Kendras (Awareness Centres) became the centres of activities for the development of concerned slums after their formation since June 1992.

4

PLAN AND PROCEDURE

INTRODUCTION

It is evident from the related literature presented in Chapter-2 that this study is an attempt to study the level of educational development and changing interests, attitudes, perceptions and behaviours as well as educational and social needs, which are highly essential to suggest for need-based and effective programmes for further development. The present chapter provides details of the plans and procedures adopted for the study, which include approach, data required, sources of data, sample, tools and techniques, procedure of data collection, and scheme of data analysis for the present study.

APPROACH OF THE STUDY

The collected data in the present study are in two forms—qualitative and quantitative. Both types of data are useful depending upon the context, nature and perspective of the study.

In the context of the impact of literacy programme on slum women, both qualitative and quantitative types of data were required. But the major category of data was of qualitative. Because as an empirical study; its approach is of phenomenological type which is 'the intellectual under current to qualitative research' (Alan, 1992). For this the nature and objectives of the study demanded to study and understand human behaviour, feelings, visions and realities, etc., from the actors' own experience frame or reference as it was without being influenced by purposes, goals, pre-dispositions or already pre-existing theories of reality. Also the study needed to examine as to how the world is experienced, for his the reality is what people imagine it to be.

With regard to the behaviour, life style, social relationship, socio-economic status and background of the slum women, which were of typical and of heterogeneous type, only mere quantification of data may not be helpful to discern and understand them. It is also essential to understand their social and personal problems, realities, experiences and feelings in the societies that they are grounded. Rather, the experiences and understanding of their own situation when expressed uninterruptedly would unravel many facts and information which otherwise cannot be obtained through the structured tools or any quantitative measures. So the investigator tried to know and understand the neo-literate slum women personally through frequent field visits. Participant observations in various natural life situations, in-depth discussions, unstructured interviews, and perceive them as they were developing their own definitions of the world. Such data are qualitative in nature. Data collected from official records for this study were also qualitative in nature.

However, data pertaining to reading, writing, numeracy and level of awareness developed among the neo-literature slum women were quantitative in nature. Hence, taking into consideration the context, nature, objectives and perspectives of the present study, phenomenological-cum-positivistic approaches have been followed by the investigators.

DATA REQUIRED FOR THE STUDY

On the basis of the objectives, data both of qualitative and quantitative type were required and they are presented below.

To know the efforts and activities made by Rourkela Saksharata Samiti for the educational development of slum-dwellers of Rourkela in general and women in particular, a comprehensive list of activities done by the Samiti was required. Types of activities and various categories of people involved with those activities in different slums were also required. Opinions and observations of the people from different sectors of living, visitors and participants to the campaign on various occasions, and the volunteers and organisers of different types of activities were also required. Strategies adopted by Rourkela Saksharata Samiti to identify woman volunteers, activists and learners were also the data needed for the first objective of the study.

To know the problems and constraints faced by the organisers and functionaries in organising, mobilising, monitoring and in identifying the women activists and learners in different slums; information related to the problems, types of problems and constraints, methods and procedures of overcoming the problems and constraints were required.

To know the impact of literacy programmes on the slum women, their level of achievement in reading, writing, numeracy and awareness; and their application in their day-to-day life, changing attitudes towards their life and life style, development of self-confidence, self-image, and power of decision-making in them, their participation in socio-cultural and economic activities were needed.

To find out the causes of under development of slum women, their family history, nature of problem, opinion of the neighbours, family members, friends and employers (if working), etc., were required for study.

To make suggestions for future development and course of action of the campaign, findings and suggestions of the evaluation reports of different literacy campaign districts including the present one pertaining to the impact of the literacy programme on the women, suggestions of the experts, resource persons activists and volunteers learners and neo-literates organisers local people etc. were required.

SOURCES OF DATA

Data required for the present study mentioned above were available from various sources mentioned below.

For Objective No. 1 : Activities and Efforts made by RSS

For this objective, data were mainly available in the documents and records dealing with the efforts and activities of Rourkela Saksharata Samiti for the development of education especially among the slum women in Rourkela. These data were in the form of Government and non-Government records like status reports day-to- day activities, and progress reports of Rourkela Saksharata Samiti, zone level progress and activities, report of the Samiti, activities report of the Basti Chetana Samities, status reports of Rourkela submitted to State Literacy Mission, Government of Orissa, NLM and State Resource Centre, reports of the medical camps organised by Rourkela Government Hospital, Sub-divisional Hospital, Panposh, Ispat General Hospital in collaboration with Rourkela Saksharata Samiti report of Shramik Vidyapith. Community Welfare Centre, *i.e.* "Sevasadan".

Survey report of the Rourkela Municipality monthly reports of the field workers and supervisors of Urban Basic Services and ICDS, involved with the activities of Rourkela Saksharata Samiti, reports of the involved high schools, colleges and cultural organisations and troops, records and reports of BGVS state as well as local units, District Inspector of schools, enrolment register of the Basti Chetana Samiti and the primary schools near by different slums and various organizations, narrative/ descriptions documented by eminent personalities, visitors, evaluations, government officers, leaders and journalists participated in the activities of the programme at various point of time.

Grass-root workers, volunteers, senior activists, working group members, controller, secretary and president of Rourkela Saksharata Samiti, members of different government and non- government organisations involved with these activities, (including cultural artists, basti people etc.) were also the sources of data. Saksharata samachar, video cassettes, photo albums, audio cassettes recording of All India Radio, Doordarshan programmes dealing with efforts and activities of the Samiti were also the sources of information.

For Objective No. 2 : Problems and Constraints Faced by the Organisers of RSS

Sources of data mentioned above under objective-1 constituted some of the sources of data for objective-2 also. Other sources of data were :

- Minutes, proceedings of the meetings conducted in the bastis, zones and central level to overcome the problems of mobilisation, monitoring etc. available in the literacy control room, records of Bastis, Chetana Samities, and other concerned organisations like Shramik Vidyapeeth etc.
- Volunteers, organisers and members of monitoring team, trainers of Shramik Vidyapeeth, leaders and volunteers of the concerned centres, were also the sources of data to deal with the problems and constraints faced by them for mobilization monitoring and identification of women learners and activists and the procedure of overcoming those problems.

For Objectives No. 3 : Impact of Literacy Programme on Slum Women

Regarding the impact of literacy programme, the level of achievement in reading, writing, numeracy and awareness of the neo-literate, the slum women, and dropout learners were the sources of data. Their way of living, pattern of behaviour, observance of small family norms, cleanliness of their own houses and the environment, their participation in different types of socio-cultural and developmental activities and in decision-making activities of the families and the basti, taking interest for enrolment of their children by sending them to formal school or to NFE centers, etc., were also the sources of data available with the slum women.

The slum leaders, social workers, family members, neighbours, local public, shop-keepers, contractors of the wage earners, middlemen of the dumping yards, supervisors and field workers of UBS and ICDS, volunteers, programme coordinators were sources of data regarding the changes and development found in the slum women through the literacy programme.

For Objective No. 4

Regarding the causes for underdevelopment of the women in slums, their history, family history, opinion of their family members, neighbours and friends, the slum women themselves, volunteers, programme coordinators were the sources of data available for the study.

For Objective No. 5

Findings and suggestions of the external evaluation reports of the different literacy programme including the present one; suggestions and opinion of the dedicated volunteers and activists involved deeply with the programme, visitors to the campaigns like, people of NLM, SRC, BGVS, etc.; cultural troops, expert group, local people, learners and neo-literates, organisers, were the sources of data available for this study.

SAMPLE

The slum areas of Rourkela city having twelve literacy zones as decided by the Rourkela Saksharata Samiti were the population or universe for the study. Out of the total one hundred ninety six slums under twelve literacy zones predominantly inhabited by disadvantaged people of different caste, culture, religion and socio-economic background sixteen slum areas in Rourkela city were selected for collecting the data. Considering the convenience of access and feasibility for conducting investigation, the investigator selected the following sixteen slum areas of different literacy zones. The units of the samples were selected on the basis of the following criteria.

TABLE 4.1
Sample Selection from Different Slum Areas of Literacy Zones of Rourkela

Sl. No.	*Name of the Slum Area*	*Zone No.*	*No. of Slum Women*
1.	Gangadhar Palli	I	9
2.	Rajeev Basti	I	8
3.	Narayani Palli	II	6
4.	Gudia Tola	III	4
5.	Oram Para	III	6
6.	Haripur Basti	III	5
7.	Laltanki	IV	6
8.	Khariabahal	V	6
9.	Ruputola	VI	6
10.	Shanti Nagar (Sec.14)	VII	9
11.	Tilkanagar	VIII	6
12.	Jhariabahal-Uttambasti	IX	5
13.	Gopabandhu Palli	IX	5
14.	Domapada	X	7
15.	Pump House Colony	XI	7
16.	Narla Road-Hasanpur	XII	8
Total	16 Slum areas	12	103

Note : Total illiterate population : 93,867

Male : 32,619

Female : 61,248 (According to the re-survey Report of RSS, 1992)

Total illiterate made literate : 65,782

Male : 23,024

Female : 42,758

Still in the campaign . 5,444 (during re-survey)

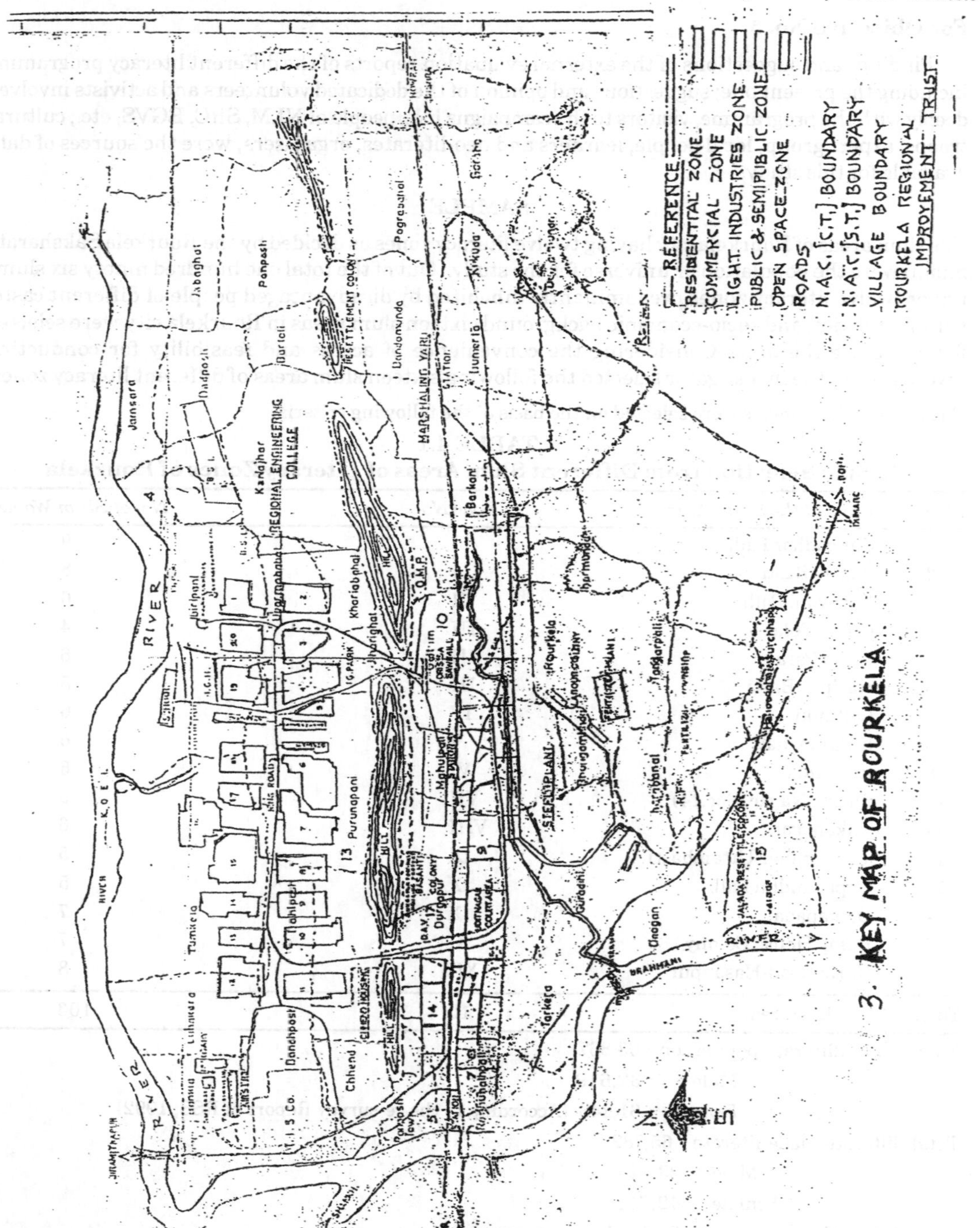

Map. 4.1 : Key Map of Rourkela

Achievement Level of the Neo-literate and Semi-literate Slum Women

To know their level of achievement in literacy and awareness, a number of 103 neo-literate slum women participated in literacy programme of Rourkela Saksharata Samiti from the above stated slums, and were selected in the field as representatives of the literacy zones.

Volunteers, Motivators and Grass-Root Workers

In order to make the study broad based, 23 samples from different slums under the literacy zones were selected from the grass-root level volunteers *i.e.* the teaching volunteers, motivators programme organisers at the grass-root level purposively.

Senior Activists and Resource Persons

Sixteen senior activists, resource persons, programme coordinators, mobiliser and members of central monitoring team were selected purposively to know their opinions about the activities and efforts of the Samiti; impact of the literacy programme experience and observed among the slum women; strategies and methods adopted for resource mobilisation and monitoring; and, problems in mobilisation of the resources, and their remarks and suggestions for further activities of the literacy programme.

Government and Non-government Functionaries

Thirty one samples of different types of people like cultural artists, organisers, medical officers, employers of the slum women (those who are working), shop-keepers, social activists, government officials concerned with literacy activities, neighbours and family members of the neo-literate women, political leaders, governing-body members of the Samiti, advocates, representatives of the concerned NGOs and women organizations, etc., were selected purposively for interviews and in-depth discussions to know their views regarding the literacy activities and efforts made by the Samiti and their impact on the slum women in changing their attitudes, behaviour and life style and also to know their suggestion for future course of action.

Two underdeveloped slum women, who, despite their participation in the literacy programme, have not achieved either the NLM expected proficiency level in learning skills or even developed the desired level of awareness, were purposively selected from two different slums for case studies to know and find out their causes of underdevelopment.

The Chairman and Secretary of Rourkela Saksharata Samiti, Secretary, Bharat Gyan Vigyan Samiti, Controller of Rourkela Literacy Control Room, the Ex-Chairman and Controller of Rourkela Saksharata Samiti, National Executive Body Member of Samata (Women wing of BGVS) were taken purposively as sample to know their opinion on the impact of the programme and suggestions for future course of action.

The number of sample units mentioned above was decided in the field at the time of data collection after a thorough study and observation of the field situation at the initial stage of the study.

TOOLS AND TECHNIQUES

Based on the types of information required for the nature and objectives of the study the investigator has made use of different tools and techniques, which are presented below :

(1) Interview schedule (Semi-structured)

(2) Achievement Test

(3) Open-ended Questionnaires

(4) Participant and Non-participant Observation

(5) Un-structured Interview Schedule

(6) In-depth Discussion

(7) Case Study

Procedure of Tool Construction

These tools were constructed keeping in view the several aspects of literacy programme and its impact on slum women to be covered. Before constructing the tools the investigator had gone through the literature pertaining to literacy programme, evaluation of literacy programme, research journals and dissertations on tool construction and NLM guidelines in details. Further, she had thoroughly studied the literacy primers, post-literacy primer, supplementary literature, and Saksharata Samachar meant for the learners along with the records and documents related to the literacy activities of Rourkela Saksharata Samiti. She had gone to the field, established rapport and discussed with the neo-literates informally about their development through literacy programmes. She had also met some of the organizers, resource persons and volunteers of various types and had conducted informal interviews related to the activities of RSS and impact of the literacy programmes on slum women. After thorough study of the documents and the required literature; discussions with the organisers, activists and neo-literates, and minutes observation of the field situation, the investigator selected the necessary tools for collection of relevant data. While constructing different types of tools for data collection, the investigator tried her level best to concentrate on finding out authentic information and facts that are relevant to the study and the research questions through the statement of items in different types of tools. While preparing the tools she had consulted two experts in this field for their guidance. After construction of the draft tools covering the various aspects of literacy programme, they were given to the experts to examine the relevance, clarity, adequacy and objectivity of the items of the tools. On the basis of the assessment, tools were appropriately revised and the approved items of each tool were finalised and final forms of the revised tools were ready for administration. The details about each tool that was developed are given category-wise as under :

Interview Schedule

Two separate sets of semi-structured interview schedules for neo-literate slum women were used :

The first set of interview schedule consisting of 30 items was used to know about their background data, date of joining in the programme, cause for joining the programme, about the environment building activities of the programme, regularities of the volunteers/coordinators, timing and functioning of the programme, distribution and availability of teaching learning materials, problems in utilising the teaching-learning materials, benefits derived from the programme, utilising the benefits in day-to-day life and the types of co-operations rendered from the family members, co-operation rendered by the basti people to the volunteers and activities of the monitoring team.

For developing this interview schedule the investigator had gone through different types of semi-structured interview schedules, which had already been prepared by different researchers for their studies. Taking ideas from the previous research literature and interview schedules, and after having based them on the background data of different aspects of literacy programme, the draft interview schedule was prepared and given to the experts for scrutiny. On the basis of their suggestions the interview schedule was modified, finalised and administered. In the interview schedule, the respondents were asked to express their opinion on each of the items separately and their responses recorded in schedules through its multiple choice type answers.

The second set of semi-structured interview schedule, consisting of 50 items, was used to know the impact of literacy programme in developing the level of awareness among slum women. This was prepared on the basis of the course content in the primers and supplementary literature of the neo-literate slum women. This includes family welfare, small family norms and various issues related to health concerns and sanitation, child and maternity care, environmental protection, etc., changing attitude towards evils of dowry, early marriage, drugs and alcohol, superstitions etc.(Refer Appendix 1 and 3 for a copy of both the sets). Based on the content of the primers, ideas of the previous researches and her own ideas and experiences, the investigator prepared the draft interview schedule and given to two experts for scrutiny. On the basis of their suggestions, the items of the interview schedule were revised and selected for the final form and redied for administration. While using this second set interview schedule each neo-literate slum woman was told to express her opinion separately on each of the 50 items given in the form of questions with multiple answers. The correct responses were taken into the consideration to judge the level of awareness.

Achievement Test

An achievement test in Oriya language consisting 11 questions was specially designed and developed by the investigator following the norms of National Literacy Mission, was administered to know the performance of the neo-literate slum women in terms of reading skill, writing and numeracy skills. The test schedule was designed on the basis of the course content of the Primers of Literacy Programmes (A copy of the achievement test can be seen from Appendix 2.).

Based on the content of the Primers, NLM guidelines, ideas of the previous researches and own experiences, the investigator prepared the draft achievement test and gave it to the experts to examine its clarity and suitability for the respondents. After getting suggestions from them, the test was modified and finalised for final construction and administration in the field. It took more than six months to construct the achievement test. The test was administered on 103 neo-literates of 16 slums of Rourkela city by the investigator personally. Before conducting the test, the investigator has viewed from the about the questions to know their opinion and made them understand about the instructions of the questions thoroughly (See the instructions of the test paper) as to how they had to be answered. The test comprises three aspects of literacy *i.e.*, *(i)* Reading, *(ii)* Writing, and *(iii)* Numeracy.

(i) Reading : For the reading aspect, the respondents were asked to *(i)* read a passage of six sentences of small length loudly with normal accent, *(ii)* read silently a small paragraph with understanding the messages there in relating to their working and living environment and answer four oral questions based on what they have read, and *(iii)* read with understanding the given "road signs" and "instructions" and asked to answer two oral questions related to the "road sign and instructions".

(ii) Writing : For writing aspect, they were instructed to *(i)* Write down their complete address, *(ii)* copying the given stanza of poem from their primer *(iii)* write down dictation of five familiar words or objects by the investigator, and *(iv)* write down independently *(a)* about their experiences as literates in learning something new and implementing that knowledge in their family, or *(b)* write down a letter to the friend narrating the activities of them as neo-literate women being done through the Basti Chetana Samiti for the development of their slum. This last question on writing skill was given to the respondent for their self-evaluation which requires courage and capacity along with the development of writing skill.

(iii) Numeracy : For this aspect the respondents were asked to do *(i)* Simple calculation without fraction involving addition. *(ii)* Subtraction up to three digits. *(iii)* Multiplication. *(iv)* Division while preparing the test items on numeracy, working knowledge of metric units of weights, measures, currency and distance, were taken into the consideration in the questions as content. The rating of the achievement was made in five descriptive categories of excellent, very good, good, poor and very poor.

Open-ended Questionnaire

Two separate sets of open-ended questionnaires were used to collect information from *(i)* The grass-root level volunteers, programme coordinators and organisers. *(ii)* Senior activists, resource persons, organisers and members of monitoring team to know their field experiences related to the efforts and activities of the Saksharata Samiti, impact of literacy programme on the slum women, strategy of resource mobilisation, monitoring and their suggestions and remarks.

The questionnaire meant for the grass-root level volunteers has 76 items respectively. The items of both sets of questionnaires were mostly of open-ended type with a view to allow a free response from the grass-root level volunteers, senior activists resource persons etc.(A copy of the questionnaire can be seen from Appendix-5.)

The items of questionnaires were developed by the investigator on the basis of the outcome of the informal discussions and interviews conducted with different types of people directly or indirectly involved with the literacy programme, interaction with the neo-literate slum women, rich experiences in the intensive field visit, information gathered from the slum-dwellers, records of the RSS with regards to activities of literacy programme and the ideas and knowledge acquired from the previous researches and literature in this regard. While developing the items of the questionnaires the following criteria were kept in mind to formulate the statements of each item :

(i) Statements were to be expression of desired behaviour and opinion and not statement of facts.

(ii) Statements were to be expressed in clear, concise, straightforward language. Confusing statements with double meaning or vague wording were to be avoided.

(iii) Each statement was to contain a single meaning.

After preparing the items of the draft questionnaires, they were given to the experts for scrutiny on the bases of their suggestions regarding the clarity of the statements in language suitability, validity of the questionnaire : they were modified and finalised for final form of item development and administration for collecting relevant data.

Participant and Non-participant Observation

The nature of the study demanded to know about the application of literacy and awareness developed among the neo-literate slum women in their day-to-day as well as social life under close scrutiny. To study their literacy and awareness in operation in their daily life, the investigator adopted participant and non-participant observation technique, so as to get an idea of interaction and the personal relationship of social relations of them in the group and society and a sense of process which cannot get in any other way or technique.

As a participant observer the investigator gathered information by participating in the daily life of the neo-literate slum women and the activities of the Chetana Kendras where they were involved. She watched them carefully to know what situation they ordinarily meet and how they behave in them. She entered into conversations with some of the participants in these natural situations and discovered their interpretations of the events she has observed. Also, she tried to study the participant as cases for their causes of underdevelopment or high level of achievements.

As a non-participant observer, the investigator watched the behaviour/actions of the neo-literate women without the latter knowing them that they were being watched in different situation by striving to make herself as invisible as possible. The feelings, opinions, experiences and working hypotheses of the investigator were also included with those events, participants and their activities and conversations in the setting during observation. Therefore, her interpretations of the observed occur from her perspective. The investigator tried to construct meaning for herself, which she supposed to direct the actions of the actors (slum women) in the way she perceived them. The kind of information sought through this observation without participation were more regarding participation and involvement in the activities of Government Hospital, near the Mobile Medical Van of Sevasadan, Immunization Camps, Pulse Polio Programme, Mahila Jagruti Talim Programme, Cultural Programme for awareness generation and environment building, Population Day celebration in the slums, Sakshar Holi, Sakshar Deepavali, celebration of Independence Day and Republic Day, Dumping yard, Grocery Shop, Quarry sides, Election meetings, Demonstration against anti-drugs, Alcohol, Rights for ration card and other amenities before the office of the additional district magistrate etc.

Further, she has observed their typical behaviour both directly and indirectly during the celebration of death ceremony, marriage ceremony, traditional festival like Saharul, Tusu, Karma, Tizz, Nuakhai, Raja and Raspurima etc. While observing their natural activities and behaviour pattern in various situations the investigator in their own community concentrated more and more on aspects that are relevant to the research questions. Each set of field observations were recorded in a systematic method of analyzing the actions and behaviour and even conversations of some setting of the subjects in the field diary as field notes in order to collect relevant evidence for the study.

Unstructured Interview

A number of unstructured interviews were conducted by the investigator to study and understand the specific details of the participant's perspectives and experiences regarding the efforts and activities made by RSS, and the impact of literacy programme on slum women under study without being influenced by the investigator. While conducting interviews of the respondent like volunteers, coordinators, resource persons, cultural artists, social workers, advisers to the governing body, Government officials, health personnel, shop-keepers, family members of the neo-literate women etc., the investigator tried her level best to make the interview pleasing to the interviewees and an agreeable form of social interaction. To collect rich data from the investigator provided minimal guidance and allowed considerable latitude to the interviewees and to derive greater part of her information the investigator used her own witness, induced them to talk and express their views, and feelings about the activities of the literacy programme and its impact on the slum women and having done so she embodied the gist of the oral testimony on her sheets of note in the field diary.

In-depth Discussion

The investigator felt the need of an in-depth discussion among the subjects individually as well as in small groups to understand the deeper meaning of their life experiences, their views on their own world, and how they articulate their feelings and thoughts *vis-à-vis* the essence of women education and development, problems related to the women and their solution etc. Through personal discussion she tried to find out the causes for the under-development of the slum women although they attended the literacy programme. The investigator had also gone for an in-depth discussion with the high level officials to know their opinion regarding the impact of the programme on the slum women. The investigator preferred such in-depth discussion through casual conversation with a purpose that the group/individual became a tool for reconstructing individual opinions more appropriately. It is pertinent to mention here that the in-depth group discussions meant for the neo-literate slum women were of "focus-group" type based on specific topics related to their daily life. Those discussions were based on the principle of brain-storming techniques and intro conversational method so as to know and study their creative and collective thinking about a particular problem in different dimensions. The informal conversations during in-depth discussion in the individual sitting as well as in the group were recorded by the investigator in her field notes as a part of the on-going flow of social life.

Case Study

The objectives of the study demanded an intensive investigation of the factors that contributed to the characteristics of underdevelopment of slum women, who despite their participation in the literacy programme are not developed. Therefore, two educationally underdeveloped slum women from two different slum areas under literacy zones of Rourkela city were selected for case studies by the investigator. These were conducted by her to get an actual picture of their life situation, activities, past-experiences and problems in domestic, social and centre (Literacy) context, so that the situations or factors leading to their underdevelopment could be understood and analysed properly.

These two cases were selected from among the 103 respondents administered for achievement test and were interviewed for awareness development. The test results of those slum women were the main criteria of selection for case studies who despite their participation in the literacy programme were unable to achieve either the NLM expected proficiency level in learning skills, nor developing the desired level of awareness.

To know their causes of underdevelopment, the investigator collected relevant data from the grass-root level volunteers and coordinators of the concerned slums by conducting informal interviews and in-depth discussion. She gathered information from them with regard to their enrolment in the literacy centre, attendance in the centre, performance in mid-term evaluation, and participation in different types of activities of the Chetana Kendras. The investigator verified the information through the supportive records in their favour for the concerned Chetana Kendras.

Further, she collected information about their nature of problems, physical and mental conditions, environmental force or situation, their family history and their own history from their family members, neighbours, friends, and employer (for the working slum woman) by conducting unstructured interview and informal discussion. She followed the same technique *i.e.* informal discussion, unstructured interview and observation technique to collect pertinent data from the respondents with regard to their present status, mental and physical conditions, past experiences, attitudes and interests which contributed to their individuality and behaviour. Unless the cases are studied deeply from the view point of the respondents ways-of-living by personal views to them, the investigation may be shadowed by some subjectivity through structured techniques, because in structured interviews there is less scope for free expression of the respondents. Therefore, the investigator preferred to follow unstructured techniques to get a clear and comprehensive picture.

During discussions no direct questions were asked to the respondents or to their relatives and friends or the informants by the investigator and she had tried her level best to make the discussion interesting and pleasing to the interviews and it seemed to them an agreeable form of interaction.

Two other slum women from two different slum areas of Rourkela city under literacy zones were also selected for case study due to their outstanding performances and active participation in the literacy programme. Despite poverty, family constraints, physical and other problems which run with them in their life, they have achieved the ratings of good, very good and excellent in reading, writing and numeracy skills and their general awareness about their surroundings, social issues and other aspects were found to be highly satisfactory. So these two slum women were selected for case studies on the basis of their performance in the literacy and level of their awareness. Their cases were studied and the factors responsible for their motivation and achievement were also investigated by the investigator systematically by following the same method and techniques which were adopted for the underdeveloped slum women.

PROCEDURE OF DATA COLLECTION

Data for the study were collected in three phases. These phases were spread over a long period from January 1997 to March 2000. Frequent field visits to various slums of Rourkela city were planned in these three phases. The investigator planned her study according to the requirements of certain aspects that needed participant and non-participant observation and in-depth group discussion *e.g.* during parliamentary election, slum level meetings and different socio-cultural functions like Holi, Dasahara, Karma, Cart Festival etc., pulse polio programme, legal-literacy camp, family welfare training programme and Mahila Jagruti Talim etc. These occasions were observed as they involved people of different levels in the slums and this is reflected in a natural way of certain heterogeneous characteristics such as interpersonal relationship between different groups of varied religions, culture and economic background.

Phase I **:** During the first phase of data collection the investigator established rapport with the slum people of various literacy zones in general and neo-literate slum women in particular and interacted with them wherever and whenever required. She also got introduced with the concerned officials and personnels of Rourkela Saksharata Samiti and other Government and non-government organizations. In this phase, data collection was primarily a document study at the slum, city, district and state level. In the entire process of document study, data of both qualitative and quantitative nature were collected and documents like survey reports, census reports, planning documents, list of activities, annual status report of the concerned organisation, list of participants (both learners and volunteers) were studied. Records of the Chetana Kendras (teaching-learning centres) of various slums were surveyed and data related to the environment activities, development activities, infrastructure facilities available for the learners etc. were collected. Identification of neo-literate slum women those who have completed the three primers of 1st phase of literacy programme and the grass-root volunteers as well as coordinators were made and enlisted for establishment of rapport to administer the test and questionnaire for data collection.

Phase II **:** During the second phase, data related to the impact of the programme, effort and activities of RSS and problems faced (objectives 1, 2 and 3) were collected from the slum women (Neo-literate), grass-root level workers, volunteers, coordinators, resource persons, organizers and members of monitoring team. Simultaneously participant and non-participant observations were made in different natural situations of the neo-literate slum women.

Two sets of semi-structured interview schedules for the neo-literate women were tried out and the achievement tests were administered during their leisure hours after fixing up a time with them. Open-ended questionnaire were administered to the grass-root workers, activists, senior activists, resource persons and members of monitoring team and their written responses were collected. In addition to this, people of different types like cultural artists involved with the environment building activities of the literacy programmes, visitors to the campaigns, contractors and employers of the working slum women; shop-keepers (grocery shop), family members of the slum women and Government Officials were located by the investigator, and a list of them was prepared accordingly.

Phase III : During the third phase, the investigator contracted different types of people as mentioned earlier in both slum and city level personally at their residences, clubs, shops, offices and even in the dumping yards and fixed up time with them for conducting interviews. She conducted their interviews after making them understand the purpose of the study and need for their co-operation till the investigation was completed. The time of the interview was fixed up with each person at his convenience. Accordingly the investigator conducted the interview (un-structured), and having discussed formally with each person noted the responses systematically in the field diary. It took more than three hours to conduct the interview with each person. Although it was a hectic activity to make them sit for such a long time for interview purpose, their active co-operation and responses encouraged and enlightened the investigator to understand and realize more and more about the impact and outcome of the literacy programme. Data with regard to the impact of the programme was collected from the high level officials like the Additional District Magistrate-cum-Chairman of the Saksharata Samiti, Director of Shramik Vidyapeeth-cum-Secretary of the Samiti, Editor of the Saksharata Samachar, Political Leaders, town administer of Rourkela steel plant and other officials, Secretary of Bharat Gyan Vigyan Samiti, Secretary of "Sevasadan" the community development organisation and other organisations through in-depth discussion and unstructured interview on Sundays and other holidays at their respective residences and suitable places according to their own convenience. A few of them, who have transferred or migrated to different places were also contracted and whosoever written down in the field diary. In addition to this, the literacy data, reports of the evaluations team, proceedings of the high power committees and other meetings were also collected from the records of the Saksharata Samiti and other concerned departments.

About three months time was required for interviewing these people and to collect the required documents. Despite fixing up of the data and time in advance some of the functionaries were not available on the communicated dates therefore, some of the interview could not be conducted at all.

In slum level, four grass-roots level volunteers were interviewed individually and their responses were noted along with the open-ended questionnaires administered to them. The responses about the impact of the literacy programmes in practice were also noted in the diary. These four grass-root volunteers of different slums were contracted at frequent intervals for the clarity of many doubts. Since they were slum-based, they helped the investigator to develop contact and establish rapport in various slums, which in turn helped the investigator during her participant and non-participant observations over a period of time. Certain subtle aspects of the life style of the neo-literate women and the inter-relationship that exists have been observed. Detailed information, bio-data, personal and social history, family details, past experiences, nature of problems etc., were also collected carefully from the family, friends, neighbours and the teaching volunteers through in-depth discussion, general observation and interview for case study.

A number of social functions and festivals like marriages, training and developmental programmes related to literacy and awareness generation at the slum as well as Samiti level, chit chat near municipality water pipes, grocery shop and congregation of slum meetings before and after discussion have been attended and the level and type of participation of the neo-literate women were minutely observed. In-depth individual and group discussion with them and other slum-dwellers were also made by the investigator over a period of time. The needed additional clarifications were sought by talking and discussing to people of different types like old and experienced people of the respective slums, social workers, government officers and others and field notes were recorded and maintained accordingly.

SCHEME OF DATA ANALYSIS

Data gathered from various sources under different heads were thoroughly scrutinised and systematically classified to understand the realities constructed by humans at times. Data were further stored out in terms of themes to analyse objective-wise.

Data collected have been subjected to both qualitative and quantitative analysis, to derive meaningful conclusion about the impact of literacy programme on women in urban slums. The major approach of data analysis was qualitative. However, quantitative analysis was attempted wherever possible by applying descriptive statistics.

Data collected through open-ended questionnaires about the efforts and activities of Rourkela Saksharata Samiti, problems and constrains faced by the volunteers, organizers and functionaries in organising and mobilising the programme and methods of overcoming the problems were coded according to the theme and contents were analysed thematically.

Data related to the level of achievement and performance of the neo-literate slum women in different aspects of literacy like reading, writing, numeracy and level of awareness were tabulated and percentage analysis was carried out. Self-confidence and development of the neo-literate slum women in various field of life were analysed qualitatively. Data obtained through observation (participant and non-participant), opinion and suggestions of different types of people and visitors about the activities and effort of RSS and also about the changes and development observed among the slum people, especially the women were analysed thematically. Information obtained through in-depth discussion, unstructured interview, informal discussion, report of the case studies, report of the field visit were analysed qualitatively by the method of content analysis in descriptive form. Data about the activities and efforts made by RSS, collected from different office records and documents were analysed qualitatively and presented in descriptive form.

The above stated data collected from different sources and with techniques have been used to cross-check and to substantiate some of the facts and responses of the subjects.

The next three chapters will deal with three major aspects of the study. They are : *(i)* The activities and efforts made by RSS , and the problems and constraints faced by the organizers. *(ii)* Impact of Literacy Programme on slum women in developing the level of literacy and awareness. *(iii)* Suggestions for the suitable modification in the programme for its future course of action.

5

ACTIVITIES AND EFFORTS MADE BY RSS AND CONSTRAINTS FACED BY ITS ORGANISERS

INTRODUCTION

An educated endeavour in the society cannot be considered and operated in isolation. The other sector of development like social, political and economic under currents in the society becomes powerful determinants in educational enterprise. An attempt has been made to study and understand the impact of literacy programme of Rourkela city of Orissa on the disadvantaged people in general and slum women in particular, keeping in the mind the above forces operating in the society.

In this chapters data collected through the various sources with regard to the efforts and activities made by RSS (Rourkela Saksharata Samiti) and constraints faced by the organisers in organising the programme, are presented.

ACTIVITIES AND EFFORTS MADE BY THE ORGANISERS OF RSS AND CONSTRAINTS FACED BY THEM

The literacy programme of Rourkela was conceived as a people's movement with the voluntary efforts of a large number of people and few organisations. The initiators of the programme Sri Asit Tripathy, IAA, the then ADM Rourkela, cum Chairman of RSS and D.N. Das, Director of Shramik Vidyapith, Rourkela, cum Secretary, RSS made the people as instrument and started a number of activities for the successful achievement of the programme. Data with regard to the major activities and efforts made by RSS was collected by the investigator from the documents and activity-list of RSS, records of Chetana Kendras, audio and video cassettes, photo albums etc. Further, the data was collected from the organisations and institutions involved directly or indirectly with the literacy activities of RSS. A number of interviews were also conducted from different types of people for the same. The major activities and efforts, made by RSS have been presented below along with constraints faced by the organisers while organising those activities.

Environment Building and Motivational Activities

Environment building activity was one of the most important aspects of the literacy programme to create congenial environment, to draw the attention of people towards the programme and make them aware of the broad objective and philosophy of the literacy programme. The environment building activities started on December1990 and continued for a long period even after the launching of Post Literacy Programme (PL Programme) in June 1992. After the launching of PL Programme, except a few important environment building activities, almost all the activities

were organised through 'Chetana Kendras' of the concerned slum. The RSS organised important environment building activities in central level involving all the members of Chetana Kendras and Chetana Samities for participation.

The core members of RSS approached the influential members of different organisations, institutions and various socio-cultural groups to initiate the environment building activities. The following organisations came forward and joined in organising the environment building activities.

(1) Shramik Vidyapeeth

(2) Bethel Cheritable Trust

(3) Community Welfare Society (Seva Sadan)

(4) Rourkela Municipality

(5) Spandan (Socio-cultural Organisation)

(6) Sankalp (Socio-cultural Organisation)

(7) Educational Institutions (All High Schools and Colleges)

(8) Youth Hostel Association of India.

Besides, many other organisations also joined the programme in organising the environment building activities. Among all the organisations, the Shramik Vidyapeeth being an implementing agency of NLM, not only initiated the concept of TLC in Rourkela, but also made the institution deeply involved with each and every activity of the Samiti. Its contribution to RSS can never be ignored.

The following environment building activities have been carried out by RSS during the first phase of literacy programme *i.e.* from December 1990 to May, 1992.

Padayatra (Procession on Foot)

As an environment building measure, a number of seven Padayatras were planned, organised and coordinated by the working group from time to time. The participants of the Padayatras travelled through the slum areas and local bodies making a call for literacy, especially on women literacy through street performances and talking to people about the literacy programme, which was to be implemented in the city. Initially people specially the women were not coming forward to join the Padayatras. They were also hesitant to attend the interaction programme of the activists. But when the Chairman, RSS cum ADM Rourkela came forward with the Padayatries as participant with his fellow activists and travelled on his foot in the slums, people got inspiration to come forward and join the procession. Further, the street performances during the Padayatras based on the themes of the essence of women literacy have motivated them a lot. As a result, after follow up interactions were over, a lot many people specially women joined the Padayatras and accompanied the participants from their slum to other slums. It may be noted here that out of seven Padayatras, two were exclusively organised by the women groups and girls students of high schools and college level.

Cycle and Bus Rallies

Four cycle rallies and one bus rally were organised between December 1990 to May 1992. The bus rally was organised on the eve of Independence Day celebration on 15th August, 1991 followed by a number of cultural programmes and motivational meetings in different parts of the city. A number of 20 buses were engaged for the purpose of environment building carrying learners, slum-dwellers, volunteers, cultural artists and school students etc. in four different directions of the city. This rally was quite effective in involving different type of people through its interaction programme. One all Orissa tour for literacy on cycle was organised by 8 student volunteers of RSS. They spread over the message of literacy and development throughout Orissa state. Out of the four cycle rallies organised by RSS volunteers, one rally was organised by the women volunteers. These cycle rallies were also followed by motivational meetings and cultural shows based on the themes of literacy in various slums by the participants of the rally.

Human Chain

A 10 km. long human chain was organised on 10th January, 1991 from Bishra Chowk to Panposh Chowk with the help of more than 10,000 students of different schools, colleges and organisations. Before organising the human chain, the chairman of RSS cum ADM Rourkela contacted different organisations and head of the educational institutions to participate in the activities of the programme for a greater cause and make it successful. The then collector cum District Magistrate and initiator of literacy programme of Sundargarh District, Mrs. Anita Agnihotri, IAS had inaugurated the programme of human chain and requested the people of Rourkela to make it a grand success, which boosted the participants of the human chain, specially the women to carry on the programme in a positive direction.

Oath Taking Ceremony

The oath taking ceremony took place in a public gathering on 26th January, 1991, followed by street plays organised by Shramik Vidyapeeth. In this occasion, the Chairman, Secretary, members of RSS and other people from different sectors, took oath to make the city "Sakshar Nagari, Bikasita Nagari" (Literate City, Developed City)

Wall Writings, Poster and Sticker Preparation

Wall Writing Campaigns with literacy message and slogans were organised for three times, by the organisers and volunteers of RSS in each and every sector and slum of Rourkela. Hoardings, posters (literacy) and stickers were prepared by the Samiti and distributed among the people especially in the slum and local areas of the city. Students and non-students of Rourkela were encouraged by the organisers to participate in the literacy programme by participating in the preparation and display of literacy. Posters, competition among the students and non-students of Rourkela were organised from time to time (four times) in this regard *i.e.* preparation and display of Literacy Poster. A very good number of participants participated in those competitions.

Mass Contact Programme and Public Motivational Meeting

For the successful implementation of the programme, public enthusiasm had to be sustained through out the campaign. Hence, thirteen mass contact and public motivational meetings followed with street plays, tribal folk dance and songs carrying the message of literacy were organised. In each and every motivational meeting, importance was given to women literacy as a major item of the agenda along with other. The ADM Rourkela, who used to be the Chairman of the RSS addressed the people and requested them to join the programme spontaneously as learners and volunteers. He, himself with fellow activists was visiting door to door in the slum to motivate the people. Initially they were not coming to the meetings seriously in large number. But when they saw the Chairman, Secretary and top level people at their doors for their development, they came down and joined in large numbers. Gradually, they, themselves, took initiative in organising slum level meetings and invited the Chairman and others to address the slum people for their educational development. It was observed in Orampara, Sitalpara, Gudiatoli, VSS Nagar, Tumkela and other slums.

Literacy Marathon and Mass Run

A Literacy Marathon was organised in the month of August, 1991 in which people from all sectors of life and students of schools and colleges were participated. In the same month, a mass run of women was also organised. Women from all class (top to bottom) participated in the run, carrying the message of literacy to make each and every illiterate woman, literate. Reputed ladies of the society like advocates, lecturers, doctors, teachers, artists, magistrates etc. came forward and motivated others to join the programme on this occasion.

Mass Plantation Programme

Mass Plantation Programmes were organised by RSS in various slums, like Bondamunda, Pradhan Palli, Gudiatoli and Khariabahal. During the plantation programme, women of the slums were not coming out spontaneously in Khariabahal and Bondamunda. The Secretary, Youth Hostel Association of India, Rourkela branch who used to be a volunteer of RSS, took much strain in motivating the women group and ultimately succeeded in involving them with plantation programme. Since then, the women groups of Khariabahal were taking care of the plants as well as the literacy activities. In Bondamunda also, the same problems were found. But the activists of RSS took it as a challenge and established rapport with their family members and at last the women of the slums spontaneously joined the programme. It is noteworthy to mention here that the plantation programme of Gudiatoli and Pradhan Palli were followed by other cultural activities organised mainly by the women volunteers and learners of the slums for environment protection.

Saksharata Mela (Literacy Fair)

On the eve of International Literacy Day Celebration, a Saksharata Mela of two days *i.e.* on 7th and 8th Sept., 1991 was organised by RSS in Bhanja Bhawan field. People from each and every sector of life enjoyed the programme whole-heartedly. A very good number of cultural programmes, video shows, competitions among school and college volunteers and non-school volunteers and learners were organised. The competitions were on letter writing, essay, song, spot painting, alpana, rangoli), folk dance etc. Special competitions among the women learners of the slum areas on cooking, reading books, writing letters, song, folk dance, knitting and awareness on social issues were organised in the mela. A good number of stalls were opened for the learners to exhibit their creativity by displaying literacy materials like posters, paintings, clay models, food items, craft items and handicrafts, cultural activities and so on. The control room staff of RSS, displayed essential literacy materials for the Rourkelites in separate stalls. Blood grouping and donation camps, counseling and information corners and health camps were also organised in the mela. Slum-dwellers from every slum of Rourkela visited the mela with full enthusiasm and participated there actively. The general public of Rourkela city also enjoyed the cultural and other programmes like street plays, video shows, discussion forum etc. This mela was inaugurated by the Honourable Minister of Industry, Sri Dillip Ray, Govt. of Orissa and validated by Sri C.P. Majhi Hon'ble Minister of School and Mass Education, Govt. of Orissa. Both of the Ministers have addressed the august gathering of Rourkela and requested them to join the literacy programme whole-heartedly as volunteers or learners.

Health, First Aid Training, and Malaria Detection Camps

A number of twelve health camps (eye-check-up and immunisation) were organised by the

RSS organisers with the help of Rourkela Govt. Hospital, Ispat General Hospital, Lions Club of Rourkela in various slum areas. Special camps on mother and child-care was organised in Phulbari slum of zone-VIII. In this occasion, there was a healthy baby contest among the children health camp. Participation of slum women was not highly satisfactory. But after the door- to- door motivational counseling of the organisers and volunteers, the number of participants increased. Gradually, the health camps became highly successful. Because one First Aid Training Camp and one Malaria Detection Camp were organised by the RSS organisers with the help of Malaria Research Centre, Rourkela Govt. Hospital and Ispat General Hospital to provide training to the RSS volunteers and even to the learners.

Basti Safai Karyakram (Cleaning Programme of Slum)

A number of Basti Safai Karyakram have been organised by the organisers of RSS with the help of the grass-root level volunteers and learners of Khariapara, Orampara, Khariabahal, Gangadhar Palli, Shantinagar and other slums from time to time to keep the area clean. During the initial stage of cleaning programme, the slum-dwellers of certain slums did not co-operate with the volunteers. But the friendly behaviour and rapport of the volunteers made them join the programme.

Women Convention and Focussed Group Discussion, Seminar and Workshops

One women convention and a number of seven focused-group discussion on women's problems and their solutions with special reference to the disadvantaged sections of the society were organised from time to time. Resource persons from various voluntary organisations, social workers, experts and trainers of Shramik Vidyapeeth were invited from the city and other places for these purposes. Slum women, especially the learners were the participants in those discussions. They were given scope to express their own problems by themselves, not through the volunteers. At the beginning, they were hesitant to participate in the focussed group discussion programme. But the motivation of the women volunteers of RSS inspired them to participate and gradually, they actively participated in those programmes. A number of five workshops and seminars on different social issues related to literacy and its other aspects were organised from time to time and both volunteers and learners participated in the Seminars and workshops. On the Eve of International Women's Day Celebration, on 8th March,1992 a variety of activities were organised, specially for the women learners of the slum areas. They were, street plays composed on the problems of women and their solutions discussion forum, tribal folk dance, and display of literacy poster and paintings on women issues. An exhibition-cum-sale on hand made product of food articles, tailoring materials, greeting cards, rakhee, footmats, candles etc. was also organised by the women volunteers and learners of RSS. Slum women as well as others have actively participated in the programme at Sector-20 club of Rourkela.

Literacy Stalls in Public Gathering

The RSS organisers in the public gathering opened literacy stalls during Vedvyas Mela, Basanti Mela, Ganesh Mela, Durga Puja, State and National Trade Fairs, and in Book Exhibitions etc. Posters, Paintings, Literature, books on various social issues and women's problem were displayed at the stall. Video shows, street plays and interaction programmes were also organised through the stall by the organisers for people's awareness and mobilisation.

Video Shows, Audio Cassettes and Telefilm

Video shows on different themes related to literacy and development programme were organised by the RSS volunteers, very often in each and every literacy zones to motivate the learners as well as illiterates. They have organised the shows for more than 30 times. RSS has prepared two audio-cassettes on literacy songs in Oriya and Hindi language with the help of the local singers and artists for the motivational purpose. The audio-cassettes were used, very frequently, in the slums along with the video show and other programmes. The members of the cultural organisation "SANKALP" with the help of RSS made a tele-film entitled "Ahuti" based on the theme of Literacy and Development. The tele-film was telecasted by the Steel T.V. of Rourkela many times. The cassette of the tele-film was also shown many a times in different slums with the video programme to make the environment alive and sustainable.

Cultural Activities—Street Plays, Women Kala Yatha, Trial, Folk Dance Drama and Song

In the process of environment building and motivational activities of the literacy programme of RSS, five different cultural troops such as street plays, women Kala Yatha, Tribal Folk-dance, drama and songs participated most actively. They performed for more than fifty times in different slums and public places. The cultural troops were DHOLAK team of Shramik Vidyapeeth, TEANKARU" and "DANDA NACHHA" (Folk dance with stick) of Udit Nagar Govt. High School, "NAWA KADAM (New steps), the tribal dance and drama in Sadri Language of Gudia toli, "GHASA PHOOLA" of Government High School, Jhirpani, and "SUKANNYA"—Women Kala Yatha Team of RSS. Here a mention may be made that the above stated teams were highly appreciated by the slum-dwellers and also the people of Rourkela. The cultural teams presented their performances on themes like literacy, environment, evils of drugs and alcoholism, evils of population explosion, need for small family, essence of women education and on the various problems of women. But the women of Kala Yatha team 'Sukannya' depicted the problems of women specially the disadvantaged and their solutions through their performances. It was conducted in various art forms to mobilise women's participation in the literacy programme.

Vanita Kalayatha of Kerala

The artists of Kerala Shastra Sahitya Parisad (KSSP) and cultural artists of "Vanita" Women Kala Yatha of Kerala visited Rourkela during the campaign period of literacy programme and performed their plays based on various issues of literacy and women. The themes of the plays were translated in Oriya language and presented before the women learners and volunteers for better communication by the BGVS activists of the local unit who were also the activists of RSS. The performance of "Vanita Kala Yatha" was also highly appreciated by the people of Rourkela specially the slum-dwellers of the city.

Eminent Visitors to the Campaign

Many eminent persons were invited to Rourkela during the environment building and motivation campaign to assess the progress of the campaign through its activities. During their stay at RSS, they visited different slums and, thereby, participated in the environment building process. Here a mention may be made of the pioneers of the literacy movement in Kerala as well as of the country Dr. M.P. Parameswaran, K. Krishna Kumar and Sundar Raman of Bharat Gyan Vigyan Samiti (BGVS), New Delhi as well as KSSP. Mr. Satya Narayan from Govt. of India, Dr. L.D. Mishra, I.A.S. Ex. D.G. NLM, Sri Rabi Ray, Hon'ble Ex-speaker of the Loksabha, Mr. Dillip Ray, Mr. Sarat Kar, Mr. C.P. Majhi and Dr. (Mrs.) K. Das, Ex. Ministers of the State, who came to Rourkela, during the campaign period and addressed the people of Rourkela to join the literacy programme spontaneously and to contribute their best. The then Hon'ble Governor of Orissa Sri

Y.D. Sharma also visited Rourkela in October, 1991. He addressed a large gathering of literacy activists and learners and visited some slum pockets.

The Chief Secretary, Government of Orissa visited Rourkela in March, 1992 to asses the situation. In the same month, the then Chief Minister of Orissa, Sri Biju Pattnaik also visited the Literacy camps organised by the volunteers and learners of RSS. He addressed the learners and volunteers and requested the public to extent their co-operation for this great social work. He checked the literacy skills of some of the women learners of Panposh basti (slum) and encouraged them to participate in the programme more actively. In fact, the visit and encouragement of the Chief Minister re-motivated the volunteers and learners (specially the women) to become more active in the programme.

The activists of the State BGVS, ORISSA, visited the campaign very frequently and extended their technical and resource support from time to time. They have also organised many workshops and seminars with the collaboration of RSS through the activists of the local BGVS Unit to strengthen the campaign.

TV Coverage

A team of Delhi Doordarsan reached Rourkela to have a complete video coverage of literacy programme. The local correspondents took it up as a challenge and there was a competition among the local and regional news papers for the coverage of literacy programme which influenced a lot of people towards the programme. All these environment building activities were continued even after the launching of P.L. programme in June,1992.

During the Post Literacy Phase, the nature of environment building activities were changed according to the objectives of the Post Literacy Programme. As a "Centre Based Programme", the activities of P.L. Programme were organised mainly in the "Chetana Kendras" at grass-root level for the neo-literates, dropouts, and leftouts. Chetana Kendras, their needs and interests were taken into consideration while organising those activities of the PL Programme. List of environment building activities and number of times organised were presented below in Table 5.1.

TABLE 5.1

Environment Building Activities of Rourkela Saksharata Samiti during Post Literacy Phase (from June,1992 to March, 2000)

Year	Sl. No.	Types of Environment Building Activities	Frequency of activities
1	2	3	4
June, 1992 to May, 2000	1.	Launching of Post Literacy Programme.	01
	2.	Re-survey : identification of neo-literates, dropout and leftout learners.	18 Camps
	3.	Publication and distribution of "Saksharata Samachar."	22,000 copies (22 issues
June, 1992 to May, 1995	4.	Video Shows and Tele-films.	38
	5.	Street Plays - "SAMBHAB-92" performed in different slums and public places (The street play team performed their show before the public of Maharaja Circus on the request of the circus team as guest show on 24-10-92 for people's awareness and motivation).	106

(Contd. . . .)

(Contd. . . .)

1	2	3	4
	6.	Training Seminar Orientation and Workshops for P.L. activists and resource Persons (It includes Kala Yatha and Writer's Workshops).	38
	7.	Wall Writing (Slogans and Quotations on P.L. Message).	324 places
	8.	Celebration of World Population Day (WPD) organised by RSS in Central Level at Bondamunda, Ruputola and Sec-20 Pump house colony respectively from 1992 to 1994 on 11th July of each year.	03
	9.	Celebration of Breast Feeding Week (BFW) through Shramik Vidyapeeth: Followed by a number of activities related to healthy mother and childcare in different slums of the city (BFW-93 and BFW-94).	02
	10.	Celebration of Independence Day (I.D.) at central level and grass-root level *i.e.* in each Chetana Kendra with a good number of post literacy activities like Safai Karya Kram, Prabhat Feri, Plantation Programme, Flag Hosting, Cultural activities etc. (I-D-92, ID-93 and ID-94)	03
	11.	Celebration of International Literacy Day on 8th Sept. (ILD) from 1992 to 1994 - Followed by a great variety of activities especially for the neo-literates like meeting, focused group discussion on current social issues, different types of competitions among neo-literates. Special competitions and activities organised for the neo-literate slum women like reading newspapers and books, quiz on health and social awareness debate, song and folk dance competition and rangoli and painting competition. The ILD programme of 1994 was followed with an exhibition-cum-sale of hand made product by the neo-literate women.	03
	12.	Celebration of Republic Day (RD) – in Central level as well as Chetana Kendra Level with a number of Socio-cultural activities (RD-93, RD-94 and RD-95).	03
	13.	Uttar Saksharata Mela (Post Literacy Mela) : out of the two melas, one mela was specially organised for the neo-literate Muslim slum women of Narla Road through "Saheli Mahila Samiti" and Alfathe Club of Narla Road with the help of RSS organisers. The mela was followed with a great variety of post literacy activities and an exhibition in February,1993. This was inaugurated by Dillip Ray, Honb'le Minister of Industry, of Orissa and closed down by the ADM Rourkela cum Chairman RSS.	02
	14	Mahila Jagruti Talim Camp: (Women Leadership Training Camp) It was started since 1993 especially for the neo-literate, dropout and leftout slum women.	14
June, 1992 to March 2000	15.	Celebration of International Women's Day (IWD) in different Chetana Kendras and even in Central Level with a good number of activities like discussion forum, debate and allocation competition among the slum women on various issues related to women and their development. Exhibition-cum-sale on home made product by the neo-literate slum women was organised at Sec. 20 club through Shramik Vidyapeeth on IWD-94. (IWD-93, IWD-94 and IWD-95).	03

(Contd. . . .)

(Contd. . . .)

1	2	3	4
June, 1995 to March, 2000	16.	Video shows and films, street plays (CHETANA-95).	38
	17.	Performed the cultural shows in different slums and public places for awareness generation and motivation.	43
	18.	Training, Workshop, Seminar, and Orientation for P.L. activists and Resource persons and Kabi-sammalen.	61
	19.	Celebration of "World Environment Day" (WED) on 5th June in each Chetana Kendra for environment protection by activities like discussion forum, cultural activities based on the theme of envircnment pollution and its protection etc. (Started from since June,95 to June, 99).	05
	20.	Celebration of World Population Day (WPD) followed by health camps and other activities related to small family norms and family welfare training in different Chetana Kendras special programme organised for the neo-literate slum women on competition on "healthy mother and child" among the slum women in WPD -1996. WPD-95, WPD-96, WPD-97, WPD-98 and WPD-99.	05
June, 1995 to March, 2000	21.	Celebration of Independence Day (ID) in Central level as well as in each Chetana Kendra with a great variety of Socio-cultural activities (ID-95, ID-96, ID-97, ID-98 and ID-99).	05
	22.	Celebration of International Literacy Day (ILD) followed with activities like open platform, discussion forum, workshop, people's parliament, cultural programme, different types of competition specially among neo-literate slum-women and NFE children of different Chetana Kendras (ILD-95, ILD-96, ILD-97, ILD-98 and ILD-99).	05
	23.	SISHUMELA (On the eve of Children's Day) (SM) started since, 1995 followed with a variety of activities for the NFE children of NFE centres run by the RSS. Parents of the children were specially invited by the RSS to enjoy the activities of their children in the mela. (SM-95, SM-96, SM-97, SM-98 and SM-99).	05
	24.	Celebration of World AIDS Day (WAD) (since Dec., 1995) in Central level – followed with Seminar and training programme, Focused group discussions, Health awareness camps, painting and poster competition among the volunteers and non-volunteers. (WAD-95, WAD-96 , WAD-97, WAD-98 and WAD-99).	05
June, 1995 to March, 2000	25.	Celebration of Republic Day (RD) in Central Level as well as in each Chetana Kendras—followed with a good number of activities especially for NFE children and neo-literate women of the slums (RD-96, RD-97, RD-98 and RD-99).	05
	26.	Celebration of Utkal Divas (UD) (Started since,1996) followed with activities like, Mass Rally from Literacy Control Room, A.D.M. Office to Madhusudan Statue and Bishramunda Statue (a coverage on foot of about 11 Km.). Literacy Volunteers, NFE instructors, neo-literates (both male and female) and slum-dwellers participated in the rally and other cultural activities organised at the civic centre. (UD-96, UD-97, UD-98 and UD-99).	05

(Contd. . . .)

(Contd. . . .)

1	2	3	4
	27.	Celebration of International Women's Day (IWD) followed by a good number of activities especially for the neo-literate slum women and girl children of NFE Centres. Exhibition-cum-sale was organised on home made product of the neo-literate slum women in collaboration with Shramik Vidyapeeth in Sec-20 club of Rourkela in 1997 and 1998. Besides, different types of cultural activities, women's platform for sharing experiences, and seminars were organised in central level as well as slum level. (IWD-96, IWD-97, IWD-98, IWD-99 and IWD-2000).	05
	28.	Mahila Jagruti Talim Camps: Organised for the neo-literate, leftout and dropout slum women of different literacy zone in different Chetana Kendras.	23

The above stated data on environment building activities of Rourkela Saksharata Samiti (RSS) was verified and cross checked with the documents of other concerned agencies and organisations like Shramik Vidyapith, Bethel Charitable Trust, Rourkela Municipality, Ispat General Hospital and Rourkela Government Hospital, Community Welfare Society, 'Sankalp' cultural Organisation, Rourkela Steel T.V., and the concerned schools and educational institutions. Interviews of concerned functionaries and people from different sectors of life (including slum-dwellers volunteers and the neo-literate slum women) were conducted with this regard. Majority of the interviewees (87.09%) had informed the investigator about their knowledge on environment building activities of RSS for motivation and awareness generation in slum areas as well as the public places since 1990 to 2000.

It was found that during the initial stage of the campaigning, people in the slum areas didn't have full faith in the literacy programme. They thought that it was also like the family planning or other programmes of the government. Therefore, they were not ready to extend their co-operation whole-heartedly. They were not even attending to the activities of the programme in large number. But when they learnt that the involved volunteers and other personnel of the literacy programme were serving selflessly without any remuneration, and observed the immature high school students in survey, teaching-learning and other activities, they started believing in it to some extent. Further, the active involvement and dedication of the ADM, SP, Sub-collector and other top class people of Rourkela, acted as intermediate levers. People who were used to a bureaucratic, indifferent and mechanised culture of Governmental functioning, suddenly discovered to their utter surprise and pleasure that the relatively inaccessible mini-Gods of the government were now walking in the slums amidst slum-dwellers and were chanting slogans, holding bans and creating enough ripples in the slum areas of the city. It highlighted the value of literacy. Specially the frequent visit of the ADM, Rourkela to the slums, his friendly behaviour to every body, his deep involvement in each and every literacy activity made the people to cooperate. As a result, they came forward in organising the environment building and other activities whole-heartedly.

As resident and teaching personnel, the researcher has been involved with the socio-educational activities of Rourkela since the last two decades, and experienced the knowledge about the various environment building and motivational activities of RSS. She has also directly participated in certain activities like street plays, human chain, plantation programme, Saksharata mela, literacy rallies etc. As a researcher, she has observed the environment building activities of the PL Phase since January,1997 and has felt that RSS has made sincere efforts and adequate number of activities for the educational development for the slum people specially the women of Rourkela with the help of dedicated volunteers and activists and a few organisations like Shramik Vidyapith, Rourkela Municipality, Bethel Charitable Trust and Community Welfare Centre etc. She has observed the sincerity and dedication of the volunteers from the grass root level of control room level while organising those environment building activities for the slum-dwellers. Their way of motivation friendly behaviour and sharing of feelings with the slum-dwellers have made the thing easy to a great extent in organising the environment building activities and mobilisation of the people specially the slum women.

Literacy Survey and Re-survey

A preliminary household survey for identification of illiterates was conducted at the initial stage of literacy programme with the help of a large number of trained volunteers (about 13,000 high school students and youth). The survey covered all the slums of Rourkela city.

Initially the target illiterate population was estimated at 1,00,000 in the age groups of 10-60 years. But when an intensive re-survey was conducted by matured and trained volunteers in June,1992, *i.e.* at the beginning of the post-literacy programme, it revealed that the total illiterate population in the age group 10-60 years was 93,867. Out of which 61,248 were women. The survey also revealed that 65,444 were still in the campaign during the re-survey period.

The investigator found from the organisers of RSS that as the survey was conducted in a hurry adequate training could not be given to all the volunteers. Therefore, about 30% volunteers were not properly trained to conduct the early round of survey in the slums for the identification of illiterates.

The school volunteers, without being aware of expected proficiency in different literacy skills required for treating a person "Literate as per NLM norms", wrongly identified some learners as illiterates and *vice-versa*. Therefore, the number of illiterates found was more during the initial round of survey than the re-survey. Thus, the survey was conducted again with full preparation, and matured volunteers were involved for this purpose so as to get a concrete picture of the status of illiterates. This information was given by one of the senior activists of the RSS to the investigator. After getting the actual position of illiterates and neo-literates planning was immediately made to cover the left out illiterates particularly during post literacy phase.

Training

Unlike environment building activities, training of different types of people participating in literacy programme is also very crucial and an important effort for the success of the programme. Since literacy programme is a people's movement, each and every participant of the programme should have properly understood its philosophy and objectives. Therefore, the required training for the participants is highly essential and a must. The organisers and activists of RSS reported it and also the records indicated that all the participants in the literacy campaign were provided a basic training of three days in both literacy and post literacy phase. In this regard training was imparted in a three tires strategies, *viz.* the training of Key Resource Persons (KRP), Master Trainers (MT) and Volunteers. The volunteers were the actual teaching personnel for the learners in the field at grass-root level.

A training camp of three days was organised for 169 KRPs consisting mostly of highly qualified persons like Lecturers, Doctors, Journalists, Advocates and Head Masters of the High Schools etc. with the resource support of State Resource Centre (SRC), ORISSA, and the Government of

India in March, 1991. Similarly, the three day training camps for about 900 MTs were organised with the help of the trained KRPs by the middle of April,1991. About 13,000 volunteers (both high school students and young youth) were trained by the middle of May, 1991 with the help of trained KRPs and trained MTs (mostly the MTs) of RSS.

As a part of the training, all the categories of literacy activists were introduced to the philosophy behind this particular literacy campaign, some basic adult psychology and other general topics related to the campaign. Later, the primers were introduced to them. The lessons in the primers explained in details mainly to the teaching volunteers by their trainers, followed by discussion as to how to conduct the classes among the different sections of people specially the slum women. Special instructions guidance and motivational techniques were given to the volunteers both male and females (but mainly to the female) so that they could easily convince the slum women for learning.

Orientation courses and workshops were organised from time to time. The training and orientation programmes were organised and co-ordinated with the help of a core group of activists.

During the post literacy phase of the literacy programme, participant volunteers were provided a basic training of three days. Thereafter, two times orientation training of two days duration in a year was given to almost all the volunteers. Each volunteer was imparted training two to three times to manage the library of Chetana Kendra. Besides, they participated in various seminars, workshops, discussion forums and camps organised by RSS on the relevant subjects like Population, Education, Family Welfare, Community Health, Para Legal and Legal Rights, Leadership Training, Women's Health, Child and Maternity Care, Prevention on AIDS, First Aid Training and various issues related to women's problem and development during the Post-Literacy Programme. The training mentioned above were organised by RSS with active training and resource support of SRC, BGVS (Bharat Gyan Vigyan Samiti) and Directorate of Mass Education (DME). Though the trainings were organised by RSS centrally, but were held at different places of the city.

The investigator has enquired and cross-checked about the training with the volunteers and senior activists of RSS and learned that majority of them (73.91% volunteers and 75% senior activists) have received training for more 11 times both in Literacy and Post-Literacy Phase. It was also found that they (70% volunteers and 81.25% senior activists) were satisfied and benefited with the training they have received.

While interviewing some of the activists of the training co-ordination committee they reported that they could have imparted much better training to their volunteers and KRPs during the initial stage of literacy programme. Since Rourkela was the first of its kind in Orissa along with Sundargarh literacy campaign, no concrete training experience in this regard could be availed from any of the resource persons involved in this training programme. They were also new in certain aspects of the training, which was required in an urban project like Rourkela cosmopolitan city. It is true that the training initiated by the above mentioned was helpful to the volunteers in the field, but their training expertise was not highly applicable for the slum-dwellers of a cosmopolitan city like Rourkela. However, the Chairman, the Secretary and the trainer activists of RSS could enhance their training efficiency, and make them competent by doing the things learned from the constraints and provided field training to the volunteers. Therefore, they could make it up in the later stage.

Here mention may be made that the researcher has attended a good number of training programmes on different subjects like population, education and family welfare, NFE training for the instructors and supervisors, Environment Protection Community Health, Women's Health, Child and Maternity Care, Para Legal Training, etc., organised by RSS during her field observation and data collection. She has experienced some important points out of her observation from the training programme in different places and slums.

(i) A very good number of participants mainly women have actively participated in the trainings.

(ii) The Participant volunteers who used to be the grass-root level workers were also equally experienced like the trainers in many aspects of literacy.

(iii) The participants were highly co-operative in organising the programme with the organisers.

(iv) Their querries on various aspects of the training in each programme were appreciable.

(v) The rapport between the trainers group especially of RSS and the participants was cordial which helped the trainers to reach out to the participants easily.

(vi) Discussion, conversation, demonstration and role-play, etc., were adopted as methods of their training. On the whole, the training programmes were need-based in accordance to the field situation. It can be interpreted from the above reports, information and observations that despite a variation of opinion among the different types of respondents, and training constraints, RSS has provided a very good number of training programmes to its volunteers and activists. The trainings imparted to its volunteers were need-based and satisfactory enough to help them in teaching, monitoring and mobilising the neo-literate slum people specially women.

Preparation and Distribution of Learning Materials

The basic necessity of literacy programme was reading and Writing materials. Because without these materials the literacy centres cannot start functioning. Keeping in view the broad objectives of the literacy programme and cultural situation and language spoken in the city, it was decided to launch primers on two languages i.e. in Oriya and Hindi. The Oriya and Hindi Primers with in built tests designed by SRC, Orissa and SRC, Jamia Milia Islamia, New Delhi, respectively, were adopted by RSS for Literacy Campaign. Each set (consisting of three primers) was prepared following the method of Improved Pace Content of Learning to be taught in about 200 hours, or six months. It was supplied with a learners' kit containing a red-coloured bag containing a slate, pencil, an exercise book and Primers. The Literacy Volunteers, Master trainers and Key Resource Persons were also supplied with the three primers teaching guide-book, note-book, monitoring form, identity card and pen. Each participant was provided a badge carrying the symbol of literacy.

Two supplementary books "Hitakatha" and "Bapa Maa Nka Payen" in Oriya language were prepared by the RSS and distributed among the learners just before completion of their third primer as pre-post-literacy literature. It may be mentioned here that from the very beginning of the actual teaching learning activities, the RSS in April,1991 started publishing and distributing "Saksharata Samachar" to the learners, volunteers and others. During the initial stage of the campaign it was published and distributed weekly. When the programme took a momentum, it started publishing fortnightly. But after launching of post-literacy programme it was published and distributed specially for the neo-literates as a monthly newspaper. Provisions were always made for the women learners and neo-literates in regard to their awareness development, sharing experiences, information regarding different skill development, training and different development schemes of the government and non-government department etc. in the Samachar.

During the post literacy phase RSS prepared and distributed its own post-literacy primer "Naba Taranga" and two other supplementary books "Mo-Rourkela" and "Swastya Chetana" (Exclusively for the women) with the help of the RSS activists and local writers. Besides these books, the books entitled "Police Abom Apna," "Dowry Rules and Our Duty", "Hindu Marriage Law" and "We and our Law" etc. in the form of ten booklets were provided to each neo-literate to read, understand and implement in their practical life. It was further reported by the organisers of RSS that a number of 300 to 400 titles of Oriya books and 150 to 200 books in Hindi language were provided to the library of each Chetana Kendra in a GL box with lock and key for regular issue of the neo-literate and members of Basti Chetana Samiti. Along with the materials mentioned above a sign board showing the name of the "Chetana Kendra", registers (enrolment, stock, library books, library stock, meeting etc.). Orissa map, dot pens (both blue and red), file cover, slate, pencil, exercise books, carban packet, chalk, white paper enrolment form, black-board cloth and duster were also provided to the Chetana Kendras for he use of the neo-literates.

The field activists (grass-root level) have reported that the teaching-learning and other material was supplied by RSS to the centres in a very systematic way on the requisition of the area co-ordinator or zone co-ordinator of the concerned area or zone.

Learners of the Zones I, III, IV and VIII, IX and XII were supplied with the material from the main control room. Whereas rest of the zones i.e. Zones II, V, VII, X and XI were supplied from the branch control rooms of the sector township.

After receiving the requisition from the area co-ordinator or zone co-ordinator or in worst case from the volunteer of the concerned slum material was enlisted and supplied by the control room volunteers through their vehicles to the centre. The material was distributed according to the need of the learners in the centres by the volunteers themselves or by the area or zone co-ordinators. At the initial stage the material was distributed in the centres by the Chairman of the Samiti himself in the gatherings as functions. Even the Secretary of RSS, other senior activists and eminent personalities have distributed the teaching materials in festive occasion. But it was not always possible to do so. Therefore, the volunteers, area and zone co-ordinators or the member of monitoring team respectable person of the areas had to perform the modalities reported a senior level activist to the investigator. He further revealed that the materials were mostly supplied phase-wise. Just before completion of Primer I, Primer II was given and *vice-versa*.

It was also reported that slate, pencil and note-books were supplied to the learners more than once according to their requirement. Whereas, primers were supplied once only. During the Post Literacy Phase they were once again supplied with the note books, pencil, pen etc. along with the post literacy primer. Before supplying the PL Primer they were given two pre-post literacy or supplementary book "Hitakatha" and "Bapa Maa Nka Payen" one after another with a gap of about one month.

It was explored by the investigator from the neo-literate slum women about the types of reading materials they were supplied for and she got it confirmed that the following material mentioned below in Table-5.2 have been supplied to them.

Further, while interviewing them (the neo-literate slum women) they informed that all of them have received literacy primers (Parts-I, II and III), notebook, slate, pen and pencil during the first phase of literacy programme. Even that they have got notebook, pen, slate and pencil twice as per their requirement. Where as during the post Literacy Phase the distribution of PL Primer and other Supplementary books were not equal due to shortage of manpower in the field

TABLE 5.2
Types of Learning Materials Provided to the Slum Women during Literacy Programme (Including PL Phase)

Sl. No.	*Types of Literacy Materials Provided*
1.	Literacy Primer : Primers I, II and III
2.	Naba Taranga (P.L. Primer)
3.	Saksharata Samachar
4.	Supplementary books prepared and distributed by RSS like Hitakatha, Bapa Maa Nka Payen, Mo-Rourkela and Swasta Chetana
5.	Other supplementary books like Dowry Rules and our duty, Hindu marriage law and other books
6.	Exercise Book
7.	Pen/Pencil
8.	Slate

as well as central level for co-ordination. Therefore, about 15% (14.56%) of the respondents have reported that they have not received the PL Primer and about 20% (19.42%) have not received the supplementary book prepared by RSS. Similarly about 24% (23.30%) have not received other supplementary book and about 19% (18.45%) have reported that Saksharata Samachar was not available to them.

It is revealed from the statement of the slum women that distribution of reading material was adequate and systematic during first phase of the literacy programme and each and every learner has received the reading material. But this distribution of the material was not equal and not systematic during P.L. Phase due to shortage of main power in grass-root as well as central level for co-ordination. Therefore, some of the potential neo-literates have been deprived of availing the reading materials supplied for post literacy activities.

While enquiring about the unequal distribution of PL materials among the neo-literate slum women during the PL Phase, the organisers and Secretary of RSS informed that due to shortage of man power like volunteers, vehicles, monitoring and interaction programme have faced a lot of problems. Therefore, neo-literates could not be given PL and other material more systematically. However, majority of them have been supplied with the materials in time.

It was reported by most of the (87%) neo-literate slum women that they were satisfied with the quality and content of the reading material and these were supplied in time.

It has also been reported by a very good number of respondents 81% that they were highly satisfied with the PL Primer and Saksharata Samachar than by the TL Primers because of their need based and interesting content, bold letters, simple language, picture and conversational-cum-story type presentation. They have revealed that the supplementary literature provided to them by RSS was very much useful in their day-to-day life.

The investigator has gone for cross validation of the above said reading and other material from the Chetana Kendras and for that the quality of material was good. The writing style, content and language of primers both literacy and post literacy were satisfactory. But the content of the post literacy primer was highly satisfactory and appreciable due to its suitability to urban background and need-based content especially for the slum-dwellers.

It is important to mention here that since literacy programme of Rourkela was the leading campaign in Orissa with regard to PL activities and primer writing, no concrete guideline in the form of model was available with the writers of PL Primer while its preparation. Therefore, RSS organised a special workshop on writing of PL Primer and invited local writers, literacy activists of different types and resource persons from BGVS to discuss on the different aspects of PL Primer and its preparation. The literacy activists did share their experiences before the writers and resource persons. On the basis of the experiences which include the needs felt and interests observed, among the neo-literates contents and topic of the primers selected and the material prepared. It is also noteworthy to mention here that most of the writers were found to be RSS activists. The other supplementary literature were prepared by only the activists of Rourkela. The Saksharata Samachar, Bapa Maa Nka Payen, Hitakatha, Mo-Rourkela, and Swasta Chetana prepared by RSS were no doubt beneficial to the neo-literates especially the slum women, but the message passed through Saksharata Samachar and Swasta Chetana were of were potentials for the neo-literates to develop further.

However, despite constraints the efforts sincerely made by RSS in preparing reading material for its learners and neo-literates were quite satisfactory and the way of supply and distribution of the materials were also systematic adequate and satisfactory.

Teaching Learning Among the Learners

The most important aspect in the literacy programme is teaching the learners. Because this is the way and the means for acquiring knowledge by the learners. Learning of the learners is the end result of the whole process of action. After being trained, the volunteers were given the task of educating (teaching) a set of learners in a specific slum area under the operation of literacy programme. Care was taken to ensure that there was no overlapping in the distribution of volunteers. Women volunteers were specially trained and instructed as to how to motivate the housewives and other women of the slums for literacy classes. To get the learners for literacy class volunteers visited the slum areas and contracted the learners mostly the women during their leisure hours in the afternoon. The rapport they had earlier developed during survey with the slum-dwellers facilitated them further in teaching-learning process.

In April, 1991 teaching in ten slum areas started with an inaugural ceremony attended by 300 illiterates approximately. The ADM Rourkela cum Chairman, RSS inaugurated the ceremony and distributed learning materials to the learners. Gradually more and more number of illiterates and slum areas were covered under the programme. Mention may be made here that out of 300 illiterates covered in ten slums for teaching, more than 60% were women and a very good number of afternoon classes especially for them were opened in various slums. For other category of people evening and night classes were begun. The RSS organisers took special care for the women labourers, rag and iron pickers and other types of working women by opening evening and night classes at their own residences in small groups. Care was taken for the child labourer, rickshaw pullers, wage earners, illiterates hotel boys and rag pickers by starting mid-night literacy centres at Public places like Sec. 20 NAC market, Laxmi Market, near Ispat General Hospital (IGH) of Sector-19 and Sector-2 NAC market near Kariabahal slum. It is pertinent to mention here that special attention was also given to the street children, destitutes and orphans for their education through literacy classes by opening learning centre at Rourkela railway station. The centre was opened by some of the literacy volunteers under the dynamic leadership of senior literacy activist and Rotarian M.B. Mukharjee where some girl children also attended the literacy class.

The literacy volunteers of schools and youth had tried their level best to make the teaching interesting and effective and organised the literacy classes accordingly. It was reported to the investigator that while organising those teaching-learning activities some major constraint had come as obstacles on the way of the volunteers and organisers and affected the literacy programme badly.

CONSTRAINTS

Accommodation for Teaching-Learning Activities

It was reported by the organisers that accommodation for teaching-learning centres and Chetana Kendras was one of the major constraints faced by the organisers of RSS. Since most of the slums have come up the Rourkela Steel Plant (RSP) areas or on government land occupied illegally by slum-dwellers, RSP or government allowed no permanent construction. Hence, most of the literacy centres were running in the varandas and living rooms of the learners or local volunteers. Even in some slums literacy classes were running in the local club, UBS Mahila Samiti of Rourkela Municipality or the Chetana Kendras constructed by neo-literates and the members of Basti Chetana Samiti. But they were limited in number (18 only). The non-availability of accommodation even in the form of small room for Chetana Kendra was a great difficulty for the organisers of RSS to organise, interact and mobilise the women of the slums. The investigator enquired from the neo-literate slum women in the regard, *i.e.* place of learning during their interviews. The response of the neo-literate slum women in this regard, *i.e.* places of learning during literacy programme is given below in Table 5.3.

TABLE 5.3
Response of the Slum Women on their Place of Learning during the Literacy Programme (N=103)

Sl. No.	*Places of Teaching-learning*	*No. of Respondent Attended the Classes*	*Percentage*
1.	Own residence/varanda of the respondents	57	55.34
2.	Residence of volunteers	26	25.24
3.	Local club, UBS Mahila Samiti, and Chetana Kendra constructed by neo-literate, slum-dwellers and members of Chetana Samiti	20	19.42
	Total No. of Respondents	103	100.00

N.B. Due to lack of accommodation most of the Chetana Kendras were running in the Verandas of the volunteers. Only in 18 slums there had accommodation facilities in the form of UBS Mahila Samiti, Local club and Chetana Kendra (constructed mainly by the neo-literates and the slum-dwellers) for teaching-learning and other activities.

During her intensive field visit for data collection the investigator observed and experienced severe problems of accommodation for teaching-learning and other related activities in most of the slums of Rourkela city. The problem becomes more acute during rainy days, when they (the learners and volunteers) don't get place to step their feet in the veranda. Despite interest in teaching and learning activities they had to close down the literacy classes for days together every year.

No Common Timing for Teaching Activity

It was reported by the organisers, volunteers and even the respondents that because of the uncommon timing for teaching-learning activity, more numbers of women volunteers were required

to cover the learners in small groups at different timings in a day in each slum. More than half (53.40%) of the respondents were of earning category, working mainly as maid-servants both on part-time and full-time basis and as labourers, working under certain contractors outside and inside the steel plant. The timing of the literacy centres for most of the women (67%) was in the afternoon and were run by the girls volunteers different high schools and women's colleges. The teaching timing during after-noon as not suitable for the contract labourers and full-time maid-servants who were of 33%. Even many of the housewives and part-time maid-servants did not feel comfortable with these teaching timings in the afternoon as it was time for collecting drinking water from the distant water connection of the municipality. During the evening hours girl's volunteers were normally not allowed by their parents and guardians to go to the slums. Especially the maid-servants of certain slums like Narayani Palli, Narla Road, Shantinagar (Orampara) and Laltanki were not ready to learn with the male volunteers who were teaching in those slums during evening hours. It created problems for the volunteers and organisers to organise teaching activities.

Information gathered from the organisers and field volunteers with regard to arrangement of teaching timing according to the suitability of the slum women were crossed checked from the neo-literates in the field. Their responses in this regard are presented below in the Table 5.4.

TABLE 5.4
Response of the Neo-literate Slum Women on Arrangement of Teaching Timing (N=103)

Sl. No.	*Timing of Teaching*	*No. of Slum Women Attended the Classes*	*Percentage*
1.	**Morning**	**—**	**—**
2.	**Afternoon**	**69**	**66.99**
3.	**Evening**	**29**	**28.16**
4.	**After 7.00 p.m.**	**05**	**04.85**
	Total Nos. of Neo-literate slum women	**103**	**100.00**

It became evident from the above stated table that organisers of RSS had tried to organise teaching classes according to the leisure hours and suitability of the slum women in the afternoon, evening and late evening classes after 7 p.m. Many of them (67%) attended the afternoon class. Whereas, about one-third of the respondents were rag and iron-pickers, contract-labourers and full-time maid-servant type have attended the evening and late evening classes (can be seen from Table 5.4).

Dropping-out of School Volunteers

A good number of girls volunteers of high schools and women's colleges who participated in the literacy programme as follow-up of SUPW Scheme and NSS work dropped themselves out from the programme during the pick period, *i.e.* in the summer vacation after their examination. Since participation in literacy programme made compulsory was a part of the curriculum was taken as a burden rather than a missionary work.

While examining the facts reported by the organisers of RSS from the ex-student volunteers of some high schools they stated their feelings on their participation in the literacy programme before the investigator, which is presented below :

(a) The ex-volunteer of Udit Nagar, Govt. Girls High School informed that her parents didn't want that she go to the slum and teach the women. She also didn't like it. But since it was a part of SUPW scheme, there was no way out. Therefore, just before the examination she stopped going for literacy work and after examination question didn't arise to go for the same.

(b) A student volunteer of Town High School, Daily Market, Rourkela stated that she was really enjoying the company of the slum girls of her age. They were very much concerned about the student volunteers with regard to her teaching. But her parents were afraid of the slum environment as well as the academic career of their daughter. They didn't want that their daughter should waste her time in such type of activities rather than her own study. Therefore, just before the examination they refuse for the said work. After examination although she was interested for further literacy work, she was not allowed by her parents to go to the slum alone. Otherwise, she would have definitely continued her teaching.

(c) Another volunteer who was from Nayabazar NAC High School, Sector-21 stated that there was no problem or objection from her parent's side. Since she herself lives nearer to the slum areas of Nayabazar, there was no problem of going alone to the centre. But her health did not permit her to go for literacy work due to frequent attack of asthma. Otherwise, she was also interested to do such social activity for a great came.

Further, it is also important to note that the motivated girls volunteers went to the field for a short period in a day, and many times their stay at the field became unproductive due to the timely non-availability of their learners. They used to lose half of their time for getting the learners assembled at a place. An activist of RSS who has rejoined the programme after a gap of six years reported this. This problem of timely non-availability of learners (in case of the researcher neo-literates) was also collection. She has observed that after fixing up time with the neo-literate slum women they were not available in the slum at the fixed time due to their struggle for livelihood and other problems. Therefore, the researcher could better realise the situation of the volunteers in this regard.

However, from the statement of the reporters, it can be interpreted that pressure of the parents, lack of proper motivation, burden of examination, illness of the volunteers, prolong time duration of the literacy programme and non-availability of learners were the factors played their due roles for dropping-out of the volunteers (girls) during the peak period of the teaching-learning process which affected badly and demotivated to the women learners of the concerned slums.

Caste Hierarchy and Group Conflicts

It was reported by the teaching volunteers in the slums that the intra-slum interaction of women learners remained restricted with regard to caste hierarchy and group conflicts. Though RSS tried to increase intra-slum interaction by organising different types of intra-slum activities along the limitations persisted as the tribals, the non-tribals and muslims were hesitant in mixing with each other. Therefore, non-tribal learners were not ready to go for learning and *vice-versa.* Even women from the same caste/religion were hesitant to go to another's house due to group conflicts and community feelings. This feeling of caste hierarchy and group conflicts were found during the 1st phase of literacy programme in some slums like Orampara, Dhipatoli, Gangadhar Palli, Narla Road etc. But these feelings were substantially lowered down in the Post-Literacy Phase.

While interviewing the volunteers and neo-literates of Oram-para and Gangadhar Palli stated that during the initial stage of teaching and learning activities some caste and religion hierarchy

and group conflict. They were even able to insist and motivate the guardians of the slum learners to raise voice against intra- slum caste/religion assimilation. But the situations were boldly handled by the grass-root level women volunteers with the help of RSS organisers and other social workers in concerned slums.

While interviewing the neo-literate slum women of Dhipatoli and Narla Road they revealed that 'since they were guided by their guardians in the families they didn't dare to go against their will'. Further, they revealed that they were not much aware about the evils of casteism and group conflicts in the long run. So they were hesitant to mix with each other. But after joining this programme and participating in various literacy activities this feeling is lower down and now they are working in the group despite caste, religion, age and economic status. The investigator has also found it by observing their activities and behaviour in various situations in the slums.

Frequent Migration (In Flow and Outflow of Population from the Slum)

The floating population of Rourkela city is about 20% which has found to have the tendency of relapsing into illiteracy. Due to frequent migration of the slum-dwellers from the city to another place for livelihood, a very good number of women had to leave their learning in between. It was also reported that in many slums new illiterate women have placed those who were in the process of learning, which caused serious constraints to the RSS organisers in organising the teaching classes once again for them.

The situation of migration became precarious during the completion of RSP modernisation in 1995, when most of the temporary workers migrated from Rourkela city between 1995-1998.

This was reported by the organisers and activists of RMS (Rourkela Majdoor Sangha), Labour Organisations and some of the Union Leaders and workers. She found the information gathered from RSS was cent per cent true and learned that not only the labourers (both male and female) but also the people involved in small business of RSP and other sister organisations have left the city during this period of modernisation, which affected badly the teaching-learning process of literacy programme.

Temptation and Expectations of Volunteers

A good number of volunteers started becoming critical about the campaign when the teaching-learning activities were halfway through. They went to the extent of campaigning against the literacy programme. Because they were under the impression that their involvement in the process especially in teaching the illiterates might bring some benefit (financial and job opportunity) in future. Since it is a purely voluntary and dedicated service, the literacy volunteers (both male and female) didn't find it alluring for future prospects. Their temptation and expectation did not materialise. Thereby the literacy volunteers and activists showed dissatisfaction and discouraged others. A few of them even started writing anonymous letters to the parents of the students volunteers stating the negative aspects of the active involvement of their girls in the campaign. As a result, parents of the students specially the girls started persuading their daughters to withdraw themselves from the campaign. This was informed by some sincere MTs of the concerned high schools where the students were reading. This information was also cross-checked from the organisers of RSS. Further, the recorded documents of the parents in this regard verified and found this as a fact. After a careful study of the records and interviewing the organisers and volunteers of RSS, it was felt by the investigator that such volunteers or activists without being properly self-motivated joined the campaign out of expectation or pressure from their authorities or administration. They become the constraints of the Literacy Programme that too in the peak

period of teaching-learning process. So more attention should have been given by the RSS organisers to motivate the volunteers/activists in a better way so as to make their participation meaningful.

Lighting Facilities

While enquiring about the light arrangement in the literacy centres for teaching, it was reported by the organisers and volunteers that they have not faced any major constraints for the light arrangement in the learning centres, as there was no need of light for the afternoon centres. And for the evening and late evening classes arrangements were made in the form of lanterns and electric wire and bulbs to the centres. But it was clearly told by the RSS organisers to the learners from the beginning that they would not be provided kerosene. Therefore, kerosene was to be arranged by the learners with the help of slum-dwellers or by contributing something of their own. This was informed by the volunteers of the respective slum areas and even the neo-literate slum women. The organisers of RSS reported before the investigator that arrangement of kerosene could have been made by RSS for a certain period. But this was only a temporary arrangement. Since the active involvement of people and the community with the process (literacy movement) was equally important, RSS provided an opportunity to the people to contribute their best for their own development.

It was also reported by some of the organisers and the neo-literates that the evening centres, which were especially running in the residences of the working slum women were mostly managed by themselves. Some of them even denied receiving lantern or electric wire and bulb. Information with regard to light arrangement for teaching was cross-checked with the neo-literate slum women in the field. Their responses regarding the above stated light arrangement is presented below in Table 5.5.

TABLE 5.5
Response of the Neo-literate Slum Women on Arrangement of Light in their Centres for Teaching-Learning Activities (No=34)

Sr. No.	*Types of Light Facilities Provided by RSS to the Literacy Centre*	*Nos. of Respondents Availed*	*Percentage*
1.	Electric wire, bulb etc.	12	35.29
2.	Lantern	13	38.24
3.	Managed by their own	09	26.47
	Total Nos. of Slum Women in the evening and night classes	34	100.00

It can be interpreted from the above stated table that majority of the slum women (73.53%) have availed of the light facilities provided by RSS to the evening and night centres during literacy programme in the form of lantern, electric wire and bulb. Whereas a meagre percentage (26.47%) of respondents have not availed the facilities as the teaching-learning centres were functioning at their own residences, which proves that the statement of the organisers and volunteers regarding light arrangement of RSS was true.

Monitoring of Literacy Centres and Evaluation of Learning

The level of literacy visualised through the literacy programme was made known to all participants and volunteers during training. Accordingly, a neo-literate person should have acquired the expected proficiency in reading, writing and numeracy skills. Along with this he should have developed his/her level of awareness concerning the various aspects of life and social issues of the

society. At the same time, qualitative changes in behaviour and positive attitude towards life were also expected.

Keeping in view the above things in operation, the RSS organised a systematic monitoring, information and supervision net-working through its interaction programme by the central and zonal level monitoring team consisting of KRPs, MTs, members of the GB and working group, etc. MTs and area coordinators visited and supervised the literacy classes under their own areas and made systematic report of each literacy centre. The zone co-ordinators were monitoring the overall literacy activities of their respective zones and supervising the work of area co-ordinators. They were also taking care of different types of environment building and other developmental activities under their zones.

The central monitoring team visited and supervised literacy classes, monitored environment building and other developmental activities, interacted with the learners and the slum-dwellers. The central monitoring team prepared detailed report and presented before the weekly meeting of the core group for discussion and necessary remedial measures of the literacy programme.

During the post-literacy phase the system of monitoring and information services extended. Along with monitoring and supervision of the literacy activities, intensive interaction with the slum-dwellers especially the women and neo-literates was given priority. During this P.L. Phase, the concept of area-co-ordinator and zone-co-ordinator was also changed and the concept of sevak, sevika and co-ordinator of Chetana Kendra were introduced. The zone-co-ordinators and other senior activists (mainly the KRPs and resource persons) those who have sustained in the campaign were turned into core group members of RSS.

The core group had to monitor the activities of the Chetana Kendras, interact with the neo-literates and slum-dwellers through group discussion, and to understand their educational needs and areas of interest for further development. Accordingly, they were given guidelines to the co-ordinators and members of Chetana Kendras in planning and executing programmes especially for the sustainable development of women, neo-literates and children.

During the first phase of literacy programme internal evaluation work (mid-term) was entrusted mainly with the volunteers and area co-ordinators. They were to conduct the evaluation only in the presence of external examiners like MTs, KRPs or member of monitoring team etc. The volunteers were given training to evaluate learners. The evaluation of learning standard was made through T-1 to T-9 included in the literacy primers. A good number of women volunteers, MTs and KRPs were entrusted to monitor the evaluation of women learners especially in the Muslim and Bihari Slums like Narla Road and Hasanpur, and also for the housewives of conservative families.

The area co-ordinators were not only helping their best to the volunteers in evaluating the performances of the learners, but also in assisting the monitoring work of the monitoring team.

While enquiring about the mid-term evaluation of the P.L. Phase of the literacy programme, it was reported by the organisers of RSS (mainly the Secretary, controller and some of the senior activists) that the mid-term evaluation of the PL Phase was not undertaken by RSS because of its non-receipt of any guideline either from the NLM or from the Director of Mass Education, Government of Orissa for the same.

They informed that without waiting for the government order, the RSS has initiated several remedial and corrective measures of its own from time to time on the basis of the MIS reports. The major corrective measures were :

(i) Emphasis on vocational training and income generation activities for the neo-literate girls and women.

(ii) Provision of education (NFE) for the children of the neo-literates and the slum-dwellers.

(iii) Organising different training programme for the neo-literate and slum women like Mahila Jagruti Talim, safe Motherhood training, family counselling, training on legal rights of the women in the families and society etc.

(iv) Interaction and group discussion with the slum-dwellers especially women and emphasis was given on girls' education and on their economic development.

The senior volunteers and organisers of RSS reported that they would have done much more extensive work during the P.L. Phase. But due to some major constraints MIS networking of RSS was badly affected.

CONSTRAINTS

Inadequate Number of Volunteers

It was reported by the organisers of RSS and also observed by the investigator in the field that the volunteers associated with RSS were found to be inadequate in number to monitor the P.L. activities due to long span since 1992 to 2000. Therefore, it has become a serious problem to RSS in monitoring the activities of Chetana Kendras very frequently. The large number of volunteers (about 13,000) involved from the outset of literacy programme to work in 196 slum areas of Rourkela, could not sustain over the years. Only about 400 volunteers of all types have sustained in the campaign and are looking after 102 Chetana Kendras and P.L. Centres. Out of 400 volunteers, only about 40 senior level activists of RSS could monitor each Chetana Kendra after a gap of one or one-and-half month only. As a result literacy programme during P.L. Phase faced a shortage of sincere volunteers and this is responsible for the inactiveness of some of the Chetana Kendras of concerned slums.

It was also found that many of the volunteers gave up because of their feeling of neglected by the RSS organisers and thereby left the campaign. However, the limited volunteers and activists sustained in the RSS, were found to be working with a missionary zeal.

Problems of Vehicles

It was reported by the organisers of RSS that vehicle problem has become one of the major constraints for monitoring and interaction work of RSS during P.L. Phase. In the first phase of literacy programme monitoring work was smoothly done due to availability of vehicles. Two jeeps, two auto-rickshaws and one moped were especially meant for literacy work. But since there was no provision (financial) to hire more vehicles for literacy work during P.L. Phase, RSS was handicapped in providing adequate vehicles to its volunteers for the said purpose. It (RSS) could hire and afford only one vehicle. Therefore, it was not possible on the part of RSS volunteers to go to each slum every day for monitoring and interaction. The data related to the nos. of vehicles provided by organisers of RSS were cross-validated from the records and documents of RSS. It was also cross checked from the grass-root level volunteers, neo-literates and other slum-dwellers with regard to the frequent use of vehicle for monitoring purpose during first phase of literacy programme.

With regard to the monitoring and supervision of literacy activities and Chetana Kendras during Total literacy and post literacy phase, the investigator examined the stated information from the slum women that now often the team visited their slums to monitor the literacy activities of Chetana Kendras. Their responses in this regard have been presented in Table 5.6.

TABLE 5.6
Response of the Neo-literate Slum Women Regarding Monitoring Network of RSS (N=103)

Sl. No.	*Frequency of Monitoring*	*No. of Respondents*	*Percentage*
1.	Frequently monitored (both in TL and PL Phase)	18	17.48
2.	Not at all monitored (Both in TL and PL Phase)	—	—
3.	Negligibly monitored (Both in TL and PL Phase)	27	26.21
4.	Frequently monitored at TL Phase, but negligible at PL Phase	49	47.57
5.	Frequently monitored during PL Phase, but negligible at TL Phase	09	08.74
	Total No. of Respondents	103	100.00

It is evident from the above table that monitoring was systematically done during TL Phase but was negligible to a great extent during PL Phase. Despite proper monitoring in TL Phase some of the slum areas were not properly monitored. Further, despite negligible monitoring during PL Phase, the post literacy activities of certain Chetana Kendras were properly monitored. It might have happened due to the special attention of some of the sincere volunteers in their respective slums.

The activities of monitoring and interaction team as reported by the organisers were cross-checked in the field from the slum women by the investigator during interview. Their response in this regard is presented below in Table 5.7.

TABLE 5.7
Response of the Neo-literate Slum Women about the Activities of Monitoring Team (N=103)

Sl. No.	*Activities of Monitoring Team*	*Nos. of Respondents*	*Percentage*
1.	Just coming and seeing the teaching-learning activities of the centre.	26	25.24
2.	Supervise the activities of the volunteers.	24	23.30
3.	See the teaching-learning activities, discuss with the volunteers and other members of Chetana Samities regarding the overall development of Chetana Kendras and neo-literates specially the women and the children.	53	51.46
	Total Nos. of respondents	103	100.00

It is evident from the above table that the monitoring team laid much emphasis on discussions with the volunteers and members of Chetana Samities for the development of Chetana Kendras and the neo-literates, especially the slum women and children than only to supervise the teaching classes or to monitor and supervise the activities of the volunteers.

The investigator during her field visit has observed and participated in the discussions made by the members of monitoring team with the volunteers and the slum people *i.e.* the members of Chetana Kendras and the neo-literates. It is experienced by her that their level of discussions were not confined to teaching-learning and related activities, rather, they have discussed on different social issues, developmental schemes, schooling for children, skill development and income generation and so on. The participants specially the women took part in those discussions quite actively. The role of monitoring team in breaking the culture of silence among the slum-dwellers specially the women were really appreciable.

Provision of Non-formal Education

It was informed by the Chairman, Secretary and some of the Senior activists of RSS during interview that they have faced critical problems when neo-literate parents especially the women continued pressing and demanding education for their children (5–14 years) in formal schools. On their demand more than 700 children were accommodated into different Primary Schools during 1992, more than 400 in 1993 and about 400 during 1994 by the efforts of RSS. Despite the enrolment of a very good number of slum children in different formal schools, an attractive number of children were deprived from schooling. Because the RSP (Rourkela Steel Plant) schools did not allow the admission of non-RSP children despite the fact that seats in RSP schools remained vacant and that the municipality schools have limited seats and already over enrolled from the very beginning of the academic session. The RSS tried its best to cope with the problems by requesting the state government to open at least 5 primary schools for these educationally deprived slum children but could not succeed. Therefore, as a preventive measure of becoming adult illiterates, on the demand of the neo-literate slum-dwellers, specially the women, RSS made efforts in opening 50 Non-formal Education Centres through its Chetana Kendras as a part of Post Literacy Programme in different slums which were sanctioned by Government of India during April,1995. These 50 NFE centres took care of 1260 children who were deprived of primary education. These children were mostly working children, and 60% of them were girls.

It is important to mention here that these 50 NFE centres were also found to be insufficient for the children of neo-literates, as there were 102 Chetana Kendras covering 196 slums under 12 Literacy Zones. However, after opening of the NFE centres by RSS, many a children of the slum-dwellers enrolled in NFE centres of the concerned Chetana Kendras. While, some others enrolled in Formal Schools through RSS. Despite this effort some good number of children of various slums remained deprived from their basic educational rights. As a result, the slum-dwellers especially the women showed dissatisfaction and discouraged others, which had a negative affect in organising people for further activities in the concerned slums.

The investigator verified the reports RSS organisers with regard to their trial for the opening of Primary Schools, from the correspondence records of the Chairman, RSS cum ADM Rourkela and got confirmed.

She further cross-checked their statements from the neo-literate slum women in the field. While interviewing to a neo-literate mother, of a school deprived child, she (the mother) stated :

"Every body is talking about the schooling of our children. As if there are mushroom growth of schools in Ambagan Market (famous market in sector township of Rourkela city). Despite my hardship, I was ready to send my daughter for her schooling. But where should I send ? HSL School, or NAC school ?"

Replied the frustrated mother. She further stated that,

"I had already purchased a new frock for my daughter to send her to the school. When we went to the ILS school (Ispat Lower Secondary) the master told us that only the children of Steel

Plant Employees will be enrolled there. While going to the NAC school it was already filled up. Where should have I gone for the admission of my child ? There is no NFE centre in our basti (slum). The existing one (NFE centre) located in another basti is far from this place. I made my child understand a lot and despite distance send her to the centre. But after some days she stopped going, because the centre was not a school of her choice. I thought, that my daughter will not be a Reja (woman labourer) like me. At least she will receive education and will do something better than me. But it did not happen".

After collecting information through interviewing the dissatisfied mother the investigator visited the said NAC school of Rourkela and enquired about the student position of the school. It was stated by the Head Master of the school that due to shortage of resources they were facing a lot many problems in the school. So they cannot extend another sections. He informed that already there were more than seventy students (over-enrolled) in the class. So further additional admission in the middle of the session would not be possible. The investigator has also carefully observed the student's position and infrastructure facilities of municipality schools. She had the experiences of other municipality schools of Rourkela in the same line and understood the limitations of the Head Master. At the same time she could feel and understand the genuine frustration of the neo-literate mother who visualised a better quality of life for her child through education, which is the basic social right of each and every child as human being.

Activities in the NFE Centre

During her field visit, the investigator personally visited all the NFE centres and interacted with the children and instructors. She observed the teaching and other activities of some NFE centres minutely along with the other activities of the Chetana Kendras. The teaching-learning process that she has observed was found to be satisfactory to a great extent. The other activities of the centre like organising sports, and games, organising cultural programme Bal Sabha (children's meeting), different types of competitions among the children like drawing and spot painting, song, fancy dress, debate competition and Bal Mela (children's fair) at slum level, children exchange programme etc. were really note worthy. It could be undoubtedly said that the NFE classes of RSS were based on "Joy of Learning" principle and highly appreciable.

Constraints Faced by NFE Instructors

While interviewing to a literacy volunteer-cum-NFE instructor with regard to the problems faced by her in managing NFE class, she revealed that initially (during 1995) there was less co-operation from the people's side. Many of them were not coming forward for the enrolment of their children in the NFE centre, because they were in demand of schooling of their children in formal schools. Since NFE centres were mainly functioning in the verandas or living rooms of the instructor or in the Mahila Samitis of UBS and Chetana Kendras due to shortage of accommodation, they thought (some of them) that NFE centres were inferior to formal schools, and teaching-learning activities were also not up to the mark like the teaching-learning of formal schools. But after some days when they observed the teaching-learning activities of the centres which were interesting and even better in certain aspect than the municipality schools, they started sending their children to the centres. Even the children who went to the formal schools were also send to the centres in evening hours. Hence, the slum-dwellers themselves started extending their co-operation to the volunteers in organising the children, arranging accommodation during rainy season, assisting the instructors in celebrating different national days as well as puja, functions etc.

Despite their satisfaction on teaching-learning activities of NFE centres, they felt dissatisfied and frustrated due to lack of basic amenities like schooling (formal), medical facilities, ration card, BPL card, drinking water, electricity, etc., which created a feeling of negligence and inferiority among them that since they were slum-dwellers with low socio-economic status they were being looked down by the high level officers, and even the government. Otherwise, schooling facilities for children would have definitely been provided to them by starting schools in their slums.

Skill Development and Income-generation Training for Neo-literate Slum Women

Mere literacy may not provide bread to the neo-literates. To make literacy functional, the RSS has organised several training programmes on vocational skills and income generation especially for the women during post literacy phase through the Shramik Vidyapeeth of Rourkela, which has been extending pivotal support to RSS from its very inception. The following training programmes mentioned below in table 5.8 have been conducted during the post literacy phase for the neo-literate women of the slum areas of Rourkela:

TABLE 5.8
Number of Skill Development and Income-generation Training Programmes of RSS Through Shramik Vidyapeeth (SVP)

Year	*Sl. No.*	*Types of Training Programme*	*No. of Times*
July 1992 to March 2000	1.	Tailoring	15
	2.	Applique work	04
	3.	Embroidary (both hand and machine)	08
	4.	Hand wool knitting	04
	5.	Fabric painting	04
	6.	Door mat making	03
	7.	Rakhi making	17
	8.	Greetings card making	11
	9.	Fruits and vegetables preservation	18
	10.	Squash and sauce making	08
	11.	Pickle and papad making	08
	12.	Cake and biscuit making	13
	13.	Mushroom cultivation	08
	14.	Candle making	04
	15.	Mehandi application	04
	16.	Safe motherhood training (Since,1998)	02
	17.	Health and nutrition (Since, 1998)	02
	18.	Hygiene and sanitation (since 1998)	02
	19.	Mobile library service	08
	20.	Family counselling and legal rights (Since,1997)	03

It is seen from the Table 5.8 that a good number of training on skill development and income generation has been undertaken by RSS with the help of SVP during P.L. Phase to make the neo-literate slum women trained and skilled to add to their family income as well as save some expenditure.

The above stated skill development and income generation training programme as reported by the organisers of RSS, was cross-validated by the investigator from the neo-literate slum women as to what extent they participated in these training programmes. The responses of the neo-literate slum women revealed that most of them (about 80%, i.e. 82 out of 103) did participate in the said training programme of different types.

Constraints Faced by Neo-literates and Organisers

It was reported by the organisers of RSS and the slum women to the investigator that after receiving income generation and skill development training from SVP, the slum women of various areas have formed groups of 10-15 neo-literates to produce the items in which they had received training. They also earned some amount by making rakhi, greeting cards, food articles, doormats, applique and wall-hangings, mehendi application, etc. In spite of their production of good quality items, they were unable to market properly due to financial crisis, lack of marketing experience and exposure and advertisement in the competition market like other organised professional groups (such as, Gruhasti and Gruha Laxmi etc.) Therefore, they market their items in the exhibitions, fairs and door-to-door pushing, which has become very difficult on their part to do. As a result some of the women groups have become demotivated to continue their income generation activities further. They have also reported that regarding these marketing facilities and financial supports in the form of incentives, loans, support of materials like sewing-machine, etc., RSS has never provided the things to the neo-literates. Even the Government or NGO sectors never come forward to help these poor and neglected women. It was noticed by the investigator that if prompt action in this regard is not taken from any quarter for the neo-literate slum women, the entire effort of RSS for the skill development will be rendered meaningless and a waste.

Other Constraints Faced by RSS Organisers

During the course of discussion with the RSS Chairman, Secretary, Controller and other senior activists of RSS they informed to the investigator that the campaign would have touched the peak of success. But due to certain major constraints other than the ones mentioned above under different headings, it could not touch the peak as they expected. The constraints became so severe that it affected to the success of the campaign in its peak period. The constraints were mainly the over ambition of the neo-literates and lack of developmental schemes of Government and NGO support for the slum-dwellers.

Over Ambition of the Neo-literates

(1) Gap Between Expectation and Hard Realities

The most serious problem of literacy programme faced by the RSS organisers was when a huge gap between the expectation of the neo-literates and the hard realities they encountered emerging. There is no doubt of the fact that literacy programme has brought about many far reaching changes in the life of the neo-literates. But it is also a fact that they have become over ambitious and more demanding after becoming literate, which was not possible to fulfill by the organisers or even by the Chairman RSS cum ADM Rourkela due to his own limitations. They were also not ready to understand the limitations of the organisers of RSS. Because they were under the impression that their involvement in the literacy programme as learner would help them in availing their basic civic rights (basic amenities) through the local administrator, who is also the RSS Chairman. Therefore, they joined the programme in large number as learners. It caused serious problems when the women learners in particularly started reaching govt. offices in organised groups and started demanding civic facilities like ration card, drinking water, medical facilities, electricity and schools for their children, etc. But when these basic amenities remained out of their reach, only because of their unauthorised occupancy in the Govt. land/RSP land as slum, the neo-literate who visualised better quality of life through participation in literacy programme and it development activities became frustrated. Some of them even started non-co-operation with the organisers while organising activities. They also tried to demotivate the others who were left-out, dropout learners to participate in the programme further. This frustration of the slum women put the organisers in severe troubles.

(2) Assurance of the High Level Government Officials

Further, it is a fact that RSS organised various income-generation and skill development training programme which raised the expectations of the neo-literate slum women. But the types of incentives and supports such as loan and marketing facilities, support of materials like sewing-machines, etc. They expected from the RSS and government which could not be provided to them. They expected those things because some of the high level govt. officials of the state and national level during their visit to Rourkela literacy campaign declared to provide incentives like sewing-machines, and some other facilities to those who have participated very actively and have achieved out standing performance in both literacy and awareness. These types of incentives and supports were out of reach for the RSS to provide to the neo-literate women. Hence, a sense of demotivation and depression generated among the women learners and they lost their enthusiasm for further participation in the literacy programme.

While examining the above information of the RSS organisers from two demotivated neo-literate slum women they stated : "before joining this literacy programme they were happy with their ignorance and misery. They thought that after being literate their conditions would change and they would be treated well by others, but, it was not so. Before joining this programme they were ignorant. Therefore, they know nothing about the rights and facilities made available to the people in the society. But when they came to know about their rights and facilities they were ignored by others, especially the government and government officers. Their problems and sufferings were not heard by the leaders and administrators". These were expressed by the demotivated respondents of RSS with regard to fulfilment of their basic amenities before the investigator.

The investigator could feel and understand the emotional turbulence of the slum women. But at the same time she could also realise the limitations of the RSS organisers and the Chairman. However, whoever may be the officials, at no point of time should have assured to provide such incentive and supports to those socio-economically dejected slum women. Unnecessarily it created problems for the organisers to mobilise and organise the work further.

Lack of Developmental Schemes of Government and NGO Support for the Slum-dwellers in Rourkela

It was informed by the RSS organisers to the investigator that most of the development programmes and schemes of Govt. were meant for the people of rural and tribal areas. Only limited socio-economic development programmes were for the poor people of urban areas. The local administration was therefore handicapped in providing such facilities to the majority of neo-literates, specially the women.

The Chairman of RSS in this regard also clearly showed his limitations in providing such facilities like loan, subsidy, etc., as an administrator. He stated that despite his limitations he had tried his level best to help the neo-literates in many ways. Since there were not many developmental schemes from the government for them, he could not introduce any scheme of his own. In fact, without policy decision at government level schemes cannot be implemented for urban poor.

While discussing with the Secretary of RSS with regard to the implementation of developmental schemes of the non-governmental organisations (NGOs) for the poor people he stated that theirs is an important role of NGOs in providing supportive services to the people under-developmental programme like literacy, etc. But, unfortunately this was lacking in Rourkela city. He further stated that the NGOs which existed in Rourkela were not in a position to provide supportive services due to their rural or tribal-based objectives and activities which were not appropriate and applicable for the slum-dwellers of Rourkela city. Hence, RSS could not involve the NGOs in the literacy programme and managed it largely by itself.

CONCLUSION

From the above discussion and analysis of a varieties of data mentioned in each heading of this chapter with regard to the activities and efforts made by RSS and constraints faced by its organisers it can be concluded that,

(1) Rourkela Saksharata Samiti has made sincere efforts and organised adequate number of activities for the educational development of the slum women with the help of a group of dedicated volunteers and activists, and organisations like Shramik Vidyapeeth etc.

The efforts and activities were:

(i) Environment building and motivational.

(ii) Literacy survey and re-survey.

(iii) Preparation and distribution of learning materials.

(iv) Training Programmes for volunteers and participants.

(v) Teaching-learning among the learners.

(vi) Lighting facilities,

(vii) Monitoring of the literacy centres and evaluation of the learners.

(viii) Provision of Non-formal Education for the children of the neo-literate.

(ix) Skill development and income generation training programme for neo-literate slum women.

(2) While organising those activities, the organisers and functionaries of RSS have faced a lot many constraints as follows :

(i) Lack of accommodation for teaching-learning activities and Chetana Kendra.

(ii) No common timing for teaching-learning activities.

(iii) Dropping-out of school volunteers.

(iv) Caste hierarchy and group conflicts.

(v) Frequent migration of slum-dwellers.

(vi) Temptation and expectation of volunteers.

(vii) Problems of vehicles for monitoring and interaction.

(viii) Shortage of volunteers for monitoring.

(ix) Over ambition of the neo-literate slum women.

(x) Lack of developmental schemes of Government and NGO support for the slum-dwellers.

(3) Despite a number of serious constraints due to considerable negligence of government in implementing different types of development programmes and schemes for urban poor in general and slum women in particular, a group of dedicated activists of RSS have tried their best to carry forward the activities of the literacy programme so as to achieve the success.

The success of the literacy programme through its level of impact expected from the neo-literate slum women has been analysed and interpreted in Chapter 6.

6

Impact of Literacy Programme on Neo-literate Slum Women

INTRODUCTION

In the present chapter an attempt has been made to analyse the impact of literacy programmes on slum women *vis-a-vis* : *(i)* Level of Literacy developed in 3 Rs., i.e. Reading, Writing and Numeracy. *(ii)* Level of awareness developed with regard to family welfare, small family norms and various issues related to health and sanitation, child and maternity care, environment protection, etc. *(iii)* Changing attitudes towards evils of dowry, early marriage, alcohol, superstition etc., raising voice against exploitation and taking interest for social welfare. *(iv)* Enrolment of their children in formal schools and other systems of education like Angan-wadi and NFE centres.

Further, attempts have been made in this chapter to find out the factors responsible for the outstanding performance in literacy skills as well as development of high level of awareness and social participation among two of the respondents who have been selected as cases to be studied.

The objective no. 3 which is to study the impact of literacy programme was carried out with the help of achievement tests, interview schedules, questionnaires, observation, case study and in-depth discussion on the educational development of the neo-literate slum women. A number of 103 neo-literate slum women from 16 different slums of Rourkela city were chosen for the study. Their responses have been analysed, interpreted and discussed in this chapter. The factors responsible for the high level of achievement both in literacy and awareness of the neo-literate slum women (case studies) about which the mention has already made above, are also presented in this chapter. Two neo-literate slum women from two different slums have been selected on the basis of their achievement out of the total sample and their cases were studied for the said purpose.

SOCIAL CHARACTERISTICS OF THE RESPONDENTS

Before going to analyse the responses of the respondents with regard to the impact of literacy programme a brief description about their social characteristics and background are presented here below.

Age

It is observed that respondents were chosen from the age group 15-50 years. Although the target group for the programme was from 10 to 60 years, none of the participants were below 15 years and above. It must be mentioned here that RSS has not confined its effort to imparting literacy mostly to NLM prescribed target group beneficiaries of 15 to 35 years. Rather RSS has tried to cover the age group 10 to 60 years. But it was observed that beneficiaries mostly from 15 to 50 years have joined the programmes in a large number. The details of the distribution of sample neo-literate slum women according to their age group are presented below in Table 6.1.

TABLE 6.1
Distribution of Neo-literate Slum Women According to their Age Group

Age group	*No. of Neo-literate Slum Women*	*Percentage*
15–25	45	43.69
26–35	41	39.85
36–50	17	16.67
Total	103	100

Caste/Community

Caste/Community background of the beneficiaries revealed that Schedule Tribes represented 36 in number, Schedule Caste consisted of 24, General Caste represented 22, other backward caste made of 12 and only 9 represented the Muslim community. Table 6.2 deals with the caste/ community wise distribution of the neo-literate slum women in details.

TABLE 6.2
Distribution of Neo-literate Slum Women According to their Caste/Community Background

Caste/Community Background	*No. of Neo-literate Slum Women*	*Percentage*
Schedule Tribe	36	34.95
Schedule Caste	24	23.30
General Caste	22	21.36
Other Backward Caste	12	11.65
Muslim	09	8.74
Total	103	100

Earning/Non earning Status

About the earning and non-earning status of sample members it was found that 48 (46.6%) respondents were engaged in household work. Out of these women 03 (2.93%) were doing voluntary social work for their slum along with their own household work. Rest of the 55 (53.40%) respondents were engaged in various occupations and income generation activities like maid-servant both on part-time and full-time basis, contract labourer and daily wage earner, rag and iron bit picker in dumping yard of RSP, very small scale business of their own like selling of papad, pickle, biscuit, Indian biscuit, (mudhi) and other food items like, egg, vegetable, etc., some of the respondents were cultivating and selling green-leaf vegetable and some were engaged as helper in Anganwadi of ICDS project. Even some of them were earning by doing mehandi application during marriage season and different festivals, making greetings cards embroidery, applique and tailoring work during various occasions, making rakhee and the detail of the distribution of neo-literate slum women according to their occupational status is presented in the Table 6.3.

TABLE 6.3
Distribution of the Neo-literate Slum Women According to their Earning and Non-earning Background

Back-ground	*No. of Neo-literate Slum-Women*	*Percentage*
Earning	55	53.40
Non-earning	48	46.60
Total	103	100

Marital Status

It is revealed from the collected data that 71 (68.93%) respondents were married, 30 (29.13%) were unmarried, 01 (.97%) was a widow and 01 (.97%) was a divorcee.

IMPACT OF LITERACY PROGRAMME ON SLUM WOMEN

Level of Literacy–Reading, Writing and Numeracy

The Literacy programme of Rourkela Saksharata Samiti (RSS) aims at *inter alias* of imparting knowledge about the three R's, i.e. Reading, Writing and Numeracy and to develop the level of awareness to the identified illiterates of the slum areas in general and women in particular.

The NLM criteria of achieving proficiency in literacy skills have been followed by the investigator in rating their performances in the form of grades like excellent, very-good, good, poor and very poor.

The gradation based on NLM guidelines for the evaluation study of the literacy programme stipulated that when a neo-literate obtained excellent in total grades and at least good grade in reading, writing, and numeracy, then he/she is assumed to have achieved NLM norms of treating him/her as successful in achieving the proficiency level.

Grades obtained by the neo-literate slum women in each literacy skill through the achievement test have been presented in the tables below and interpretations have been made accordingly.

Reading

TABLE 6.4
Distribution of the Neo-literate Slum Women According to Total Grades Obtained in Reading

Grades Assigned	*No. of Slum Women Tested*	*Percentage*
Excellent	17	16.50
Very Good	34	33.00
Good	42	40.78
Poor	10	9.72
Very Poor		—
Total	103	100

It is evident from the Table 6.4 that most of the (90.28%) neo-literate slum women have achieved the expected proficiency in reading. Further it can be observed that almost half of the neo-literates (49.5%) have achieved excellent and very good grades and 40.78% have achieved the good grade rating in reading. Even a meagre percentage (9.72%) of slum women who have obtained poor grade were also found to be close to achieving the success. Mention may be made here that before the launching of literacy programme, the slum women of Rourkela in general know nothing about reading. The slum women themselves have reported to the investigator during their in depth discussion that they have learnt to read, write and compute after joining the programme. In Narla Road Muslim slum the slum women have also informed to the researcher that only two (out of nine respondents) could hardly recognise some words of "Kuran" in Arabic Language before joining the programme. Now, they are not only reading the P.L. Primers and other supplementary literature, but also reading the newspaper, Saksharata Samachar and many other books regularly.

It can be said that the level of achievement as emerged from the table showed very significant outcome of the slum women in reading and also a sizeable percentage of unsuccessful slum women would achieve a level of reading proficiency in course of time. So the programme for the slum women was very successful as it has a good impact in terms of reading.

TABLE 6.5

Performance of the Neo-literate Slum Women in Reading as per their Age Group

Sl. No.	*Grades Assigned*	*No. of Slum Women*			*Total*
		15-25	*26-35*	*36-50*	
1.	Excellent	8 (17.78)	6 (14.63)	3 (17.65)	17 (16.51)
2.	Very good	18 (40.00)	10 (24.39)	6 (35.29)	34 (33.00)
3.	Good	17 (37.78)	20 (48.78)	5 (29.41)	42 (40.78)
4.	Poor	2 (4.45)	5 (12.19)	3 (7.65)	10 (9.71)
5.	Very Poor	—	—	—	—
	Total	45 (100)	41 (100)	17 (100)	103 (100)

Note : Figures within parentheses indicate percentages.

Data presented in the Table 6.5 reveals that the neo-literate slum women in general, have achieved out standing proficiency in reading. However, the young respondents of age group 15-25 had shown extremely satisfactory results than the older two groups. This might be because : *(i)* they might have no time-bound work inside and outside home, so that they could manage their household activities, to find out some time for study, *(ii)* they might be interested to know about the information of out side the city. Hence they took interest to read newspaper etc. regularly, or *(iii)* The motivational activities of the campaign that have highly charged the respondents of younger group to learn seriously. That counts a lot for their high achievement in reading.

In case of the relatively inferior achievement of the other two age groups (26-35 and 36-50 respectively) it might be due to: *(i)* They might have get relatively less scope in the family front to revise their lessons, *(ii)* they might not have been seriously internalised the essence of education in their day-to-day life, or *(iii)* though they have attended the classes, none might have encouraged or helped them in learning. All these factors must have influenced in achieving relatively inferior result among the older age groups in reading.

Further the table reveals that a meagre percentage of respondents (9.71%) from all the age groups were found to be unsuccessful in achieving proficiency by obtaining poor grades in reading. But it is also worth mentioning here that none of the respondents from all the three age groups have not obtained very poor grades which indicates that the respondents do have potencies, but due to some reasons they have not achieved the success. The causes might be : *(i)* They might have negative self-perception about them, *(ii)* they might like to spend their time as usual without any change in their life style, or *(iii)* they might not have realised the intrinsic values of education for their development. All these reasons might have affected in achieving success in reading. However, despite a wide difference of their level of achievement, their overall performance in reading was outstanding and shows a highly positive impact of RSS on the slum women of Rourkela.

TABLE 6.6
Performance of the Neo-literate Slum Women in Reading as per their Caste/ Community Background

Sl. No.	Grades Assigned	No. of Slum Women					Total
		ST Women	SC Women	GC Women	OBC Women	Muslim Women	
1.	Excellent	6(16.66)	3 (12.05)	5(22.73)	2(16.67)	1(11.11)	17(16.51)
2.	V. Good	12(33.33)	8(33.33)	4(18.18)	5(41.67)	5(55.55)	34(33.00)
3.	Good	15(41.67)	10(41.67)	11(50.0 0)	4(33.33)	2(22.23)	42(40.78)
4.	Poor	3(8.33)	3(12.05)	2(9.09)	1(8.33)	1(11.11)	10(9.71)
5.	V. Poor	—	—	—	—	—	—
	Total	36 (100.00)	24 (100.00)	22 (100.00)	12 (100.00)	9 (100.00)	103 (100.00)

Note : Figures within parentheses indicate percentages.

It can be viewed from the Table 6.6 that most of the (90.28%) slum women of all the groups of Caste/Community background have achieved a highly satisfactory result in reading. However, the ST and OBC slum women have performed relatively better than the other three counter groups, and the SC slum women have achieved comparatively inferior result than that of the other four groups of various Caste/Community. The reasons for the high achievement among the ST and OBC respondents might be due to : *(i)* as per their cultural background, they might have availed more freedom in utilising their leisure time in reading and revising lesson, *(ii)* they might have become conscious about their supressed condition and when they got the chance through literacy programme, they must have tried to compete to get higher status in the society. In case of the SC slum women for their relatively low achievement in reading, it might be due to : *(i)* the young volunteer might not have made the respondents properly understand the lessons of the Primers, *(ii)* they might have some personal problems related to their families during the peak period of learning, or *(iii)* they might not have time due to household activities to revise their lesson in the home. All these factors must have affected in achieving high results among the ST and OBC respondents and low results among the SC respondents in reading.

Further, the table shows that a very few percentage (9.71%) of respondents from all the Caste/ Community background have not achieved the proficiency level in reading. Further it is important to mention here that none of the respondents from any Caste/Community background have obtained very poor grade in reading. It indicates that the respondents of all the Caste/Community background do have inner potentials to achieve good grades and they have developed their interest for reading.

The non-achievement of success among the few respondents in reading might be due to : *(i)* they might not know about the intrinsic value of education in their lives; *(ii)* they might have negative self-perception, or *(iii)* they might have spent their leisure hour in gossiping with the neighbouring women without any change in their living condition. All these factors must have forced them to not to achieve success in reading. It is, therefore, not fair to draw a conclusion that the level of literacy achievement in reading was only due to the Caste/Community background of the respondents. It might be one of the factors, but not the whole. However, despite a difference between the achievement levels of the slum women of various Caste/Community background, their achievement in reading was outstanding. The outstanding results of the respondents reflect the highly satisfactory impact of RSS activities on the slum women of Rourkela.

TABLE 6.7

Performance of the Neo-literate Slum Women in Reading as per Their Earning/Non-earning Background

Sl. No.	*Grades Assigned*	*No. of Slum Women*		*Total*
		Earning	*Non-earning*	
1.	Excellent	10 (18.18)	7(15.58)	17 (16.50)
2.	Very Good	18 (32.73)	16 (33.33)	34 (33.00)
3.	Good	24 (43.64)	18 (37.5)	42 (40.78)
4.	Poor	3 (5.45)	7 (14.58)	10 (9.71)
5.	Very Poor	—	—	—
	Total	55 (100.00)	48 (100.00)	103(100.00)

Note : Figures with in Parentheses indicate percentages.

It is evident from the Table 6.7 that both the earning and non-earning slum women have shown high level of performance in reading. However, the earning respondents did better than the non-earning group. This might be due to : *(i)* the hidden potentialities of the respondents, *(ii)* they had been exposed in their occupations to variety of situations, *(iii)* it is their self-interest, which was in need of an opportunity to learn, or *(iv)* the sincere efforts made by the volunteers and effective environment building activities done by RSS. These might have aroused the desire in them to study sincerely. All these factors enabled them to achieve success in reading more than the non-earning members.

The non-earning members have also achieved good results in reading, which is in fact less than the earning slum women. It may be because : (1) they might not have been interested in learning than that of the earning group, (2) they might have felt tried and fatigued after daylong household work, or (3) might have some socio-personal problems that count for their relatively lower achievement than the earning slum women.

Further, a meagre percentage of sample slum women of both earning and non-earning categories have not been able to achieve the success. It gives a clue to guess that it might be due to their : *(i)* lack of keen interest and self-motivation for reading, *(ii)* serious illness and health hazards, or *(iii)* family problems. All these have forced the few slum women for not achieving the success in reading. Therefore, it is illogical to draw a conclusion that the level of literacy achievement in reading was only due to the earning status of the respondents. It might be one of the factors for their literacy achievement but not the whole. However, despite a wider difference between the achievement levels of the earning and non-earning slum women in reading, their result was highly satisfactory as no body was found to be very poor and very few as poor in reading. It can therefore be concluded that the literacy programme had a very highly positive impact on the neo-literate slum women.

Writing

TABLE 6.8
Distribution of the Neo-literate Slum Women According to Total Grades Obtained in Writing

Sl. No.	*Grades Assigned*	*No. of Slum Women Tested*	*Percentage*
1.	Excellent	12	11.65
2.	Very Good	34	33.00
3.	Good	37	35.93
4.	Poor	18	17.48
5.	Very Poor	02	1.94
	Total	103	100

It is evident from the above table 21 that majority of the (80.58%) neo-literate slum women have achieved expected proficiency in writing of the total respondents, 44.65% slum women have obtained excellent and very good grades and 37.92% have obtained good grades in writing. Even a few slum women (17.48%) who have obtained poor grades in writing were also found to be achieving success. Only a very few (1.94%) respondents obtained very poor grades in writing. The level of achievement as observed from the table revealed quite satisfactory outcome of the slum women in writing. Therefore, it can be said that there was a good impact of the literacy programme of RSS on the neo-literate slum women with regard to writing.

TABLE 6.9
Performance of the Neo-literate Slum Women in Writing as per their Age Group

Sl.	*Grades*	*No. of Slum Women*			*Total*
No.	*Assigned*	*15-25*	*26-35*	*36-50*	
1.	Excellent	6 (13.33)	5 (12.19)	1 (5.88)	12 (11.65)
2.	Very good	17 (37.78)	13 (31.70)	4 (23.53)	34 (33.00)
3.	Good	15 (33.33)	15 (36.58)	7 (41.18)	37 (35.92)
4.	Poor	5 (11.11)	8 (19.52)	5 (29.41)	18 (17.49)
5.	Very Poor	2 (4.44)	—	—	—
	Total	45(100.00)	41(100.00)	17(100.00)	103

Note : Figures within parentheses indicate percentages.

It can be seen from the Table 6.9 that the respondents of the younger age group have achieved highly satisfactory results than that of the middle and older age groups in writing. This relatively better performance of the younger age group than others might be became of : *(i)* their self-interest for development through literacy activities, *(ii)* encouragement of the elders of the family as well as members of Chetana Kendras, or *(iii)* the effect of video shows and other cultural activities organised in the Chetana Kendras. These factors must have influenced them to be serious in learning and to practice writing. But in case of the middle age group, their performance is relatively inferior to the younger group. It might be due to : *(i)* their over-burden of the family and non-conducive environment to practice writing, *(ii)* personal health problems, or *(iii)* demotivation due to lack provision for them to avail the basic amenities like schooling, lighting, ration card etc. All there causes might have affected in achieving relatively inferior result.

It can also be observed from the table that there was a wider difference between the achievement levels of younger groups with the older group in writing. This might be because : *(i)* they might have hesitate to learn with the younger respondents, *(ii)* they might have felt shy to clarify their doubts from the young volunteers, *(iii)* might not have given more importance to writing them to reading and numeracy. That counts a lot for their inferior achievement in writing than the other two counter groups. Further, the table shows that a few number of respondents (17.49%) were found to be unsuccessful in achieving the proficiency level and a very few (1.94%) slum women were found to be failure in achievement of writing skill by obtaining very poor grades. These failures of the poor and very poor grade holders respondents might be due to their : *(i)* lack of keen interest in writing, *(ii)* lack of scope in the family for writing, *(iii)* socio-personal problem of the slum women which affected in achieving success in writing. However, the overall performance of the respondents in writing skill was satisfactory. It indicates a positive impact of RSS on the slum women of Rourkela.

TABLE 6.10
Performance of the Neo-literate Slum Women in Writing as per their Caste/Community Background

Sl. No.	*Grades Obtained*	*No. of Slum Women*					*Total*
		ST Women	*SC Women*	*GC Women*	*OBC Women*	*Muslim Women*	
1.	Excellent	6(16.67)	2(8.33)	3(13.64)	1(8.33)	—	12 (11.65)
2.	Very Good	11(30.56)	10(41.67)	7(31.82)	3(25.00)	3(33.33)	34 (3.00)
3.	Good	12(33.33)	8(33.33)	8(36.36)	5(41.67)	4(44.45)	37 (35.92)
4.	Poor	5(13.89)	4(16.67)	4(18.18)	3(25.00)	2(22.22)	18 (17.48)
5.	Very Poor	2(5.55)	—	—	—	—	2(1.94)
	Total	36 (100.00)	24 (100.00)	22 (100.00)	12 (100.00)	9 (100.00)	103 (100.00)

Note : Figures within parentheses indicate percentages.

Data presented in the Table 6.10 reveals that the SC slum women have done well among all the other groups. Even the ST respondents who are considered as lower caste group have performed relatively better than the GC category in obtaining excellent and very good grades. The GC category might have achieved relatively inferior grades than the SC and ST categories, due to their superiority complex, that they belong to the so-called higher caste category, and whatever they know and practice were sufficient for them. As a result they neglected their learning and secured relatively inferior grades. It can be said that the ST and SC respondents, who have been supressed by the higher caste people for a long time might have been highly motivated by the sincere efforts and activities of the RSS volunteers and made themselves determined to avail of the opportunities that are provided by the government through the literacy programme for their up liftment. So their determination and efforts of RSS count for the high achievement of SC's and ST's.

Further, it can be observed (Table 6.10) that despite highly satisfactory result among the Muslim respondents, none of them has obtained either excellent or very poor grades in writing. All the successful respondents (77.78%) have secured very good and good grades, and a few of respondents were found to be unsuccessful. It indicated that they do have potentialities, but might be due to some reasons like as they belonged to Muslim community, socio-culturally they have had lets privileges than the others. Therefore, none of the family members might have encouraged or helped them in learning and household and other activities while they were studying. All these count a lot for their non-achievement of excellent grade and even relatively lower achievement than the SC, ST and GC categories in writing. Hence, such a comparison cannot lead to the conclusion that the difference in achievement levels of the respondents in writing is due to their Caste/Community background only. Rather, it can be thought that if opportunities are given, constant efforts will be made in arousing the self-interest of the slum women, no Caste/Community will make a difference in the impact of literacy programme.

It is pertinent to mention here that, the respondents of Narla Road Slum were not able to write a single word either in Hindi or in Oriya language. It was observed by the investigator that they are now writing letters and even writing applications to the local administration in Oriya language demanding for education of their children and other basic amenities.

However, despite the difference of the achievement levels of the neo-literate slum women of the mentioned Caste/Community background, their levels of achievement in writing skills were quite satisfactory which indicates a positive impact of the literacy programme on the slum women of Rourkela.

TABLE 6.11

Performance of the Neo-literate Slum Women in Writing as per their Earning/Non-earning Background

Sl. No.	*Grades Assigned*	*No. of Slum Women* *Earning*	*Non-earning*	*Total*
1.	Excellent	6 (10.90)	6 (12.50)	12 (11.65)
2.	Very Good	21 (38.18)	13 (27.08)	34 (33.00)
3.	Good	19 (34.55)	18 (37.50)	37 (35.92)
4.	Poor	8 (14.55)	10 (20.83)	18 (17.48)
5.	Very Poor	1 (1.82)	1 (2.08)	2 (1.94)
	Total	55 (100.00)	48 (100.00)	103 (100.00)

Note : Figures within parentheses indicate percentages.

It can be viewed from the Table 6.11 that the earning women have achieved more outstanding result than that of the non-earning slum women. This might be due to : *(i)* their exposure in various situations due to occupation, *(ii)* need for writing in vocational training programme of Shramik Vidyapith, *(iii)* Inspiration and scope given by the employer in working field, *(iv)* self-interest for development. All these factors must have contributed to their outstanding performance in writing more than the non-earning slum women.

In case of non-earning slum women, they have also achieved satisfactory results that is in fact less than the earning slum women. It may be due to : *(i)* lack of self-confidence in writing, *(ii)* might have mental tension due to family problems, or *(iii)* the volunteers might have neglected to the non-earning slum women while teaching. That affects their relatively inferior result. Further a few per cent (17.48%) of sample slum women of both the categories have not been able to achieve the success. And a very few respondents 1.94% (only two) of each category have obtained very poor grades in writing. The failure among the unsuccessful respondents (both poor and very poor grade holders) in writing might be caused due to : *(i)* their lack of self-motivation and determination to develop writing skill, *(ii)* wretched poverty and its related tension, *(iii)* lack of cooperation in household activities, or *(iv)* negligence of the demotivated volunteers as they were slum-dwellers. These factors might have affected adversely in their literacy achievement. It is important to mention here that out of the two very poor grade holder respondents, one is from earning background. Which indicates that her occupational nature and skill or background were not found to be highly useful in achieving success in writing skill. However, despite a greater difference between the achievement level of the earning and non-earning respondents in writing, their performance was quite satisfactory. Therefore, it can be said that there was a highly positive impact of literacy programme on the slum women of Rourkela.

Numeracy

TABLE 6.12
Distribution of the Neo-literate Slum Women According to Total Grades Obtained in Numeracy

Sl. No.	*Grades Assigned*	*No. of Slum Women tested*	*Percentage*
1.	Excellent	46	44.66
2.	Very Good	26	25.24
3.	Good	22	21.36
4.	Poor	6	5.83
5.	Very Poor	3	2.91
	Total	103	100.00

It can be seen from the Table 6.12 that most of the neo-literate slum women (91.26%) have achieved the NLM prescribed proficiency in numeracy. Out of the total respondents, almost 70% have achieved excellent and very good grades and 21.36% have achieved good grades in numeracy. Only a few numbers of respondents (5.83% and 2.91% respectively) were found to be unsuccessful by obtaining poor and very poor grades in numeracy. The level of achievement as derived from the above table showed a highly satisfactory result of the neo-literate slum women in numeracy. This indicates a healthy impact of the literacy activities of RSS on the slum women of Rourkela.

TABLE 6.13
Performance of the Neo-literate Slum Women in Numeracy as per their Age Group

Sl. No.	*Grades Assigned*	*No. of Slum Women* 15-25	26-35	36-50	*Total*
1.	Excellent	18 (40.00)	26 (63.4)	2 (11.76)	46(44.66)
2.	Very Good	11 (24.44)	7 (17.07)	8 (47.06)	26(25.24)
3.	Good	11 (24.44)	5 (12.20)	6 (35.29)	22(21.36)
4.	Poor	3 (6.67)	2(4.88)	1 (5.89)	6(5.83)
5.	Very Poor	2 (4.45)	1(2.44)	—	3(2.91)
	Total	45 (100.00)	41 (100.00)	17(100.00)	103(100.00)

Note : Figures within parentheses indicate percentages.

It can be observed from the Table 6.13 that the respondents of the older age group have performed better than the middle and younger age group, and the middle age groups have performed better than the younger age group in numeracy. This relatively better performance of the older age group than that of other might be due to : *(i)* their age long practical experiences in domestic affairs related to finance, budgeting, expenditure etc., or *(ii)* their family members might have taken special care for their literacy development. But, in case of the younger group of 15-25, they might not have got better scope to practice their knowledge of numeracy which was learnt in the Chetana Kendra by budgeting, calculating, purchasing etc., *(iii)* they might not have been keenly interested in calculation and numeracy than that of other aspects of literacy. Therefore, they have achieved relatively inferior result than the other two counter groups.

Further, it can be seen that although the respondents of older age group have achieved the highest among the three groups in NLM prescribed proficiency in numeracy, but relatively lower in obtaining excellent and very good grades as compared to the other two groups. It can be noted that a great majority (more than 80%) of the respondents of the middle age group have obtained excellent and very good grades. This shows their outstanding performance in numeracy. It might be due to : *(i)* their nature of job which needs frequent calculation (in case of earning women), *(ii)* they might have been habituated in keeping daily accounts, or *(iii)* might be the efforts made by RSS volunteers in developing habit of savings or depositing their money in the women's group or in the co-operative bank. These factors might have been instrumental in achieving high level of achievement and excellent and very good grades in numeracy.

Further, one can see from the table that a very low percentage of the respondents from all the three age groups have not been able to achieve the proficiency level. This might have happened due to their : *(i)* lack of interest in numeracy, or *(ii)* wretched financial conditions. These factors must have affected their proficiency level. Although the slum women of different age groups differ from one another, there is no doubt that their level of achievement in numeracy was highly satisfactory. Which indicates a highly positive impact of the literacy programme of RSS on the neo-literate slum women of Rourkela.

TABLE 6.14
Performance of the Neo-literate Slum Women in Numeracy as per their Caste/ Community Background

Sl. No.	*Grades Assigned*	*No. of Slum Women*					*Total*
		ST Women	*SC Women*	*GC Women*	*OBC Women*	*Muslim Women*	
1	Excellent	16 (44.44)	12(50.00)	8(36.36)	6(50.00)	4(44.44)	46(44.66)
2	V. Good	8(22.22)	5(20.83)	8(36.36)	3(25.00)	2 (22.22)	26(25.24)
3	Good	8(22.23)	5(20.83)	4(18.18)	2(16.67)	3(33.34)	22(21.36)
4	Poor	2(5.56)	2(8.34)	1 (4.55)	1 (8.33)	—	6(5.83)
5	V. Poor	2(5.56)	—	1 (4.55)	—	—	3(2.91)
	Total	36 (100)	24(100)	22(100)	12 (100)	9 (100)	103(100)

Note : Figures within parentheses indicate percentage.

It can be viewed from the Table 6.14 that a great majority of the respondents (91.26%) of all the groups of Caste/Community background have shown high level of performance by achieving

NLM prescribed proficiency in numeracy. However, the Muslim respondents did better than that of their counter-groups by showing cent per cent result in numeracy. The respondents of ST category have achieved relatively inferior result (88.89%) than the other four groups. Mention may be made here that both Muslim and ST respondents are considered as special categories as per the social parameter for development. Therefore government both at the Central and States level have been trying for their upliftment through various schemes and programmes. In case of ST women, although they are socially under-estimated and oppressed (to an extent) by the so-called higher caste people, they enjoy maximum freedom and rights in their families and even in their own communities. Whereas in case of Muslim women, they are socio-culturally under-privileged and have more family restrictions. Therefore, it was assured that under constrains the Muslim women would not achieve better than that of the women of other caste categories. On the contrary it was not found to be true. The cent per cent result among them (Muslim women) might be due to : *(i)* their strong will-power for self-development through literacy achievement, *(ii)* special care taken by the literacy volunteers for numeracy development, *(iii)* effect of the powerful message of the street plays organised by RSS on evils of illiteracy with regard to the different aspects of literacy. All these factors must have affected in achieving cent per cent result among Muslim women in numeracy. In case of ST women although they may not have faced the problems in their families, but have faced constrains in the literacy centres like *(i)* accommodation for learning during rainy season (which was the peak period for learning) as it was one of the greatest problem for RSS in organising literacy activities, or *(ii)* might be due to the immatured school/volunteers who were unable to clarify the doubts of the ST respondents properly. Therefore, they must not have achieved comparatively better results in numeracy than other groups.

Further the table reveals that few respondents have achieved poor result and a very few respondents have shown very poor performance in numeracy. It is important to mention here that out of three respondents (2.91%) of the very poor grade holder, two (1.94%) respondents have also achieved the very poor grade in other aspects of literacy and their cases have been studied. But in case of the rest of the unsuccessful respondents it gives a clue to guess that it might be due to : *(i)* their unwillingness to change their present condition, *(ii)* lack of inspiration from the family members, *(iii)* demotivation due to lack of infrastructure facilities like suitable accommodation for learning, mainly during monsoon and winter season, or *(iv)* demotivated volunteers who were unable to arouse urge for learning among the slum women. All these reasons might have affected the few slum women for not achieving success in numeracy. Therefore, it cannot be said that Caste/Community is the dominating factor for literacy achievement. It might be one of the factors, but not the whole for literacy achievement. It is important to mention here that before joining the literacy programme of RSS, they were (the respondents) not keeping their family accounts properly. Even they were not calculating properly in the grocer's shop while purchasing their groceries. As a result, they had to be cheated many a times. But after joining the literacy programme, they have not only become calculative while purchasing anything, but also keeping their family accounts regularly. Further, they saved some amount every week. This was reported by the slum women of pump house colony and Rajeev basti during in depth discussion for data collection to the investigator. However, in spite of a difference between the achievement levels of respondents of various Caste/Community in numeracy, their performance was highly satisfactory, which indicates highly positive impact of literacy programme on the slum women of Rourkela.

TABLE 6.15
Performance of the Neo-literate Slum Women in Numeracy as per their Earning/ Non-earning Background

Sl. No.	*Grades Assigned*	*No. of Slum Women*		*Total*
		Earning	*Non-earning*	
1.	Excellent	27 (49.09)	19 (39.58)	46 (44.66)
2.	Very good	15 (27.27)	11 (22.92)	26 (25.24)
3.	Good	10 (18.18)	12 (25.00)	22 (21.36)
4.	Poor	2 (3.64)	4 (9.33)	6 (5.83)
5	Very Poor	1 (1.82)	2 (4.17)	3 (2.91)
	Total	55 (100)	48 (100)	103 (100)

Note : Figures within parentheses indicate percentages.

It can be viewed from the Table 6.15 that both the earning and non-earning slum women have achieved high level of result in numeracy. However, the earning slum women have performed better than the non-earning respondents. A number of factors like : *(i)* encouragement of the employers and literate friend circle in the working field, *(ii)* occupational need, that compelled to be serious in calculation, *(iii)* self-eagerness of the slum women to know, learn and practice, or (iv) the rigorous efforts made by RSS organisers, must have been responsible for their high achievement in numeracy on than the non-earning respondents.

The non-earning respondents have also achieved good results in numeracy is in fact less than the earning slum women. It may be due to : *(i)* their lack of self-interest for learning, especially numeracy aspect of literacy, *(ii)* irregularities of the immature volunteers, *(iii)* non-cooperation of the family members that counts for their relatively inferior achievement than the earning slum women.

Further, it can be observed that a meagre percentage respondents (5.83%) have shown poor result and a very few (2.91%) have shown very poor result in numeracy. The causes for the failure of the unsuccessful respondents might be due to *(i)* their negligence to practice numeracy after the literacy class *(ii)* lack of time and facilities to practice in the home due to household burden, or *(iii)* socio-personal problems of the respondents. It is also pertinent to mention here that out of the 2.91% of the very poor grade holder respondents, one (0.97%) was from working category. Which gives a clue to guess that her nature of occupation might not have helped in achieving success in learning numeracy. Therefore, it cannot be said that the level of literacy achievement in numeracy might be only due to the earning status of the respondents. It might be one of the dominating factors for literacy achievement but not the whole. However, despite a marked difference between the achievement level of earning and non-earning slum women in numeracy, their result was outstanding. It indicates the success of RSS in developing numerical skills of literacy among the slum women of Rourkela.

Discussion

The distribution of 103 sample respondents, *i.e.* neo-literate slum women in terms of their competency level in Reading, Writing and Numeracy have already been presented in the preceding section. The analysis of the data revealed that the respondents who have obtained excellent, very good and good grades in different aspects of literacy, *i.e.* in Reading, Writing and Numeracy have been considered as successful in achieving the prescribed level of proficiency in competency area (as per the NLM guideline). It is evident from the data analysis that 90.29% respondents have achieved excellent, very good and good grades in Reading, 80.58% in Writing and 91.26% in Numeracy. So far as the literacy skills are concerned, the respondents bettered their performance in Reading and Numeracy skills than that of Writing skills, and there found a difference between the reading skill with writing and numeracy with writing skill was not nominal. The difference found was 9.71% and 10.68% respectively. Whereas, the difference observed between the reading and numeracy skills was found to be not even 1% (.97%).

This relatively less success of respondents in writing skill might be due to the lack of practice and attention on regular writing in Chetana Kendras (Post Literacy Centres) as well as in daily life which needs to be upgraded among the neo-literates. They might have also faced the problems of lack of time due to their various household responsibilities as well as work outside the home for income generation activities. So they might not have regularly attended the literacy classes during the campaign period or in the post literacy phase.

It is important to mention here that all the respondents have not achieved the NLM expected proficiency level in literacy skills, although they have completed the Primers (Primers I, II and III). They were evaluated in mid-term evaluation and considered as neo-literates. Further, they were also expected to have gone through the P.L. Primer and other supplementary literature as their names and details were found in the list of the neo-literates and concerned documents of Chetana Kendras.

However, despite a relatively wide difference between the achievement in writing skill of the respondents and the reading and numeracy skills of literacy, the impact of literacy programme on neo-literate slum women was reported to be highly satisfactory in all the three aspects or literacy, *i.e.* Reading, Writing and Numeracy of Literacy Achievement.

Based on the research findings of Literacy House, Lucknow (1969), Directorate of Adult Education (1973), Agnihotri (1979), Shah (1978), Council for Development of the Scheme of Functional Literacy (1984), Aikara (1984), Chakraborty (1988), Gupta (1988), Pathak (1991), Khatun (1991) and Sachidananda (1992), which have been reviewed in Chapter-2 on impact of literacy programme in developing literacy skills among the neo-literates, it was expected that there would be a very low impact of the literacy programme on the respondents. On the contrary, there found a highly satisfactory impact of the literacy programme in achieving the level of literacy among the neo-literates. Rather, the findings of the researches of Kudesia (1973), Vankataih (1977), Rao (1992), Laxminarayan (1982), Ganguli (1985) and Singh (1996) supported the present study that majority of the respondents who used to be the participants of literacy programme have shown highly positive impact with regard to literacy skills by obtaining excellent, very good and good grades in Reading, Writing and Numeracy.

This high impact of literacy programme in developing literacy skills among respondents might be due to their keen interest in learning which leads to their active participation in the teaching learning programme or high level of motivation and environment building efforts and activities by the volunteers and organisers, or the needs of respondents themselves. It might also be due to the encouragement of the family members or special care taken by the teaching volunteers in making them regular in the literacy classes which have affected the achievement level of the neo-literate slum women, because Natrajan (1982), Seth (1983), Seth (1984), and Rao (1992) have found relationship between the participation of the learners with the programme and their achievement in Literacy Skills.

Impact of Literacy Programme of RSS as per the Age Group of the Slum Women

The analysis of data as per age group-wise achievement of the respondents in different aspects of literacy skills can be seen in Tables 6.5, 6.9 and 6.13 that the respondents from the age group 36-50 have although achieved inferior result in reading and writing skills, but have still achieved excellent result in numeric than that of their other counter groups. The respondents from the age group 15-25 have achieved excellent result in reading and writing than the age groups 26-35 and 36-50. But at the same time they have achieved relatively less satisfactory result than the age group 26-35 and 36-50 in numeracy skill. It might be due to their lack of interest in numeracy skill or due to lack of dealing with financial activities like budgeting, purchasing, etc., in their day-to-day life in the home. The respondents from the age group 26-35 have achieved moderately satisfactory results in all the three aspects of literacy *i.e.* reading, writing and numeracy.

On the basis of the research findings of Natrajan (1982) and Brahma Prakash and Chaturvedi (1983) it was assumed that there will be effect of age on achievement level of the respondents of younger age group (15-35 years) in achieving higher standard in reading, writing and numeracy than the older (above 35 years) age group. This is in line with the findings of the present study that the achievement level in reading and writing skills of the respondents of the younger group is better than the older group. But with regard to numeracy skill they found a contradictory result from the older group of the respondents (36-50). They have achieved an excellent grade in numeracy than that of the younger groups of 15-25 and 26-35 years. This might be due to : *(i)* dealing with financial activities like, budgeting, expenditure etc. in the home and in the work field (in case of working women), *(ii)* might be due to keen interest in counting, *(iii)* they might have in need of accounts due to their nature of job, *(iv)* might be due to the special efforts of the volunteers in developing numeracy skill among the learners which have been reported.

It is evident from the above discussion based on the analysis of the data that age is one of the factors which effects in differentiating the level of achievement of the respondents to some extent in different aspects of literacy. However, in spite of difference in achievement level of the respondents based on age-wise performance, there was recorded a great impact of literacy programme on respondents different age groups.

Impact of Literacy Programme of RSS as per Caste/Community of the Slum Women

Data with regard to caste/community-wise achievement of the respondents in different aspects of literacy have already been presented in Tables 6.6,6.10 and 6.14 of the preceding section and analysed accordingly. The analysis of the data indicated that the ST and OBC respondents have achieved excellent result in reading than that of from the respondents of the SC, GC and Muslim Category. The difference found between the respondents of ST and OBC categories with SC, GC and Muslim respondents was just nominal. These corresponding categories, *i.e.* SC, GC, and Muslim have also achieved highly satisfactory result in reading. The high level of achievement of ST and OBC categories might be due to their family members who had a little education and may be encouraging and helping them in learning, or the high level of motivational programme of the RSS organisers affects in developing keen interest for learning sincerely.

In terms of writing skills respondents from SC category have achieved excellent grade and their result was relatively better than ST and GC categories and for better than OBC and Muslim Categories. The difference found between SC with ST and GC Categories was just nominal, whereas there was found a wide difference in the achievements of SC respondents with OBC and Muslim categories. The excellent result of the respondents of SC category in writing skill might be due to their keen interest in writing as well as regular practice in day- to- day life. In case of ST and GC. Categories they might be interested in writing but might not have practiced writing skill in their day-to-day life due to lack of time and family support which counts for their relatively lower achievement than the SC respondents. Further, the wide differences found in the SC Category with OBC and Muslim might be due to their lack of interest in writing, or after the day's practice writing, which counts for their comparatively lower achievement level in writing skill than other SC and other categories.

Further, the difference between SC respondents with OBC respondents was found to be wider than that of the Muslim respondents. This might be due to the interest of the Muslim respondents which was relatively more than the OBC category, or they must (the Muslim respondents) not have been willing to miss the opportunities in spite of their day's long hard labour which count for their relatively better result in writing than the OBC category.

Even there found a difference of the achievement between the ST and GC respondents with the OBC and Muslim respondents. Despite this difference in the achievement level in writing skill, the achievement of Muslim and OBC categories was quite satisfactory, as they have achieved 77.78% and 75% respectively.

So far as the numeracy skill is concerned, the respondents from the Muslim category (sector) have shown extraordinary performance by showing 100% result in numeracy skills, although they have achieved a low grade in reading and writing skills than the other respondents. The achievement of other respondents, *i.e.* ST, SC, GC. and OBC were although not extraordinary in comparison to the Muslim respondents still were outstanding in numeracy skill as they have achieved 88.89%, 91.67%, 90.90% and 91.67% respectively.

However, from the above discussion it can be said that despite a very low level of difference among the respondents from different categories of caste with regard to their achievement in different aspect of literacy, *i.e.* reading, writing and numeracy, their overall performance was outstanding, which shows highly positive impact of the literacy programme on the neo-literate slum women of different categories of caste background. Hence, caste background of the respondents is not a prominent factor to differentiate the given achievement level.

The review of the research findings of Khawja Peer (1978) and Malhotra (1991), which was in this tune supported to this present study and strengthened the statement given above. Rather, the expectation which was based on the review of the research findings of Sarkar (1981), Chugani (1987), Siddiqui (1989) and Reddy (1991) reveal contradictory results that wide difference would be found in the performance of respondents from different caste background.

Further, it was expected from the research findings of Sarkar (1981) that the growth of education among the higher caste Hindus was the highest and among the Muslim the lowest, and SC women were less motivated. These findings have further revealed contradictory results with that of the present study. Because it is seen from the analysis that the respondents from the GC. Category (higher caste background among the respondents) have not achieved outstanding or excellent result than the respondents of ST, SC, OBC and Muslim Category in all those three aspects of literacy. They have simply achieved moderately satisfactory results. The respondents from Muslim background who were having the lowest growth of education in the findings of Sarkar (1981) and Siddiqui (1989) have achieved extraordinary result by obtaining 100% result in Numeracy. Further they have achieved quite satisfactory results in Writing. This might be due to the constant efforts made by the sincere volunteers of RSS specially for the Muslim neo-literate women of Narla Road slum for their upliftment which arose strong determination in the respondents to develop their literacy skills, or they might be in need of calculation in their home front and in work field that count a lot in achieving extraordinary result in numeracy as well as reading and writing.

The SC respondents achieved excellent in writing and highly satisfactory in reading and numeracy. This performance of the SC respondents once again contradicts to the research findings of Sarkar (1981). Further, the respondents of ST category who used to be the disadvantaged group of the society have achieved excellent results in both reading and writing skills. They have also achieved highly satisfactory result in numeracy, and the OBC category have achieved excellent in reading, highly satisfactory. This might be because of the government programmes like literacy and adult education, which have been trying to uplift these ST, SC, OBC and other downtrodden people from a pitiable condition so that they may become conscious to develop their status in the society. Moreover, people from higher caste have supressed them for a long time. So they might have taken more interest in learning than the higher caste people and must not have been willing to miss the opportunities given through the literacy programme, that counts for their higher level of achievement.

It is important to mention here that the respondents from OBC and ST category who used to be the socially lower caste people of the society have achieved the highest in writing, and the Muslim respondents have achieved the highest in numeracy. Whereas the respondents from the GC category (so-called higher caste category among the respondents) have not achieved the highest in any of the aspects of literacy, *i.e.* reading, writing and numeracy.

The high level of achievement among the respondents of ST, SC, OBC, Muslim and even the GC category shows the highly positive impact of literacy programme on the respondents. Further, this high level of achievement among the respondents specially the disadvantaged and Muslim background proves that higher caste background is not at all a differentiating factor in the achievement level of the neo-literates in different aspects of literacy. Hence, almost all the neo-literate slum women from different caste/community background have been highly effected by the impact of literacy programme. The conjecture put forward was that it was the sincere efforts and highly motivational and need-based activities of RSS through its sincere volunteers which count much to arouse strong will power and determination among the respondents for active participation in the literacy programme, which results for their better/higher achievement. Further, it was reported by majority of the respondents (80.58%) that the quality of teaching was satisfactory and volunteers were sincere. The teaching-learning materials were satisfactory and of good quality. These also count for their high level of achievement. Otherwise, respondents like Muslim slum women who were supposed to be more oppressed due to socio-cultural background than that of the other caste and cultural background would not have come forward and achieved extraordinary results in numeracy and satisfactory in reading and writing. However, despite a differences in achievement level of the respondents as per their caste/community background there found high impact of literacy programme on the slum women.

Impact of Literacy Programme of RSS as per the Earning Status of the Slum Women

It was found from the analysis of data on achievement of the earning and non-earning status of the respondents in different aspects of literacy presented in the table (see Tables 6.7, 6.11 and 6.15) of the present chapter that the slum women of earning category had higher level of achievement in all the three aspects of literacy, *i.e.* reading, writing and numeracy than that of the non-earning category. It is important to mention here that although both earning and non-earning groups of respondents had achieved the minimum NLM required proficiency levels, still the respondents of earning category did better than the non-earning respondents which shows the high level of impact of RSS on the earning women than that of the non-earning women.

Based on the research findings of Mali (1974) and Siddiqui (1989) it was expected that there was no relationship between the occupation of the adult learners and their level of achievement in literacy skill. Further, the study of Siddiqui (1989) specifically revealed that the respondents belonging to non-working group achieved higher level of impact in reading, numeracy and agriculture, which was quite contradictory from the findings of the present study. Rather, the findings of Rao's study (1983) pointed out that occupation was a positive factor for higher level of achievement. This high level of achievements might be due to : *(i)* the self-motivation and interests of the respondents *(ii)* exposure of their inner-potential qualities due to occupation, *(iii)* sincere efforts and qualitative teaching of the RSS volunteers and *(iv)* their nature of occupation which counts for their high level of achievement. So we cannot fully accept that the level of literacy development or achievement was due to the earning status of the respondents. It might be one of the attributes for their achievement but not the whole. At the same time we cannot discard that respondent's levels of achievement have been associated with different types of factors like facilities they might be getting at home and work field, adequate and need-based learning material as well as good teaching facilities they might have received in the Chetana Kendras and their economic background.

Whereas in case of the non-earning respondents of relatively low level of achievement it may be assumed that this might be due to : *(i)* low level of self-motivation, interest and attainment in reading, writing and numeracy, *(ii)* non-satisfactory teaching and irregularities of volunteers in the Chetana Kendras (which has been reported by 19.00% and 8.74% of respondents respectively), *(iii)* chronic illness of the respondents, and *(iv)* financial constraints due to lack of source of income etc. in comparison to the earning respondents, which counts for their relatively low achievement than that of their counterpart earning respondents.

However, despite a wide variation between the achievement level of earning and non-earning respondents, there was a high level of impact of literacy programme on them in developing their level of literacy in its different aspects *i.e.* reading, writing and numeracy.

Conclusion

The above discussion with regard to the achievement of neo-literate slum women in different aspects of literacy leads to the conclusion presented hereunder.

(i) The overall performance of the neo-literate slum women with regard to reading, writing and numeracy was quite satisfactory. In spite of their high level of achievement (overall) it was also found that they have fared better in numeracy and reading as compared to writing.

(ii) The impact of literacy programme was although highly positive on the respondents of different age group, the junior most group (15-25 years) faced for better in reading and writing than the other two counter groups.

(iii) The respondents of senior age group, *i.e.,* 36-50 years did outstandingly only in mathematics. Whereas, they have achieved relatively low in reading and writing than the other counter groups.

(iv) The respondents of middle age groups. *i.e.,* 26-35 have shown satisfactory level of achievement in all the aspects of literacy.

(v) With regard to the Caste/Community background, no specific difference in the achievement level of the respondents was noticed other than the Muslim respondents. That too, the achievement level in numeracy, in which they have achieved cent per cent result.

(vi) Regarding earning and non-earning status of the respondents, it was found that the earning slum women have achieved relatively better than the non-earning slum women in all the three aspects of literacy, *i.e.* reading, writing and numeracy. However, despite a difference between the levels of achievement between the two groups their achievement in literacy skills were highly satisfactory.

Level of Awareness Developed Among the Neo-literate Slum Women

This section deals with the awareness level of slum women indifferent aspects of life such as need for environmental protection, Family Welfare, Child and Maternity care and Personal Health and Hygiene.

Problems of population explosion, environment pollution and small family norms have been the burning issues in India for last few decades. Therefore, the strategies of population control, environmental protection and family welfare activities (techniques) have been prioritised by Indian planning. The nature and dimensions of their problems are such that unless there are linked to various developmental and educational programmes, their chances of success become minimal. Therefore, as implementing agencies of educational programme, literacy campaigns are creating awareness on there issues among the respondents by supplying reading material, organising

TABLE 6.16
Awareness about Population Explosion—Scarcity/ Misery

Sl. No.	*Background*	*Effects of Large Family*			*Nos. of Respondents*
		Income Increases A	*Scarcity Increases* B	*Misery Increases* C	
	Age Group				
1.	15-25	—	23(51.11)	22(48.89)	45
2.	26-35	—	24(58.54)	17(41.46)	41
3.	36-50	—	7(41.18)	10(58.82)	17
	Status				103
1.	Earning	—	30(54.55)	25(45.46)	55
2.	Non-earning	—	24(50.00)	24(50.00)	48
	Caste/Community				103
1.	Scheduled Tribe	—	18(50.00)	18(50.00)	36
2.	Scheduled Caste	—	13(54.17)	11(45.83)	24
3.	General Caste	—	11((50.00)	11(50.00)	22
4.	Other Backward Caste	—	7(58.33)	5(41.67)	12
5.	Muslims	—	5(54.56)	4(44.44)	09
	Total nos. of Respondents	—	54(52.43)	49(47.57)	103

Note: Figures within parentheses indicate percentages.

health awareness campaigns and discussion series among the neo-literate slum women about the family welfare activities.

As an implementing agency, RSS has been organising programmes on these aspects for the awareness development of the people in general and slum women in particular since 1990-91. Data collected in this regard from the slum women has been analysed by descriptive statistics and inter pretations are made accordingly and presented below.

It is seen from the Table 6.16 that more than half of the slum women are aware that population explosion leads to scarcity, and less than half of the respondents irrespective of their age, caste/ community and earning status are aware that it increases misery. And none of them have expressed that it increases their income. It is pertinent to mention here that before the RSS started functioning, there was a notion among the slum women that increase in population leads to increase income of the family, and this idea has been found to be changed among them. It means the RSS is successful in developing awareness among the neo-literate slum women.

TABLE 6.17
Awareness about Population Explosion—Environment Pollution

Sl. No.	*Background*	*Effects of Population Explosion on Environment*			*Nos. of Respondents*
		Environment remains Clean A	*Environment becomes Polluted* B	*Nothing happens* C	
	Age Group				
1.	15-25	—	44(97.78)	1(2.22)	45
2.	26-35	—	41(100.00)	—	41
3.	36-50	—	16(94.18)	1(5.88)	17
	Status				103
1.	Earning	—	55(100.00)	—	55
2.	Non-earning	—	46(95.83)	2(4.17)	48
	Caste/Community				103
1.	Scheduled Tribe	—	35(97.22)	1(2.78)	36
2.	Scheduled Caste	—	23(95.83)	1(4.17)	24
3.	General Caste	—	22(100.00)	—	22
4.	Other Backward Caste	—	12(100.00)	—	12
5.	Muslims	—	9(100.00)	—	09
	Total nos. of Respondents	—	101(98.06)	2(1.94)	103

Note : Figures within parentheses indicate percentages.

It can be observed from Table 6.17 that almost all the respondents irrespective of age, Caste/ Community and earning and non-earning background have expressed their opinion that environment gets polluted due to population explosion. Only 1.94% (two only) of respondents have expressed that nothing happens out of population explosion. Mention may be made here that these ignorant respondents were from ST and SC and non-earning categories respectively. Further, they belong to the younger and the older age groups, it means that since they belonged to non-earning category—

(i) They might not have been exposed to the many situations which would have made them aware of the causes of environmental pollution.

(ii) It might be due to their family background, which was not conclusive to attend the discussion classes and programmes regularly with regard to awareness generation, or

(iii) Their mental immaturity (in case of the respondent of younger age group), or

(iv) Negligence of the respondent (in case of the respondent of older age group) in attending the awareness programmes. These factors seem to count for their un-awareness. However, about cent per cent responses of the slum women indicate the success of RSS in developing high level of awareness among slum women.

TABLE 6.18

Awareness about Population Explosion—Land and Human Resources

Sl. No.	*Background*	*Evils of Over Growth of Population in the Centre*			*Nos. of Respondents*
		Increases the Scarcity of Agricultural Land A	*No Harm on the Increase of the Scarcity of Agricultural Land* B	*Increases Human Resources* C	
	Age Group				
1.	15-25	42(93.33)	1(2.22)	2(4.45)	45
2.	26-35	39(95.12)	1(2.44)	1(2.44)	41
3.	36-50	15(88.24)	1(5.88)	1(5.88)	17
	Status				103
1.	Earning	52(94.55)	1(1.81)	2(3.64)	55
2.	Non-earning	44(91.67)	2(4.17)	2(4.17)	48
	Caste/Community				103
1.	Scheduled Tribe	34(94.44)	1(2.78)	1(2.78)	36
2.	Scheduled Caste	22(91.67)	2(8.33)	—	24
3.	General Caste	21(95.45)	—	1(4.55)	22
4.	Other Backward Cast	11(91.67)	—	1(8.33)	12
5.	Muslims	8(88.89)	—	1(11.11)	09
	Total nos. of Respondents	96(93.20)	3(2.91)	4(3.88)	103

Note: Figures within parentheses indicate percentages.

Data presented in Table 6.18 shows that most of the respondents are aware about the fact that over growth of population leads to the increase of scarcity of agricultural land. Only a meagre percentage of respondents, irrespective of their age, caste/community and earning and non-earning status were found to be unaware with the evils of population explosion by expressing their opinion that : *(a)* there is no problem on the increase of the scarcity of agricultural land, and (b) population explosion increases human resources.

Their unawareness might be due to : *(i)* lack of self-interest in developing awareness. *(ii)* lack of time due to household and other activities to participate actively in the awareness generation camps, *(iii)* lack of follow-up discussion with family members and friends. These factors might have caused the slums women's unawareness. It may be noteworthy to mentioned here that many of the respondents have informed to the investigator that before joining the literacy

TABLE 6.19

Awareness about the Control of Over Crowding in Public Places

Sl. No.	*Background*	*Control of Over Crowding in Schools, Colleges, Roads and Transport*			*Nos. of Respondents*
		By Increasing more human reourcer A	*By controlling population growth* B	*No need of doing anything* C	
	Age Group				
1.	15-25	2(4.45)	42(93.33)	1(2.23)	45
2.	26-35	—	41(100.00)	—	41
3.	36-50	1(5.88)	15(88.24)	1(5.88)	17
	Status				103
1.	Earning	1(1.82)	54(98.18)	—	55
2.	Non-earning	2(4.17)	44(91.67)	2(4.17)	48
	Caste/Community				103
1.	Scheduled Tribe	1(2.78)	35(97.22)	—	36
2.	Scheduled Caste	1(4.17)	22 (91.67)	1(4.17)	24
3.	General Caste	1(4.55)	21(95.45)	—	22
4.	Other Backward Caste	—	11 (91.67)	1(8.33)	12
5.	Muslims	—	9(100.00)	—	09
	Total Nos. of Respondents	3(2.91)	98(95.14)	2(1.94)	103

Note : Figures within parentheses indicate percentages.

programme they were not so aware about the harm of over growth of population in relation to agricultural land. Now they have realised the fact, however, there is no doubt about the fact that RSS has been able to develop awareness among the slum women with regard to the evils of population explosion.

Here public places refer to schools, colleges, roads and transports. About the awareness of slum women with regard to over-crowding in public places it can be seen from the Table 6.19 that almost all the slum women irrespective of their age, caste/community and earning-non-earning status are aware about the check of over-crowding in public places by controlling population growth. Only a few slum women from almost all the caste/community background (except Muslim) were not found to have developed their awareness by expressing that over-crowding can be checked : *(i)* by increasing more human resources, *(ii)* there is no need of doing anything. This unawareness of the very few respondents might be due to their negative attitudes or self-images which resulted in their inactive participation. *(iii)* the timing for the awareness programmes might not be suitable to the respondents, or *(iv)* their chronic illness which counts a lot. In case of the cent per cent awareness level among the respondents of the age group 26-35 and also the Muslim women, it can be said that : *(i)* since the slum women of the said age group are quite young and matured, they might have taken active participation in those awareness activities, *(ii)* they might have been supported by their family members and friends in follow up discussion and household chores. All of these helped them to develop their awareness level. In case of Muslim women, they are suppressed by the family and society. So when they got the chance to attend the awareness programmes of RSS, their eyes must have opened to a greater extent. This resulted in their development of cent per cent awareness level. The above table also shows a highly satisfactory level of awareness developed among the slum women. It indicates highly positive impact of the awareness generation activities of the RSS on the slum women of Rourkela.

TABLE 6.20

Awareness about Mechanism to Protect Environment

Sl. No.	*Background*	*Mechanism to protect environment*			*No. of Respondents*
		Deforestation of the Social Forstry A	*Hues Plantation* B	*To Eastablish a Number of Industries and Factories* C	
	Age Group				
1.	15-25	—	44(97.78)	1(2.22)	45
2.	26-35	—	41(100.00)	–	41
3.	36-50	—	16(94.180)	1(5.88)	17
	Status				103
1.	Earning	—	54(98.18)	1(1.82)	55
2.	Non-earning	—	47(97.92)	1(2.08)	48
	Caste/Community				103
1.	Scheduled Tribe	—	35(97.22)	1(2.78)	36
2.	Scheduled Caste	—	23(95.83)	1(4.17)	24
3.	General Caste	—	22(100.00)	—	22
4.	Other Backward Caste	—	12(100.00)	—	12
5.	Muslims	—	9(100.00)	—	09
	Total Nos. of Respondents	—	101(98.05)	2(1.94)	103

Note : Figures within parentheses indicate percentages.

It can be viewed from the above Table 6.20 that almost cent per cent respondents irrespective of their age, caste/community and earning status are aware of the mechanism to protect environment by expressing their views on hues plantation. Only a very few (1.94%) respondents from both younger and older groups (one from each group) have shown their ignorance by responding to establish a number of industries and factories as protectional mechanism for environment. Such response of the slum women may be because of the following :

(i) The respondents belong to the poor class and always think for their livelihood in the social environment. They might have thought that a number of industries would be helpful for them in providing job opportunities and financial security and help them to protect in the social environment. They might not have thought about the natural environment.

(ii) The respondents of younger age group might not have critically thought about the protectional mechanisms as one of the respondent was immature.

(iii) In case of the respondent of older age group, the other respondent might be hesitating to participate in the awareness programme actively. That caused low level of awareness. It is important to mentioned here that a good number of plantation programmes have been

organised by RSS through the Chetana Samities from time to time in different slums during the RSS programmes. The members of Chetana Samities and neo-literate slum women have actively participated in all those programmes. The investigator herself has experienced their plantation in Bondamunda, Pradhan Palli, Gudiatoli and Khariabahal slums during her field visit for data collection. The active involvement of slum women in plantation programmes and extremely satisfactory responses of the respondent presented in Table 6.20 indicate the highly positive impact of RSS in developing high level of awareness among the slum women of Rourkela.

TABLE 6.21
Awareness about Family Welfare and Small Family Norms

Sl. No.	Background	Number of Children in the Family Depends				Nos. of Respondents
		Upon Both Father and Mother A	Upon Father Only B	Upon Mother Only C	Upon God D	
	Age Group					
1.	15-25	43(95.56)	1(2.22)	1(2.22)	—	45
2.	26-35	39(95.12)	1(2.44)	—	1(2.44)	41
3.	36-50	16(94.12)	1(5.88)	—	—	17
	Status					103
1.	Earning	53(96.360)	2(3.64)	—	—	55
2.	Non-earning	45(93.76)	1(2.08)	1(2.08)	1(2.08)	48
	Caste/Community					103
1.	Scheduled Tribe	34(94.44)	2(5.56)	—	—	36
2.	Scheduled Caste	22(91.67)	—	1(4.17)	1(4.17)	24
3.	General Caste	21(95.450)	1(4.55)	—	—	22
4.	Other Backward Caste	12(100.00)	—	—	—	12
5.	Muslims	9(100.00)	—	—	—	9
	Total Nos. of Respondents	98(95.14)	3(2.91)	1(0.97)	1(0.97)	103

Note : Figures within parentheses indicate percentages.

It is evident from the Table 6.21 that almost all the respondents irrespective of their caste/ community and earning and non-earning status are aware about the fact that the number of the children in a family depends upon both father and mother.

A meagre percentage (85%) of respondents from all the age group, and different caste/community like ST, SC and GC and even from earning and non-earning background were found to be unaware about this fact that the number of children in a family depends upon both the parents.

It may be mentioned here that the respondents of GC category who always feel themselves superior, and under-estimate the ST, SC and others are also unaware like ST and SC respondents. It might be due to their superiority complex that by birth they are superior as they belong to higher castes families, and might not have wanted to mix and discuss with the respondents from SCs and STs of which they are ashamed of, count for their unawareness.

It might have so happened that the unaware respondents from all the categories might have been interacted to discuss about the related issues on small family norms but since their volunteers were male they could not have clarified their doubts and remained unaware.

Further, it can be seen from the table that the respondents from OBC and Muslim community have developed cent per cent awareness in this regard. It gives a clue to guess that both OBC and Muslim respondents are considered as disadvantaged group of the society. And in case of Muslim they are less privileged than the others. When they (both the group) got the scope to develop their awareness level through the activities of RSS they might have taken more interest for active participation in the programme, which resulted for their high level of awareness development. However, as observed from the above table it can be said that the level of awareness among the respondents for the above mentioned aspect was quite high and indicated the successful programming of RSS in developing awareness among the slum women.

TABLE 6.22
Awareness about Family Welfare and Small Family Norms

Sl. No.	*Background*	*Responsible for the Birth of Femate Child*			*Nos. of Respondents*
		Mother A	*Father* B	*Both of them* C	
	Age Group				
1.	15-25	7(15.56)	28(62.22)	10(22.22)	45
2.	26-35	6(14.63)	27(65.85)	8(19.51	41
3.	36-50	3(17.65)	9(52.94)	5(29.41)	17
	Status				103
1.	Earning	7(12.73)	36(65.45)	12(21.82)	55
2.	Non-earning	9(18.75)	28(58.33)	11(22.92)	48
	Caste/Community				103
1.	Scheduled Tribe	5(13.89)	23(63.89)	8(22.22)	36
2.	Scheduled Caste	4(16.67)	15(62.5)	5(20.83)	24
3.	General Caste	3(13.64)	14(63.64)	5(22.73)	22
4.	Other Backward Caste	2(16.67)	7(58.33)	3(25.00)	12
5.	Muslims	2(2.22)	5(55.56)	2(2.22)	09
	Total Nos. of Respondents	16(15.53)	64(62.13)	23(22.33)	103

Note : Figures within parentheses indicate percentages.

Awareness about family welfare and small family norms-responsible for the birth of a female child.

It can be viewed from the Table 6.22 that majority of the slum women, irrespective of their age, caste/community and earning and non-earning status have shown awareness by expressing their views that father is responsible for the birth of a female child, and a very low percentage of them have expressed their unawareness by responding that the mother is responsible for the birth of a female child. Whereas, a low percentage of slum women have shown their unawareness by viewing on both father and mother to be responsible for the birth of a female child. Thus about 40% unaware slum women from all types of back of round : *(i)* might not have been sincere in the awareness generation activities/discussion forms, or *(ii)* after knowing about the actual fact also they might not have believed and might not have changed their pre-occupied belief that both father and mother one responsible for the birth of the female child. That resulted for their unawareness.

It is pertinent to mention here that even in some of the educated families it is seen that they are not aware of the fact that father is responsible for the birth of a girl child. In this situation when more than 60% slum women are aware about the same, it can be said that it is not a small achievement. Rather, it shows a high level of understanding along with the awareness among the slum women and indicates the success of RSS in developing awareness among slum women.

TABLE 6.23

Awareness about Family Welfare and Small Family Norms—Number of Children in the Family

Sl. No.	*Background*	*Number of Children in a Family*			*Nos. of Respondents*
		No. Fixed Limit A	*One or Two* B	*More Than Two* C	
	Age Group				
1.	15-25	—	41(91.11)	4(8.89)	45
2.	26-35	—	38(92.68)	3(7.31)	41
3.	36-50	—	14(82.35)	3(17.65)	17
	Status				103
1.	Earning	—	51(92.73)	4(7.27)	55
2.	Non-earning	—	42(87.5)	6(12.5)	48
	Caste/Community				103
1.	Scheduled Tribe	—	33(91.67)	3(8.33)	36
2.	Scheduled Caste	—	21(87.5)	3(12.5)	24
3.	General Caste	—	20(90.90)	2(9.10)	22
4.	Other Backward Caste	—	11(91.67)	1(8.33)	12
5.	Muslims	—	8(88.89)	1(11.11)	09
	Total Nos. of Respondents	—	93(90.30)	10(9.70)	103

Note : Figures within parentheses indicate percentages.

It can be seen from the Table 6.23 that most of the respondents irrespective of age, caste/ community and earning status are in favour of small family norms with one or two children. And none of the respondents have given their view for a family with no fixed limit of children. Only a meagre percentage of respondents from all the background have expressed their opinion that there should be more than two children in the family. They might have expressed such responses because : *(i)* some of them might have experienced the death of infants in their own families, *(ii)* they might have thought of getting support from their children in future, *(iii)* the amateur school volunteer might not have been able to convenience about the deep-rooted effects of over growth of population. All these factors might be responsible for their low level of awareness.

It was expected that the slum women specially from Muslim community would not have developed favourable attitude towards small family norms due to their socio-cultural restrictions. But it was found that they have also developed favourable attitude towards small family norms with one or two children. Even in practice also they have adopted such ideas in their own life with family opposition. Not only the Muslim, but the respondents of other caste/community background have adopted such ideas in practice. Even the respondents of older age group have encouraged the younger generations of the slum to adopt small family norms. The investigator has cross-verified the fact from the family welfare unit of URS, pass post Government Hospital of Rourkela. The Officer-in-charge of the medical unit has also informed to the investigator that the number of family planning operation has been increased in the slum areas of Rourkela then that of the previous years after implementation of the literacy and awareness programme in Rourkela.

He further informed that some of the respondents have gone for family planning operation even after the birth of one of two daughters.

The highly satisfactory response of the slum women as emerged from the above table not only shows the high level of awareness among the respondents, but also it indicates the success of RSS in developing high level of awareness among the neo-literate slum women in Rourkela.

TABLE 6.24

Awareness about Child and Maternity Care—Diet of the Pregnant Mother

Sl. No.	*Background*	*Diet of the Pregnant Mother*			*Nos. of Respondents*
		Food Rich in Fats A	*Food Rich in Protein* B	*Food Without Vitamins* C	
	Age Group				
1.	15-25	7(15.56)	36(80.00)	2(4.44)	45
2.	26-35	7(17.07)	33(80.49)	1(2.44)	41
3.	36-50	3(17.65)	13(76.47)	1(5.88)	17
	Status				103
1.	Earning	11(20.00)	44(80.00)	—	55
2.	Non-earning	10(20.83)	38 (79.17)	—	48
	Caste/Community				103
1.	Scheduled Tribe	7(19.44)	27(75.00)	2(5.56)	36
2.	Scheduled Caste	5(20.83)	18(75.00)	1(4.17)	24
3.	General Caste	2(9.09)	19(86.36)	1(4.55)	22
4.	Other Backward Caste	2(16.67)	10(83.33)	--	12
5.	Muslims	1(11.11)	8(83.89)	—	09
	Total Nos. of Respondents	17(16.50)	82(79.61	4(3.88)	103

Note : Figures within parentheses indicate percentages.

Data presented in the Table 6.24 reveals that a great majority of respondents irrespective of their age, caste/community and earning status are aware of the diet of the pregnant mothers that they should take protenious food. Whereas, a meagre percentage of slum women from all the background have expressed their unawareness by responding on food rich in fats for the pregnant mothers. Such response of the slum women may be because of the following : *(i)* They might not have differentiated the type of food properly due to lack of acquaintance with such kind of food in their daily life, *(ii)* They might have a preoccupied notion in the mind that food rich in fats would be more beneficial for the pregnant mother, or *(iii)* The volunteer might not have discussed about the diet before the respondents properly with illustrations or examples due to lack of practical experiences. There factors must have affected for their unawareness. Further, the table reveals that very poor (3.88%) percentage of respondents have shown their unawareness by responding to food without vitamins for the pregnant mother. Such type of response of the respondents might be due to : *(i)* their unwillingness to know about the different types of diet specially for the pregnant women, *(ii)* their wretched poverty might not have helped them to think about nutritious food during pregnancy, *(iii)* they might have some notion in the mind that a very good diet (nutritious food) during pregnancy leads to an overgrowth of the foetus and can be the reason for complicacies during delivery. That caused for low level of awareness among the slum women. However, despite differences, the satisfactory responses of a great majority of responses show a high level of awareness among them and indicates a positive impact of RSS in developing satisfactory level of awareness among the slum women of Rourkela.

TABLE 6.25
Awareness About the Advantages of Breast-Feeding

Sl. No.	*Background*	*Effect of Brest Feeding*			*Nos. of Respondents*
		Mother becomes weak A	*Infant becomes healthy by increasing immunity power* B	*It makes no differences on the health status of the mother and the Infant* C	
	Age Group				
1.	15-25	2(4.44)	43(95.56)	—	45
2.	26-35	1(2.44)	40(97.56)	—	41
3.	36-50	3(17.65)	14(82.35)	—	17
	Status				103
1.	Earning	2(3.64)	53(96.36)	—	55
2.	Non-earning	4(8.33)	44(91.67)	—	48
	Caste/Community				103
1.	Scheduled Tribe	1(2.78)	35(97.22)	—	36
2.	Scheduled Caste	2(8.33)	22(91.67)	—	24
3.	General Caste	1(4.55)	21(95.45)	—	22
4.	Other Backward Caste	1(8.33)	11(91.67)	—	12
5.	Muslims	1(11.11)	8(83.89)	--	09
	Total Nos. of Respondents	6(5.83)	97(94.17)	--	103

Note : Figures within parentheses indicate percentages.

It can be viewed from the Table 6.25 that most of the slum women irrespective of their age, caste/community and earning non-earning status were found to be aware about the affect of breast-feeding, and none of the respondents showed their unawareness by responding that it makes no differences on the health status of the mother and the infant. Further, the table shows that a very few percentage of respondents from all the categories were not found to have developed their awareness as they responded on the statement that the mother becomes weak due to breast-feeding. Such a response of the slum women might be due to : *(i)* the teaching volunteer in the

Chetana Kendra might be a young and shy boy who did not want to discuss openly about the advantages of breast-feeding before the young slum women, *(ii)* they might have some prejudices for breast-feeding that the mother becomes weak for the same, or *(iii)* they might not have the exposure to mass media especially T.V. on its advertisement on merits of breast-feeding. That count a lot for their unawareness.

Mention may be made here that every year RSS had been celebrating the breast-feeding week with a very good number of health related activities in the slum areas of Rourkela. A number of neo-literate slum women had been participating in those activities actively. The investigator herself has observed their activities, behaviour and level of awareness in the field during the celebration of breast-feeding week and found them highly aware with the many sensitive benefits of breast-feeding related to the spacing of children.

However, the highly satisfactory responses of most of the respondents indicate a high level of awareness among the neo-literate slum women. It can therefore, be said that the literacy activities of RSS had a healthy impact in generating highly satisfactory level of awareness among the slum women of Rourkela.

TABLE 6.26
Awareness about the Medical Registration of the Pregnant Women

Sl. No.	*Background*	*Timing for the Medical Registration of the Pregnant Women*			*Nos. of Respondents*
		Within 7/8 Months of Pregnancy A	*Within 4/5 Months of Pregnancy* B	*No Need of Registration* C	
	Age Group				
1.	15-25	10(22.22)	35(77.78)	—	45
2.	26-35	7(17.07)	34(82.93)	—	41
3.	36-50	5(29.41)	12(70.59)	—	17
	Status				103
1.	Earning	12(21.82)	43(78.18)	—	55
2.	Non-earning	10(20.83)	38(79.17)	—	48
	Caste/Community				103
1.	Scheduled Tribe	8(22.22)	28(77.27)	—	36
2.	Scheduled Caste	7(29.17)	17(70.83)	—	24
3.	General Caste	5(22.73)	17(77.27)	—	22
4.	Other Backward Cast	2(16.67)	10(83.33)	—	12
5.	Muslims	2(22.22)	7(77.78)	—	09
	Total Nos. of Respondents	22(21.36)	81(78.64)	—	103

Note : Figures within parentheses indicate percentages.

Data presented in the Table 6.26 shows that a majority of respondents irrespective of their age, caste/community and earning status were found to be aware of the need and timing for medical registration of the pregnant women, and none of the respondents had shown their unawareness by responding to the answer no need of medical registration of the pregnant women. It is further seen from the table that a meagre percentage of respondents from all the background

TABLE 6.27
Awareness about the Immunisation of the Pregnant Women

Sl. No.	Background	Timiing for Giving Tetanus Toxoid to Pregnant Women			Nos. of Respondents
		No Need of TT TT A	Within 5/6 Months of Pregnancy B	Just Before the Delivery C	
	Age Group				
1.	15-25	—	41(91.11)	4(8.89)	45
2.	26-35	—	39(95.12)	2(4.88)	41
3.	36-50	—	14(82.35)	3(17.65)	17
					103
	Status				
1.	Earning	—	50(90.90)	5(9.10)	55
2.	Non-earning	—	44(91.67)	4(8.33)	48
					103
	Caste/Community				
1.	Scheduled Tribe	—	33(91.67)	3(8.33)	36
2.	Scheduled Caste	—	22(91.67)	2(8.33)	24
3.	General Caste	—	20(90.91)	2(9.09)	22
4.	Other Backward Caste	—	11(91.67)	1(8.33)	12
5.	Muslims	—	8(88.89)	1(11.11)	09
	Total Nos. of Respondents	—	94(91.26)	9(8.74)	103

Note : Figures within parentheses indicate percentages.

were not found to be aware as they responded that the timing for the medical registration should be with in 7/8 months of pregnancy. This type of response of the slum women might be because : *(i)* they might not have keen interest to know the details about the medical check-up and guidance for the pregnant women, *(ii)* they might not have changed their rigid attitude of avail medical facilities made available for the pregnant women, or *(iii)* they might not have understood properly the essence of medical registration of the pregnant women. All these factors must be responsible caused for their unawareness. However, the highly satisfactory response of the great majority of respondents shows highly satisfactory level of awareness among the slum women and indicate the successful programming of RSS in developing awareness among the slum women.

It is evident from the Table 6.27 that most of the slum women irrespective of their age, caste/community and earning status are aware about the need and timing for giving tetanus toxoid to pregnant women. It is also seen from the table that none of the slum women have expressed their unawareness by responding that there is no need of giving tetanus toxoid to pregnant women. Further, the table shows that a low percentage of respondents from all the categories are found to be unaware by showing their unawareness that tetanus toxoid should be given just before the delivery. It means they are aware about the need of tetanus toxoid for the pregnant women, but are not aware about the timing for giving T.T. to them. Such type of unawareness among the few respondents might be due to : *(i)* their negligence of knowing and enquiring about the immunisation etc. of the pregnant women, *(ii)* they might not have keen interest to be aware about such information, *(iii)* they might not have been informed about the timing very properly. All these factors must have affected for their unawareness about the timing of giving tetanus toxoid. It will not be out of place to mention here that the slum women of Rourkela have become more conscious about their own health status after joining the literacy programme. They have reported to the investigator about the regular vaccination and medical check-up of the pregnant women of their slums.

It is clear that most of the slum women (see Table 6.27) have high level of awareness which shows a highly positive impact of RSS activities in developing awareness among the neo-literate slum women of Rourkela.

TABLE 6.28
Awareness about the Diseases of the Infants and their Immunisation

Sl. No.	*Background*	*Possible Dangerous Diseases Vulnerable to Infants*			*Nos. of Respondents*
		Cancer, Plague, Jaundice, Diptheria A	*Polio, Tetanus, Whooping Cough* B	*Small Pox, Skin Diseases, Cholera* C	
	Age Group				
1.	15-25	1(2.22)	44(97.78)	—	45
2.	26-35	1(2.44)	40(97.56)	—	41
3.	36-50	—	15(88.24)	2(11.76)	17
	Status				103
1.	Earning	—	54(98.18)	1(1.82)	55
2.	Non-earning	2(4.17)	45(93.75)	1(2.08)	48
	Caste/Community				103
1.	Scheduled Tribe	1(2.78)	35(97.22)	—	36
2.	Scheduled Caste	—	23(95.83)	1(4.17)	24
3.	General Caste	1(4.55)	21(95.45)	—	22
4.	Other Backward Caste	—	11(91.67)	1(8.33)	12
5.	Muslims	—	9(100.00)	—	09
	Total Nos. of Respondents	2(1.94)	99(96.11)	2(1.94)	103

Note : Figures within parentheses indicate percentages.ppp

It can be observed from the Table 6.28 that almost all the respondents irrespective of their age, caste/community and earning status were found to be aware of the diseases in infants. Only a few per cent (two only) of respondents from younger and middle age group, and non-earning background were found to be unaware by responding on cancer, plague, jaundice and diptheria as possible dangerous diseases of the infants. Further, one of the respondent was from ST and GC background respectively.

The table also shows that a very few respondents (only two) of older age group with both earning and non-earning background from SC and OBC categories were also found to be unaware by showing their unawareness on the response small pox, skin disease and cholera as the possible disease for infants. It is pertinent to mention here that a very few respondents (only four) from all the age groups, earning and non-earning background and most of the caste/community background (except Muslim) have shown their unawareness in two different responses. Whereas the Muslim respondents have shown cent per cent awareness for the same. The unawareness among the respondents of different age, caste and earning categories might not be due to their background variables, but might be due to the following : *(i)* they might not have experienced such diseases of infants in their families, *(ii)* might have lack of interest to know about their infant diseases as they have crossed the age of fertility (in case of the respondents of older age group), and *(iii)* might be the only respondent of young age group was too immature to differentiate the common disease with diseases of infants. All these factors might have led to ignorance with the possible infant diseases among the slum women. In case of the cent per cent awareness among the Muslim slum women might be due to : *(i)* active participation on in the health camps organised by RSS through "Seva Sadan" very frequently, *(ii)* keen interest of the women to know about the child care and its related issues including infants diseases, etc., or *(iii)* the support provided by their family members to know more and more about different aspects of infant growth and development through various other programmes organised by other organisations. Their reasons might have affected in generating cent per cent awareness level among the Muslim slum women.

It is, therefore, illogical to draw a conclusion that age, caste and earning back-ground of the respondents are responsible for the awareness development of the slum women. They might be influencing in developing their awareness level to some extent, but not the whole. However, the satisfactory response of the slum women as observed from the above table indicates the high level of awareness among the respondents and there is no doubt about the fact that RSS has been able to develop awareness in the slum women with regard to child and maternity care.

TABLE 6.29
Awareness about the Essential Vaccines for the Infants

Sl. No.	*Background*	*Essential Vaccines for the Infant to be Given Immediately After the Birth*			*No. of Respondents*
		Measles vaccines A	*BCG and DPT* B	*Polio booster* C	
	Age Group				
1.	15-25	—	43(95.56)	2(4.44)	45
2.	26-35	1(2.44)	39(95.12)	1(2.44)	41
3.	36-50	3(17.65)	11(4.70)	3(17.65)	17
	Status				103
1.	Earning	2(3.62)	51(92.73)	2(3.64)	55
2.	Non-earning	2(4.17)	42(87.5)	4(8.33)	48
	Caste/Community				103
1.	Scheduled Tribe	2(5.56)	33(91.67)	1(2.78)	36
2.	Scheduled Caste	1(4.17)	21(87.5)	2(8.33)	24
3.	General Caste	1(4.55)	20(90.90)	1(4.55)	22
4.	Other Backward Caste	—	11(91.67)	1(8.33)	12
5.	Muslims	—	8(88.89)	1(11.11)	09
	Total Nos. of Respondents	4(3.88)	93(90.29)	6(5.83)	103

Note : Figures within parentheses indicate percentages.

It can be viewed from the Table 6.29 that more than 90% respondents irrespective of their age, caste/community and earning, non-earning status are aware of the essential vaccines for the infants. Only a few per cent of respondents from all the backgrounds are not aware that BCG and DPT vaccines should be given to the infants immediately after birth. Therefore, 3.88% of respondents from middle and older age group with both earning and non-earning status with ST, SC, and GT caste/community background have responded on measles, vaccines, and 5.83% of respondents irrespective of age, caste/community and earning status have expressed their view on Polio-Booster to be given to the infants immediately after birth. This ignorance among the very few respondents might be due to : *(i)* lack of attendance and sincerity in the health awareness programme on child and maternity care, *(ii)* they did not feel the necessity of knowing about such vaccines as many of them have crossed this stage for childcare and nourishment, *(iii)* the health awareness programmes of RSS might not have been organised very properly with follow-up discussion, or *(iv)* the respondents in those awareness activities due to over family burden. All these reasons might have influenced the respondents to remain unaware about the essential vaccines for infants.

However one can see from the above Table 6.29 that a high level of awareness among the slum women about diseases in infants have been generated in the neo-literate slum women of Rourkela.

TABLE 6.30
Awareness with Regard to the First Polio Dose to the Infants

Sl. No.	*Background*	*First Dose of Polio Drop should be Given to the Child*			*Nos. of Respondents*
		Immediately After Birth A	*After Six Weeks of Birth* B	*Just at Sixth Weeks of Birth* C	
	Age Group				
1.	15-25	41(91.11)	2(4.44)	2(4.44)	45
2.	26-35	38(92.68)	2(4.88)	1(2.44)	41
3.	36-50	15(88.24)	1(5.88)	1(5.88)	17
	Status				103
1.	Earning	51(92.72)	2(3.64)	2(3.64)	55
2.	Non-earning	43(89.58)	3(6.25)	2(4.17)	48
	Caste/Community				103
1.	Scheduled Tribe	34(94.44)	1(2.78)	1(2.78)	36
2.	Scheduled Caste	22(91.67)	1(4.17)	1(4.17)	24
3.	General Caste	20(90.90)	1(4.55)	1(4.55)	22
4.	Other Backward Caste	10(83.34)	1(8.33)	1(8.33)	12
5.	Muslims	8(88.89)	1(11.11)	—	09
	Total Nos. of Respondents	94(91.26)	5(4.85)	4(3.88)	103

Note : Figures within parentheses indicate percentages.

It is evident from the data presented in the Table 6.30 that most of the slum women irrespective of their age, caste/community and earner status have realised the need for administering polio drops to their infants and they are aware about the timing for the first dose of polio drops to be given to the infants by expressing their views on immediately after birth. Only a very few respondents (five only) from all the categories have been found to be unaware as they expressed their opinion that first dose of polio should be given to the infant after six week of birth. Further a very few respondents (four only) of all the age groups with both earning and non-earning categories from ST, SC, GC. and OBC caste/community background have been found to be unaware about the timing of giving first polio dose to infants by responding on just six week of the birth of infant. The unawareness among both the groups of unaware respondents might be due to : (i) their lack of interest in health aspect of literacy programme, (ii) lack of exposure to various discussion forum/programme related to health and immunisation programme, (iii) lack of time due to overwork load in the family and outside for follow-up discussion related to health aspect of the child, or (iv) the volunteer himself/herself was unable to inform very accurately about the timing for first dose of polio. All these factors might have compelled them to be unaware with such situation.

It is important to mention here that the respondents have reported to the investigator about the regular immunisation of their children. Further, it was informed that every child was administered polio drops. It was also noticed that they have become more conscious, about the health, nutrition and immunisation of their children. As a result, the IMR rate has been checked in Rourkela slums. It was found from the records and reports of Anganwadi workers, field supervisors and CDPO of ICDS project that the IMR of the city (especially in the slum areas) has come down from 98 (in the year 1991) to 56 (in the year 1999) (per 1000). According to them, the control of IMR rate of the city was possible only due to the efforts of RSS.

TABLE 6.31
Awareness of Personal Health and Hygiene : Risk of Attending of Nature's call in the Field

Sl. No.	*Background*	*Risk of Attending Nature's call in the Field*			*Nos. of Respondents*
		Getting Disease by Hookworn A	*Environment Becomes Polluted* B	*Spreading of Diseases like Cholera and Diarrhoea* C	
	Age Group				
1.	15-25	35(77.78)	10(22.22)	—	45
2.	26-35	33(80.49)	8(19.41)	—	41
3.	36-50	10(58.82)	7(41.18)	—	17
	Status				103
1.	Earning	42(76.36)	13(23.64)	—	55
2.	Non-earning	36(75.00)	12(25.00)	—	48
	Caste/Community				103
1.	Scheduled Tribe	29(80.56)	7(19.44)	—	36
2.	Scheduled Caste	17(66.67)	7(33.33)	—	24
3.	General Caste	17 (77.27)	5(22.73)	—	22
4.	Other Backward Caste	8(66.67)	4(33.33)	—	12
5.	Muslims	7(77.78)	2(22.22)	—	09
	Total Nos. of Respondents	78(75.73)	25(24.27)	—	103

Note : Figures within parentheses indicate percentages.

However, the above table also shows a high level of awareness developed among the respondents. It indicates a highly positive impact of literacy programme of RSS on the neo-literate slum women of Rourkela.

It is viewed from the Table 6.31 that three-fourth of the respondents irrespective of their age, caste/community and earning and non-earning status were found to be aware about the effects of visiting open fields to attend nature's call by responding on getting disease by hookworm, and none of the respondents had shown their unawareness by responding to spreading of diseases like cholera or diahorrea as consequences of visiting open field to attend nature's call. Whereas about one-fourth of the respondents from all the background had shown their unawareness by responding on environmental pollution as the affect of attending nature's call in the open field. Such responses of the neo literate slum women might be due to the following :

(i) They might be absent from the literacy centre due to some personal reason on the very particular day when discussion was made on evils of visiting open field to attend nature's call.

(ii) They might not be interested in participating in such discussion forum which seems to be very common and known to every body, or

(iii) They might have some pre-occupied belief that environment gets polluted due to the same.

All these causes might have caused the low level of awareness among the unaware slum women.

However, the response of majority of the slum women as stated in Table 6.31 shows satisfactory level of awareness among them and indicates a positive impact of literacy programme of RSS on the neo-literate slum women.

TABLE 6.32

Awareness about Personal Health—after Visiting Latrine

Sl. No.	*Background*	*Maintenance of Cleanliness After Attending Nature's Call*			*Nos. of Respondents*
		Nothing Doing A	*Using Soap to Clean Hands and Feet* B	*Washing Hands and Feet by Using Clay or Ash* C	
	Age Group				
1.	15-25	—	44(97.78)	1(2.22)	45
2.	26-35	—	41(100.00)	—	41
3.	36-50	—	15(88.24)	2(11.76)	17
	Status				103
1.	Earning	—	54(98.18)	(1.82)	55
2.	Non-earning	—	46(95.83)	2(4.17)	48
	Caste/Community				103
1.	Scheduled Tribe	—	35(97.22)	1(2.78)	36
2.	Scheduled Caste	—	23(95.83)	1(4.17)	24
3.	General Caste	—	22(100.00)	—	22
4.	Other Backward Caste	—	11(91.67)	1(8.33)	12
5.	Muslims	—	9(100.00)	—	09
	Total Nos. of Respondents	—	100(97.08)	3(2.91)	103

Note: Figures within parentheses indicate percentages.

Data presented in the Table 6.32 reveals that almost all the slum women irrespective of their age, caste/community and earning and non-earning status are aware of using soap after visiting the latrine. Only a very few (2.91%) slum women of both young and older age group with earning and non-earning status from ST, SC and OBC caste/community background have shown their unawareness by responding to use clay or ask after visiting latrine. Such responses of the slum women may be due to : *(i)* their age old practice of using clay or ash might not have been changed till now (in case of the slum women of older age group and tribal women, *(ii)* they might not have though of using soap so seriously, or *(iii)* they might not have been made to understand properly the reason of using soap instead of any other thing. These factors might have caused their unawareness regarding the use of soap for the same. It is important to mention here that none of the slum women have shown their unawareness by responding to "nothing to be done after visiting latrine." It means they are aware that something should be used for cleanliness. But what should be used for cleaning purpose or purpose of sanitation was not exactly known to the very few unaware respondents.

Further, it can be seen that the slum women of GC and Muslim background have shown cent per cent awareness in this regard. This might be due to: *(i)* they might have been working in educated families (in case of earning women), *(ii)* family members might be literate and conscious about personal health, *(iii)* volunteers might have taken special care to make the Muslim women understand about the personal health (in case of Muslim slum women), or *(iv)* they themselves might have taken much interest to know about personal health. These factors must have counted in achieving cent per cent awareness level among GC and Muslim slum women. It is important to

TABLE 6.33
Awareness about Personal Hygiene—to get Purified Water from Well

Sl. No.	Background	To be Done to get Purified Water from Well			Nos. of Respondents
		Putting Lime in the Well A	*Use of Clean Bucket* B	*Not Washing Clothes Near the Well* C	
	Age Group				
1.	15-25	20(44.44)	7(15.56)	18(40.00)	45
2.	26-35	18(43.90)	6(14.63)	17(41.47)	41
3.	36-50	8(47.05)	3(17.65)	6(35.30)	17
	Status				103
1.	Earning	24(43.64)	9(16.36)	22(40.00)	55
2.	Non-earning	22(45.83)	7(14.48)	19(39.48)	48
	Caste/Community				103
1.	Scheduled Tribe	16(44.44)	5(13.89)	15(41.67)	36
2.	Scheduled Caste	10(41.67)	3(12.5)	11(45.83)	24
3.	General Caste	10(45.45)	4(18.18)	8(36.37)	22
4.	Other Backward Caste	6(50.00)	2(16.66)	4(33.34)	12
5.	Muslims	4(44.44)	2(22.22)	3(33.33)	09
	Total Nos. of Respondents	46(44.66)	16(15.53)	41 (39.80)	103

Note : Figures within parentheses indicate percentages.

mention here that a very good number of slum women have admitted before the investigator during indepth discussion that before joining the literacy programme they were not particular to use soap for cleanliness after attending call of nature. However, the responses of the slum women as presented in the above table shows a high level of awareness among almost all the respondents and indicate a highly positive impact of RSS activities in generating awareness among the neo-literate slum women in Rourkela.

It is seen from the Table 6.33 that a good number of respondents irrespective of age, caste/community and earning status are aware that by putting lime in the well, purified water can be obtained and about 40% respondents of all the background have expressed their unawareness by responding not to wash clothes near by the well to get purified water. Further a meagre percentage of respondents (15.53%) from all the categories have expressed their unawareness by responding to use of clean bucket to get purified water.

It is pertinent to mention here that less than half of the respondents have been found to be fully aware about the use of lime to get purified water, and more than half of the respondents have not been found to be much aware about the proper way or technique to get purified water. Therefore, they have responded on the secondary strategy to get purified water. Their low level of awareness with this regard might be due to the following : *(i)* They might not have the scope to use a well in their day-to-day life as they are found very few in numbers in the urban areas, *(ii)* They might be habituated to use tap water or water from tube well for drinking purpose, *(iii)* They must be using for household and odd purpose. Therefore, they might not have been much conscious about the purification of water, *(iv)* due to wretched poverty they might not have money to purchase lime to put into the well for purification, or *(v)* the volunteer might not have discussed about the process of getting purified water from the well properly. These factors must have affected for the low level of awareness among the slum women.

The responses of the slum women presented in the stated in the Table 6.33 show a medium level of awareness developed among the respondents, that indicates simply a positive impact of RSS in generating awareness among the neo-literate slum women regarding purified water.

TABLE 6.34

Awareness About Personal Hygiene : Affect of Fly-infected Food

Sl. No.	*Background*	*Risk of Eating Fly Infected Food*			*Nos. of Respondents*
		Spreads jaundice *A*	*Spreads cholera* *B*	*Nothing happens* *C*	
1	2	3	4	5	6
	Age Group				
1.	15-25	—	45(100.00)	—	45
2.	26-35	—	41(100.00)	—	41
3.	36-50	—	17(100.00)	—	17
	Status				103
1.	Earning	—	55(100.00)	—	55
2.	Non-earning	—	48(100.00)	—	48
	Caste/Community				103
1.	Scheduled Tribe	—	36(100.00)	—	36

1	2	3	4	5	6
2.	Scheduled Caste	—	24(100.00)	—	24
3.	General Caste	—	22(100.00)	—	22
4.	Other Backward Caste	—	12(100.00)	—	12
5.	Muslims	—	9(100.00)	—	09
	Total Nos. of Respondents	—	103(100.00)	—	103

Note : Figures within parentheses indicate percentages.

It can be observed from the Table 6.34 that cent per cent slum women have been found to be aware that cholera spreads by eating fly-infected food. This cent per cent awareness among the slum women irrespective of their age, caste/community and earning status might be due to : *(i)* their keen interest to be aware about personal hygiene and its related aspects, *(ii)* there might have been frequent discussions on evils of taking fly-infected-food in the Chetana Kendra among the slum women, *(iii)* the literacy volunteer might have projected slide shows, video shows and pictures with this regard before the slum women during discussion so as to make the discussion more effective, *(iv)* they might have been exposed to the media like T.V. and radio programme with regard to health awareness and personal hygiene. These factors seem to count for their cent per cent awareness. However cent per cent responses of the slum women indicate the success of RSS in developing high level of awareness among the neo-literate slum women.

TABLE 6.35

Awareness About Personal Hygiene : To Get Rid of Mosquito

Sl. No.	*Background*	*To Get Rid of Mosquito*			*Nos. of Respondents*
		To Spread Smoke Regulariy in the House A	*Using Mosquito Net* B	*Keeping the Environment Clean* C	
	Age Group				
1.	15-25	2(4.44)	40(83.89)	3(6.67)	45
2.	26-35	2(4.88)	37(90.24)	2(4.88)	41
3.	36-50	2(11.76)	13(76.48)	2(11.76)	17
	Status				103
1.	Earning	2(3.64)	50(90.90)	3(5.46)	55
2.	Non-earning	4(8.33)	40(83.34)	4(8.33)	48
	Caste/Community				103
1.	Scheduled Tribe	2(5.56)	32(88.88)	2(5.56)	36
2.	Scheduled Caste	2(8.33)	20(83.33)	2(8.33)	24
3.	General Caste	1(4.55)	20(90.90)	1(4.55)	22
4.	Other Backward Caste	1(8.33)	10(83.89)	1(8.33)	12
5.	Muslims	—	8(88.89)	1(11.11)	09
	Total Nos. of Respondents	6(5.83)	90(87.37)	7(6.79)	103

Note : Figures within parentheses indicate percentages.

It can be viewed from the above Table 6.35 that a majority of respondents irrespective of their age, caste/community and earning status were found to be aware of the fact that to get rid of

mosquito, mosquito net should be used. It is also seen from the table that a meagre percentage (6.79%) of respondents were found to be less aware by responding to keeping the environment clean. And a very few percentage (5.83%) of the respondents were found to be very less aware by responding to spread smoke regularly in the house. This low level of awareness among both the group of respondents irrespective of their age, caste/community and earning status might be due to : *(i)* unawareness about the causes of Malaria, *(ii)* non-attendance in the discussion class due to lack of self-interest, *(iii)* their poverty might not have permitted to use mosquito net. Therefore, the alternatives they usually have adopted, have been responded by them, *(iv)* they might not have liked to use mosquito net due to the feeling of suffocation, *(v)* their age old practice of spreading of smoke and keeping the environment clean might not have been changed despite their participation in literacy programme. These factors must have affected their low level of awareness. However, the satisfactory responses of the slum women indicate that RSS has been able to generate high level of awareness among the neo-literate slum women in terms of personal hygiene.

Attitudinal Changes Found Among the Neo-literate Slum-Women

Under this heading it is intended to analyse and interpret the data pertaining to the changes found in the attitudes of neo-literate slum women in various aspects of life. They are evils of alcohol, superstitions, child marriage, dowry, status of girl child in the family, advantages of girls education, attitude towards political participation of women and helping husband, raising voice against exploitation, interest for social welfare and communal harmony, knowledge about property, right of women, various developmental schemes of government and social functionaries etc. The details of analysis and interpretation of data is presented here under :

TABLE 6.36
Changing Attitude Towards Evils of Alcoholism and Drug Abuse

Sl. No.	*Background*	*Effect of Drinking Alcohol*					*No. of Respondents*
		Individual Loses his sense A	*Individual Feels Active* B	*Increase of Social Prestige* C	*Health of Individual Improves* D	*Health of Individual Deteriorats* E	
	Age Group						
1.	15-25	9(20.00)	—	—	—	36(80.00)	45
2.	26-35	7(17.07)	—	—	—	34(82.93)	41
3.	36-50	5(29.41)	—	—	—	12(70.59)	17
	Status						103
1.	Earning	11(20.00)	—	—	—	44(80.00)	55
2.	Non-earning	10(20.83)	—	—	—	38(79.17)	48
	Caste/Community					103	
1.	Scheduled Tribe	7(19.44)	—	—	—	29(80.56)	36
2.	Scheduled Caste	5(20.83)	—	—	—	19(79.17)	24
3.	General Caste	3(13.64)	—	—	—	19(86.36)	22
4.	Other Backward Caste	4(33.33)	—	—	—	8(66.67)	12
5.	Muslims	2(22.22)	—	—	—	7(77.78)	9
	Total Nos. of Respondents	21(20.39)				82 (79.61)	103

Note : Figures within parentheses indicate percentage .

Table 6.36 reveals that majority of the respondents have changed their attitudes towards a positive direction by expressing their opinion that health of the individual deteriorates by consuming alcohol. Only a few respondents (about 20%) irrespective of their age, caste/community and earning status, have shown relatively less changes of their attitudes by expressing views that individual loses his sense by taking alcohol, and none of the respondents have supported the statements that by drinking alcohol : *(i)* individual feels active, *(ii)* his social prestige increases, and *(iii)* his health improves. It means that each and every respondent is aware about the evils of drinking alcohol. But the levels of awareness among them and their perceptions differ from one another. However, the healthy attitudes observed among a great majority of respondents may be attributed to : *(i)* the effect of street plays and cultural medias on the theme of evils of drinking alcohol, content of the P.L. Primer on evils of alcohol, door to door campaigning of the literacy volunteers in making the people understand about evils of drugs and alcohol or the demonstrative effects of the experienced person shared before the neo-literates about the serious effect of alcohol, *(ii)* they might have experienced serious effect of health problems or even death in their own families due to the consumption of alcohol, *(iii)* they themselves might have experienced the evils of drinking alcohol by getting their health status down, *(iv)* their self-interest to change their living condition. All these factors must have affected in changing their attitudes in a positive way.

The relatively less perceptible changes found among the respondents might be due to: *(i)* they must not have experienced the serious effect of alcohol related to health in their families, *(ii)* very few members of their family might have been drinking alcohol occasionally. So they might not have faced serious health problems other them loosing their senses, *(iii)* since alcoholism drinking is very common in the slum areas and even in higher societies where they are working as labourer, they might not have thought about evils of drinking alcohol so seriously, or *(iv)* they might not have seen the street plays or participated in the discussion forum in this regard as they joined the programme in the later stage. These factors count a lot for their relatively less perceptible changes in attitudes.

It would not be out of place to present here a few observations made by the investigator as a Rourkelite and researchers during her pre-field study for data collection. Normally in the slum-setting majority of the people are not habituated in drinking alcohol. In an industrial city like Rourkela, that too situated in the tribal district of Sundargarh, there is an additional impact of country liquor on the common people, especially on the tribals. Therefore, country liquor, and rice beer are very commonly needed by the slum-dwellers of both male and female (specially the tribals) of Rourkela slum. But it has been observed and experienced by the investigator as well as some of the local people (from whom she has collected required data regarding the impact of RSS) that most of them have started changing their living style and attitude after joining the literacy programme. During participant and non-participant observation in various cultural functions and ceremonies the investigator has observed that the women have not touched alcohol of any kind, but some male members have taken during "Tusu" and "Saharul" function, but they were under control.

During in-depth discussion two slum women of Dhipatoli and Kariabahal have confessed before the investigator that they were addicted to drink "Handia" (rice beer) before joining the programme. But after watching the street plays "Tenkarn" based on the theme of evils of alcohol and the women "Kala Yatha" "Sukannya", they could visualise the horrible consequences in future. So gradually they stopped drinking.

The teaching volunteers, cultural artists and members of Chetana Kendras have also reported to the investigator during interview that the message of the cultural plays on evils of drinking

alcohol were so powerful and influential that people (both male and female) become emotional and start weeping while watching the consequences of drinking alcohol. It was also reported by the informants and respondents that some of the slum-dwellers have stopped doing the business of rice beer after observing the street plays in Laltaki slum and Uttambasti.

This indicates that there was direct impact of the message of street plays and cultural activities of RSS on the people in changing their attitudes.

However, the satisfactory responses of the majority of the slum women as presented in the above table show a positive attitude towards evils of alcohol and indicate the success of RSS in changing their attitudes.

TABLE 6.37
Changing of Attitude towards Evils of Alcohol-Business of Country Liquor

Sl. No.	*Background*	*Evil of Doing the business of country liquor in the Slums*			*No. of Respondents*
		There is no harm of doing liquor business	*It lures the people*	*It helps to improve the economic condition of the country*	
		A	*B*	*C*	
	Age Group				
1.	15-25	—	43(95.56)	2(4.44)	45
2.	26-35	—	40(97.56)	1(2.44)	41
3.	36-50	—	16(94.11)	1(5.89)	17
	Status				103
1.	Earning	—	53(96.36)	2(3.64)	55
2.	Non-earning	—	46(95.83)	2(2.17)	48
	Caste/Community				103
1.	Scheduled Tribe	—	34(94.44)	2(5.56)	36
2.	Scheduled Caste	—	23(95.83)	1(4.17)	24
3.	General Caste	—	21(95.45)	1(4.56)	22
4.	Other Backward Caste	—	12(100.00)	—	12
5.	Muslims	—	9(100.00)	—	9
	Total Nos. of Respondents	—	99(96.11)	4(3.89)	103

Note : Figures within parentheses indicate percentages.

It can be viewed from the Table 6.37 that most of the respondents irrespective of their age, caste/community and earning status were found to have changed their attitudes in a healthy way by expressing their views that business of country liquor in the slums. Lures the people towards wrong direction, and none of the respondents have expressed their views that there is no harm in doing liquor business. It means every respondent know that there is harm of doing liquor business. This type of awareness found among the respondents might be because of the following : *(i)* the effect of "Street Plays", cultural activities, discussion forum and door to door campaigning on evils of alcohol and alcohol business, *(ii)* they themselves might have suffered a lot due to the drinking habits of their family members like, *(a)* all of their money might have been spend on alcohol and thereby their wretched poverty, *(b)* their husbands might have tortured them physically

after getting drunk, *(c)* they (family members) might have ill treated their children and outsiders after getting drunk, *(d)* they (the drunkards) might have committed criminal activities after getting drunk, *(e)* some of them might have done the liquor business (rice beer or country liquor) and experienced their down fall, and *(iii)* their self-interest and determination to change their situation might have caused for their attitudinal changes.

Further, the table shows that a few per cent (3.89%) respondents from all the age group with earning and non-earning status were found to have unchanged their attitudes towards the evils of liquor business by expressing their views that it helps to improve the economic condition of the country. This might be due to the following : *(i)* lack of interest and self-motivation of slum women to know about the evils of alcohol and alcoholic business, *(ii)* since half of the unaware respondents belong to younger age group, they may not have critically thought about the consequences due to immaturity, *(iii)* since they belong to the economically backward group of the society, they must have given priority to the in-coming of money. They might not have thought about the source of in-coming. Whether the source was healthy or not, *(iv)* they might not have been exposed to the cultural media or the discussion forum organised by RSS in this regard, as they have joined the campaign in a later stage. These factors seem to count for their unchanged attitudes.

It is worth mentioning over here that women group of various slums were taking an active part to closed own some of the country liquor shops in certain slums. It is also recorded that neo-literate tribal slum women of Ruputola, Kariabahal and Gudiatola slums have organised processions from time-to-time and were demanding the closure of country liquor shops in their slums and the city.

From the above it can be said here that RSS has been able to change the attitude of slum women to a greater extent with regard to evils of alcohol.

TABLE 6.38
Attitude Towards Evils of Superstition

Sl. No.	*Background*	*Person to be Consulted During Disease*				*Nos. of Respondents*
		Leaving on Fate A	*Doctor* B	*By Worshipping Goddess* C	*Consulting Black Magician* D	
	Age Group					
1.	15-25	—	43(95.56)	2(4.44)	—	45
2.	26-35	—	41(100.00)	—	—	41
3.	36-50	—	17(100.00)	—	—	17
	Status					103
1.	Earning	—	55(100.00)	—	—	55
2.	Non-earning	—	46(95.83)	2(4.17)	—	48
	Caste/Community					103
1.	Schedule Tribe	—	35(97.22)	1(2.78)	—	36
2.	Schedule Caste	—	23(95.83)	1(4.17)	—	24
3.	General Caste	—	22(100.00)	—	—	22
4.	Other Backward Caste	—	12(100.00)	—	—	12
5.	Muslims	—	9(100.00)	—	—	9
	Total Nos. of Respondents	—	101(98.05)	2(1.94)	—	103

Note : Figures within parenthesis indicate percentages.

It can be observed from the Table 6.38 that about cent per cent respondents irrespective of their age caste/community and earning status were found to have shown their positive attitude by expressing their view that doctor should be consulted in sickness and none of the respondents have expressed their unchanged attitude by expressing their opinion on leaving on fate or consulting to the black magician in getting sick. Mention may be made here that before joining the literacy programme most of the slum women were hesitant to consult doctors for any physical problems. They were not going to the hospital for their treatment. Rather they consulted to the black magicians even for serious deceases. Many of them were worshipping goddess. It was reported by the health officer of Rourkela Municipality that their magico-religious believes have been controlled to a greater extent after their participation in literacy programme. As a result instead of consulting a black magician or performing a Puja (worshipping) they go to the hospital for any of their health problem.

This highly favourable change in the attitude of the almost all the respondents must be due : *(i)* the follow-up discussion and interaction with the doctors, *(ii)* impact of the cultural media like folk dance, folk drama, street plays on the themes of evils of superstitions, *(iii)* the volunteers must have properly made them understand about the evils of superstitions, *(iv)* superstitions may not helped them in reality. All these factors must have forced to bring changes in the attitudes of the neo-literates.

The table further reveals that a very few respondents (only two) from the young age group were found to have maintained their attitude towards evils of superstitions. This might be due to : *(i)* their mental immaturity to think about the matter critically, *(ii)* they might not have been exposed to various cultural shows based on the theme of evils of superstitions, *(iii)* they might have lacked interest to change their attitude, *(iv)* their family members might have worshipped to

TABLE 6.39

Attitude Towards Child Marriage—Perception about Mothering at an Early Age

Sl. No.	*Background*	*Consequence of mothering at an Early Age*			*Nos. of Respondents*
		The Baby Becomes Healthy A	*The Mother Becomes Weak and Diseased* B	*The Mother Remains Healthy* C	
	Age Group				
1.	15-25	1(2.22)	43(95.56)	2(4.44)	45
2.	26-35	—	41(100.00)	—	41
3.	36-50	—	17(100.00)	—	17
	Status				103
1.	Earning	—	54(98.18)	1(1.22)	55
2.	Non-earning	—	47(97.42)	1(2.8)	48
	Caste/Community				103
1.	Scheduled Tribe	—	35(97.22)	1(2.78)	36
2.	Scheduled Caste	—	24(100.00)	—	24
3.	General Caste	1(4.55)	21(95.45)	—	22
4.	Other Backward Caste	—	12(100.00)	—	12
5.	Muslims	—	9(100.00)	—	9
	Total Nos. of Respondents	1(0.97)	101(98.06)	1(0.97)	103

Note : Figures within parenthesis indicate percentage.

the goddess during the illness of any family members. All these factors seem to count for the unchanged attitudes towards evils of superstitions. However, RSS has changed the perceptions of women in superstition.

It is evident from the above Table 6.39 that almost all the respondents irrespective of their age, caste/community and earning and non-earning status were found to have shown favourable attitudes towards the evils of child marriage by presenting their opinion that women get weak and diseased, when they become mothers at an early age. This highly perceptible change in the attitudes of the slum women might be attributed to the points as follows : *(i)* their interaction with the volunteers and medical personnel of the health camps organised by RSS on various occasions in different slums, *(ii)* they might have experienced the consequences of child marriage in their own life, or among to their friends and in family, *(iii)* they might have been exposed to the advertisement of the T.V. and other cultural media. These factors seem to count for their perceptible change in attitudes. It is also seen from the table that a very poor percentage of slum women (only two) have shown their unchanged attitudes towards evils of child marriage by responding on : *(i)* baby becomes healthy and *(ii)* mother remains healthy, by becoming mother at an early age. It is important to mention here that these two unaware respondents were from younger age group. Their attitudes might not have changed due to the following: *(i)* mental immaturity, *(ii)* irregularity and absent in RSS programme, *(iii)* lack of keen interest, *(iv)* uncomfortable to discuss with young RSS volunteers.

All these things might have caused them to remain unchanged their attitudes. However, although two women have not changed their attitude, it can be said that RSS has caused drastic changes in the neo-literate slum women's attitudes towards evils of child marriage.

TABLE 6.40
Attitude Towards Minimum Age of Marriage for Girls

Sl. No.	*Background*	*Minimum Age of Marriage for Girls*			*Nos. of Respondents*
		25 Years A	*18 Years* B	*15 Years* C	
	Age Group				
1.	15-25	5(11.11)	40(88.89)	—	45
2.	26-35	4(9.76)	37(90.34)	—	41
3.	36-50	3(17.65)	14(82.35)	—	17
	Status				103
1.	Earning	6(10.90)	49(89.10)	—	55
2.	Non-earning	6(12.5)	42(87.5)	—	48
	Caste/Community				103
1.	Scheduled Tribe	3(8.33)	33(91.67)	—	36
2.	Scheduled Caste	4(16.67)	20(83.33)	—	24
3.	General Caste	2(9.10)	20(90.90)	—	22
4.	Other Backward Caste	1(8.33)	11(91.67)	—	12
5.	Muslims	2(22.22)	7(77.78)	—	9
	Total Nos. of Respondents	12(11.65)	91(88.35)	—	103

Note : Figures within parentheses indicate percentages.

Data presented in the Table 6.40 shows that more than ninety per cent (a great majority) slum women irrespective of their age, caste/community and earning status have been found to have changed their attitudes in a positive way by expressing their views on statement that 18 years should be the actual age of marriage for the girls, and a meagre percentage of respondents from all the background have expressed their views that girls should get married at the age of twenty five. None of them have expressed that the actual age of marriage for girls should be fifteen years. It is important to mention here that before launching of the literacy programme of RSS, there was a trend of early marriage of girls in the slum areas of Rourkela. It was observed in the Muslim and Bihari slums that this trend has been found to be changed. They have strongly opposed to early marriage many of them have suggested before the investigator for delayed of girls. They feel that this will help them to be self-dependent and self-decissive.

Mention may be made here that the trend of child marriage which was very common in Muslim and Bihari slums like, Hasanpur Narla Road, Narayani Palli, etc., was found to have changed. "It was possible due to the involvement of slum women in developmental and literacy activities of Chetana Kendra", replied the husband of a neo-literate slum women during indepth discussion.

It can therefore be said that the marked change found among the neo-literate slum women is because of the activities of RSS.

TABLE 6.41
Attitude Towards Evils of Dowry

Sl. No.	*Background*	*Result of Taking or Giving Dowry*			*Nos. of Respondents*
		Social Status of the Person Increases A	*Improves the Economic Condition* B	*Gives Birth to Crime* C	
	Age Group				
1.	15-25	3(6.67)	2(4.44)	40(88.89)	45
2.	26-35	2(4.88)	2(4.88)	37(90.24)	41
3.	36-50	4(23.53)	3(17.65)	10(58.82)	17
	Status				103
1.	Earning	4(4.27)	4(4.27)	47(85.46)	55
2.	Non-earning	5(10.42)	3(6.25)	40(83.33)	48
	Caste/Community				103
1.	Scheduled Tribe	—	1(2.78)	35(97.22)	36
2.	Scheduled Caste	4(16.67)	2(8.33)	18(75.00)	24
3.	General Caste	3(13.64)	2(9.10)	17 (77.27)	22
4.	Other Backward Caste	1(8.33)	1(8.33)	10(83.34)	12
5.	Muslims	1(11.11)	1(11.11)	7(77.78)	9
	Total Nos. of Respondents	9(8.74)	7(6.79)	87(84.47)	103

Note : Figures within parentheses indicate percentages.

It can be observed from the Table 6.41 that a large majority of respondents irrespective of their age, caste/community and earning status were found to have perceived the idea that giving or taking dowry gives birth to crime. And a meagre percentage of respondents of all the age group, with earning and non-earning status from among the all caste/community (except ST background) were found to have perceived the idea that by giving or taking dowry, the social status of the person increases. They might have perceived this because of the following : *(i)* they might not have considered dowry as an evil, *(ii)* they might not have understood the deep-rooted effect of giving and taking dowry, or *(iii)* dowry might be very common in their caste/community. These factors might be responsible for the diseased perception of the respondent.

In case of ST respondents they have not perceived dowry as a symbol of prestige or social status of the person. It might be due to the influence of their own tradition and culture. Because it is seen in the ST Communities that they don't demand dowry at the time of marriage from the bride's parents. On the other hand, they offer some gift to the bride during marriage as token of love. This concept of providing gift to the bride might have influenced the ST respondents to perceive in a different way them the other respondents. Further, the table reveals that a very poor percentage of slum women from all the background were found to have perceived the idea that economic condition of the person gets improved by taking dowry. This might be due to the following reason : *(i)* demanding or taking dowry might have been considered as one of the easiest way to gain some handsome money without hard labour, *(ii)* they might have experienced some cases, who have improved their economic condition by taking dowry at the time of marriage, *(iii)* since they belong to poverty striken class, they might not have thought beyond property to remove poverty, *(iv)* they might not have realised the evils of dowry in a broader prospective due to lack of advanced outlook, or *(v)* the volunteers and organisers might not have been able to make them convenience about the evils of dowry. All these reasons seen to be attributable for their negative perception towards evils of dowry.

TABLE 6.42

Attitude Towards the Status of Girl Child—Perception on the Birth of a Baby Girl in the Family

Sl. No.	*Background*	*Thoughts of Family Members on the Birth of a Baby Girl*			*Nos. of Respondents*
		Burden to the Family A	*Blessings to the Family* B	*Makes no Differences* C	
	Age Group				
1.	15-25	—	18(40.00)	27(60.00)	45
2.	26-35	—	16(39.02)	25(60.98)	41
3.	36-50	—	8(47.05)	9(52.94)	17
					103
	Status				
1.	Earning	—	22(40.00)	33(60.00)	55
2.	Non-earning	—	20(41.67)	28(58.33)	48
					103
	Caste/Community				
1.	Scheduled Tribe	—	23(63.89)	13(36.11)	36
2.	Scheduled Caste	—	5 (20.83)	19(97.17)	24
3.	General Caste	—	8 (36.36)	14(63.64)	22
4.	Other Backward Caste	—	4(33.33)	8(66.67)	12
5.	Muslims	—	2(22.22)	7(77.78)	9
	Total Nos. of Respondents	—	42(40.78)	61(59.22)	103

Note : Figures within parentheses indicate percentages.

However, the healthy perception among the majority of respondents as reflected the data in the presented in the above table indicates a highly positive impact of RSS on the slum women of Rourkela.

It is seen from the Table 6.42 that majority of the respondents were found to have developed favourable attitudes towards the status of a girl child in a family by expressing their views that the birth of a baby girl makes no difference among the family members, and about forty per cent respondents irrespective of their age, caste/community and earning status have also shown their favourable attitude towards the status of a girl child in the family by responding on the birth of a girl child as the blessings to the family. None of them have expressed their view that the birth of a baby girl is a burden to the family. It means all the respondents have changed their attitudes toward a positive direction. It would not be out of place to mention here that before the RSS started functioning, it was noticed in the Bihari, Berhampuri and Muslim slums that the birth of baby girls were not been happily accepted by the family members because of dowry problem. But it was found that women have changed their attitude, of course, it is also a fact that birth of a baby girl is always welcomed in tribal families. It might have also been able to influence other respondents in changing their attitudes. However, the favourable attitudes found among the respondents to change the attitude of the slum women towards a favourable direction regarding the status of a girl in the family.

TABLE 6.43
Attitude Regarding Female Education

Sl. No.	*Background*	*Priority should be Given to the Education of*			*Nos. of Respondents*
		Daughter A	*Son* B	*Both* C	
	Age Group				
1.	15-25	13(28.89)	—	32(71.11)	45
2.	26-35	11(26.83)	—	30(73.17)	41
3.	36-50	8(47.05)	2(11.76)	7(41.18)	17
	Status				103
1.	Earning	18(32.72)	—	37 (67.27)	55
2.	Non-earning	14(29.17)	2(4.17)	32 (66.67)	48
	Caste/Community				103
1.	Scheduled Tribe	20(55.56)	—	16 (44.44)	36
2.	Scheduled Caste	4(16.67)	1(8.33)	19(79.17)	24
3.	General Caste	4(18.19)	—	18(81.81)	22
4.	Other Backward Caste	1(8.33)	1(8.33)	10(83.33)	12
5.	Muslims	3(33.33)	—	6(66.67)	9
	Total Nos. of Respondents	32(31.07)	2(1.94)	69(66.99)	103

Note : Figures within parentheses indicate percentages.

It can be viewed from the Table 6.43 that majority of the respondents were found to have developed a favourable attitude to give importance to the education of both son and daughter, and more than thirty per cent (about one-third) respondents irrespective of their age, caste/community and earning status were found to have shown their positive attitudes by giving importance to the education of daughter. Whereas a few (only two) per cent of respondents were found to have shown their interest by giving importance to the education of the son. It shows that they have not yet changed their age long traditional and 1 rigid attitude towards boy's education. It is important to mention here that the two unchanged respondents were from the older age group with non-earning background. This might be due to the following : *(i)* they might have thought that spending money for the education of daughters would be a great loss since they go to their in-laws after their marriage, *(ii)* they might not have realised the benefit of girls education till now due to lack of exposure to different medias and situations, *(iii)* they might not have changed their attitude due to their rigid thinking and traditional values that the son would run the family in future, or *(iv)* they might not have been regular in the centre to participate in the discuss in forum due to their socio-personal problems. All these attributes might be responsible for their unchanged attitudes for the same.

The responses of the majority of slum women as reflected in the above table show a positive impact of RSS in bringing attitudinal changes among the neo-literate slum women.

TABLE 6.44
Attitude Towards Over Emphasis of the Education of Son than that of Daughter

Sl. No.	*Background*	*Reason for Over Emphasising of the Education of Sons than that of the Daughters*			*Nos. of Respondents*
		Because the family Burden is Borne by the Sons	*Since the Girls Leave for their Inlaws Families after Marriage, the Amount Spent for their Education goes waste*	*There is Development in the Girl and Her Family*	
		A	B	C	
	Age Group				
1.	15-25	—	2(4.44)	43(95.56)	45
2.	26-35	—	1(2.44)	40(97.56)	41
3.	36-50	—	2(11.76)	15(88.24)	17
					103
	Status				
1.	Earning	—	1(1.82)	54(98.18)	55
2.	Non-earning	—	4(8.33)	44(91.67)	48
					103
	Caste/Community				
1.	Scheduled Tribe	—	1(2.78)	35(97.22)	36
2.	Scheduled Caste	—	2(8.33)	22(91.67)	24
3.	General Caste	—	1(4.55)	21 (95.45)	22
4.	Other Backward Caste	—	1(8.33)	11(91.67)	12
5.	Muslims	—	—	9(100.00)	9
	Total Nos. of Respondents	—	5(4.85)	98(95.15)	103

Note : Figures within parentheses indicate percentages.

Data presented in the Table 6.44 reveals that most of the respondents irrespective of their age, caste/community and earning status have shown favourable attitudes towards girls education by expressing their views that by receiving education, there is development in the girl and her family.

This favourable attitudes might have taken place due to : *(i)* the impact of various cultural activities, discussion, forum, training programes, video show and street corner meeting on theme of the benefits of girls education organised by RSS, *(ii)* their self-interest to change their thinking process according to the change of time and society, *(iii)* the effective and message oriented content of the reading materials in the form of stories and short plays provided by RSS during their learning. All these reasons seem to count a lot for their highly favourable attitude towards female education. It is also seen from the table that none of the respondents have laid stress upon the education of son by responding on the statement because the family burden is borne by them. It means the respondents are aware that the total responsibility of the family does not depend on the son only.

Further, the table shows that a very few percentage of respondents (4.85%) have shown their favourable attitudes towards the education of sons by expressing their opinion that since the daughters leave for their in laws after marriage, the money spend for their education goes waste. This might be due to : *(i)* their lack of outlook and exposure to various situations and different media, *(ii)* their environment might not be conclusive to think in a broader prospective for the education of the daughters, *(iii)* they might have some preoccupied belief about the education of the girls, (iv) they might have seen in most of the families that the family burdens were borne by the sons only. *(v)* They might not have been properly communicated about the merits of girls education. All these reasons might have forced them to be unchanged in their attitudes. However, the highly favourable responses of the respondents for the education of daughter indicate that RSS is successful in developing favourable attitude among the slum women towards the education of girls.

TABLE 6.45
Attitude Towards Literate and Aware Parents

Sl. No.	*Background*	*Advantage of Literate and Aware Parents in the Family*			*Nos. of Respondents*
		The family becomes large and unhappy A	*It makes no difference* B	*The family becomes happy* C	
	Age Group				
1.	15-25	—	6(13.33)	39(86.67)	45
2.	26-35	—	4(9.76)	37(90.24)	41
3.	36-50	—	2(11.76)	15(88.24)	17
	Status				103
1.	Earning	—	3(5.45)	52(94.55)	55
2.	Non-earning	—	9(18.75)	39(81.25)	48
	Caste/Community				103
1.	Scheduled Tribe	—	4(11.11)	32(88.89)	36
2.	Scheduled Caste	—	3(12.5)	21(97.5)	24
3.	General Caste	—	2(9.09)	20(90.91)	22
4.	Other Backward Caste	—	2(16.67)	10(83.33)	12
5.	Muslims	—	1(11.11)	8(88.89)	9
	Total Nos. of Respondents	—	12 (11.65)	91(88.35)	103

Note : Figures within parentheses indicate percentages.

It can be viewed from the Table 6.45 that about ninety per cent (a great majority) of the slum women were found to have agreed that the family becomes happy if the parents are literate and aware. It is also seen from the table that a few number of respondents (only twelve) irrespective of their age, caste/community and earning status were found to be agreed to the statement that it makes no difference in the family if the parents are literate and aware. This type of unperceptible changes in the attitude of respondents might be due to : *(i)* lack of interaction with different types of people other than the family members, *(ii)* they might not have interest in learning seriously, (iii) they might have some socio-personal problems, *(iv)* they might not have participated in different types of training programme like Mahila Jagruti Talim, Family Welfare Camps, Discussion Forum due to certain problems, or *(v)* they might not have self-interest to know about the effect of education in family life.

All these causes count a lot for their unperceptible changes in attitude. However, the highly favourable responses of the respondents presented in the table show that there is no doubt of the fact that RSS is successful in developing healthy attitudes among the neo-literate slum women with regard to the need for educaticn and awareness of the parents in the family.

TABLE 6.46
Attitude Towards Literate and Aware Mother

Sl. No.	*Background*	*Advantage of Literate and Aware Mother in the Family*			*Nos. of Respondents*
		There is an increase in disturbances in the family	*The possibilities of alround development of of the family increases*	*Only education of the children gets facilitated*	
		A	*B*	*C*	
	Age Group				
1.	15-25	—	41(91.11)	4(8.89)	45
2.	26-35	—	37(90.24)	4(9.74)	41
3.	36-50	—	14(82.35)	3(17.65)	17
	Status				103
1.	Earning	—	52(94.55)	3(5.45)	55
2.	Non-earning	—	40(83.33)	8(16.67)	48
	Caste/Community				103
1.	Scheduled Tribe	—	32(88.89)	4(11.11)	36
2.	Scheduled Caste	—	22(91.67)	2(8.33)	24
3.	General Caste	—	20(90.91)	2(16.67)	22
4.	Other Backward Caste	—	10(83.33)	2(16.67)	12
5.	Muslims	—	8(88.89)	1(11.11)	9
	Total Nos. of Respondents	—	92(89.32)	11(10.68)	103

Note : Figures within the parentheses indicate percentages.

It can be observed from the Table 6.46 that most of the slum women (more than 90%) were found to have developed a highly favourable attitude towards having a literate and an aware mother in the family by expressing their views that all round development of the family is possible

by a literate and an aware mother. It can be seen that none of the respondents have expressed their negative attitude towards literate and aware mother by responding on the statement that disturbance increases in the family due to a literate and an aware mother. It means all the respondents have developed a favourable attitude towards having a literate and an aware mother. Only their level of perception varies from person to person. Further, the table reveals that a meagre percentage (10.68%) of respondents in respective of their age group, caste/community and earning status were not found to have developed highly favourable attitude towards literate and aware mother by expressing their opinion that only the education of the children gets facilitated by the literate and aware mother. It means that respondents do have a favourable attitude towards a literate and an aware mother. But their level of perception is not up to mark. This might be due to : *(i)* their inactive participation in various developmental activities of the literacy programme with regard essence of education of the mother, *(ii)* they themselves might not be interested for various developmental work of the family, *(iii)* they might have a pre-occupied thought in their mind that only education of the children gets facilitated by literate mother, *(iv)* the volunteers might not have been able to provide more details about the merits of literate and aware mother in the family due to her/his immatured state of mind, or *(v)* they might have observed some literate women in their work field (income of earning member) always busy with the education of their children. All these factors seem to affect the development or relatively less favourable attitude among the respondents.

However, a highly positive change of attitude among the slum women towards literate and aware mother was observed as causes by RSS.

TABLE 6.47

Attitude Towards the Education of Married Women

Sl. No.	*Background*	*Effect of Learning of the Married Daughter and Daughter-in-laws*			*Nos. of Respondents*
		Problem arises in household chores A	*family is benefitted* B	*Problems donot arise in the household chores* C	
	Age Group				
1.	15-25	5(11.11)	22(48.89)	18(40.00)	45
2.	26-35	4(9.76)	24(58.54)	13(31.70)	41
3.	36-50	3(17.65)	8(47.05)	6(35.29)	17
					103
	Status				
1.	Earning	5(9.09)	30(54.55)	20(36.36)	55
2.	Non-earning	7(14.58)	24(50.00)	17(35.42)	48
					103
	Caste/Community				
1.	Scheduled Tribe	2(5.56)	15(41.67)	19(52.78)	36
2.	Scheduled Caste	3(12.5)	14(58.33)	7(29.17)	24
3.	General Caste	4(18.18)	11(50.00)	7(31.82)	22
4.	Other Backward Caste	2(16.67)	6 (50.00)	4(33.33)	12
5.	Muslims	1(11.11)	5(55.56)	3(33.33)	9
	Total Nos. of Respondents	12(11.65)	54(52.43)	37(35.92)	103

Note : Figures within parentheses indicate percentages.

It can be viewed from the Table 6.47 that more than half of the slum women have shown a positive attitude towards the education of the married women by responding that family gets benefit if the married daughter and daughter-in-laws go for education. More than one-third (35.92%) have also shown their favourable attitude by expressing their views on the statement that problem does not arise in household chores if married a daughter and daughter-in-law go for education. Whereas, a few women irrespective of their age, caste/community and earning status have expressed their unchanged attitudes by expressed their views that problem arises in household chores if the married daughter and daughter-in-law go for education. This unchanged attitudes among the few slum women may be attributed to : *(i)* their lack of self interest and determination for education, *(ii)* their family members might not have encouraged and co-operated in household chores, *(iii)* they might have been tortured a lot by their family members due to some (little) negligence in household chores during their learning in the centre, *(iv)* they might not have been able to manage time and home in a better way, or *(v)* they might not have been able to motivate their family members for extending co-operation in household chores. These reasons might have caused an unfavourable attitude towards education of married women. It is important to mention here that respondents irrespective of their age group, caste/community and earning status have shown their highly favourable, favourable, and even unfavourable attitudes towards the education of married women. Respondents from not a particular age group, caste/community and even earning and non-earning status have shown their highly favourable, favourable, and unfavourable attitudes towards education of married women. It gives a clue to guess that attitudinal changes

TABLE 6.48
Attitude Towards the Benefit/Advantage of Girls' Education

Sl. No.	*Background*	*Advantages of Girls' Education*			*Nos. of Respondents*
		They become self-reliant and don't brother anybody A	*They utilize the facilities meant for them* B	*They change the economic condition of the family by becoming self-dependent* C	
	Age Group				
1.	15-25	—	12(26.67)	33(73.33)	45
2.	26-35	—	14(34.15)	27(65.85)	41
3.	36-50	2(11.76)	6(35.29)	9(52.94)	17
	Status				103
1.	Earning	—	15(27.27)	40(72.73)	55
2.	Non-earning	2(4.16)	17(35.42)	29(60.42)	48
	Caste/Community				103
1.	Scheduled Tribe	—	11(30.56)	25(69.44)	36
2.	Scheduled Caste	1(4.16)	7(29.17)	16(66.67)	24
3.	General Caste	1(4.55)	6(27.27)	15(68.18)	22
4.	Other Backward Caste	—	5(41.67)	7(58.33)	12
5.	Muslims	—	3(33.33)	6(66.67)	9
	Total Nos. of Respondents	2(1.94)	32(31.06)	69 (66.99)	103

Note : Figures within parentheses indicate percentages.

among the respondents are not due to their background variables like age-group, caste/community and earning status, but due to their interests strong determination and urge to learning along with the sincere efforts and facilities made for them for their education. Therefore, it cannot be concluded that the level of attitudinal changes were possible only due to the increase of age, caste/community background and earning status. They might be contributing towards changing their attitudes to some extent, but not the whole. However, despite a differences between the changes of attitude among the slum women, it was found to be favourable towards the education of married women. It indicates the success of RSS in changing the attitude of slum women for the same in a positive direction.

Data presented in the Table 6.48 reveals that majority of the slum women have shown a highly favourable attitude towards the advantage of girls' education by expressing their view that by getting education girls become self-dependent and they change the economic condition of the family. Whereas, more than thirty per cent slum women irrespective of their age, caste/community and earning status have shown their relatively less favourable attitude by responding on the statement that they (educated girls) utilise the facilities meant for them. This might be due to : *(i)* lack of exposure among the slum women to certain developmental activities and people involved therein, *(ii)* lack of faith on educated women due to some pre-occupied belief , *(iii)* they might not be sincere in the discussion forum of awareness generation programmes, *(iv)* the immature student volunteers might not have communicated the advantages of girls' education properly. These factors might be responsible for their relatively, less favourable attitude towards girls' education.

Further the table shows that two respondents (1.94%) of older age group and from non-earning status have shown their negative attitudes by expressing their views that by getting education the girls become self-reliant and don't bother for anybody. This type of negative attitude of the slum women might not have changed due to the following, *(i)* since they belong to the older age group, they might have expected respect from the younger generation, which was not always possible in modern times, specially in cosmopolitan urban slums, *(ii)* since they were not earning and not exposed to different situation of life and its related problems they might not have the realisation of the essence of girls' education, *(iii)* they might have experienced some cases in their life, who have not bothered for anybody after being literate, *(iv)* they might not have self-interest and determination for learning. Therefore, they might have reflected their beliefs in aim a negative way.

Mention may be made here that most of the slum women after being literate have developed interest in becoming economically self-sufficient (mostly the non-earning). Therefore, they have undergone a variety of income generation and skill development training organised by RSS with the active support of Shramik Vidyapith, and now earning some good amount by preparing standard quality of food articles, embroidery and applique items, rakhee, foot-mates, candles and greeting cards etc. Parents of some of the young respondents have reported to the investigator that after receiving income generation training, the economic conditions of their families have got improved due to their daughters and daughter-in-laws. However, the favourable responses of the majority of slum women as emerged from the table indicate the success of RSS in changing attitude of the neo-literate slum women towards the advantages of girl's education.

It is evident from the Table 6.49 that more than half of the slum women have shown a highly favourable attitude towards literate and economically self-sufficient girls by expressing their opinion that the value of the girls increases in the society when they become literate and economically independent. Where as less than half of the slum women irrespective of their age group, caste/

TABLE 6.49
Attitude Towards Economically Independent Girls

Sl. No.	*Background*	*Economically Independent Girl*			*Nos. of Respondents*
		The need to give dowryceases A	*Their value in the society increases* B	*Prestige of the family is hampered* C	
	Age Group				
1.	15-25	21(46.67)	24(53.33)	—	45
2.	26-35	20(48.78)	21(51.22)	—	41
3.	36-50	8 (47.05)	9(52.94)	—	17
					103
	Status				
1.	Earning	27(49.09)	28 (50.91)	—	55
2.	Non-earning	22(45.83)	26 (54.17)	—	48
					103
	Caste/Community				
1.	Scheduled Tribe	12(33.33)	24(66.67)	—	36
2.	Scheduled Caste	13(54.17)	11(45.83)	—	24
3.	General Caste	12 (54.55)	10(45.45)	—	22
4.	Other Backward Caste	7(58.33)	5 (41.67)	—	12
5.	Muslims	5(55.56)	4(44.44)	—	9
	Total Nos. of Respondents	49(47.57)	54(52.43)	—	103

Note : Figures within parentheses indicate percentages.

community and earning status have also shown a favourable attitude by agreeing with the statement that there is no need of giving dowry when the girls become literate and economically independent. And none of them have expressed that prestige of the family gets hampered for the same. It means all the respondents were having favourable attitude towards literate and economically self-sufficient girls. But the majority of the respondents possessed positive attitude than that of their counter respondents who have responded to no need of dowry. Such response of the respondents might have found for the following : *(i)* they might have experienced in their own slum and in working field (in case of earning that literate and earning girls might not have taken dowry during their marriage than that of the illiterate and non-earning girls, *(ii)* the volunteer might have given more stress on dowry aspect as the advantage of women education during their follow up discussion, or *(iii)* it might be a self-perception of the slum women that since they are literate and economically independent there is no need of dowry. These factors might have caused for such response of the respondents.

However, despite a little difference in the attitudes of the respondents of various age group, caste/community background and earning status, attitudes of slum women towards literate and economically independent girls were found be quite healthy. This healthy attitudes of the respondents reflect the satisfactory impact of RSS activities on the neo-literate slum women of Rourkela.

TABLE 6.50

Attitude Towards Helping Husbands in Household Chores

Sl. No.	*Background*	*Extending help to the Wives in Household Chores by the Husbands*			*Nos. of Respondents*
		Family prestige is hampered	*Self-prestige of the males is affected*	*The house-wives get co-operation and family peace prevail in the family*	
		A	B	C	
	Age Group				
1.	15-25	6(13.33)	15(33.33)	24(53.33)	45
2.	26-35	4(9.76)	12(29.27)	25(60.98)	41
3.	36-50	4(23.53)	6 (35.29)	7 (41.18)	17
	Status				103
1.	Earning	6(10.91)	13(23.64)	36(65.45)	55
2.	Non-earning	8(16.67)	20(41.67)	20(41.67)	48
	Caste/Community				103
1.	Scheduled Tribe	3(8.33)	5(13.89)	28(77.78)	36
2.	Scheduled Caste	3(12.5)	10(41.67)	11(5.56)	24
3.	General Caste	4(18.18)	10 (45.45)	8(36.36)	22
4.	Other Backward Caste	2(16.67)	5 (41.67)	5 (41.67)	12
5.	Muslims	2(22.22)	3(33.33)	4(44.44)	9
	Total Nos. of Respondents	14(13.59)	33 (32.04)	56(54.37)	103

Note: Figures within parentheses indicate percentages.

It can be observed from the Table 6.50 that more than half of the respondents were found to have a positive attitude towards helping husbands in household cores. Whereas, the rest of them irrespective of their age, caste/community and earning status were found to be rigid and unchanged their attitudes towards the same. The attitude has not changed among the respondents because of the following : *(i)* effect of the deep-rooted socio-cultural tradition, *(ii)* there might have some notion among the respondents with this regard, *(iii)* the male members of the family might not have shown their interests despite several request of their wives to co-operate in household chores as they have not been acquainted with such activities, *(iv)* the husbands might have become aggressive with their wives when they ask for help in household chores, by passing remarks that their self-prestige gets affected, *(v)* the volunteers might not have made them understand about the essence of co-operation of the husbands in household chores, *(vi)* this aspect of the literacy programme might not have been projected/demonstrated by the cultural artists of the street plays or video films through their cultural activities effectively.

However, despite a marked difference in the attitudes of the respondents of various age group, caste/community and earning status, there was a positive attitude of slum women towards the assistance of husbands in household activities to the wives, as more than half of them have responded on the desired responses.

It indicates positive impact of RSS activities on the slum women for the same.

TABLE 6.51

Attitude Towards the Decision-making Right of Women

Sl. No.	*Background*	*Resasons as to why women should not have the right to take decision like men*			*Nos. of Respondents*
		From mental and physical point of view they are much weaker than the men A	*They also manage all sorts of social responsibilities unlike the men* B	*Family cannot run smoothly without women* C	
	Age Group				
1.	15-25	2(4.44)	20(44.44)	23(51.11)	45
2.	26-35	2 (4.88)	19(46.34)	20(48.78)	41
3.	36-50	1(5.88)	7 (41.18)	9(52.94)	17
					103
	Status				
1.	Earning	2(3.64)	26 (47.27)	27 (49.09)	55
2.	Non-earning	3(6.25)	20(41.67)	25(52.08)	48
					103
	Caste/Community				
1.	Scheduled Tribe	1(2.78)	18(50.00)	17(47.22)	36
2.	Scheduled Caste	1(4.17)	10(41.67)	13(54.17)	24
3.	General Caste	2(9.09)	8 (36.36)	12(54.55)	22
4.	Other Backward Caste	—	6 (50.00)	6(50.00)	12
5.	Muslims	1(11.11)	4(44.44)	4(44.44)	9
	Total Nos. of Respondents	5 (4.85)	46(44.66)	52(50.49)	103

Note : Figures within parentheses indicate percentages.

Data presented in the Table 6.51 reveals that more than half of the respondents were found to have developed favourable attitudes towards decision-making rights of women by expressing their views that family cannot run smoothly without women. Which indicates that the decision-making rights of the women should be protected in family matters. Whereas, less than half of the respondents irrespective of their age group caste/community and earning status have also shown their positive attitudes by expressing their opinions that they (women) also manage all sorts of social responsibilities unlike the men. It also indicates their favourable attitudes in the social context that their decision-making right should also be protected in the social field. The table also shows that a very poor percentage (4.85%) of respondents were found to have remained unchanged in their attitudinal level by responding that women are much weaker than the men from mental and physical point of view.

This might be because they might not have recognised their own potentials till now : *(i)* they might have considered themselves inferior than men both mentally and physically, *(ii)* they might have been dominated by/under estimated by them male members of their family, neighbourhood or even in the working field (in case of working women), *(iii)* they might have suffered from certain chronic diseases, *(iv)* they might not have exposed to different situations, media and cultural activities which provide a wider vision to the women. All their unchanged attitude. It is pertinent to mention here that before the RSS started functioning, it was very difficult to unite the women for any sorts of work. They would not even come forward to give their family details during the

survey work of census or even for any developmental work. This was reported by the members of some of the voluntary socio-cultural organisations like Spandan, Sevasadan, Bethel Cheritable Trust and Shramik Vidyapith, concerned with slum activities prior to literacy programme. Literacy programme has been able to break their culture of silence. It has been observed by the investigator that they have become more objective with regard to assess some of their socio-cultural practices. Now they are taking active participation not only in the decision-making process of their families, but also in their social setting like the male members. As a result, grass-root level leadership among the slum women have been developed through various activities of Chetana Kendras. A number of women groups have also come up in different slums.

However, the responses as emerged from the above table showed a healthy attitudes of neo-literate slum women towards the decision-making rights of them and indicates a highly positive impact of RSS towards awareness generation.

TABLE 6.52

Attitude Towards Work Participation of Sons than Daughter in Household Chores

Sl. No.	*Background*	*Resasons as to why daughters should help their mothers in household chores and not sons*			*Nos. of Respondents*
		Since sons are more intelligent, they should study instead of household chores A	*Son and daughter both should do the household activities* B	*Participation in household activities lowers the prestige of sons* C	
	Age Group				
1.	15-25	8(17.78)	27(60.00)	10(22.22)	45
2.	26-35	6(14.63)	28(68.29)	7(17.07)	41
3.	36-50	5(29.41)	7(41.18)	5(29.41)	17
	Status				103
1.	Earning	8(14.55)	37(67.27)	10(18.18)	55
2.	Non-earning	11(22.92)	25(52.08)	12(25.00)	48
	Caste/Community				103
1.	Scheduled Tribe	3(8.33)	30(83.34)	3(8.33)	36
2.	Scheduled Caste	5(20.83)	12(50.00)	7(29.17)	24
3.	General Caste	6(27.27)	9(40.91)	7(31.82)	22
4.	Other Backward Caste	3(25.00)	6(50.00)	3(25.00)	12
5.	Muslims	2(22.22)	5(55.56)	2(22.22)	9
	Total Nos. of Respondents	19(18.45)	62(60.19)	22 (21.36)	103

Note : Figures within parentheses indicate percentages.

It can be observed from that a majority of the slum women were found to have developed favourable attitudes towards equal work participation of both sons and daughters in the household activities. Whereas a few respondents irrespective of their age group, caste/community and earning status were found to have unchanged their attitudes by expressing their views that participating in household activities lowers the prestige of sons. This types of attitude among the slum women might not have changed because of the following : *(i)* the volunteers might not have been serious about this aspects of literacy programme during their teaching to the respondents, *(ii)* the pre-

occupied socio-traditional belief in their mind to give more emphasis on males (sons) of the family, *(iii)* their own rigid and fatalistic attitude to not to change themselves with the change of the time, or *(iv)* lack of exposures of different kinds like advertisement of T.V., video show of RSS, discussion of Chetana Kendra, Mahila Yagruti Talim Camp, Cultural activities in this regards etc. These factors might have attributed for their unchanged attitudes.

Further, the table shows that a meagre percentage of respondents have shown their unchanged unfavourable attitudes towards equal work participation of both sons and daughters in household activities in a different way by expressing their opinions that since sons one more intelligent, they should study instead of doing household chores. This might be due to : *(i)* lack of outlook with regard to the intelligence of daughters, *(ii)* the content of the literacy primers might not have discussed, in a reflective way by the volunteer, *(iii)* their poor self-image as women, *(iv)* lack of proper training among the volunteers to communicate the message properly, *(v)* since the women have been under-estimated in many ways by the members of the family as well as by the outsiders, they might have reflected their state of suppression on their daughters, *(vi)* they might not have been able to judge the intelligence of their daughters due to lack of scope and exposure to different situation, or *(vii)* impact of age old socio-cultural tradition. These factors seem to count for their unfavourable attitude for the same.

However, the favourable responses of the more than half of the respondents indicate that RSS was able to change attitude among the slum women in a positive way towards the equal work participation of both sons and daughters in house-hold activities.

TABLE 6.53

Awareness About the Parental Property Rights of Women

Sl. No.	*Background*	*Legal provisions made for the women to get a share of their parental property*			*Nos. of Respondents*
		They have no right to have a share in a share in the parental property A	*They can avail of equal property rights like sons* B	*There is no specific law to get a share in parental property* C	
	Age Group				
1.	15-25	12(26.67)	24(53.33)	9(20.00)	45
2.	26-35	10(24.39)	23(56.10)	8(19.51)	41
3.	36-50	6(35.29)	5 (29.41)	6(35.29)	17
	Status				103
1.	Earning	10(18.18)	34(61.82)	11(20.00)	55
2.	Non-earning	13(27.08)	18(37.5)	17(37.42)	48
	Caste/Community				103
1.	Scheduled Tribe	7(19.44)	19(52.78)	10(27.78)	36
2.	Scheduled Caste	6(25.00)	10(41.67)	8(33.33)	24
3.	General Caste	5(22.73)	12(54.54)	5(22.73)	22
4.	Other Backward Caste	3(25.00)	6(50.00)	3(25.00)	12
5.	Muslims	2(22.22)	5(55.56)	2(22.22)	9
	Total Nos. of Respondents	23(22.33)	52(50.49)	28(27.18)	103

Note : Figures within parentheses indicate percentages.

It is observed from the Table 6.53 that more than half of the respondents were found to be aware of availing equal rights of their parental property and a few respondents (more than one fourth) irrespective of their age group, caste/community and earning status were found to be unaware about the property rights of women from their parental property by expressing their views that there is no law to get parental property for the women. Further, a meagre per cent (less than one-fourth) of respondents have expressed their unawareness by presenting their opinion that they won't get any right of parental property. There about half of the respondents were found to be unaware about the property rights because of the following. Most of the respondents in the slum areas are found to be from the wretched poverty sector, and a very few of them do have some land in their distant native villages. Since they were unable to earn their livelihood from the small pieces of land, they migrated to the industrial city for better prospect, and started dwelling over encroacher's land of RSP or the land of Govt. of ORISSA. When they don't have their own legal occupancy for residence as slum-dwellers, under circumstances how could they think to avail their property rights from the landless parents.

Therefore, they must not have thought about it. This might be the main attribute to their unawareness towards property rights. Mention may be made here that, the content of the PL primer has clearly emphasised on the property right of women from the parental property in one chapter entitled "Neta-Re-Dukha-Gala". The primer was written in the middle of 1992 and got approved and published by the starting of 1993. By that time the legal code on property rights of women (the latest one) was not implemented. So the volunteers have taught and discussed the topic before the learners with additional and supplementary literature in this regard. So the respondents have also responded on the basis of the knowledge/awareness developed through that primers and discussion. So this has been taken care of while collecting data.

TABLE 6.54
Awareness About Different Developmental Schemes of Bank of India

Sl. No.	*Background*	*Awareness of special schemes introduced by Bank of India for women to improve their financial condition by starting small scale Business*			*Nos. of Respondents*
		Indira Vikas Yojana A	*Nehru Yojana* B	*Priyadarshini Yojana* C	
	Age Group				
1.	15-25	27(60.00)	10(22.22)	8(17.78)	45
2.	26-35	29(70.73)	7(17.07)	5(12.20)	41
3.	36-50	7(41.18)	6(35.29)	4(23.53)	17
	Status				103
1.	Earning	35(63.64)	11(20.00)	9(16.36)	55
2.	Non-earning	28(58.33)	12(25.00)	8(16.67)	48
	Caste/Community				103
1.	Scheduled Tribe	20(55.56)	9(25.00)	7(19.44)	36
2.	Scheduled Caste	16(66.67)	5(20.83)	3(12.50)	24
3.	General Caste	15(68.18)	4(18.18)	3(13.64)	22
4.	Other Backward Caste	7(58.33)	3(25.00)	2(16.67)	12
5.	Muslims	5(55.56)	2(22.22)	2(22.22)	9
	Total Nos. of Respondents	63(61.17)	23(22.33)	17 (16.50)	103

Note : Figures within parentheses indicate percentages.

Awareness registered developed among more than half of the respondents with regard to property right of the women from parental property as reflected through their responses is not encouraging. However, it was found to be satisfactory and indicates a positive impact of the literacy programme on the slum women of Rourkela.

Data presented in the Table 6.54 reveals that majority of respondents were found to be aware of the special scheme introduced by Bank of India to improve the financial condition of women by starting small-scale business as they have responded that they are aware of Indira Vikas Yojana. Whereas a few respondents irrespective of their age group, caste/community and earning status have shown their low level of awareness in this regard by responding on Nehru Yojana, and a meagre percentage of respondents have also shown their unawareness by responding on Priyadarshini Yojana. The low level of awareness among respondents in this regard might be due to the following : *(i)* they have confused with the scheme NRY with Nehru Yojana due to lack of familiarities with these types of terms and schemes, *(ii)* since most of the schemes are meant for the rural poor and for the tribals and a very few schemes are implemented for the slum-dwellers, they might not have developed much interest on these type of schemes. Therefore, they might have guessed the name of the scheme and respondents, *(iii)* they might not have interest to know much about different schemes and programmes, *(iv)* volunteer himself/herself might not be aware about different developmental schemes of government or she/he might not have discussed with the respondents thoroughly. All these reasons might have attributed for their low level of awareness regarding special developmental scheme introduced by Bank of India.

TABLE 6.55
Raising Voice Against Exploitation

Sl. No.	*Background*	*Steps to be taken against women sufferings*			*Nos. of Respondents*
		One should tolerate tolerate A	*It should be reported to the police* B	*After being self-aware and make others aware voice should be raised jointly* C	
	Age Group				
1.	15-25	—	18(40.00)	27(60.00)	45
2.	26-35	—	14(34.15)	27(34.15)	41
3.	36-50	—	9(52.94)	8(47.06)	17
	Status				103
1.	Earning	—	19(34.55)	36(65.45)	55
2.	Non-earning	—	22(45.83)	26(54.17)	48
	Caste/Community				103
1.	Scheduled Tribe	—	14(38.89)	22(61.11)	36
2.	Scheduled Caste	—	8(33.33)	16(66.67)	24
3.	General Caste	—	9(40.91)	13(59.09)	22
4.	Other Backward Caste	—	6(50.00)	6(50.00)	12
5.	Muslims	—	4(44.44)	5(55.56)	9
	Total Nos. of Respondents	—	41(39.80)	62 (60.20)	103

Note : Figures within parentheses indicate percentages.

It is important to mention here that many the slum women of different slums areas were aware of certain development schemes like Swarna Sahari Yojana, TRYSEM, DWCRA, etc., meant for the weaker section of people. They have expressed these names of the schemes during the in-depth discussion with the investigator in the field.

However, the responses as presented in the table shows a satisfactory level of awareness among the slum women with regard to developmental schemes, and indicated that RSS has been able to generate awareness among the neo-literate slum women for the same.

It can be seen from Table 6.55 that majority of the slum women were found to be aware as to how to raise voice against exploitation and women torturing by responding that after being self-aware and making others aware, voice should be raised unitedly. Whereas about forty per cent of the slum women irrespective of their age, caste/community and earning status have also shown satisfactory level of awareness by expressing their views that it should be reported before the police officer. It is important to note here that none of the respondents from any category have expressed their opinion that one should tolerate the exploitation of torturing. It means all the respondents are aware of raising voice against exploitation. It will not be out of place to present some of the observations made by the investigator in this regard. Due to the negligence of a night shift doctor of Govt. Hospital, Rourkela, (who was incidentally a Gynaecologist) a newly born baby of a slum women of Balughat, was declared dead before the actual death. When this fact was disclosed the neo-literate slum women of Balughat didn't remain silent. They organised themselves and raised their voice against the doctor before the Medical Superintendent, Police Superintendent and Additional District Magistrate. As a result disciplinary action was taken against the concerned doctor and nurse.

Further, it was also observed by the investigator during her field visit that they have become assertive in many places. They were raising their voice in their own family, if necessary. In the words of Nuri Begun, a neo literate women of Hasanpur slum.

"We were like the cows of the cow shed. We didn't have any choice to live or voice to say 'No' to our Sohar (husbands) for anythings. They think that we are meant to be submissive before them, and to please them at any cost. Like machines we would be giving birth to their children every year."

She further stated:

"After joining this programme, mixing with other people in the centre, we realised that we do have our own lives to lead, and our choices to take care off. So why should we tolerate them unnecessarily against our will. So first we learnt as to how to say "no" to injustice and gradually we practiced in our family to say "no" to anything which are against our will and justice."

However, the highly satisfactory responses of a great majority of respondents as emerged from the above table shows a healthy impact of literacy programme of RSS on the slum women of Rourkela.

It can be viewed from Table 6.56 that cent per cent respondents were found to have developed their social awareness regarding different functionaries by expressing their views that thieving in the house or in the slum should be reported in the police department. This cent per cent desired responses among the respondents might be attributed to the following : *(i)* they might have experienced theft in their house or in the slum, for which they might have reported in the Police Station, *(ii)* they might have experiences of Police investigation in their slum in connection

TABLE 6.56
Social Awareness About Different Functionaries : Reporting for Thieving

Sl. No.	*Background*	*Theft in the house or in the Slum should be reported to*				*Nos. of Respondent*
		Town Services *A*	*Health Department* *B*	*Town Administration* *C*	*Police Department* *D*	
	Age Group					
1.	15-25	—	—	—	45(100.00)	45
2.	26-35	—	—	—	41(100.00)	41
3.	36-50	—	—	—	17(100.00)	17
	Status					103
1.	Earning	—	—	—	55(100.00)	55
2.	Non-earning	—	—	—	48(100.00)	48
	Caste/Community					103
1.	Scheduled Tribe	—	—	—	36(100.00)	36
2.	Scheduled Caste	—	—	—	24(100.00)	24
3.	General Caste	—	—	—	22(100.00)	22
4.	Other Backward Caste	—	—	—	12(100.00)	12
5.	Muslims	—	—	—	9(100.00)	9
	Total Nos. of Respondents	—	—	—	103(100.00	103

Note : Figures within parentheses indicate percentages.

with the search of thief or the theft materials, *(iii)* this aspect of awareness generation might have taken a lot of care by the RSS organisers through discussion, role play, dramatisation etc. during their learning, *(iv)* they might have much exposed to T.V., Cinema, Street Plays and Video Shows etc. in this regard, *(v)* they might have developed self-interest to know about different functionaries so as to facilitate their work in time. All these factors might have helped them in developing cent per cent awareness level. However, their cent per cent desired responses as emerged from the above table indicates the success of RSS in generating social awareness among the slum women.

It can be viewed from Table 6.57 that more than half of the respondents were found to be aware about the proper functionary, where they should apply for tube-well to be set-up in their slum. Whereas, more than one-third respondents irrespective of their age group, caste/community and earning status were found to have shown their low level of awareness by expressing their views that to set-up tube well in their slum they should apply to the local administrator. This relatively low level of awareness among the few respondents might be due to multiple factors like : *(i)* lack of keen interest about different types of functionaries, departments and outer activities, *(ii)* they might not have gone for the follow-up discussion properly among their own women's group after the literacy class due to the tight schedule of their household activities, *(iii)* they might have seen people demanding their basic amenities before the ADM and got the work done by him. All these causes might be responsible for their low level of awareness. Further, the table reveals that a very low percentage (6.80%) of respondents have expressed their very low level of awareness by presenting the opinions that they should apply to the health department to set up

TABLE 6.57
Social Awareness About Different Functionaries : Applying for Tube Well

Sl. No.	*Background*	*To install tube well in your slum you should apply to*				*Nos. of Respondents*
		Police Department A	*Health Department* B	*Local Administration* C	*Town Services* D	
	Age Group					
1.	15-25	—	3(6.67)	17(37.78)	25(55.56)	45
2.	26-35	—	2(11.76)	13(31.71)	26(63.41)	41
3.	36-50	—	2 (11.76)	8 (47.06)	7 (41.18)	17
	Status					103
1.	Earning	—	3 (5.45)	17(30.91)	35(63.64)	55
2.	Non-earning	—	4(8.33)	21(43.75)	23(47.92)	48
	Caste/Community					103
1.	Scheduled Tribe	—	3 (8.33)	11(30.56)	22(61.11)	36
2.	Scheduled Caste	—	2 (8.33)	10(41.67)	12(50.00)	24
3.	General Caste	—	1 (4.55)	8 (36.36)	13(59.90)	22
4.	Other Backward Caste	—	1(8.33)	5(41.67)	6(50.00)	12
5.	Muslims	—	—	4(44.44)	5(55.56)	9
	Total Nos. of Respondents	—	7 (6.80)	38(36.89)	58(56.31)	103

Note : Figures within the parentheses indicate percentages.

tube well in their slum. And it is pertinent to mention here that none of them have responded on police department for the same. The very few numbers of respondents might not have developed their desired level of awareness in this regard may be attributed to the following. *(i)* they might not have been exposed to various practical situation of life, *(ii)* they might not have keen interest in participating different types of social activities in which they would have to be thought about different functionaries, *(iii)* since tube well provides purified water, which is prime to good health, they might have thought that health department would have been taking care of to set up tube well, or *(iv)* their volunteer might not have been thorough about the functions of different functionaries. All these factors seem to count for the development of very low level of awareness among the slum-dwellers. However, the satisfactory responses as have been shown in the above table by more than half of the respondents, indicate a positive impact of the literacy programme in arousing awareness among the slum women with regard to different functionaries.

Data presented in Table 6.58 reveals that more than half of the slum women were found to have developed a very healthy attitude towards political participation of women by expressing their opinion that country develops when they also possess equality of political rights like men and less than half of the slum women were also found to have developed on healthy attitude towards political participation of women by expressing their views that social status of women increases by their political participation. Whereas a very poor (only three) percentage of respondents of all the age group and earning and non-earning status with SC GC and Muslim Community were not found to have changed attitudes for the same by showing their attitudes in responding

TABLE 6.58
Attitude Towards Political Participation of Women

Sl. No.	Background	Reason for Political Participation of Women			Nos. of Respondents
		Their social status increases A	*By entering politics their social prestige is hampered* B	*The country develops when they possess equality of political rights like men* C	
	Age Group				
1.	15-25	22(48.89)	1(2.22)	22(48.89)	45
2.	26-35	14(34.15)	1(2.44)	26(63.41)	41
3.	36-50	8 (4.06)	1(5.88)	8(4.06)	17
					103
	Status				
1.	Earning	22(40.00)	1(1.82)	32(58.18)	55
2.	Non-earning	22(45.83)	2(4.17)	24 (50.00)	48
					103
	Caste/Community				
1.	Scheduled Tribe	16(44.44)	—	20(55.56)	36
2.	Scheduled Caste	12(50.00)	1(4.17)	11(45.83)	24
3.	General Caste	8 (36.36)	1(4.55)	13(59.09)	22
4.	Other Backward Caste	5(41.67)	—	7(58.33)	12
5.	Muslims	3(33.33)	1(11.11)	5(55.56)	9
	Total Nos. of Respondents	44(42.73)	3(2.91)	56(54.37)	103

Note : Figures within parenthesis indicate percentage.

their opinion that social prestige of women gets hampered by their political participation. This may be attributed to: *(i)* they might have some pre-occupied thoughts in the mind on political participation of women, *(ii)* they might not have been exposed to the political activities the women in their slums, *(iii)* they might have listened something wrong about some of the women politician, *(iv)* they might be knowing nothing about the political activities/involvement of women in politics due to mental immaturity (in case of the respondents of younger age group). All these causes might have affected for their unchanged negative attitudes towards political participation of women. It is note-worthy to mention here the important impact of literacy programme on the slum women is that their direct involvement in politics and decision-making activities after joining the literacy programme. It is found that due to the development of grass-root level leadership among the neo-literate slum women their attitude towards politics and political personalities has changed. They have politics and political activities. Therefore many of them have joined in different political groups and trying their best to involve themselves in decision-making process. It has become evident from the last Municipal Election when women from Ruputola area contested for slum-dwellers.

However, the healthy attitudes among the majority of the slum women as reflected from the above table indicate a highly positive impact of RSS on slum women of Rourkela with regards to their political participation.

TABLE 6.59
Interest to Take Part in Different Training Programme

Sl. No.	*Background*	*Your interest to participate in the training programme of*				*Nos. of Respondent*
		Mahila Jagruti Talim **A**	*Training in child and maternity care* **B**	*Training in women and law* **C**	*Income generation training* **D**	
	Age Group					
1.	15-25	13(28.89)	7(15.55)	8(17.78)	17(37.79)	45
2.	26-35	16(39.02)	9(21.95)	6(14.63)	10(24.39)	41
3.	36-50	6(35.29)	3(17.64)	2(11.76)	6(35.29)	17
	Status					103
1.	Earning	18(32.73)	8(14.54)	7(12.73)	22(40.00)	55
2.	Non-earning	17(35.41)	11(22.92)	9(18.75)	11(22.92)	48
	Caste/Community					103
1.	Scheduled Tribe	13(36.11)	7(19.44)	5(13.89)	11(30.56)	36
2.	Scheduled Caste	9(37.5)	4(16.67)	3(12.5)	8(33.33)	24
3.	General Caste	8(36.36)	4(18.18)	3(13.64)	7(31.82)	22
4.	Other Backward Caste	3(25.00)	2(16.67)	3(25.00)	4(33.33)	12
5.	Muslims	2(22.22)	2(22.22)	2(22.22)	3(3.33)	9
	Total Nos. of Respondents	35(33.98)	19(18.45)	16(15.53)	33(32.04)	103

Note : Figures within parentheses indicate percentages.

It can be seen from Table 6.60 that one-third of the slum women irrespective of their age group, caste/community and earning status were found to have shown their interest to participate in Mahila Jagruti Talim for their development as well as for the development of the women of their slums. Whereas about one-third respondents have shown their interest in income generation training programme. Mention may be made here that, despite their wretched poverty they didn't show their interest to join income generation training programme in large number. It might be due to the following : *(i)* they might have already gone through the income generation training in the past. Therefore, they have not shown their interest for further training, *(ii)* their income generation training might not have proved fruitful in practical situation, *(iii)* they might not have been properly motivated for the training, *(iv)* since more than half of the respondents were found to be from earning category; they may not have felt the necessity of it. These factors might have affected them in showing lack of interest towards income generation training.

Mention may be made here that during her data collection 80% of the respondents (82 out of 103), have reported to the investigator that they have participated in various income generation and skill development training programme of RSS through Shramik Vidyapeeth. They have informed to the investigator that they have formed group of 10-15 neo-literate women to produce the items in which they have got training. The investigator has also interacted with the groups in Gangadhar Palli, Pump House Colony, and saw their production *viz.*, (pickles of different types,

badi muduku, Sance and squash etc. good articles) embroidery, applique and other items like wall hanging, pillow cover, greeting cards, rakhee, candle, foot-mat and even cultivation of mushroom.

It was also observed in Narla Road Muslim slum that some of the neo-literate slum women were making a good amount by mehandi application which they have learned from SVP during their training programme.

The investigator has also observed the involvement of the slum women in skill development and income generation activities during her data collection. The slum women have exhibited and sold their produced materials with great zeal in various occupations like literacy melas, programmes on International Literacy Day, International Women's Day, Women Convention and even in the Trade Fair organised by local administration. Their production items were found to be of standard quality.

In spite of their production of good quality items, they were unable to market properly due to financial crisis and lack of marketing experience. Therefore, it has become difficult on their part to sustain those activities, (reported by the slum women of Gangadhar Palli and Sector-20 Pump House Colony). They market their items in the exhibitions and by door to door punching. It has become very difficult on their part to do so. Therefore, many of them have become demotivated to continue their income generation activities, and they didn't even show their interest for future training with regard to income generation.

The table further shows that a percentage of slum women have shown their interest in training on child and maternity care and a meagre percentage of respondents have shown their interest in training on women and law. This might be due to the following : *(i)* they might have given more stress to participate in Mahila Jagruti Talim, which an integrated training programme covering all the aspect like child and maternity case/paralegal training, skill development, and awareness generation in various concerning issue etc. *(ii)* they might not have keen interest on child and maternity care then that of other training, *(iii)* they might not have interested in terms of law and legal rights due to lack of exposure to certain situation, *(iv)* they might not have been encouraged by their family members to participate in those training, *(v)* they might have found those training much effective than that of the income generation training and Mahila Yagruti Talim, *(vi)* due to their immaturity (in case of the respondents of younger age group) they might not have critically thought about their affect in future life, *(vii)* since majority of volunteers in the first phase of the programme were from high school level (students of class IX and X), they might not be able to make the respondents convenienced about the effectiveness of the training programme in their day to day life.

All these factors might have caused for showing their relatively less interest in the training programmes like child and maternity care and women and law.

However, the responses of the slum women as given in the table shows that RSS has been able to arouse interest among the respondent to take active participation in different types of training programme for their development as well as the development of their slum areas.

TABLE 6.60
Attitude Towards Communal Harmony and National Integration

Sl. No.	*Background*	*Irrespective of caste, colour, creed and religion all should stay in the slum areas unitedly because*			*Nos. of Respondents*
		People of different castes and religions should live separately A	*People of all religions should live together* B	*There is no harm in living, who ever may the person be, wherever he wants to live* C	
	Age Group				
1.	15-25	3(6.67)	25(55.55)	17 (37.78)	45
2.	26-35	2 (4.88)	26 (63.41)	13(31.71)	41
3.	36-50	2 (11.76)	7 (41.18)	8(47.05)	17
	Status				103
1.	Earning	3(5.45)	31 (56.36)	21(38.18)	55
2.	Non-earning	4 (8.33)	27(56.36)	17 (35.42)	48
	Caste/Community				103
1.	Scheduled Tribe	--	23(63.89)	13 (36.11)	36
2.	Scheduled Caste	1(4.17)	14 (58.33)	9(37.5)	24
3.	General Caste	3(13.64)	11(50.00)	8(36.36)	22
4.	Other Backward Caste	1(8.33)	6 (50.00)	5(41.67)	12
5.	Muslims	2 (22.22)	4(44.44)	3(33.33)	9
	Total Nos. of Respondents	7(6.8)	58(56.31)	38 (36.89)	103

Note : Figures within parentheses indicate percentages.

It is evident from Table 6.60 that majority of the slum women have shown their highly favourable attitude towards communal harmony and national integration by expressing their opinion that people of all caste and religion should five together unitedly, and more than one-third of the slum women irrespective of their age, caste/community and earning status have expressed their views that there is no harm of living whoever man be the person wherever he wants to live. Whereas, only seven respondents (6.8%) of all the age group with earning and non-earning status and from almost all the caste/community background (except ST) have shown their unchanged negative attitude by expressing their views that people of different caste and religion should live separately. Their attitudes might not have changed because of *(i)* age old practice of living in separate sectors according to their caste category and religion might have made them rigid and fatalistic, *(ii)* they might not have discussed openly with other about the evils of casteism and communal disorder, *(iii)* they might not have exposed to different cultural media, T.V. programmes, discussion forum with regard to the advantages of communal harmony and national integration or demerits of communal riots, *(iv)* their feelings of superiority (in case of the GC respondents) and inferiority (income of so called lower caste category respondents) complexes might have blocked their mental levels to think for living separately. All these factors were seen to count for their unchanged attitudes.

It is also seen from the table that all the respondents of ST background have shown their favourable and highly favourable attitude towards communal harmony.

It gives a clue to guess that this might be due to : *(i)* the special efforts made by the activists of RSS in making the learners as well as other slum-dwellers involved with different community development programme despite their caste, colour, sex, religion and age status, *(ii)* effect of the special dance drama and street plays like "Naya Kadam" in Tribal Script (Sadri language) organised by RSS, *(iii)* their own inner will and determination to change themselves for their development, *(iv)* since they enjoy maximum freedom in their family and community, they might have got much scope and time to participate in those discussions made in this regard, *(v)* effect of the primer which is written in the form of story and drama on communal harmony and national integration, *(vi)* all these factors might have caused for their highly favourable attitude towards the same. It was assumed that caste background would play an important role for the attitudinal changes of the respondents. Specially in case of ST it was expected that they might prefer to live separately as they do have a separate culture and specific living style. But it was not found true. Rather all the ST respondents did show a favourable attitude towards a united living. It is therefore illogical to draw such a conclusion that caste background might be one of the reason for change of attitude, but not the whole.

However, the perceptible changes found among most of the neo-literate slum women indicate the success of RSS in bringing attitudinal changes among them towards communal harmony and national integration.

Awareness about the Enrolment of Slum Children in Formal School and Other System of Education

Under this heading it is intended to analyse and interpret the data pertaining to the awareness developed in the neo-literate slum women about the enrolment of their children in formal schools and other system of education like Anganwadi and NFE Centres etc. The details of analysis and interpretation of data is presented hereunder.

TABLE 6.61

Awareness About the Enrolment of Children/School-going Age of the Children

Sl. No.	*Background*	*Children should be send to the school for primary education at the age of*			*Nos. of Respondents*
		Three Years A	*Five Years B*	*Six Years C*	
	Age Group				
1.	15-25	10(22.22)	33(73.33)	2(4.44)	45
2.	26-35	7(17.07)	34(82.93)	—	41
3.	36-50	5(29.41)	11(64.71)	1(5.89)	17
					103
	Status				
1.	Earning	13(23.64)	41(74.55)	1(1.82)	55
2.	Non-earning	9(18.75)	37(77.08)	2(2.17)	48
					103
	Caste/Community				
1.	Scheduled Tribe	7(19.44)	28(77.78)	1(2.78)	36
2.	Scheduled Caste	5(20.83)	18(75.00)	1(4.17)	24
3.	General Caste	5(22.73)	17(77.27)	—	22
4.	Other Backward Caste	3(25.00)	8 (66.67)	1(8.33)	12
5.	Muslims	2(22.22)	7(77.78)	—	9
	Total Nos. of Respondents	22(21.36)	78 (75.73)	3(2.91)	103

Note : Figures within parentheses indicate percentages.

It is evident from Table 6.61 that more than three-fourth of the respondents were found to be highly aware about the school going age of the children that children should be send to school for primary education at the age office, and more than one fifty of the respondents irrespective of their age, caste/community and earning status have shown their relatively low level of awareness by expressing their opinion that children should be send to the school at the age of three. This relatively low level of awareness might be due to the following: *(i)* they might not have self-interest to know about the school-going age of the children as they are young and unmarried (in case of young and unmarried respondents), *(ii)* they might have been sending their children to the nearly Oriya medium nursery schools, *(iii)* they might be sending their children to the Anganwadi at the age of three, *(iv)* they might have seen the children going to the English Medium Schools at the age of three, *(v)* they might have been working in the nursery schools with the children as aaya (in case of earning women), or *(vi)* they might not have discussed with the volunteer and other slum women regarding the actual school-going age of the children. All these factors seem to count for their relatively low level of awareness. Further, the table shows that only three respondents (2.91%) of lower and higher age group with both earning and non-earning status and from ST SC and OBC background were found to have very low level of awareness by showing their awareness that children should be send to the school at the age of six. This might be because of the following : *(i)* they might be careless about the school-going age of the children because of the formal schooling problems in their slums, *(ii)* they might be sending their children to the NFE centres of RSS at the age of six, *(iii)* they might not have developed interest for the same due to lack mental immaturity (in case of the respondents of young age group), *(iv)* they might have crossed this stage of sending children to the school as their children have already group up (in case of the respondents of older age group), *(v)* they might have given emphasis to NFE centres for schooling of their children than that of the formal setting due to their poverty timing and nature of work. All these reasons might have attributed to their very low level of awareness for the same.

It is pertinent to mention here that some of the slum women of Giridharipada Jhariabahal, and Uttam Basti were sending their children to the near by "Saraswati Sishu Mandir" at the age of three for education. It was also observed that many of the slum women of various slum areas were sending their children to the Anganwadi at the age of three to four years. And even some of them were sending their children to the NFE centers of RSS to make their children acquainted with the environment non-officially at the age of three instead of six. But most of the respondents do send their children to the schools (formal) at the age of five. It has been cross verified from the school records of the concerned schools. It was also reported by the headmasters of concerned primary schools that the enrolment rate of their schools have increased after the launching of literacy programme. If at all they don't get chance to avail a seat in the school, they still send the children to the NFE centers for the next session as the enrolment age of NFE centre is six.

However, the highly satisfactory responses of the slum women with regard to school-going age of the children show the success of RSS in generating awareness among the neo-literate slum women.

Data presented in Table 6.62 shows that all respondents have shown perceptible changes in their attitudes in three different way. About three-fourth of the respondents have perceived

TABLE 6.62
Perception About the Prime Responsibility of Sending Children to the School in Time

Sl. No.	Background	Prime responsibility of sending children to the school in time			Nos. of Respondents
		Mother A	*Both father and mother* B	*Father* C	
	Age Group				
1.	15-25	32(71.11)	8(17.78)	5(11.11)	45
2.	26-35	35(85.37)	4(9.76)	2(4.88)	41
3.	36-50	10(58.82)	5(29.41)	2(11.76)	17
					103
	Status				
1.	Earning	45(81.82)	6(10.90)	4(7.27)	55
2.	Non-earning	32(66.67)	11(22.92)	5(10.42)	48
					103
	Caste/Community				
1.	Scheduled Tribe	26(72.22)	5(13.89)	5(13.89)	36
2.	Scheduled Caste	18(75.00)	4(16.67)	2(8.33)	24
3.	General Caste	17(72.22)	4(18.18)	1(4.56)	22
4.	Other Backward Caste	9(75.00)	2(16.67)	1(8.33)	12
5.	Muslims	7(77.78)	2(22.22)	—	9
	Total Nos. of Respondents	77(74.76)	17(16.50)	9(8.74)	103

Note : Figures within parenthesis indicate percentage.

mother's responsibility as prime to send the children to the school in time. Whereas, a meagre percentage of slum women irrespective of their age group caste/community and earning status have perceived that both father and mother are mainly responsible for sending the children to the school in time. And a very poor percentage of respondents (8.74%) have shown their perception by expressing their views that father is mainly responsible for sending children to the school in time. This types of perception among the slum women might be due to the following : *(i)* they might not have perceived the thing critically due to immature state of mind (in case of respondents of younger age group), *(ii)* the fathers of the children mighty be mostly available in the house during the school-going time either due to their nature of job or unemployment, *(iii)* the fathers of the children might have been over-dominating in the families with regard to the education of their children, *(iv)* the mothers might have been engaged either in their work in the workfield (in case of earning) or in the household chores (income non-earning) during the school going time of the childness, *(v)* the fathers might have shown their special interest in sending the children to the school in time, *(vi)* the mothers might not be interested to take up responsibility of sending the children in time, *(vii)* this responsibility aspect of father and mother or mother or the father might not have discussed clearly before them, or *(viii)* the P.L. Primer and other literature might not have reflected properly for the same. All these factors seem to count for such type of perception among the neo-literature.

However, the perceptible changes as observed from the presented data in the table show a healthy attitude of slum women developed through the activities of RSS. Which also indicates the success of the literacy programme.

TABLE 6.63

Awareness About the alternative Education for the Children of Poor and Labour Class People

Sl. No.	*Background*	*Children of poor and labour class people those who are unable to go to format school would Learn at*			*Nos: of Respondents*
		Literacy centres A	*Non-formal education centres* B	*There is no justification for their education* C	
	Age Group				
1.	15-25	15(33.33)	30(66.67)	—	45
2.	26-35	12(29.27)	29(70.73)	—	41
3.	36-50	8(47.06)	9(52.94)	—	17
	Status				103
1.	Earning	17(30.91)	38(69.09)	—	55
2.	Non-earning	18(37.50)	30(62.50)	—	48
	Caste/Community				103
1.	Scheduled Tribe	11(30.56)	25(69.44)	—	36
2.	Scheduled Caste	8(33.33)	16(66.67)	—	24
3.	General Caste	8(36.36)	14(63.64)	—	22
4.	Other Backward Caste	5(41.67)	7(58.33)	—	12
5.	Muslims	3(33.33)	6(66.67)	—	9
	Total Nos. of Respondents	35(33.98)	68(66.02)	—	103

Note : Figures within parentheses indicate percentages.

It is evident from Table 6.63 that cent per cent respondents have shown their awareness regarding the education for the children of poor and labour class people, those who are unable to join the formal school. Majority of them have shown their high level of awareness by expressing their opinion that children of poor and labour class should learn at NFE centres, and one-third of the respondents irrespective of their age group, caste/community and earning status have also shown their relatively low level of awareness by expressing their view that they should learn at the literacy centres. None of them have shown their unawareness by expressing that there is no justification of their education, which indicates that all the respondents were aware about the need for education of their children. Their awareness regarding non-formal education centre for poor children might attributed to : *(i)* their interaction with the literacy volunteers, NFE coordinators and monitoring team of RSS, who have been engaged and activated for the awareness generation and development of the slum people specially the neo-literates since long. *(ii)* their keen interest for the educational development of their children. *(iii)* the activities of the NFE centres might have attracted more than the formal schools. All the reasons might have attributed for their high level of awareness for NFE centres as an alternative for the poor children.

The reasons for preferring literacy centres as an alternative for the poor children by the respondents might be due to the following : *(i)* the target group of the literacy programme was 10 to 60 years. So children upto the age group 10 to 60 could have been enrolled,*(ii)* there were no facilities of NFE centres in every slum due to its limited sanction, where as literacy centres were found in each and every slum areas, *(iii)* their self-interest for the education of their children at any centre within their reach. These causes might have affected to select literacy centres as alternative for poor children to learn.

However, the highly satisfactory level of awareness as emerged from the responses of the majority of slum women presented in the table shows positive impact of the literacy activities of RSS on the neo-literates slum women.

TABLE 6.64
Awareness Regarding the Education for the Child Labourer

Sl. No.	*Background*	*Children labourer those who are unable to go to the formal school should learn at—*			*Nos. of Respondents*
		Literacy centers A	*Non-formal education centres* B	*No need of to educate them* C	
	Age Group				
1.	15-25	20(44.44)	25(55.56)	—	45
2.	26-35	13(31.71)	28(68.29)	—	41
3.	36-50	8(47.06)	9(52.94)	—	17
	Status				103
1.	Earning	19(34.55)	36(65.45)	—	55
2.	Non-earning	22(45.83)	26(54.17)	—	48
	Caste/Community				103
1.	Scheduled Tribe	14(38.89)	22(61.11)	—	36
2.	Scheduled Caste	10(41.67)	14(58.33)	—	24
3.	General Caste	8(36.36)	14(63.64)	—	22
4.	Other Backward Caste	5(41.67)	7(58.33)	—	12
5.	Muslims	4(44.44)	5(55.56)	—	9
	Total Nos. of Respondents	41(39.81)	62(60.19)	—	103

Note : Figures within parentheses indicate percentages.

It is seen from Table 6.64 that more than half of the slum women were found be highly aware that child labourers, those who are unable to go to the schools, should learn at the NFE centres, and less than half (forty per cent) of the slum women irrespective of their age, caste/community and earning status were also found to be aware of education for the child labourers to some extent that they should learn at the literacy centres. The table also shows that none of the respondents showed their unawareness by expressing their views that there is no need of education for the child labourers. It indicates that each and every slum women are now aware of the essence of education for the children, whether he is a child labourer or not. The respondents who have shown their relatively low level of awareness might be due to : *(i)* non-availability of NFE centres in each slum, *(ii)* lack of keen interest to know in details about the alternative education for child labourers, *(iii)* the timing of the literacy centres might be more suitable to the child labourers than the NFE centres, *(iv)* they might not have the detailed ideas about the difference between the objectives and functions of both the types of centres, *(v)* they might not have got the chance to enrol in the NFE centres due to a limited sanctioning of seats. All these factors might have forced the respondents to prefer literacy centre for the child labourer.

It is important to mention here that before the launching of literacy programme there was no alternative educational provision for the education of the children of poor and labour class people, or even for child labourers those who were unable to go to the formal schools. On the constant demand of the neo-literates, especially the slum women, fifty NFE centres had been opened by RSS in different slums for the education of the poor children (including child labourers). It was noticed by the investigator that the literacy volunteers cum NFE instructors were taking special care of the centres and the education of the children.

Their sincere and dedicated efforts have not only made the people convinced to send their children to the schools and NFE centres, but also been able to develop high level of aspiration among the poor slum children and child labourers to dream for further education after completion of their NFE course. Mention may also be made here that most of the NFE centres were having a good number of child labourers as learners. It was also observed that the teaching-learning activities of the centres were interesting and even better in certain aspect than that of the municipality schools.

While discussing with the slum-dwellers and the neo-literate slum-women about the standard of teaching of NFE centres they have shown a high degree of satisfaction with the activities and teaching of the centres and also on the volunteers/instructors.

However, the highly satisfactory responses of a majority of slum women presented in the table not only shows the impact of literacy programme of RSS on them but also indicate the success of RSS in arresting the illiteracy among the future adults. Who used to be the learners of NFE centres.

TABLE 6.65

Awareness Towards the Continuation of Writing Practice/ Letter Writing

Sl. No.	*Background*	*Number of letter writing in a month to your friend and relatives*			*Nos. of Respondents*
		Not at all A	*One or two* B	*Regularly* C	
	Age Group				
1.	15-25	8(17.78)	20(44.44)	17(37.78)	45
2.	26-35	9(21.95)	19(46.34)	13(31.71)	41
3.	36-50	4(23.53)	9(52.94)	4(23.53)	17
	Status				103
1.	Earning	13(23.64)	23(41.82)	19(34.54)	55
2.	Non-earning	8(16.67)	25(52.08)	15(31.25)	48
	Caste/Community				103
1.	Scheduled Tribe	5(13.89)	18(50.00)	13(36.11)	36
2.	Scheduled Caste	6(25.00)	9(37.50)	9(37.5)	24
3.	General Caste	5(22.73)	9(40.91)	8(36.36)	22
4.	Other Backward Caste	3(25.00)	7(58.33)	2(16.67)	12
5.	Muslims	2(22.22)	5(55.56)	2(22.22)	9
	Total Nos. of Respondents	21(20.39)	48(46.60)	34(33.01)	103

Note : Figures within parentheses indicate percentages.

Data presented in Table 6.65 reveals that about one-third of the respondents irrespective of their age, caste/community and earning status were found to be in touch with their writing practices by regular writing of letters to their friends and relatives. Whereas about half of the respondents from all the background have expressed that they use to write letters to their friends and relatives once or twice in a month. This might be due to : *(i)* their lack of time in house hold chores as well as other activities, *(ii)* feeling of fatigue after day long hard work in the household activities and at work field, *(iii)* lack of encouragement from the family members, *(iv)* lack of keen interest in writing. All these factors might be responsible for their occasional writing of letter to keep up the writing practice.

The table further reveals that hundred and fifty of the respondents from all the background have expressed that they don't write any letter to their friends and relatives. It indicates that they were not in touch with their writing practice. This might be due to their lack of interest and motivation, and no habit to write letter. These factors might have led to their non-practice of writing habit by letter writing.

However, the highly satisfactory responses of the majority of slum women as shown in the above table indicate the regularities of their writing practices by letter writing. There is no doubt in the fact that RSS has been able to develop awareness about the regularities of writing practices among the neo-literate slum women for their further learning.

Discussion

Data with regard to the development of the awareness level of slum women in different aspects of life, changes taken place in their attitude, and enrolment of their children in formal and non-formal education system have already been analysed in the proceeding section.

It is evident from the data analysis that a great majority of respondents (more than 80%) irrespective of their age, Caste/Community and earning status have shown very high, high and satisfactory level of awareness and very highly positive, highly positive and positive changes in attitudes in different aspects of life. Their level of awareness development and attitudinal changes found in different aspects of life are discussed hereunder.

Awareness with Regard to Population Explosion, Environmental Protection and Small Family Norms

It is evident from the data analysis that most of the (more than 90%) respondents irrespective of their age, caste/community and earning status have shown very high level of awareness towards evils of population explosion, environmental protection, and family welfare and small family norms. Mention may be made here that no much differences were found between their level of awareness in those aspects of life. It was expected on the basis of the research findings of Agnihotri (1974), Rao (1983), and Siddiqui (1989) that low level of awareness with regard to the above mentioned aspects found among the slum women of adult literacy programme; but, their findings did not support the present study in drawing such a conclusion. On the contrary, the present study has been supported by the research findings of Singh (1979), Council for Social Development (1982), Behera (1993) Menon (1993) and Mishra (1999). All of them have ascertained a very high level of awareness among the neo-literate with regard to different aspects of life like evils of population explosion, environmental protection and adoption of small family norms and family planning among the respondents who have attended the adult literacy classes and awareness generation programmes.

Further, it was expected on the basis of the research findings of Sarkar (1981), Siddiqui (1989) and Reddy (1991) that a very low level of awareness would be found in the Muslim respondents with regard to evils of population explosion, family planning and environmental protection. These research findings did not support to draw a logical conclusion for the present study. On the contrary, it was found in the study that the Muslim respondents have shown relatively better level of awareness than that of the respondents of other caste/community background. They have shown cent per cent awareness in many sub-aspects like effects of population explosion (Table 6.17), awareness about the control of overcrowding in public places (Table 6.19), mechanism to protect environment (Table 6.20) and awareness about family welfare and small family norms (Table 6.21). It is pertinent to mention here that they have even shown relatively better level of awareness than that of the respondents of general caste category in some of the aspects mentioned above (can be seen in the tables 6.19 and 6.21) this high level of awareness development among the Muslim respondents towards the above mentioned aspects of life can be attributed to the following factors :

(1) The sincere efforts and regular motivational activities of RSS volunteers have aroused a keen interest in the Muslim respondents to be regular and active in literacy classes as well as awareness generation activities of the Chetana Kendras.

(2) Since they were socio-culturally less privileged than others, when they got the scope for their development they didn't want to miss it and took more interest for their level of development.

(3) The content of the PL Primers and Supplementary literature has been highly useful with regard to the same.

(4) The message of the street plays, Mahila Kala Yatha and video shows and might have been highly powerful to the respondents.

(5) They must have attended regularly the health camps, Mahila Yagruti Talim, Family Welfare Counselling, Income Generation Training and other programmes. All these have affected in developing high level of awareness among the Muslim slum women of Rourkela.

It is, therefore illogical to draw a conclusion that age, caste/community and earning background of the respondents are the responsible factors for their high level of awareness development. They influence in developing their awareness level to some extent, but not entirely.

It will not be out of place to present here the views of different types of people interviewed by the investigator during the course of the study on impact of literacy programme on slum women with regard to various aspects of their life style.

The medical officer of Family Welfare Unit of URS (Urban Revamping Scheme), Panposh, Rourkela and his trained multipurpose health workers (female) have informed the investigator that when the scheme (URS) was implemented during 1987, it was very difficult to convince the people (specially the illiterate slum-dwellers) about the need for family planning. They were thinking that more people means more money. Therefore, they were not ready to listen anything on family planning. There was no such provision for motivational and environment–building activities in the scheme so as to activate them for the same, as it is a government scheme. Thus, they were handicapped in doing anything for motivation. Therefore, in the family planning camps there was rush among the educated and semi-educated people only. It was horrible in Muslim areas like Hasanpur, Narla Road, Imaratisaria, Madhusudan Palli and Gopabandhu Palli. Women of the Muslim slum areas were not even ready to go for family planning operation after having seven to eight children. Their husbands and mother-in-laws did not give them permission in the family for the same.

"After launching of RSS, they have made our job easier" said the medical officer during discussion. Now after joining the programme through its various media they have become aware about the need of small family norms. As a result, now they themselves are coming to the camps for operation, spacing and even for counselling in this regard. Population growth of the slum areas of Rourkela have therefore been controlled to a better extent.

The officer-in-charge of social forestry of Panposh have been found to be grateful to the RSS activists and the slum-dwellers for their co-operation for huge plantation in various dry areas of Rourkela. He reported to the investigator that after launching of RSS, he had been sending different types of plants to various Chetana Kendras regularly as per the requisition of RSS for plantation. Prior to RSS, no seriousness was marked among the people specially the slum-dwellers in this regard. Government was also not serious about plantation, although there is a steel plant in the city and huge plantation is utmost required for the same. RSP was concerned about the beautification of its sector township. But after launching of the programme and involvement of the department of social forestry with RSS, this was made possible and successful by its neo-literates and volunteers.

It can be said from the views of the medical officer and his field staff of URS, Rourkela, and the officer, in-charge of social forestry, Panposh, that RSS has been trying its level best to develop the awareness level of slum women through constant efforts. As a result, they have been able to develop their high level of awareness in various aspects of life. Which shows a highly positive impact of RSS in developing their awareness level.

Awareness with Regard to Child and Maternity Care and Personal Health and Hygiene

It was found from the data analysis that a large majority (about 90%) of respondents were found to be highly aware about the different sub-aspects of child and maternity care and personal health and hygiene, irrespective of their age, caste/community and earning status.

Based on the research findings of Siddiqui (1989), External Evaluation Report of NIRD (1992), Naik (1994) and Parikh (1995) it was assumed that simply positive level of awareness will be found among the respondents with regard to the different aspects of life like child and maternity care and personal health and hygiene. Further, it was expected from those studies that wide differences will be found in the awareness level of different caste/community background. The respondents of higher caste or general caste background will be shown better level of awareness than that of the ST and slum categories.

But in the present study it was not found so. Rather, the research findings of Panwar (1978), Khaja Peer (1978), Menon (1993), Behera (1993), Mishra (1999) and GIDSL (2000) have supported the present study in drawing a conclusion that those who have attended the literacy classes regularly and participated in the awareness programmes actively and sincerely have shown high level of awareness in different aspects of life like child and maternity care and personal health and hygiene.

On the contrary, it was observed in the present study that the ST slum women have shown relatively better or equal level of awareness in almost all the sub aspects of life mentioned above (can be seen from Tables 6.25 to 6.31 and 6.34) than that of the respondents of general caste and other background.

These differences of the level of awareness development between the respondents of general caste category and ST category was observed probably due to the following reasons: (1) Respondents of GC background must have over-estimated them selves as they belong to so called higher caste category and their condition was a little better than others. They must have thought that whatever they know was more than sufficient to lead a good life. Therefore, they didn't want to mix and learn with the respondents of ST and other categories. As a result they didn't develop higher level of awareness than others. (2) In case of ST respondents, they were supressed by the so-called higher caste people of the society since long back. So when they got the chance through literacy programme of RSS to uplift their condition, their eyes must have opened to a greater extent and didn't want to miss the opportunities for development. Further, the sincere and rigorous efforts of RSS volunteers, powerful messages of the street plays, and reading materials have made them determined to be sincere and active in those awareness activities. That resulted in their very high level of awareness development than that of others with regard to child and maternity care and personal health and hygiene.

Mention may be made here about the opinion of the CDPO of ICDS Project and her field supervisors and Anganwadi workers, and also the views of the project officer and supervisors of UBS, Rourkela Municipality. They have reported before the investigator regarding the impact of the literacy programme of RSS on slum women with regard to the above mentioned aspects of life that before launching of literacy programme (prior to 1990) their participation in immunisation programme was very poor. A very few number of slum women were coming to the hospital for their medical registration and immunisation. The rate of still birth was also high among the women of slum areas. Infant mortality rate was also observed high in those days (during 1990-91 it was 98 and has come down to 56 in the year 1999 per thousand). Keeping pigs was a very common practice in slum setting, which was controlled to a greater extent. But after their participation in literacy programme and different types of activities, they have gradually changed their attitudes and become aware about various aspects of life. They have become more particular to the regular immunisation of their children and regular vaccination and medical check-up of the pregnant women. They themselves are coming forward to the immunisation camps for the administration of polio-drops to their children, which was a dream one decade back.

They have given their view that only due to efforts and rigorous activities of RSS it was being possible.

During her course of data collection (over a long period in three phases from January, 1997 to March, 2000) the investigator has also observed many far reaching changes among the slum women of Rourkela. They have not only become conscious about the health of their children or themselves, but also have developed fellow feelings for others and taking care off others accordingly. They are now maintaining cleanliness in their houses as well as in their bastis. It was also observed that they are cleaning their wells, drains and road of their slums through "Safai Karyakram" (Cleaning Programme) of Chetana Kendras. Further, they are participating on the Pulse-polio and other immunisation programmes quite enthusiastically. All of the respondents have reported to the investigator that every child had been administered pulse polio-drops, and all the mothers had preferred to breast-feed to their infants. The investigator has not found any specific level of discrimination in awareness development between the higher caste respondents and others.

Hence, it cannot be concluded that the high level of awareness development is only because of their caste/community background and their impact on the respondents. It might be one of the important factors affected for their level of awareness development. On the other hand, the conjecture put forward was that it was the impact of literacy programme of RSS that count a great deal for the high level of awareness development among the slum women.

It can therefore, be said that the literacy activities of RSS had a healthy impact in generating highly satisfactory level of awareness among the neo-literate slum women of Rourkela with regard to child and maternity care and personal health and hygiene aspects of their lives.

Changing Attitudes Towards Evils of Alcoholism, Superstition, Child Marriage and Dowry

It can be deduced from the data analysis and interpretation that a great majority of respondents (about 90%) irrespective of their age, caste/community and earning status were found to have developed highly positive attitudes towards evils of alcoholism, superstition, child marriage, dowry and their effects on the society. There was an expectation of the investigator on the basis of the research findings of Naik (1994) that a very low level of changes will be found in the attitudes of the slum women with regard to different social issues like evils of alcohol, superstition, early marriage and dowry. But it was found that a large majority of the slum women of all the categories have shown highly positive attitudes towards the same. On the contrary, the research findings of Rao (1983) and Shukla (1988) have supported the present study in drawing a logical conclusion. Further, there was an assumption on the basis of the study of Naik (1994) that the respondents of younger groups (15-25 age) will be shown highly positive attitudes than of the older age group (25-45) in the concerning social issues. But on the contrary it was found that irrespective of their age groups, large majority of the slum women have shown highly positive attitudes towards the same. Rather, the respondents of middle age group (26-35) have shown relatively better level of awareness and more positive attitudes than that younger and older age groups in almost all the aspects of life and concerning issues. This relatively high level of attitudinal changes in a positive direction among the middle-aged respondents must have attributed to the following : *(i)* the effect of the message of the cultural media, reading material and constant efforts of the RSS activists, *(ii)* their self-motivation and hidden potential for self development, *(iii)* their own experiences with regard to the effect of evils of dowry, alcohol, child marriage or superstitions, *(iv)* Support and constant inspiration from the family members, friends and relatives.

All these factors must have affected in changing their attitudinal level in a highly positive direction than that of the other age groups.

Further, the relatively low level of attitudinal changes found among the respondents of younger and older age group in a positive direction might be due to the following reasons : *(i)* lack of keen interest to participate in the awareness generation activities actively and sincerely, *(ii)* lack of exposure to different situations of life and various medias like cultural, T.V., printing etc. *(iii)* poor self-image about themselves, (iv) their traditional and fatalistic nature of thinking and living (mainly in case of older respondents), (v) mental immaturity (in case of younger respondents), *(vi)* hesitant to discuss with young RSS volunteers (about the evils of child marriage and its effect etc.) All these causes have affected them and are responsible for the relatively lesser changes of attitudes in a highly positive direction than the respondents of middle age group.

However, despite a relatively very low level of difference among the respondents of all the age group, the slum women have shown a highly positive attitude towards the evils of different social issues as mentioned earlier.

It will not be out of place to mention the opinion of different types of people interviewed by the investigator in this regard during her data collection. It was reported by the excise inspector of

Udit Nagar, some social workers and local public of Rourkela that alcohol abuse and its business (business of country liquor) has been checked to some extent in tribal slums of Rourkela. Further the local people have informed that alcohol abuse, which was very common among the tribal slum women has been controlled to a greater extent. Prior to the establishment of RSS, business of country liquor was very common and open in most of the slums. Even the slum women were also into the business of selling Handia (rice beer). After joining RSS and its literacy activities, the slum women of various areas of literacy zones started developmental activities by closing down country liquor shops and liquor distilleries from their slums. The constant efforts of the women groups (consist of both neo-literate and grass-root volunteers) have also been able to control the alcohol consumption by the slum people in various areas. The alcoholic habit in the slum women (tribal), which was very common, has been totally checked in various areas like Orampara, Gudiatoli, Dhipatoli, Kariabahal etc. The investigator also observed the same during her data collection. It is important to mention here that the women's groups of Orampara and Gudiatoli were imposing high amount of fines on the owners of the distilleries whenever were found working in the slums for alcohol. Even the drunkards here penalised heavilt through the Chetana Kendras. The same principle has also been applied to the parents of the girls who were organising the marriage of their daughter before eighteen or offer dowry to the bridegroom's family. They also fined the parents of the bridegroom who demanded dowry. All these problems were resolved through the Chetana Kendras in the presence of monitoring team and senior activists. In worst case, the RSS secretary or chairman interfere and settle down the matter. The investigator has experienced those many a time during her field visit. Hence, it cannot be concluded that the high level of awareness development was due to their age or Caste/community background or earning status. They might be some of the influential factors for their awareness development, but not the whole. On the other hand, it can be said that it was the impact of the constant activities of RSS, there its sincere grass-root level volunteers and activist that affect a lot for the high level of awareness generation of slum women. Based on the information of different types of people, field experiences of the investigator and above all the result of data analysis, it can be concluded that the literacy programme of RSS has been able to develop a high level of awareness among the slum women with regard to evils of alcohol, superstition, child marriage and dowry, which one the burning issues in the present day society.

Attitude Towards the Status of Girl Child and their Education, Political Participation of Women and Raising Voice Against Exploitation

The analysis of data reveals that a great majority of the respondents (more than 80%) irrespective of their age, caste/community and earning status have shown highly positive attitude towards status of girl child and their education, political participation of women and raising voice against exploitation. It is important to mention here that no much difference were found between the levels of attitudes between the respondents of different age groups, caste/community and earning status. Further, no wide gap of differences were observed between the above started aspects of life of the slum women. Kudesia (1973), Brahma Prakash (1976, 1983), Khatun (1991) and Ramesh (1991) have found in their studies that a very low level of attitudinal changes among the respondents will be deduced in different aspects of their life. Further, the findings of Kudesia (1973) and Ramesh (1991) presented a base to theorise that adult literacy programme failed in respect of imparting political knowledge and consciousness into the minds of the adult learners. On the contrary, the researcher found highly positive attitude among the respondents for the same. The research findings of Planning commission (1969), Bastia (1982), Rao (1992), External

Evaluation Report of Pondichery (1993), Parikh (1994 and 1995) and Pati (1996) have supported to draw a concrete conclusion for the same.

It was further concluded on the basis of the findings that there was no relationship between the occupation of the learners and their attitudinal change and level of awareness development. The research findings of Saldhana (1992) has also supported to the hypotheses that there was no impact of occupation on the learners for the same.

Further, the findings of their studies did not help the researcher to derive a logical conclusion for the present study. On the contrary, the studies conducted by Rao (1983) and Siddiqui (1989) were found to be supportive to some extent in drawing a logical conclusion for the same that occupations of the learners help them in changing their level of attitudes to some extent. It was found in the present study that the earning women have shown relatively better level of attitudes than that of the non-earning women in almost all the aspects of life and concerned issues. Further, they were found to be relatively more aware in most of the aspects of life than the non-earning category. Mention may be made here that both the group (earning and non-earning) have shown positive attitudes towards in status of girl child and need for their education, political participation of women and raising voice against exploitation. But the earning respondents were found to be more divergent than that of non-earning group in all the aspects except raising voice against exploitation. It is important to mention here that none of the respondents (both earning and non-earning) have shown negative attitude towards raising voice against exploitation. Both the groups were possessed positive attitudes towards the same.

This relatively better level of attitude among the earning women must have developed due to the following reasons : (1) their hidden potential and self-interest for attitudinal change, (2) Effect of the working atmosphere, nature of work, encouragement of the employer and the co-workers, interaction with very many people concerned with the occupation, (3) Family support and encouragement, (4) Exposure to various life situation, and (5) The sincere efforts and powerful messages of various types of activities of RSS and its volunteers. All these factors have attributed to them in changing a relatively better level of attitudes in them than the non-earning slum women. But in case of non-earning slum women, (1) they didn't have strong desire to change their attitude, (2) their fatalistic and traditional nature of thinking and living, (3) non-co-operation from family members and friends in household cores, (4) mental tension and wretched poverty due to non-supplementary income from them, (5) chronic illness and family disturbances, might have affected to their relatively less level of attitudinal changes in them.

Hence, it cannot be said that the relatively better level of attitudinal changes found among the earning slum women than that of the non-earning slum women was only due to the earning background of the respondents. It is true that occupation is a dominant factor for attitudinal change of the learners but is not the only factor. Rather the sincere efforts made by the RSS volunteers, their active participations in the campaigns, and the powerful messages of the reading and cultural media seem to count to a greater extent for the same.

Mention may be made here that both earning and non-earning slum women were found to be actively participated in politics and other developmental activities of the slum areas of Rourkela. It was also observed by the investigator in the field during her data collection that both earning and non-earning slum women have actively raised their voices against exploitation whenever necessary. This active participation of slum women in different types of activities specially in politics, raising voice against exploitation, taking special interest for the education of their girls

were not found prominently among the slum women before the launching of literacy programme. The grass-root level volunteers, local people and the slum women themselves have reported it to the investigator. The investigator has also recorded those things in the field. Thus, it can be said that it was the sincere efforts and activities of the organisers and volunteers of RSS, which count a lot in bringing attitudinal changes in a positive direction among the neo-literate slum women towards the status of girl child and their education, political participation and revising voice against exploitation.

Knowledge about Property Right, Decision-making Right, Different Developmental Scheme and Attitude Towards Communal Harmony and Helping Husband in Household Chores

It is deduced from the data analysis that a large majority of the respondents (more than 85%) irrespective of their age, caste/community and earning status have developed a highly positive attitude towards communal harmony and national integration, decision-making rights of women and interest to take part in social welfare. Whereas more than half of the respondents (less than 60%) irrespective of their age, Caste/community and earning status were found to be developed simply positive attitudes towards helping husband in household chores and aware about property right of women and different developmental schemes.

It was expected on the basis of the research finding of Aikara and Henriques (1985), Mohanty (1988), Tantry (1990) and Thakre (1991) and Trivedi (1992) that a very low level of social awareness will be ascertained among the respondents of this study. But it was not so happened. On the contrary, it was found that respondents irrespective of their age, caste/community and earning status of the present study have developed a positive attitude towards their active participation in social activities and communal harmony and national integration, which shows the high level of their social awareness. Rather, on the studies of Sukla (1988), Rao (1992) and GIDSL(2000) have ascertained in drawing a conclusion for the same.

Further, the findings of the study of Murthy (1988) gave an impression that adult literacy programme will be helpful in developing high level of awareness among the participants regarding income generation schemes etc. The results of the study of Dhanbal (1991) also ascertained in this line that the respondents of the study were much aware about different loan facilities and majority of them (67%) have repaid the loan in time. These findings have not supported to a greater extent to the present study. The findings of the research studies of Mohanty (1988) and Pushpa (1992) ascertained that the respondents were not found to be much aware about the schemes for income generation implemented by Govt. and different agencies. The findings of the study by Mohanty (1988) revealed that only 46 per cent respondents were aware about developmental schemes of Govt. But in the present study it was observed that more than fifty per cent of the slum women (56%) and 61% respectively, Table 6.54 and 6.57) were found to be aware about different social so functionaries and developmental schemes of the government.

Based on the research findings of Rao (1992) it was assumed that a great majority of the respondents will be highly aware about their decision-making right and right to parental property. Further they were expected to have developed very highly positive attitudes towards helping husbands in household chores. On the contrary, except about their decision-making rights, they were not found to be highly aware about their right of parental property and highly positive attitude towards helping husbands (can be seen in Tables 6.53 and 6.50). Only more than half have shown their awareness and positive attitudes towards the same. Whereas, regarding decision-

making rights of women a large majority of slum women irrespective of the age, caste/community and earning status have shown highly positive attitude (can be seen in Table 6.51).

This relatively low level of awareness regarding right of parental property, different developmental schemes of the government and less positive attitude of women towards helping husband must have attributed to the following factors : *(i)* lack of keen interest to know about legal and property rights and different developmental schemes, *(ii)* lack of interest to change their attitudes due to their fatalistic and traditional thinking, *(iii)* lack of exposure to different life situation and medias, *(iv)* inactive participation in various discussion forum and their follow-up programmes, *(v)* lack of co-operation from the family members and in work field that leads to demotivation for active participation, *(vi)* effect of immature school volunteers, who themselves were unaware about different schemes of govt. and legal rights. All these factors seem to count a lot for their relatively lesser development in their awareness as well as attitudinal level.

Further, their highly positive attitudes towards communal harmony and national integration, and interest to take part actively in social welfare and decision-making rights must have affected by : *(i)* their self-interest and motivation, *(ii)* their exposure to different life situation and various cultural medias, *(iii)* encouragement from the family and work field to take active participation in the programme, *(iv)* inner potential which was in need of an opportunity to come out, *(v)* the special efforts and activities of RSS volunteers and organisers, and *(vi)* The powerful message of the reading materials and environment building ac ivities. All these factors have affected a lot in developing high level of awareness and highly positive attitudinal change among the respondents.

It is observed by experts that the literacy programme has been able to break the culture of silence among the slum women. Now they have become more objective in decision-making process of their families as well as in their social-setting like male members. Further they have become conscious about their basic and legal rights. It is surprising to note that the Muslim slum women of Narla Road and Hasanpur have come forward from their "BURKHA" on a procession to the A.D.M. office to fight for their basic rights like, ration card, drinking water, electricity etc. The tribal women of Dhipatoli, Khariabahal and other slums have also demonstrated before the A.D.M. Rourkela for their basic rights.

It is noteworthy to mention here that some of the respondents from conservative Muslim and Bihari families have taken their own decisions and have gone for family planning operation even after the birth of one or two daughters. It was reported by the officer-in-charge of the family welfare centre of Rourkela.

The active role of neo-literate slum women as agents of socio-cultural integration and communal harmony during the communal flare-up of 1992-93 at Muslim dominated areas like Narla Road and some of the areas of Madhusudan Palli was historic. The leading role played by a neo-literate Muslim slum women-cum-volunteer was remarkable. Her contribution in organising people and bringing harmony with the help of other neo-literates (mainly women group) proves their level of social awareness in this regard.

Further, the social responsibilities performed by the neo-literate slum women of various slums during Latur earthquake (1993), Super Cyclone of Orissa (1999) and for the victims of Gujarat (Kutch) earthquake (2001) is noteworthy. It was found that they collected cash and kind from door-to-door and sent it to the victims. During super cyclone of Orissa a representative group of slum women had gone to the area along with the grass-root level volunteers and senior activists for their service and served there for more than two weeks selflessly. It was directly experienced by the investigator in the field.

Based on the reports of different types of people concerned with the activities of RSS, information gathered from different functionaries concerned in this regard and the observations of the investigator herself, it can be said that there might be the affect of various factors on the development of awareness level and attitudinal changes of the respondents to some extent but not the whole. It is the sincere and constant efforts and activities of RSS with its dedicated volunteers which count maximum in developing their high level of awareness and attitudinal changes towards communal harmony, decision-making rights etc. It shows a highly positive impact of RSS on the slum women for the same.

Awareness About the Enrolment of Children and Continuation of Writing Practice

It is evident from the data analysis that almost all the neo-literate slum women irrespective of their age, caste/community and earning status were found to be aware about the education of their children. their own responsibility to send their children to the school in time and about the NFE centre as alternative arrangement for the education of poor children and child labourers of the slum. Further, it was found that majority of them (more than 70% Table 6.65) irrespective of their age, Caste/community and earning background were found to be in touch with their writing practices.

Based on the research findings of Thakre (1991), Naik (1994) and Parikh (1994) it was assumed that there will be a low level of awareness found among the slum women regarding the enrolment of their children. But these findings did not support to the present study in drawing such a conclusion. On the contrary, the research findings of Planning Commission (1969), Rao (1992), Saldhana (1992) and GIDSL (2000) ascertained to draw a conclusion for the present study that the participants of literacy programme have realised the importance of education to a great extent and therefore, started educating their children in formal or non-formal system of education. This high level of awareness development among the slum women was possible because of the following reasons : *(i)* Their inner urge to make their children educated and developed. *(ii)* Sublimation of their own desires and feelings for education through their children, *(iii)* Encouragement of the employers (in case of earning slum women), *(iv)* Their wretched poverty and social conditions. *(v)* Exposure of different media and advertisements, *(vi)* Constant efforts and effective activities of RSS for the literacy and educational development of the disadvantaged slum-dwellers. All these factors seem to be responsible for their high level of awareness in this regard.

In terms of the regularities of the writing practice of the slum women it must have continued due to the following : *(i)* Their self-interest to keep writing practice through letter writing to their relatives and friends, (ii) Nature of work (in case of earning members), *(iii)* Budgeting habit in the family, *(iv)* Encouragement from the family members etc., *(v)* Further efforts of the volunteers/ organisers through various activities of Chetana Kendra to retain their writing skills. All these factors must have encouraged them to keep their writing skills alive and active.

Mention may be made here that before launching of literacy programme, there was no over-enrolment in primary and upper primary schools of Rourkela (Municipality and Government Schools). A very few number of children from the slum areas of Rourkela were coming to the school for their education. Most of the children of school-going age were found in the dumping yards of RSP during school hours to pick up iron bits. But after launching of literacy programme when the mothers of the children were involved with the programme and made literate, they realised the need of education for their children. Of course, the role of the volunteers in generating urge for the education of their children is noteworthy. As a result they started sending their children to the schools. The increasing rate of enrolment in Primary and Upper Primary Schools were the evidence for it. It was also noticed from the records of the schools and report of the DI of schools that the dropout rate especially among the girls dropped down considerably and regular attendance of the schools, located in and around slum pockets, went up significantly. In other educational systems like Anganwadi NFE centres of RSS, the enrolment rate of the children have also been increased significantly. Further, the frequent demand and demonstration of slum women before the ADM Office for opening of more Primary Schools and NFE centres prove their awareness and craze for the education of their children.

It is also important to present the observation of the investigator with regard to the writing practice and skills of the respondents in various occasions. During her data collection over a period of three years (from January, 1997 to March, 2000) in three phases, the investigator has attended a number of programmes organised by RSS in various occasions. The programmes were Celebration of International Literacy Day, International Women's Day, different training programmes, health camps etc. Almost all the functions were followed with a good number of literacy activities like writing competitions, reading competitions, Mathematic test, Alpana and Rangoli competition, general knowledge, song, debate and so on.

In writing competitions it was observed that a number of respondents were participating in those competitions with great zeal. Their writing performances in general were also found to be satisfactory. Many of them were even able to write short stories, poems, experiences as neo-literates. Which proves their interest and keeping touch practice with writing skills. During in-depth discussion many of them expressed their gratitude to the organisers of the competitions.

Further, the informants (including the slum women) have reported that prior to literacy programme they were unaware of very many aspects of life and the concerning issues. They were rigid, conservative and fatalistic; therefore, they were not sending their children to the school or other institution. They themselves were also not thinking for their education. After joining this programme, they got a common platform to start their journey of life in a better direction through their developed awareness and changed attitudes.

Hence, it can be thought that the high level of awareness and positive attitudinal changes marked in the neo-literate slum women was due to the impact of the literacy programme through its selfless volunteers and their constant efforts that count much for the same.

CONCLUSION

On the background of the above discussion the following can be derived as conclusion :

1. The over all impact of literacy programme on slum women in developing their level of awareness and changing their attitudes towards various aspects of life and issues were found to be highly positive.
2. The slum women were found to be highly aware in the aspects like population and pollution, health and sanitation, child and maternity care, communal harmony, status of girl child and their education, raising voice against exploitation, education of their children, political participation of women, evils of superstitions, alcohol, dowry and child marriage than that of property rights women, various developmental schemes and social functionaries and attitude towards helping husband in household chores.

3. Age, caste/communication back round didn't play any significant role in developing their level of awareness or attitudinal changes. There found some influence of occupational background of the respondents in developing very high level of awareness or attitudinal changes among the respondents.
4. It was found that the respondents of middle age group have shown relatively better than the younger and the older and the ST, SC and Muslim have shown relatively better than the GC. and OBC in many aspects of life and concerning issues, and the earning respondents in general have shown relatively better than the non-earning category.

However, the overall impact of the literacy activities of RSS was found to be highly satisfactory in generating high level of awareness and changing the attitudes of the slum women in Rourkela through its networking and sincere and dedicated volunteers.

CASE STUDIES

Introduction

Attempts have been made in this section to present the case studies of four neo-literate slum women (two unsuccessful and two successful) out of 103 so as to find out : *(i)* their causes of under development (as per the objective No. 4 of the study), and *(ii)* factors responsible for their outstanding performances in literacy skills as well as level of awareness development, attitudinal changes and social participation despite their family constraints, personal problem and wretched poverty. The name of the cases have been changed for confidentiality and presented hereunder.

Causes for the under development to Neo-literate Slum women

Mention may be made here that these two slum women have achieved the lowest both in literacy skills and in level of awareness development among the 103 neo-literate slum women.

CASE 1

Name	— Ujarabati Majhi	— Age		— 16 years	
Caste/Community	— ST	— Marital Status		— Unmarried	
Occupation	— Nil	— Income		— Nil	
Name of the Slum	— Haripur basti	— No. of Literacy		— Zone 3	

Ujarabati, is the only daughter of her parents in Haripur basti. Her father is a daily labourer under a steel plant contractor; his condition is a little better than that of other slum-dwellers of Haripur basti. Therefore, his wife didn't have to go for supplementary earning for their livelihood, and taking care of the household as well as Ujara, who was an asthma patient from her very childhood.

Ujara was an over-protected child from her very birth as she was born after the thirteen years of married life of her parents. The mother reported to the investigator that to get a child they had gone to many temples, consulted many saints and black magicians and worshipped the goddesses. Only then they were blessed with Ujara. Therefore, despite poverty they took special care of Ujara, and provided the best medical treatment for asthma and even consulted many black magicians and saints for the same. Since the Municipal School was half-a- kilometer away from their slum, they therefore, didn't send her for education during her childhood. As a result, like her parents, she also remained illiterate till the literacy programme was launched in Rourkela.

During the survey work of literacy programme, she was identified as an illiterate and motivated to learn by the volunteers of RSS, who used to be the students of Udit Nagar Government high school and the nearby youth club.

She was enrolled in the literacy centre of Haripur basti for the afternoon class. Initially she was regular in her literacy classes. But she was never interested to participate in-group discussion with regard to awareness generation in various aspects and issues of life. After a couple of days of her joining the classes she neglected coming to the literacy centre and also didn't show keen interest for learning. As she was a sick child suffering from asthma, her parents also could not force her to go to centre regularly.

While testing her literacy skills the investigator has observed that she was just able to read the paragraph of the topic "Neta Ra Dukha Gala" from the PL Primer "Nabataranga" by spelling alphabets. She could read the given passage for comprehension with a little difficulty, but she was unable to comprehend the questions correctly. Further, she was not even able to recognise the road symbols given in the test question properly.

Regarding writing, she was some how able to copy the paragraph with much difficulty, but she could not complete writing her personal address. With regard to word dictation, out of five words dictated, she could write only two words correctly. Her speed of writing was very slow and quality of writing was also very poor.

Regarding letter writing she could not write her experiences in the letter correctly and properly. She could write only three lines for the same.

On the numeracy test, except subtraction, she did not do well in addition, multiplication and division. Overall her performance in literacy skills was found to be very poor.

Regarding her level of awareness development and attitudinal changes, the investigator observed that she was unaware with most of the aspects of life and concerning issues like effects of population explosion, need for environmental protection, child and maternity care, evils of superstitions, advantage of literate parents, work participation of sons in household work, awareness on property rights of women from her parental property, different develop parental schemes and social functionaries and the enrolment of poor children in different educational system.

She was found to be aware about evils of alcohol, dowry, early marriage, raising voice against exploitation and she had a positive attitude towards political participation of women and communication harmony and national integration.

When the investigator wanted to know about her future planning, she could not say anything. She had a negative self-image about the life of women. She didn't have any interest for any sorts of training to be undergone, not even for income generation training for her future. But she expressed her feelings that she would have learnt in the centre regularly, if her volunteer had been sincere and regular and her health would have been better. She reported that at many times she felt uneasy in the centre. Therefore, she could not sit there for long time. Further, the absence of the volunteer demotivated her. Therefore, she was irregular in later part of the literacy programme. Her illiterate parents reported it to the investigator,

"If she is not interested to learn, why should we force her repeatedly ? After all she is our only daughter, and there is no meaning to hurt her by going against her will for education. Whatever will be in her fate, will happen".

Ujara also thinks in the same line. Only she was apprehensive about her would be husband that he should not be a drunkard and that he should be ready to live with her parents in Haripur basti. Why should she think about her future, since her parents are alive?

After a detail investigation about the case study of Ujarabati Majhi, the investigator could visualise that constant illness, over protection of the illiterate superstitious parents, lack of self-motivation and keen interest of the respondents and irregularities of the school volunteers in the literacy centres were the causes responsible for the unsuccessfulness of Ujarabati Majhi.

CASE 2

Name	— Kumari Majhi	— Age	— 22 Years
Caste/Community	— Scheduled Caste	— Marital Status	— Married
Occupation	— Maid Servant	— Income	— Rs.500
Name of the Slum	— Narayani Palli	-- No. of Literacy	— Zone 5

Kumari Majhi, is a married neo-literate slum woman from 'Golghar' literacy centre of Narayani Palli slum areas under literacy zone no. 5. She is a maid-servant, working in the staff quarters of State Bank of India colony, Sector-8 and earns Rs. 500 per month. Her husband Raghu Majhi about 35-years-old is a drunkard and gambler. He works in one of the sister plants of RSP as a labourer and earns about Rs. 2000 per month. Kumari lives with her husband and mother-in-law in a rented, Jhupudi (hut) by paying Rs. 300 per month. Kumari was the second wife of Raghu. Raghu's first wife left him after one year of their married life because of his gambling and alcoholic nature and physical torture. He then married to Kumari, who was only sixteen-years-old at that time. To get relieved from dowry, her alcoholic parents organised the marriage of Kumari, without enquiring any details about Raghu. Kumari thought that after marriage she will be at least in a better state of mind than that of her parents' house. But her dreams didn't come true, and Raghu tortured her both mentally and physically. Despite physical and mental torture, she was staying with Raghu. Seeing her condition, her neighbour Golapi has helped her in arranging those jobs of maid servant before joining literacy programme. So that she could at least relieve from the home for sometimes.

She joined the literacy class immediately after the launching of the programme. During her childhood she didn't get a chance to go for education due to her alcoholic parents and wretched family condition. So she had a desire to learn.

Thereby when the volunteers of RSS came to their slum for environment building activities and identification of illiterates, without consulting to her husband and mother-in-law, she enlisted her name as illiterate and expressed her will to join the literacy class. Her husband and mother-in-law did not like this. They thought that by joining literacy class she will be leaving her job, and they will be losing her earning. However, despite their opposition and non-co-operation of her mother-in-law in the household activities, she attended the classes regularly and taking active participation in those awareness generation programme. Although her learning time was not always suitable to her, she could manage it by convincing her employers. But gradually they also didn't co-operate her as their work neglected due to late coming of Kumari. With the increase of physical and mental torture to her, the workload of home and at work field also increased and she became irregular in the class and inactive those programmes.

In the literacy test, Kumari was rated good in reading. Because, she was able to read a paragraph of the P.L. Primer "Naba Taranga", and also could read the paragraph for comprehension. But

she was unable to comprehend the questions correctly. But with regard to the recognition of symbols, she could recognise the traffic symbols very easily and answered the given questions correctly.

In the written test she could copy the given passage with much difficulty. She wrote her personal address incorrectly. Regarding dictation, she could write only two correct words out of five words dictated to her. Further, she tried to write her experience as a neo-literate through letter writing but could not complete the letter. Whatever she wrote was also not correct. Hence, her writing skill was also found to be very poor.

In numeracy test, she did well in addition and subtraction, and committed one mistake in multiplication out of the two. Whereas, she was found to be very poor in division. On the whole her performance in numeracy was found to be good. This has been possible probably due to her nature of job and exposure to working situation. In aggregate, her performance in literacy skills was found to be poor.

Regarding awareness development and attitudinal changes, she was found to be unaware with many important aspects of life and concerning issues. Although she generated her income, she did not develop a highly positive attitude towards evils of dowry, superstition, different developmental schemes and social functionaries, assistance of husband in household work, political participation of women, communal harmony and national integration. She was ignorant about the sub-aspect of effects of population explosion, child and maternity care (immunisation of the pregnant mother and child), but she was found to be aware of some aspect of environmental protection, evils of population explosion, personal hygiene and cleanliness, evils of alcohol, need for girls education and raising voice against exploitation. Overall, her awareness level was also found to be not satisfactory.

During in-depth discussion, Kumari reported to the investigator that Raghu was unfaithful to her as he indulged in extramarital affairs with a Reja (female labourer). This greatly distressed and depressed her. This was further aggravated when she was underwent abortion due to extreme physical and mental torture of her husband. Since then, she had been severe depression and she has neglected her study. Because of her fatalistic and traditional nature, she could not leave Raghu. In fact, once she decided to leave the "Jhupudi." But where to go was a big problem before her. She also could not go back to her alcoholic and poor parents as they were living in a wretched condition in a near by a village *viz.*, Lathikata". Her two younger sisters and one brother, who were supported by her before marriage, were still to be independent. Therefore, she stopped thinking of leaving the house.

She had a desire to get peace of mind and happiness. She was not happy with her life. She felt that if Raghu could be changed, everything would be changed. She wanted to get relieved from mental tension and physical torture, but at the same time did not want to go for a divorce and second marriage. She was apprehensive of the fact that if the second one would be again alcoholic like her father or Raghu her life would be more of a hell. Therefore, she reconciled to her present way of life.

The investigator could visualise that she could be re-motivated to learn for living. After a thorough study of the profile of Kumari Majhi, the investigator came to a conclusion that poverty, alcoholic parents and husband, tensed family environment, day-long hard labour in the family and work place, non-co-operation of the family members and inconvenient teaching learning hour unsuccessfulness of Kumari Majhi of Narayani Palli slum.

Factors Responsible for Outstanding Performance of Neo-literate Slum Women

CASE 1

Name	— Ahalya Barik	Age	— 21 (At present)
Caste/community	— SC	Marital Status	— Unmarried
Occupation	— Nil	Income	— Nil
Name of the Slum	— Gangadhar Palli	No. of Literacy	— Zone 3

Ahalya Barik, a physically challenged neo-literate woman, is the daughter of Sri Bipra Barik of Gangadhar Palli slum area. Bipra Barik, being visually challenged is dependent totally on his wife Sula, who is a maid-servant, earns about five hundred rupees per month. Both Bipra and Sula had four children, two sons and two daughters. Ahalya was the youngest one. Their elder daughter was married and lived with her family in the interior corner of Kalahandi district of Orissa. Whereas, their other two elder married sons were also staying separately in two different slums of Rourkela with their families. They had never bothered about their old parents and the handicapped sister. They were not concerned about the treatment for their blind father or handicapped sister.

At the age of about 11 years, while cooking food for her blind father in the absent of Sula, Ahalya got severely burnt in the burning firewood and almost lost her both legs. This incident happened just before the launch of literacy programme. Due to wretched poverty and lack of proper guidance they didn't go for the better treatment of Ahalya. As a result, her legs got infected and thereby Ahlaya lost her hope for further treatment and zeal of living.

During the survey work of the literacy programme, the local grass-root level volunteers Bichitra Kumari Barik identified her as an illiterate. By that time Ahalya was able to crawl a little for her own movement with the help of crotches. Bichitra tried her level best to motivate Ahalya for her enrolment in the literacy centre, which was supposed to run in her house. Initially Ahalya was reluctant to learning. As she was a physically challenged and that her condition was also not good for movement, she denied joining the campaign. But the grass-root level worker without losing her patience tried her level best to motivate Ahalya with the help of other volunteers of RSS and ultimately were able to convince her to enroll her name in the centre.

Bichitra was able to create urge in Ahalya for living through learning in literacy programme of RSS. The moral support of the RSS organisers (specially some of the senior level activists) aroused interest in her to develop strong will power. As a result, she could complete all the three primers along with the issues of Saksharata Samachar before the time frame. She was also able to develop her level of awareness accordingly. In the meantime, Bichitra with the help of RSS organisers could arrange some source for the treatment of Gandharbi in Rourkela Government Hospital and was looking forward for further treatment and operation. But till 1995 no such facilities could be made available for her better treatment. In between Ahalya made herself strong to exist with great difficulty. She regularly attended the P.L. classes and the activities at the Chetana Kendras of Gangadhar Palli in a State of crawling with two wooden supporters. The painful picture of her state of crawling from her Jhupudi (hut) to the Chetana Kendra had been seen by the investigator during her data collection in the field. Despite, her physical problem, she participated in almost all the competitions organised by RSS during different occasions both at their slum level and central level. She had also been awarded for her outstanding performances in patriotic song competition, Rangoli competition, allocation and debate competitions, numeracy test and letter writing competition etc.

In the year 1995, she personally requested to the Chairman of RSS, and ADM Rourkela for her treatment. She expressed her desire before him during his field visit to Gangadhar Palli that she wanted to stand and walk on her own feet. Once again Bichitra and the other senior activists of RSS, and the members of Chetana Samiti of Gangadhar Palli tried their best for her treatment. Mr. N.K. Das, the then ADM of Rourkela sanctioned five thousand rupees for her from the Red Cross fund and encouraged the RSS volunteers to carry on the missionary work. Although the amount was very small for this purpose this became the instrument of inspiration for extending help from the volunteers and learners. Observing her strong will power for existence some of the senior activists took the case as a challenge and providing financial as well as other support whole-heartedly. Of course, the school and grass-root level volunteers, and the neo-literates have also contributed their best in the form of, cash, kind and services in the hospital. Although, Ahalya was in desire of her artificial limbs, but was not ready for amputation once again she was motivated and in Feb. 1996 her operation and amputation was done successfully with the full co-operation of the doctors and other staff of Government Hospital, Rourkela. She was hospitalised for about four months for her treatment.

During her treatment in the hospital she didn't forget to read and write she kept her regular practice of reading local newspaper in Oriya "YugaVarta and "Utkalmail", Saksharata Samachar, and different library books of Chetana Kendra provided by the grass root volunteer Bichitra Bank. She kept intimating about her progress of health condition to the Secretary and Chairman of RSS as well as the neo-literate friends of Chetana Kendras of different zones.

After coming back from the hospital, she started motivating people to join in the post-literacy programme by citing her own example, encouraging mothers to send their children to the NFE centres or to the schools, and helping indirectly to Bichitra in her motivational work for the PL activities. As her case was complicated, she was advised to wait for another a few months for the setting of artificial limbs. In the mean time, due to various reasons and the false assurance of some eminent personalities, nothing could be properly materialised to go for the setting of her artificial limbs and operation. Since it was quite expensive despite the interest of some senior activists of RSS, they also could not dare to do it single handedly.

However, her struggle came to an end at the arrival of Sri Aurobindoo Padhi, IAS who joined as ADM Rourkela-cum-Chairman of RSS. After learning about Ahalya and her family condition, he took over her case almost immediately for further treatment and setting of artificial limb, etc. With an active co-operation of the Artificial Limb Centre, Rourkela, some senior level RSS activists and grass-root volunteers like Bichitra, her operation was successfully done in March, 2001. Artificial limbs were set in October 2001 before Puja vacation. She had a dream in her life to enjoy Durga Puja by moving on her own feet. With the efforts of different levels of RSS volunteers co-operation and best wishes of the people of the slum and Basti Chetana Committee and above all her strong will power and determination in all her dreams came true.

The investigator during her in-depth discussion and observation in various situation found that Ahalya had become mentally strong and bold with strong determination. She desires to be economically self-sufficient by undergoing income generation training at Shramik Vidyapith of Rourkela. For this, she has already requested to the Director of Shramik Vidyapith through an application written by her in Oriya language.

The investigator while administering the literacy test on her, came to know that Ahalya had already finished almost all the library books of Chetana Kendra. In addition, she had gone through a series of books written on different religions and patriotism. While testing her, it was observed by the investigator that she was very good in reading. She was able to read the paragraph of "Naba Taranga" without any mistake and after reading the paragraph for comprehension and answer to all the questions satisfactorily. Also she was able to read and recognise the road symbol given in the test question. But she took some more time in recognising the road symbol. It might be due to her lack of exposure in practical field, as she was a handicap and she had less scope to move on the road. However, her overall reading skill was found to be highly satisfactory as she was rated very good for the same.

Regarding her writing skill, she was able to copy the given passage and write down her personal address completely and correctly, she was also able to write five words of dictation correctly. Further, she could write her personal experiences as a neo-literate focusing on her development of awareness level. Her standard of writing the personal experience was very satisfactory. Overall, her writing skill was very good.

In numeracy test, she was rated excellent. Because, she was able to do the addition, subtraction, multiplication and division. Overall, her performance in literacy skill was found to be highly satisfactory as she secured very good and excellent grades in reading, writing and numeracy.

Regarding her development of the level of awareness, she was found to be aware of most of the aspects of life and concerning issues. But was not much aware with regard to child and maternity care (specially in the sub-aspect of registration of pregnant women, advantages of breast-feeding, diseases of the infants etc.) But she was found to be highly aware in the aspects like the need for women education and its advantages, decision-making rights of the women, enrolment of poor children in different education system, evils of dowry, superstition, alcohol, child marriage, explosion of population and environmental protection, different developmental scheme and legal rights. She was also found to be very keen to personal hygiene and sanitation. It might be due to her regular visits to the hospital and repeated hospitalisation which has made her keen to sanitation.

Although she was having a positive attitude towards the work participation of son in the household activities of the family, she could not have supported very strongly to the assistance of husband in household chores of the wives. This might be due to the effect of her family background as her father was dependent upon her mother for everything. Overall, her development of awareness level was found to be quite satisfactory.

While interviewing Ahalaya about her future plan she has clearly responded to the investigator say, "I was like a dead cow. People used to come and see me like they come and see an animal. Which was unbearable. My own family never sympathised with me. Many a time, I wanted to give up my life. Bichitra didi and other brothers and sisters of RSS have given me a new lease of life. I, therefore, can never think about anything other than RSS and its work. The rest of my life will be for the poor people and the people like me. But first of all I would like to earn something and be self-sufficient."

After careful observation of her profile, the investigator came to the conclusion that constant and sincere efforts of the self-less, RSS volunteers of different types (including the chairman), self-motivation, coupled with the will power and determination of Ahalya, and the involvement and co-operation of the people of Basti Chetana Samiti, were mainly responsible for the outstanding performance of Ahalya as well as her unique success in life.

CASE 2

Name	— Aisha Begun	Age	— 34 Years
Caste/Community	— Muslim	Marital Status	— Married
Occupation	— Housewife and social work	Income	— Nil
Name of the slum	— Gopalbandhu Palli	Literacy Zone	No. IX

Aisha Begam, the wife of Rajak Abdul, was a neo-literate slum woman. Her husband was a worker in Rourkela Steel Plant. They were leading a happy life with their six children (four daughters and two sons) in their own house at Gopabandhu palli slum. Being a Muslim girl of an orthodox family, she was not given an education during her childhood. She was only allowed to learn some alphabets of Arabic language so that she could read "Kuran Sarif". Although her father was a fourth class Bank Employee in Calcutta, there was no impact of the advanced culture of the city on him. He was a rigid and orthodox Muslim. Therefore, he organised the marriage of Aisha with Rajak at the age of fourteen only. By heart Rajak was a mild and considerate person. So, at the time of marriage, he didn't take any dowry from Aisha's father, and after marriage he tried his level best to make Aisha happy with his very limited income. Aisha also tried her best to oblige Rajak by performing her family responsibilities and additional duties like taking care of her dependent sister-in-law who was a widow and her two children (one daughter and one son). Despite her peaceful family life, Aisha was tortured mentally by her sister-in-law. Rajak also could not say anything against his widow sister, and remained silent. Her sister-in-law was very much traditional, fatalistic and rigid in her attitude. She was not in support of the family planning operation. Therefore, she didn't allow Aisha to go for the same. Her Khawuish (will) of delivering a male child for the Biradari (family) was therefore fulfilled. As a result, in spite of her unwillingness Aisha had to become the mother of half a dozen children at the age of about 26.

From the very beginning Aisha was very social and sympathetic to the poor and disadvantaged. Abdul was also a man of that type. So when the literacy movement started in Rourkela, she got a chance to fulfill her inner desire.

Inspired by father John of "Sevasadan" voluntary organisation, who was also a volunteer and zone co-ordinator of literacy zone no. IX, she joined in the programme as a learner, and at the same time motivated other illiterate women of the slum to join the programme. Gradually, she became a learner-volunteer of the area. Her husband supported and inspired her a lot in this regard. As a result, within two months, she could complete her primers and developed the required level of awareness in various aspects of life and the concerning issues. After being literate, she started helping the volunteers in teaching and other activities of the centre as well as the developmental activities of the slum.

Gopabandhu Palli, situated just back to the Railway godown and yard was well known for criminal activities. There was evidence of rape cases even in the broad day light before the launching of the literacy programme. Therefore, women of the slum, specially the Biharis and the Muslims did not dare to step out of their houses so easily. Hence Aisha organised a group of women, who were the learners of the literacy centre and started protesting against the criminal activities of the slum like, gambling, alcohol business, and about the unsecure condition of women etc. She started this type of work with the full co-operation of the then ADM-cum-Chairman of RSS Sri Asit Tripathy, IAS, who was the initiator of the literacy programme. Her husband also supported her in her activities. For this work, many a times she had to visit the police station and to the court to give evidence. But, she has never bothered about her consequences and continued her work as it is.

Now, Aisha has been identified in her slum as a social worker, who works for the development of her slum. She has not joined any political party, but has been invited to all sorts of decision-making activities of the slum by each and every political party and other groups.

Role of Aisha as an agent of Socio-cultural integration during the communal flare-up of 1992-93 at Muslim dominated Narla Road slum and some of the areas of Madhusudan Palli was remarkable. When the local administration and police failed to bring the situation under control, they took the help of the local RSS volunteers. Aisha along with other RSS volunteers and matured neo-literates handled the situation and restored complete normalcy by doing door to door campaigning.

While testing, the literacy skills and awareness level of Aisha, the investigator came to know that she has also learned a little English from the literacy volunteer (NFE instructor). Now she is able to write her name and even address in English.

In her test of reading skill, she was found to be excellent. She was able to go through the passage from the PL Primer "Naba Tarang" fluently. She could also equally read the passage of comprehension and able to comprehend it by answering all the given questions. She could recognise the symbols and answered the related questions very easily.

Regarding her writing skill, she could copy down the passage and write down her personal address completely and correctly. She was also able to write five words of dictation. But there was spelling mistake in one of the dictated words. Further, she could write her personal experiences as a neo-literate based on her knowledge of awareness with spelling mistakes. She was very slow in writing, and her style of writing was not so systematic. However, her writing skill was rated quite good.

In the numeral test, she was found to be excellent because of her eligibility of doing correct addition, subtraction, multiplication and division.

Regarding her development of awareness level, it was observed that she was very much aware about different aspects of life and concerned issues. Rather, she was found more aware in certain aspects like different developmental schemes, social functionaries, immunisation of the children and pregnant women and so on then that of the local volunteer. It might be due to her direct involvement that the indifferent agencies also started activities for the beneficiaries of her slum. She was equally aware of the evils of population explosion, need for environmental protection, evils of alcohol, dowry, superstition, and need for the education of girls and other aspects like communal harmony and national integration, enrolment of poor children in educational system, raising voice against exploitation. But it was also observed by the investigator that, although, she was aware about personal hygiene, she was not found to be highly practical in her day-to-day life. This might be due to her large family and lack of time due to household chores and literacy work.

However, she was found to be highly aware in almost all the aspects of life. Overall, her performance, in literacy skills and awareness level, were found to be highly satisfactory in all respect.

During the in-depth discussion in a women's group of Gopabandu Palli, the participants of the group reported that she is the "torch light" of their slum. Without her no development work, like widow-pension, ration card, education of their children, water supply, basti-co-operation and so on could have been achieved.

The counselor of the ward and other elders have also highly appreciated her selfless and developmental work for the slum. Once (three years back) she was involved in a voluntary organisation with only little remuneration. But when she came to know that the organisation had exploited her voluntary social spirit, she immediately gave up the work and made herself free from the bondage.

Her husband says, *"Aisha should have been born in a Khandani family (royal family). Literacy movement has given her a platform to grow and expose herself and her inner qualities. The support, the co-operation and the opportunities which have been extended by RSS, would not have been given by anybody, not even by me"*.

Aisha also pays her deep sense of gratitude to RSS and its organisers, who have given her a scope to be literate and provided her a common platform, co-operation and moral support to fulfill her inner desire as a social worker. She has a dream for her slum that each and every child of the slum (who one row in the school and NFE Centre) should go to the college. They should not be recognised as criminals in the future. Further, she wants that her elder daughter who studies in the college would be a doctor. So that she can serve her slum in a better manner through her daughter.

Now she regrets her foolishness of becoming the mother of six children. She says *"If this programme would have launched earlier, I would not have listen to any body of my family and would have gone for family planning operation after the birth of my second daughter. But as they have already come on this earth, I would not let them miss the chance for education. I will try my best for their educational development and I would not give a single paisa at the time of their marriage as dowry"*.

If they want, they can go marry anybody of their own choice in religion but not before they are twenty.

After studying the profile of Aisha, the investigator learned that immense will-power, inner potential and self-interest of Aisha, moral support and encouragement of her husband, the acute problems of her slum and above all the efforts, scope, co-operation and various support extended by the organisers of RSS were the responsible factors for her literacy achievement and success as a neo-literate social worker.

CONCLUSION

From the four cases it can be concluded that :

(a) Constant illness, over protection of the illiterate and superstitions parents, lack of self-motivation and immature school volunteers were the main causes for the unsuccessfulness of case no.1 (Ujarabati Majhi) and wretched poverty, alcoholic parents and husband, tensed family environment, day long hard labour, non-co-operation from the family and the unsuitable timing for learning were the main causes for the unsuccessfulness of case no. 2 (Kumari Majhi).

(b) It was found that sincere and selfless efforts of the grass-root level volunteers as well as RSS organisers, strong will-power of the respondent, involvement and co-operation of the community people through Basti Chetana Samiti were mainly responsible for the success of case no.1 (Ahalya) and immense will power and inner potentials, support of her husband, internalising the problems of her slums and above all the sincere efforts and co-operation of RSS in every steps have helped in achieving success of Aisha (case no. 2) as a neo-literate social worker.

7

SUGGESTIONS FOR FURTHER IMPROVEMENT OF LITERACY PROGRAMME OF RSS

INTRODUCTION

Any developmental programme needs to be evolved with suggestions to facilitate interactive process of its further improvement and future course of action. Literacy programme of RSS, as a developmental programme of NLM is intended to eradicate illiteracy and to develop the educational level among the disadvantaged slum-dwellers, through its networking also needs to be reformed and evolved through suggestions for its further improvement. An attempt has been made in this chapter to deal with the suggestions rendered by different types of respondents, like 103 slum women, 23 grass-root level volunteers, 16 senior literacy activists and organizers and 31 people from different sectors of life like social workers, cultural-artists, NGO representatives, visitors to the campaign, government and non- government employees, employers of the carning slum women, government members etc. on the basis of their experiences, needs felt and problems overcome in the field for further development of slum women and the future course of action.

Suggestions Made by the Slum Women, Grass-root Level Volunteers, Senior Literacy Activists and Others Concerned with the Activities of RSS

TABLE 7.1

Retention of Literacy Skills

Sl. No.	*Suggestions*	*Total No of. Slum Women 103*	*Total No. of Volunteers 23*	*Total No.of Senior Activists 16*	*Total no. of other type of people 31*
1	2	3	4	5	6
1.	Neo-literate slum women to be recharged to keep their literacy skills in practice.	NA	NA	3(18.75)	16(58.06)
2.	Their regular participation in the activities of Chetana Kendra, which work like community center.	NA	NA	4(25.00)	17(54.84)
3.	Continuation of literacy programme through post literacy and implementation of CE.	NA	14(60.86)	16(100.00)	16(54.61)

(Contd. . .)

1 2	3	4	5	6
4. Increase of duration of teaching timing according to the suitability of the slum women.	22(21.36)	NA	NA	6(19.35)
5. Pilot experiment on new ideas with regard to literacy and other development.	NA	NA	NA	2(6.45)
6. Modification and development of reading and wriring materials in regional language and reflection of local culture in those materials.	NA	1(4.35)	NA	4(12.90)

Note : Figures with in parentheses indicate percentages.

It can be deduced, from Table 7.1, that the senior level of literacy activists and people from different sectors of life were concerned deeply with RSS activities have felt the need for recharging of the slum women to retain their literacy skills. Thus, they should be contacted even after their course content is over. Roy and Kapoor (1975) have mentioned in their studies that ex-literacy class adults were more susceptible to relapse into illiteracy than the school learners. Therefore, continuity of the programme should be given due importance. Practical assignments on the use of literacy skills are more useful for permanent learning of the slum women. Post literacy and continuing education facilities can help them to retain the learning of the literacy classes and not to relapse into illiteracy. Moreover, the literacy volunteers can try to motivate and attract them to come to the Chetana Kendra regularly through their activities. Therefore, the Chetana Kendra should be like the community centre of slum areas, where all sorts of facilities would be available. It is important to mention here that a very good number of respondents (can be seen from Table 7.1) have also suggested in this line that Chetana Kendra should function as community centre of the slum areas. Further, a few respondents have suggested that the duration of teaching timing should be increased, so that the participant will get some more time to practice their literacy skills in the centre which may not be possible at their home.

To tackle the problem of retention, especially on writing efficiency, the slum women should be motivated in the Kendra to participate in different types of writing competition among themselves like writing poems, short stories, proverbs, letters, applications, experiences in their family life or in working field etc. They should be encouraged to start their own wall magazine in the Chetana Kendra. It should be mentioned here that it has been experimented in two slums of Rourkela as pilot studies at Gudiatola and Shantinagar by some senior level literacy activists and were found to be encouraging. The table also reveals that a few respondents have also suggested for such type of pilot experiments on new ideas in this regard at different slum levels simultaneously. Hence, the RSS organizers and other senior activists should consider it and do the needful.

An important suggestion was given by some respondents (volunteers and resource persons) with regard to the modification of reading materials of the adult learners. It will not be out of place to highlight here that more than one-fourth per cent of the population of Rourkela is tribal and one-third of the respondents of this study is also from tribal background. Since Rourkela is coming under the tribal district of Sundargarh, and a good percentage of learners of literacy programme are also from tribal background; their culture, tradition, language and life style should definitely be reflected in the reading materials. It is true that there is a need of common language for the purpose of communication. But since they were under-developed, and now they are coming out for their development, they should also be encouraged through their culture and traditional media for further development. A mention may be made here that people are highly satisfied with the primers specially the PL one, and other literature for their effective stories writing style etc. But the literature lacks the reflection of tribal culture and living style which would have been more effective to the tribal learners.

Further it is suggested by the respondents (see Table 7.1) that reading materials on various issues, lives of great women, successful women from the grass-root levels and their success stories, about different types of people and their way of development should be written (developed) by RSS in regional language and they should be encouraged to go through the reading materials. Further, they should be guided by the volunteers to discuss among themselves in the group on the content and on various issues related to their lives. Thereby, they can retain reading skills along with other skills.

The table further reveals that cent per cent senior activist, majority of the grass-root level volunteers and more than half of the different types of people have seriously emphasized on the immediate implementation of continuing education programme along with PL activities. It should be mentioned here that the ground work of CE programme was already taken care of to a large extent by the RSS during the PL Phase itself. The achievement of TLC and PLC phone were in a way instrumental in introducing the objectives of CE. Moreover, it was observed that "reading and writing" cannot be continued in an isolated way because the natural fatigue had developed among the neo-literates towards the usage of primers. Therefore, a variety of activities were planned and organised for the people in different slums who, in fact, asked for them and also actively co-operated in the organisation of the activities. Despite a very strong level of ground work for CE. Programme, funds for the CE. Project was released by August, 2001 by Govt. of India through State Govt. As a result, the volunteers and senior activists of RSS were anxious for the implementation of CE programme. By this time, the funds for the CE. Project must have released, otherwise the RSS Chairman, Secretary and other senior members should do the needful for the future course of action.

Problem of accommodation has been a crucial one before the RSS organizers, volunteers and slum women from the beginning of the programme. It has already been highlighted in chapter 5 that due to lack of accommodation, more than 80 per cent literacy classes were conducted in the verandahs of the learners or in the living rooms of the local volunteers during TL/PL phase with much difficulties.

Therefore, a large number of respondents (see Table 7.2) have seriously felt the need of accommodation in the form of a room for the purpose of Chetana Kendra in each slum. Hence, they suggested for the same. So that teaching-learning and other developmental activities of RSS for the slum people specially the neo-literates came to be organized systematically in time. It is important to mention here that this problem of accommodation becomes acute during rainy season. It was also seen that the volunteers of certain slums used to teach their learners under the open sky during mid winter nights. Some of the volunteers had to teach their learners just near the pig-shed of the house owner. These were seen by the investigator during the different phases of her data collection. Since literacy activity of RSS is not a over night show, there are fair chances for the continuation of different programme like post literacy and continuing education etc. The organizers of RSS should consider the suggestion and think the matter seriously. The suggestions given by the slum women and volunteers regarding the construction of UBS Mahila Samiti in

TABLE 7.2
Accommodation for Chetana Kendra

Sl. No.	*Suggestions*	*Total No. of Slum Women 103*	*Total No. of Volunteers 23*	*Total No. of Senior Activists 16*	*Total No. of Other Type of People 31*
1.	Infrastructure support to be given to the slum people to construct Chetana Kendra by extedning people's co-operation from the slum.	79(76.70)	12(52.17)	16(100.00)	NA
2.	Construction of UBS mahila samiti room in each slum for the developmental and entertainment prog-ramme of slum women.	19(18.74)	4(17.39)	4(25.00)	NA
3.	Smaller bodies like word council be the unit for TL/PL activities center in urban areas like Rourkela.	NA	NA	3(18.75)	NA

Note : Figures within parentheses indicate percentages.

each slum for developmental activities may also be considered in this regard as a supplementary arrangement of accommodation for the same. Mention may be made here that the slum-dwellers, specially the neo-literates of Guidatoli and others, have constructed Chetana Kendras in their slums at their own effort by collecting some amount from each house of their areas. The same strategy can also be adopted by the people of other slums. Therefore, RSS organizers are suggested to provide accommodation facilities for Chetana Kendra or to provide infrastructure so that they can make it a base to construct the same with the help of community participation.

The table further reveals that some senior level activists have suggested for a smaller body like ward council as the unit of TL, PL and CE activities centres in each urban areas like Rourkela. Mention may be made here that the Rourkela Municipality had been associated with RSS from the very beginning. So it should not be an objection before the council in co-operating with RSS for the same. The suggestion is also sorting out the problem of accommodation for Chetana Kendra to a great extent. Therefore, the RSS Chairman should consider the suggestion and co-ordinate the work as an alternative arrangement of Chetana Kendra. So that people's participation in the programme will also be increased and the suggestions made by senior activists with regard to Chetana Kendra to be the community development centre of the slum (see the table) will be fulfilled.

It can be viewed from Table 7.3 that a very good percentage of respondents from different categories, as mentioned above have suggested for the frequent environment building activities of different types in the slum areas of Rourkela. Because "EB activities promotes willingness to act, to work and serve the literacy programme for realizing the objectives of TLC/PLC according to their own capacities, interest, station and office of the people" (Seetharamu, 1997). Further, they (respondents) have suggested a number of activities like special health camps and programme for women and adolescent girls (see the table). The senior activists and volunteers have realized

TABLE 7.3
Environment Building

Sl. No.	*Suggestions*	*Total No. of Slum Women 103*	*Total No. of Volunteers 23*	*Total No.of Senior Activists 16*	*Total No. of Other Type of People 31*
1.	Frequent environment building through various activities including cultural programmes like, street play, kala yatha etc.	56(54.36)	11(47.82)	9(56.25)	16(51.61)
2.	Special health camps and programmes for women and adolescent girls.	NA	NA	4(25.00)	11(35.48)

Note : Figures within parentheses indicate percentages.

interaction and monitoring work can be done in a better manner and they will be able to go for following activities. It is important to note here that after the performance of "Chetana-95" which was continued till 1997, no other cultural troops or "Kala Yatha" team have performed their cultural excellence in the slum areas of Rourkela. Since its one of the effective media for motivation and communication of the messages to the general man, it should be seriously taken care of. The cultural troops of RSS and other concerned organizations should also be revived, organized and further reactivated so that it could spread over the message of literacy, post-literacy and continuing education programme at different angles in each and every slum of Rourkela.

Tables 7.4 reveals that the majority of the respondents have suggested infrastructural support and provision of loan facilities to the slum women for their economic development. This has also

TABLE 7.4
Economic Development of Slum Women

Sr. No.	*Suggestions*	*Total no. of slum women 103*	*Total no. of volunteers 23*	*Total no.of senior activists 16*	*Total no. of other type of people 31*
1.	Financial and infrast-ructural support, loan and marketing facilities and opening of women's cooperative.	62(60.19)	14(60.86)	13(81.25)	22(70.97)
2.	Involvement of more number of NGO's voluntary organisa-tions and government deptts.	NA	5(21.74)	7(43.75)	16(51.61)
3.	Need based vocational skill development training and income generation activities in both center and Chetana Kendra level to the ne-oliterates slum women.	63(61.17)	15(65.22)	16(100.00)	16(51.61)

Note : Figures within parentheses indicate percentages.

the essence of environment building activities in each slum through cultural activities like street plays, women kala yatha, and folk dance and drama based on burning social issues. So that their been suggested by the senior activists, volunteers and the slum women themselves. It should be mentioned here that majority of the respondents have realized that although the slum women were found to have developed their literacy skills and level of awareness to a greater extent, they have not yet developed their own economic condition, which is highly necessary. Therefore, the respondents have suggested for the deep involvement of more number of NGOs, voluntary organizations, Government and non-government departments with RSS so as to extend their co-operation in developing the economic standard of the slum women. They have also suggested that RSS can initiate women's co-operative at the central level with the help of all types of members like activists, volunteers, neo-literates and members of Chetana Kendras etc. The co-operative can be developed through the savings group at slum level. This type of suggestion was made by the respondents on the basis of the experiences gathered from different women's saving group (financial) of Pump House Colony, Gangadhar Palli, Shantinagar and Narla Road etc. This suggestion should be considered as remedial measures of financial support to the slum women. A mention may be made here that problems with regard to different types of financial schemes and loan provisions etc. for slum women were also major constraints before RSS organizers during the literacy and post literacy phase of the programme.

Due to the lack of financial and infrastructural facilities and support, many of the neo-literate slum women have become demotivated and are loosing their zeal to work further. The vocational and income generation training provided by Shramik Vidyapith was quite satisfactory, but not sufficient. Further, their needs could not be fulfilled by Shramik Vidyapith, as it is not a funding agency to provide financial support to the slum women. They can provide only the training for the same. Therefore, RSS organisers should co-ordinate certain agencies or the Government and non-Government, organisation (those who work in this line) to provide such training, loan and infrastructural facilities to the disadvantaged slum women.

It can also be seen from the table that respondents of all the types have suggested to market the facilities of the materials produced by the slum women through RSS. Because, it has been experienced by the neo-literate slum women that in spite of their production of good quality items, they were unable to market properly due to financial crisis, lack of marketing experience and exposure and advertisement in the competition market like other organised professional groups (such as Gruhasti and Gruha Laxmi etc.) Therefore, they sell their items in the exhibitions or by door to door pushing. Hence, their cases (Marketing Problems) should be taken care of seriously by the Chairman of RSS, who is also the ADM of Rourkela, and deeply involved with "Sahayog" co-operative unit and the like. Once they would be introduced in the market through "Sahayog" and other organizations means they will get scope for their existence and gradually they will pick-up with their situation.

It can be deduced from Table 7.5 that both grass-root level volunteers and the senior level activists have felt the need of vocational and income generation training and loan facilities to the sincere unemployed volunteers of grass-root level for their sustainable development. A mention may be made here that a large number of youth joined the literacy programme at the beginning with some aspiration and expectation of getting materials and other support (mainly job). But when they didn't achieve the same, they left the campaign. Only the dedicated and sincere volunteers with social spirit were left in the campaign and serving there without material gain. Despite their family and socio-personal problems, they have been serving since last few years with missionary zeal. They have spent their entire youth for the literacy development of the disadvantaged people of the society. Instead of going for additional qualifications for their job

TABLE 7.5
Recognition and Infrastructural Support to the Volunteers and Encouragement for Middle Level Leadership and Training

Sr. No.	Suggestions	*Total no.of slum women 103*	*Total no. of volunteers 23*	*Total no. of senior activists 16*	*Total no. of other type of people 31*
1.	Vocational and income generation training facilities and loan facilities to the unemployed dedicated volunteers.	NA	4(17.39)	3(18.75)	NA
2.	Remuneration or hono-rarium to the unemployed sincere and selfless volunteer.	NA	NA	9(56.25)	15(48.39)
3.	Recognition and reward to the selfless senior activists and volunteers.	NA	12(52.17)	14(87.50)	16(51.61)
4.	Involvement of more number of activists and volunteers and their training.	NA	4(17.39)	8(50.00)	13(41.93)
5.	Encouragement for middle level leadership among women in a positive direction.	NA	NA	5(31.35)	10(32.26)

Note : Figure within Parentheses indicate Percentages.

opportunity, they contributed their best to the slum-dwellers. It is further noticeable that none of the grass-root level volunteers have suggested for their honorarium. They have only suggested for their vocational training and loan facilities. This idea about honorarium or financial support have been emerged and suggested by senior level activists which is quite genuine. Because the spirit of volunteership may not continue among the volunteers for another few years, if they will not be able to satisfy their basic requirements. A mention may be made here that a number of fifty four grass-root level volunteers of RSS did join its NFE Project as instructors and supervisors (fifty instructors and four supervisors) according to their educational qualification and field experience by getting Rs. 200 and Rs. 500 respectively as honorarium. Rest of the volunteers were serving in the field as literacy workers and assisting their instructor friends and supervisors of NFE centres in the field. But, they didn't get any, thing from the RSS. Since they have accepted the literacy work as social work, they remain silent. Therefore, their condition should be internalized and their voluntary spirit should be properly considered and respected by the RSS Chairman and Secretary. Further, some of the respondents have given their opinion that once the volunteers will get remuneration they will be lose their voluntary spirit and will become money minded. Their work will be mechanical. Therefore, they should be given priority in job opportunity, loan facilities and recognition and reward. However, they (volunteers) should not be the worst sufferers and their dedication should not go waste. Since their service is utmost required in future, they should be recharged and be motivated to work further, and their cases should be taken care of accordingly. The table further reveals that a large majority of respondents of all the types (except neo-literates) have felt the need of recognition, reward and moral support from the

RSS organisers and thus, suggested the same. It is genuine on their part to suggest. It is important to mention here that those who have joined the literacy programme of RSS as activists or volunteers from the beginning and sustained there till now have not taken any financial or material support from the samiti. Rather, they have contributed their best as volunteers, resource persons, writers, senior activists, programme organisers etc. So, those who were in jobs or engaged somewhere, have suggested for recognition and reward to the volunteers and activists. Others (more than half) have suggested for loan facilities or job opportunities. But in case of senior activists and organisers, almost all are employed and well settled. Many of them are holding high posts like principalship of higher secondary schools, lecturership in Government colleges, and are doctors, high school head masters, steel plant-executives and engineers etc. They have joined the programme from the very beginning and they have been contributing their best after their normal office duty hours without any vested interests. It is also important to mention here that many of the senior activists were the founder members of the literacy movement of Rourkela as well as Orissa. Their voluntary spirit to work for the development of the slum people should therefore be recognised by the Chairman, Secretary and other Senior Members of RSS, because, they need nothing but moral support and encouragement from the RSS. It will not be out of place to mention here that during in depth discussion with some of the dropout grass-root level volunteers and senior activists of RSS, it was reported by them to the investigator that they have left the RSS because of the negligible attitudes of some of the RSS organisers. Even, some of the sustained volunteers and activists have expressed their feelings in the same line. They have reported to the investigator that they feel neglected by some of the senior activists and organisers during decision-making process of RSS activities. If this tendency among the RSS organisers will continue, it will be very difficult on the part of the RSS to get dedicated volunteers in future. Therefore, their suggestions should be considered seriously and steps should be taken according by the RSS Chairman, Secretary and other senior organisers.

The table further reveals that a very good number of respondents (except slum women) have suggested that more number of volunteers should be involved in RSS, and they should be given adequate training from time to time in different aspects of literacy, post literacy and continuing education and other concerned aspects of the literacy programme.

It is also viewed from Table 7.5 that the senior level of activists and people from different sector of life have suggested that there should be encouragement for middle level of leadership among women in a right direction. It was seen that grass-root level leadership have already been highly emerged in the slums of Rourkela among the neo-literates and volunteers (women). But in middle level their numbers are relatively lower than the grass root level leaders. Since this middle level leaders or the activists are the real programme implementers, organisers and coordinators, their number should be increased accordingly. They should be encouraged to come forward to take leadership in a positive direction. RSS should take special care for it and involve more and more motivated volunteers and activists for the same and adequate leadership training facilities should be made for them. This has also been suggested by a good number of respondents (can be seen in the table).

It is evident from Table 7.6 that a major percentage of neo-literate slum women have suggested for the regularity of volunteers in the centres as well as suitable timing for their teaching. A mention may be made here that their numbers are very few. Regarding regularity of the volunteers, no grass-root volunteers or even the senior activists who used to be the members of monitoring team would have suggested for the same, if it would have been a major problem. However since

TABLE 7.6
Further Training and Campaign Visits of the Volunteers and Activists

Sl. No.	*Suggestions*	*Total No. of Slum Women 103*	*Total No. of Volunteers 23*	*Total No.of Senior Activists 16*	*Total No. of Other Type of People 31*
1.	Regularity of volunteers.	18(17.47)	NA	NA	NA
2.	Regular training to the grass-root level volunteers/activists and newly involved volunteers in different aspects of literacy, post literacy, continuing education and other concerned aspects.	NA	9(39.13)	8(50.00)	NA
3.	Scope be given to the volunteers and senior activists to visit different successful literacy campaign of the state as well as outside state to gain experience.	NA	4(17.39)	5(31.35)	NA
4.	Scope be given to the neo-literate slum women to visit successful literacy campaign for further motivation and encouragement.	12(11.65)	4(17.39)	4(25.00)	NA

Note : Figure within parentheses indicate percentages.

irregularity of volunteers are also found to some extent, it should also be taken care of. There should be a suitable timing for teaching neo-literates. Each and every adult learner should get the chance to learn according to her own timings. Since about one-fifth of the slum women have given the suggestion for the same means. It is not a small matter. Because more than half of the slum women struggle for livelihood and one-fifth sample respondents are from earning category so their cases should be considered accordingly and evening classes (as per their opinion) should be organized for them. Further, the activists of Chetana Kendra should be tagged accordingly so that they will get more scope to participate.

The table further reveals that both grass-root level volunteers and the senior activists have felt the need of various types of training in different aspects of literacy programme like literacy, post-literacy and continuing education, and on other concerning aspects frequently. It is important to mention here that a very good number of training programmes in different dimensions of literacy and its concerned aspects have been organised by RSS in different phases of the programme and most of the volunteers and senior activists have attended the training programme many a times. This has been presented with data in Chapter 5. Since learning is a continuous process from various situations and environment, the respondents want to develop their knowledge and experiences from various training workshops and situations. So that they can make their knowledge up to date and informative, thereby helpful to the campaign as well as the neo-literacy. Thus, various types of training programme should also be organised by RSS very frequently. Further, they should be given scope to go and participate in different types of training programme in this regard from different places. It will not only encourage them but also enlighten them with many more ideas of literacy and its development.

The table further reveals that both senior activists and the grass-root level volunteers were of the opinion that they should be given scope to visit different successful literacy campaigns of the state and out of the state to exchange their ideas, acquire practical knowledge and adopt different types of strategies for the RSS. The neo-literate slum women have also expressed their desire that they should also be given scope to visit different literacy campaign and rise with the neo-literate slum women to know their process of development level of leadership development etc. The grass-root level volunteers and senior activists have also given stress on their interests as suggest. Therefore, they have suggested for the same.

It was found that a group of volunteers and activists have already visited the literacy district of Birbhum, West Bengal in 1996. After coming back from the field visit, they tried to give more time and resource to the Samiti and by March, 2000 they were found active in the campaign. Further, it was observed in the field that they had been able to organize the programmes more systematically and confidently. Their field visit had helped them in developing their organisation capacity. This change among the volunteers activists should also be taken into the consideration as strategy development for the campaign. Further, it was also reported by the senior activists that many of them had visited various literacy districts of India at their own expenses to acquire knowledge and to internalize the field situations of other literacy campaigns. They have also been accompanied by the neo-literates to many places. Their field experiences, their expertise skills and resources had been utilised for RSS. So, these personal efforts of the activists should be given to the sincere volunteers, activists and the potential neo-literates for field visit to different literacy campaigns.

TABLE 7.7

Monitoring, Feedback Mechanism and Fresh Survey

Sl. No.	*Suggestions*	*Total No.of Slum Women 103*	*Total No. of Volunteers 23*	*Total No. of Senior Activists 16*	*Total No. of Other Type of People 31*
1.	Frequent monitoring of activities and interaction with the slum dwellers and proper feedback mechanism.	52(50.48)	9(39.13)	11(68.75)	15(48.38)
2.	Fresh survey of the neo-literates and identification of dropouts and illiterates and evaluation of the programme.	NA	NA	2(12.52)	5(16.13)
3.	Provision of more vehicles for monitoring and intervention.	NA	NA	11(68.75)	13(41.93)
4.	Involvement of experienced and educated people in monitoring team even the politicians.	NA	4(17.39)	8(50.00)	12(38.71)

Note : Figures within parentheses indicate percentages.

It can be viewed from Table 7.7 that a very good number of respondents of all the types have suggested for frequent monitoring of the activities and interaction with the people from all the areas. They have given stress on the improvement of the feedback mechanism under the organizational structure of PLC and CE. Because, a sound feedback mechanism is very much needed for making on objective assessment of the achievement and shortcomings of the programme (Behera, 1993). Further, few respondents of senior activists and resource persons have felt the essence of fresh survey of the status of neo-literates, illiterates, semi-literates, dropouts and the leftouts. So that, the mopping up operation can be carried out to bring the leftout and illiterate categories to the NLM level. The dropouts and other categories can be involved in the post literacy and continuing education programme. It was found from the table that the same respondents have also suggested for the internal evaluations of the activities of the programme from time to time. External evaluation of the programme is also essential for future course of action.

The table further reveals that the respondents of senior activists and other categories (resource persons, cultural artists, social workers etc.) have suggested for the arrangement of more vehicles for the purpose of monitoring by RSS organizers. Because, during the first phase of literacy programme monitoring and interaction programme of RSS were done very frequently by a very good number of senior activists in the team. This was possible because transportation facilities were available. However, this facility was neglected during post literacy phase due to shortage of vehicles and man power. Since monitoring of the activities and interaction with the slum-dwellers (specially with the neo-literates) are at the most, requirement for feedback mechanism, data collection about the progress of the programme as well as development of the slum women, should be properly taken care of.

It is true that monitoring and interaction were inspiring to more than half of the slum women. It might be an unnecessary interference to the activities of many of the volunteers, as one-third of them have suggested for the same. However, after observing the field situation and the needs of the slum women, suggestions can be made for the frequent monitoring and interaction in the field. Provision for more vehicles should be made for this purpose by the Chairman of RSS and its Secretary. To sort-out the problem of man power the volunteers, senior activists and other categories of people involved with the activities of RSS have suggested the involvement of different types of experienced people.

It was a general observation of the investigator during her data collection that a limited number of women have been associated in the decision-making process of RSS at higher level. The same feeling was expressed by many of the senior activists of RSS during their interview for data collection and they have also mentioned it as a suggestion (it can be seen from Table 7.7). This type of feeling was not found among the grass root level volunteers or the neo-literate slum women. Because in the slum, grass-root level leadership among the slum women in very good number have already been developed through Chetana Kendras. Slum women and volunteers both take active participation in decision-making process of Chetana Kendras. Hence, they don't feel for the same.

Further the table reveals that respondents of all the categories (except the resource persons etc.) have suggested the involvement of the members of Chetana Kendras in the decision making process of RSS. They also suggested for the active involvement of RSS with the activities of Chetana Kendras as well as the slums. It have been reported by the respondents that many a times the exact problems of the Chetana Kendras as well as the slums are not properly exposed before RSS by the representative volunteers of concerned areas. Since the problems are not the personal problems of the volunteers, they don't give much importance to them. Only they are put before the RSS as a formality.

TABLE 7.8
Decision-making Process

Sl. No.	Suggestions	Total No. of Slum Women 103	Total No. of Volunteers 23	Total no. of Senior Activists 16	Total No. of Other Type of people 31
1.	Involvement of more number of women in decision-making process of RSS in central level.	NA	NA	6(37.5)	NA
2.	Involvement of the member of Chetana Kendra in decision-making process of RSS and more involvement of RSS with the activities of Chetana Kendra.	32(31.07)	5(21.73)	5(31.35)	NA

Note : Figures within parentheses indicate percentages.

Therefore, the members of Chetana Samities along with their volunteers should represent in decision-making process of RSS, so that the RSS organizers will get the exact picture of the problems as well as their needs and any matter of the concerned areas.

TABLE 7.9
Fulfilment of Basic Amenities

Sl. No.	Suggestions	Total No. of Slum Women 103	Total No. of Volunteers 23	Total No. of Senior Activists 16	Total No. of Other Type of People 31
1.	Fulfillment of the basic requirement of the slum women like, water, electricity, ration card, BPL card, widow pension etc.	67(65.05)	11(47.82)	10(62.5)	NA
2.	Opining of primary schools in the slum areas and increase of NFE centers and supply of play materials to the NFE centers.	54(52.43)	5(21.74)	NA	14(45.16)
3.	Special provision for the enrolment of the children of the neo-literates slum women in formal schools.	48(46.60)	9(39.13)	5(31.35)	NA
4.	Medical facilities (health care) in each slum and provision of free medicine for slum women and their children.	40(38.83)	4(17.39)	3(18.75)	7(22.58)

Note : Figures within parentheses indicate percentages.

It can be deduced from Table 7.9 that majority of the slum women and senior activists and about half of the volunteers have suggested for the fulfilment of the basic needs of the neo-literate slum women like water, electricity, education of their children, medical facilities, BPL card , widow pension etc. It was observed that problems of the fulfilment of basic amenities for the slum-dwellers were found to be the most important constraints before the RSS organizers. This problem has already been stated in Chapter 5. Based on these problems, it can be suggested that since the Chairman of RSS is also the ADM of Rourkela, he should co-ordinate with government and concerned departments to fulfill the minimum requirements like drinking water facilities, ration card, BPL card etc. If sincere and daring steps would be taken, some of their basic needs could be fulfilled. Regarding the fulfillment of basic need like education of the children in formal schools, it can be seen from the table that a good number of respondents from each category (as mentioned above) have felt the essence of primary schools in each slum areas of Rourkela. Therefore, they have suggested for the same. Further, it can be viewed from the table that slum women, volunteers and the senior activists have suggested for the special provision of admission for the children of neo-literate slum women in formal schools. Because of lack of provision in RSP schools for non-RSP children and less seats and over-enrolment problem of municipal schools, a very good number of slum children do not get scope for formal schooling. Further, due to the sanction problem of NFE centres, only 50 centres have been opened by RSS in various slums. Many a times, children those who don't get admission in formal schools, don't get enrolled in NFE centres due to its limited seats and sanctions. As a result, the neo-literate slum women become demotivated. Therefore, some quotas or provisions should be made for the same, so that a good percent of future illiterates would be arrested.

Realizing the importance of primary schools in the slum areas, RSS has been trying its level best in opening few (at least five) primary schools since 1992-93. But due to lack of political will and co-operation from so-called highly educated society, the government is also not able to take it seriously. It should be a public demand. It is not the responsibility of only RSS. When RSS didn't get success in opening schools, it started functioning its NFE centers as an alternative for the poor slum children. Further, the respondents who have suggested for the opening of primary schools have also suggested to increase the number of NFE centres of RSS in different Chetana Kendras. Hence, the children of the slum areas, specially the children of neo-literates will get scope for education. This has also been suggested by the volunteers and slum women. The table further reveals that a few volunteers and NFE instructors have realized the need of play materials for the children of NFE centers of RSS. So that they will be interested to remain in the center and concentrate on reading. Further, other dropouts and leftout children will also be interested to join center for education. Therefore, they have (volunteers) suggested for the same. Hence, the RS organizers should consider this suggestion as important.

It can also be seen from Table 7.9 that respondents of various types like slum women, volunteers and senior activists have suggested for the availability of medical facilities to the slum women to their own slum. It is important to mention here that these suggestions have been made for the people of the slum areas of Rourkela which are more than ten kilometers away from the Government Hospital. The mobile health service of "Sevasadan" also does not function in those areas. Further, they don't have the users' medical card of IGH (Ispat General Hospital) or any health centre of RSP as they are not the RSP employee. If at all they will be going there (health center or IGH), they will have to pay the consultancy fee etc. Therefore, the respondents have sincerely suggested for the health centers in remote slums and free medicine facilities. Co-ordination between RSS and the health centers RSP should also be made, and they should be requested to extend their services to the neo-literate women and their children. The organizer of Mobile Health Service of "Sevasadan" should also be coordinated by RSS in this regard to extent their services. Further, RSS should try to generate political will and create interest among the highly educated people through its net-working. Hence, public demand for school, medical facilities and fulfilment of other basic needs of the urban poor can be fulfilled.

TABLE 7.10
Media Services and Proper Maintenance of RSS Record

Sl. No.	*Suggestions*	*Total No. of Slum Women 103*	*Total No. of Volunteers 23*	*Total No. of Senior Activists 16*	*Total No. of Other Type of People 31*
1.	Media services be properly done by broadcasting telecasting the activities of RSS.	NA	11(47.82)	9(56.25)	NA
2.	Proper maintenance of record on each and every activity of RSS and Chetana Kendras.	NA	2(8.76)	5(12.5)	NA

Note : Figures within parentheses indicate percentages.

It was a feeling of both grass-root volunteers and senior activists that the message of the activities of RSS has not been properly communicated before the different sectors of people of outside Rourkela through different media. Being the first literacy campaign of Orissa and that to the first separate urban project, it should have been acted by Radio, TV etc. properly. It is true that at a point of time the activities of RSS were telecasted and flashed in the newspapers quite regularly. But now when the actual result of the programme has come out as impact in a developmental form of the down-trodden people specially the women, medical services have remained silent. The slum dwellers, who have come out from their "Handia Dubni" (pot of alcohol) (gave up alcohol) have not been highlighted. This change among the people, neo-literates, should be highlighted by media services through T.V., Radio and printed in materials. So that not only the slum women, volunteers and activists of RSS but also the participants of other literacy campaign would be encouraged and inspired to work further. Their exposure to medias are highly required. Therefore, the senior activist and volunteers have suggested for the same. RSS Chairman and other organizers should take care of it properly. Being the 1st citizen of the city and representative of the government in Rourkela, the ADM can initiate the process time and again for the sustained growth and development of RSS.

Further the table reveals that, meagre percentage of volunteers as well as senior activists have felt that each and every activity of RSS and the Chetana Kendras should be recorded and stored properly. It is true that RSS office has been maintaining the detail list of activities with special care. But since it has long been started (more than one decade), it will not be possible to record the every movement in detail. Rather, it can be recorded in the CDs in the control room of RSS. Further, the activities in various occasions, which have already been recorded in audio and video cassette, should be properly maintained and utilised in time for re-motivation of people during C.E. programming. However suggestions for recording of the important events of RSS and Chetana Kendras should be given importance by the organisers.

It is seen from Table 7.11 that the slum women and grass root level volunteers have suggested for the legal support (administrative and police) during their activities against any forms of socio-criminal problems of the slums. Further, they have suggested to take steps against the practice of unnecessary interference of corrupt police officers. It can be mentioned here that some police officers were habituated to take their monthly/weekly quota from the owner of country liquor

TABLE 7.11
Legal Support

Sl. No.	*Suggestions*	*Total No. of Slum Women 103*	*Total No. of Volunteers 23*	*Total No. of Senior Activists 16*	*Total No. of Other Type of People 31*
1.	Administrative and police support to the women while doing protest agaisnt any criminal and unsocial activities in the slum.	24(23.30)	2(8.76)	NA	NA
2.	Disciplinary action against corrupt and harassing police officers.	8(7.77)	2(8.79)	NA	NA

Note : Figures within parentheses indicate percentages.

shop or liquor distillery in certain slums. When the members of Chetana Kendra, especially the neo-literate women, go to the shop of distillery to request the owner to close down the distillery, these police men come in their ways and interfere unnecessarily. As a result instead of closing down the liquor shop and distillery in the slum, liquor is openly sold. It is true that the women groups do not remain silent, they go to the police superintendent and even to the excise superintendent and report against them. What these women want is that they should be supported legally by the administration or police department. Hence as their cases and suggestions are very sensitive, they should be given protection for the disciplinary growth of the society.

Further, the table reveals that some of the senior level activists have suggested for legal settlement on women exploitation through RSS. A mention may be made here that Chetana Kendra, being the centre of activities at the slum level also, works like a settlement camp of legal matters of the slum. All sorts of exploitation (mainly the women) at slum level are being settled with the help of senior activists of RSS. In the worst cases, the Chairman of RSS also interferes in these matters. It was also seen that some of the senior level activists have already started family counselling as a part of the developmental activities of PL and CE. Programme at their own group level with the moral support of the senior organisers of RSS. It needs to be the legal settlement of the government on women exploitation either by RSS or by any other concerned organisations. The investigator also feels that legal settlement activities on women exploitation should be done by RSS with the dynamic leadership of the local administration. Therefore, the RSS organisers and others should consider the above suggestions for their future course of action.

It can be seen from Table 7.12 that respondents of all categories have felt the need of family and legal counselling slum women in the form of group discussion in Chetana Kendra very frequently. It was the feeling of some of the respondents that due to lack of skills of communication among the slum women they are not been able to make their family members convinced about many of their problems, rights and even freedom. They should be therefore, given counselling with regard to their family problems and the legal matters related to property rights, marriage act, divorce act, consumer's act etc. in practical setting through group discussions and demonstrations (through direct exchange of experiences). They should also be given scope to visit the family court and other concerned places. During hearing RSS organisers should take the responsibility through the senior women activists and the others. Further, they have suggested that parents should be made aware in giving freedom to their daughters for the choice of their

TABLE 7.12
Family and Legal Counselling

Sl. No.	Suggestions	Total No. of Slum Women 103	Total No. of Volunteers 23	Total No. of Senior Activists 16	Total No. of Other Type of People 31
1.	Family and legal counselling to slum women : freedom of choice for marriage of the girls and decision making right with regard to the number of children in the family.	18(17.47)	4(17.39)	5(31.35)	6(19.35)
2.	Counselling for the adopting of family planning operation by male members (Vasectomy)	NA	NA	NA	4(12.90)

Note : Figures within parentheses indicate percentages.

own life partner. A mention may be made here that except tribal women/girls, there is less freedom among the girls of other categories to select their life partners. Many a time, they have to marry against their own will. Further, the respondents have suggested that the women should get scope in taking decisions regarding the number of children in their family. All there things should be discussed in the Chetana Kendra in family and legal counseling camps. Therefore, RSS should organise the family counseling properly and the counselling camps should function in those directions.

It is interesting to mention here that four male respondents (see Table 7.12) out of 31(12.90%) have suggested that RSS should encourage the family planning operation of the male members (Vasectomy) through its family counselling and other net-working. A mention may be made here that this concept has already been developed by the RSS organisers since long back while developing the PL Primer "Naba Tarang" where one topic is totally devoted to this concept. It has also been reported by the volunteers of grass root level that hardly few people have gone for vasectomy despite much discussion and propagation of the concept. Still, this is one of the genuine suggestions made by the respondents. Hence, more and more advertisement, family counselling camps and discussion in this regard need to be done by RSS.

Some of the respondents (senior activists and govt. and non-government officials) have felt that the neo-literate slum women have become over ambitious after being literate. They have become more demanding and non-compromising. This has become a problem for RSS organisers, which has been mentioned in Chapter 5. Many a times they don't understand the reality and go for demonstration, because there are many things which cannot be done through the local administration or by RSS, or cannot be done over night, like opening of schools (primary), implementation of Government loans etc. It was also reported by one of the Directors of Urban Co-operative Bank that a group of slum women went to the Bank Manager for sanction of loan. The Manager denied to do so as they were the residents on encroacher's land. When they came to know the fact, they started quarrelling and complained against the Manager before the Chairman and Board of Directors and also to the local administrator.

Thus, during the interaction programme, group discussions in the meetings of the slum the limitation of RSS should be very clearly discussed before the slum-dwellers and the neo-literates.

TABLE 7.13
Limitations of RSS

Sl. No.	*Suggestions*	*Total No. of Slum Women 103*	*Total No. of Volunteers 23*	*Total No.of Senior Activists 16*	*Total No. of Other Type of People 31*
1.	Making aware to the slum women about the limitations of RSS in fulfilling their demands.	NA	NA	2(12.50)	5(16.13)

Note : Figures within parentheses indicate percentages.

So that they will not be demotivated at the end. However, they should not also be demoralized from the beginning. Other wise, it would be difficult to include them in future course of action.

CONCLUSION

Based on the suggestions made by different types of people, senior level literacy activists, grass root level volunteers, slum women and the experiences of the investigator herself during her data collection, the following suggestions can be derived :

1. To retain the literacy skills of the neo-literate slum women, they are to be recharged through various activities of Chetana Kendra according to their suitable timings.
2. Provision of accommodation for Chetana Kendra is to be made by RSS with the community support, UBS Mahila Samiti, or Ward Council may be utilised for the same.
3. Chetana Kendra is to be functioned like community centre of the slum with a varieties of facilities and activities like library, entertainment, etc. for the slum women.
4. Regular environment building activities are to be made and continued like follow up discussions, mass meetings, health camps, celebration of festive occasions and above all the cultural programmes like women Kala Yatha, Street Plays and Folk Dance and Drama bearing the message of social problems.
5. Provisions for need based income generation training facilities and financial and infrastructural facilities in the form of loan etc. are to be provided to the slum women. Marketing facilities for their production material are to be made by RSS.
6. Active involvement of different NGOs, Voluntary Organizations, Government Departments, Different Women's Group and RSP with RSS are to extent their support for the slum women.
7. Implementation of Women's Co-operative by RSS in each slum in the form of "Savings group".
8. Encouragement, recognition and reward to the dedicated volunteers and senior level activists in different occasions for their selfless contribution to the RSS.
9. Financial support in the form of honorarium, loan facilities or vocational training to the selfless and sincere unemployed volunteers.
10. Priority of employment to the neo-literates and sincere volunteers according to their qualification and nature of employment.
11. Regular monitoring and interaction with the activities of Chetana Kendra and neo-literate slum women and slum-dwellers.

12. Fresh survey of neo-literates, illiterates, dropouts and left-outs are to be included for further activities of the programme and steps be taken for the evaluation of NFE, PL and other activities of RSS time to time.
13. Creation of interest among the highly educated people for literacy work and involvement experienced people in monitoring team of RSS.
14. Fulfilment of the basic amenities like water, electricity, medical facilities, education, BPL card, ration card etc. of the slum women through the co-ordination of RSS with other concerned departments.
15. Generation of political will for the fulfilment of the basic needs of the disadvantaged slum people.
16. Steps to be taken for the opening of more Primary Schools and NFE Centres in the slum areas public demand be made for this purpose.
17. Implementation of Continuing Education Programme as a follow up programme of TL and PL activities.
18. Involvement of more number of middle level volunteers and adequate leadership training to them.
19. Encouragement for both high and middle level of women leadership as well as their direct involvement in decision-making process.
20. Media services to be effective and implementive in communicating the activities of RSS.
21. Family and legal counselling are to be organised regularly for slum women and their family members with those activities for bringing rapport and girls should be given freedom of choice for their life partner.
22. Male members of the slum women are to be encouraged through family counselling and other networking of RSS to go for vasectomy.
23. Legal support is to be given the women and grass root volunteers while taking any steps against illegal, unsocial or criminal activities of anybody in the slums.
24. Pilot experiments on new ideas with regard to literacy and other development of slum women and downtrodden are to be made in different slum areas.
25. Development of sufficient reading materials in different aspects of literacy and life of the people are to be made in regional language and reflection of the local tribal culture, traditions, language and unique feature of the society be presented there.
26. Success stories of women from different parts of the country from the grass-root level to higher level are to be developed and be given to the slum women for reading. Follow up discussion are to be made accordingly on the topic after completion of the materials in the focused group.
27. Training to the volunteers, activists and other members of RSS with regard to teaching primers, monitoring, evaluation etc. are to be given from time to time.
28. Arrangement of field visit of volunteers/activist and slum women to different successful literacy campaigns of the state or out side for encouragement and further learning.
29. The neo-literate slum women be made aware about the limitation of RSS in fulfilling their demands.

8

FINDINGS AND IMPLICATIONS OF THE STUDY

INTRODUCTION

In this chapter the findings of the study have been embodied along with their educational implications for proper planning and co-ordination, modification and necessary actions in different literacy programmes of the state as well as the country. This chapter also deals with further research required in various aspects of adult education and literacy programmes.

FINDINGS OF THE STUDY

The findings of the study presented as per objectives are as follows :

Efforts and Activities of RSS

1. **It was found that RSS had undertaken extensive and effective activities viz., environment building and motivational, survey and resurvey of the illiterate and neo-literates, preparation of reading materials, distribution teaching-learning materials, training of the volunteers and others, teaching-learning and other developmental activities, monitoring interaction and evaluation income generation and skill development trainings, opening of NFE centres for the children of slum-dwellers etc. during literacy and post literacy phase of the literacy programme for the educational development of the learners, especially the slum women.**
2. **All those activities and efforts of RSS were made with the help of group of dedicated grass-root level volunteers and activists, and organizations like Shramik Vidyapeeth, Bethel Charitable Trust, "Sevasadan" of Community Welfare Centre, Spandan, and lot many government and non-government organisations. But the contribution of Shramik Vidyapeeth was found to be highly appreciable for literacy achievement, awareness generation, material preparation (publications of Saksharata Samachar) and other development of the neo-literate slum women as well as the organisational structure of RSS.**
3. **The neo-literate slum women, slum-dwellers, grass-root level volunteers, senior activists, resource persons and different types of people have reported their awareness and active participation in those environment building and other literacy activities of RSS.**
4. **Environment building activities like cultural programmes, workshops and meetings, celebration of different important days, organising different competitions among learners, literacy melas, conventions, video shows, marathons, sports, padayatras (procession on foot), human chain, plantation programme, safai karyakram, health camps, mahila jagruti**

Talim, bus rally, cycle rally, paralegal training camps, focused group discussions etc. were organised by RSS from time to time. Literacy tele-films were also made and telecast through steel TV of Rourkela.

5. Special cultural programme for slum women like street plays composed on women's problem and their solution were organised frequently. Special women Kala Yatha "Sukannya" was completely organised and performed by women artists and volunteers of RSS. Women Kala Yatha "Banita" from Kerala was invited and their performance had been utilised to motivate and build-up the self-image of slum women.
6. A very good number of discussion forums on women issues related to evils of illiteracy, health camps on child and maternity care, advantages of breast-feeding were organised in both slum and central level. Special Mahila Pada Yatra, Mahila Rallies, Mahila sports and various intra slum competitions were organised. A Literacy Mela was completely organised by Muslim, slum women and literacy volunteers of Narla Road slum through "Saheli" Mahila Samiti which resulted in to a greater intra-slum movement and cultural assimilation with environment building.
7. It was found that conduct of survey work for the identification of illiterates, mass mobilisation of people and functionaries from different sectors of life and organisation were also made simultaneously for their active participation in the programme. Further, after completion of first phase of literacy programme the resurvey work was conducted to know about the status of neo-literates for their further enrolment in PL phase of the programme.
8. The training of the grass-root level volunteers, master trainers, key-resource persons and activists during TL and PL programmes was found to have been imparted by RSS for a period of three days separately. Special instructions and guidelines were given to the volunteers to make it convenient for slum women to learn. Further, they were given orientation on PL and NFE activities and other aspects of literacy from time to time. It was also found that majority of the trainees were satisfied on the training programmes of RSS.
9. Keeping in view the culture and language spoken in the city, primers in two languages, *i.e.* Oriya and Hindi were provided to the learners during TL Phase. It was that the learners preferred to have gone through Oriya Primer than the one in Hindi. During PL phone RSS developed and provided its own primer "Naba Taranga" in Oriya language along with other supplementary literature. "Saksharata Samachar" was also specially published by RSS (after launching of literacy programme) for learners, volunteers and others. But after launching of PL phase, the Saksharata Samachar was especially meant for the neo-literates carrying the message of various social issues and their solution, different developmental schemes, information etc.
10. The teaching learning material supplied to the centres was found to be adequate, systematic and in time. Majority of the slum women have reported their satisfaction on learning material. They have also reported their high level of satisfaction on the reading material like the PL Primer 'Naba Tarang', Saksharata Samachar and other supplementary literature for their relevant content, style of presentation and lucidity.
11. It was found that sincere and concerted efforts were made by RSS to teach the slum women according to their own time during the afternoons, evenings and even during the

nights (for the daily labourers) by different types of volunteers. About 13,000 high school students and youth were deployed for teaching, learning and other activities. Majority of the slum women were found to be satisfied with the teaching of the RSS volunteers. Further, it was found that the school volunteers were dropped after their examination and launching of PL phase was difficult.

12. Sincere and concerted efforts were made for the systematic and proper monitoring, interaction and feed-back mechanism of RSS activities in different slums during TL phase. Sufficient vehicles and a large number of volunteers, activists and organisers were engaged for the same. But during PL phase, only limited Chetana Kendras and slum areas were monitored systematically with the special attention of some of the local volunteers of the respective slums. Only one vehicle and a limited number of senior activists were engaged for the same.
13. Efforts were also made by RSS to conduct mid-term evaluation of the learning achievement of the learners during TL phase with the help of large number volunteers, activists, coordinators and organisers in each and every centre sincerely.
14. As a preventive measure of becoming adult illiterates, on the demand of the neo-literate slum-dwellers, RSS made efforts in opening 50 NFE centres through its Chetana Kendras as a part of post-literacy programme in different slums. The slum-dwellers were found to be satisfied with the efforts of RSS. It was also found that the teaching-learning and other activities of NFE centres were satisfactory.
15. It was found that a very good number of training on skill development and income generation has been undertaken by RSS with the help of Shramik Vidyapeeth during PL phase to train the slum women to develop their financial status. Several organised group activities by neo-literate slum women were found to have come up for income generation.

Problems and Constraints Faced by RSS

Despite adequate and regular efforts and activities made by RSS, the activists and organisers of RSS while organising different activities have faced a number of problems and constraints. The constraints as reported by the grass-root level volunteers, organisers and the activists and even the neo-literate slum women are presented below :

1. It was found that most of the slums have come up on the unauthorised land occupied illegally by the slum-dwellers. They had their non-permanent accommodations. Hence, most of the literacy classes for women and the Chetana Kendras were run in the Verandas and living-rooms of the learners or local volunteers. Lack of accommodation for Chetana Kendra was a serious problem to the RSS volunteers for interacting with women of the slum during TL and PL phase.
2. It was found that the timings of the literacy centre for women were mostly in the afternoon as the volunteers were girls of different high schools and women's college. This timing of learning was not suitable mainly for the contract and daily-wage labourers. Even this timing was not suitable for many housewives and maid-servants, as it was time for collecting drinking water from the distant water connection. In the evening girls were not allowed by their family members to the slums, and women learners were normally not ready to learn with male volunteers.
3. A large number of female volunteers who were from schools and colleges dropped-out from the programme after their course work (SUPW and NSS). These volunteers were

not having a missionary zeal and therefore the RSS programme was affected badly as it demotivated women learners of the concerned centres.

4. Despite the sincere trial of RSS to increase intra slum interaction, it was observed that the limitation persisted as tribal, non-tribal, and Muslim were hesitant in mixing with each other during the pre-stage of the literacy programme. But these feelings were found to be substantially lowered down at the post-literacy phase.
5. The floating population of Rourkela city is estimated 20% which was found to have the tendency of elapsing into illiteracy because of frequent migration of the slum-dwellers from the city to another city/town for better earning. Therefore, a good number of slum women had to quit their learning in between.
6. A good number of volunteers and activists were under the impression that their involvement in the process might bring some benefit in future. Since literacy work is a purely voluntary service, the volunteers did not find it alluring for future prospects. Their temptations and expectations did not materialise. Thereby, the deprived volunteers showed dissatisfaction and discouraged others, which had a very bad effect on the mobilization of people.
7. It was found that due to availability of sufficient vehicle, the first phase of literacy programme could be monitored properly. But during PL phase RSS could hire only one vehicle. Therefore, the RSS volunteers and activists could not monitor the activities of each slum frequently. This drastically curtails the feedback mechanism by way of MIS.
8. It was found that the volunteers associated with RSS were inadequate in number to monitor the PL activities. It resulted in a serious problem and frequent monitoring could not be done with limited volunteers and only one vehicle, RSS could monitor each Chetana Kendra after a gap of one or one and half month only.
9. Most of the neo-literates were under the impression that they will be able to avail of their civic rights after being literate. Therefore, they joined the programme. After becoming neo-literate, they started demanding civic facilities like ration card, drinking water, BPL card, medical facilities and education, etc., which was beyond the reach of RSS to fulfill. Hence, they (slum women) started reaching the concerned government offices to demand civic facilities, which caused serious problem.
10. It was found that the RSS organisers faced critical problems when neo-literate parents specially the women were demanding and demonstrating for education of their children. Some of their children enrolled in NFE centres of RSS while soon others in formal schools. Despite vacancies in schools, RSP did not enroll non-RSP students. Since the municipality schools have limited seats, it was again a problem for their enrolment. The RSS tried to cope with the problem by requesting the state government to start some more schools, but could not succeed.
11. It was found that the income generation and skill development programme organised by RSS raised hope to get infrastructural support like, loan, seed money, etc., for their improvement of their financial condition this sense of expectation from RSS or govt. could not be met. Hence a sense of demotivation and depression prevailed among the slum women.
12. The role of NGOs is normally to provide supportive services to literacy projects, which was unfortunately found to be lacking in Rourkela city due to their limited numbers.

Hence RSS could not involve the NGOs in the programme and managed it largely by itself.

IMPACT OF LITERACY PROGRAMME

Level of Literacy

1. **The overall performance of the neo-literate slum women irrespective of their age, caste/ community and earning status with regard to reading, writing and numeracy was found to be quite satisfactory as 90.29% have achieved the NLM proficiency in reading, 80.50% in writing and 91.26% in numeracy.**
2. **Despite high level of achievement (overall) it was also found that they have achieved better in numeracy and reading as compared to writing.**
3. **There was satisfactory level of literacy achievement among the respondents of all the age groups. The respondents of younger age group did better in reading and writing and the respondents of older age group did outstanding in numeracy. The respondents of middle age group shown satisfactory level of achievement in all the aspects of literacy skills.**
4. **In spite of high level of literacy achievement among the respondents of all the caste/ community background, the slum women of Muslim community have shown relatively better performance in numeracy by achieving cent per cent result.**
5. **Despite highly satisfactory performance among the respondents of earning and non-earning categories, the earning slum women have shown relatively better result in all the three aspects of literacy than that of the non-earning category.**

Level of Awareness and Changes of Attitudes

1. **It was found that most of the neo-literate slum women (more than 90%) irrespective of their age, caste/community and earning status have shown their high level of awareness towards evils of population explosion, environmental protection and small family norms. It was also found that the slum women have become conscious about environmental protection by doing hues plantation in various slums from time to time. To cut the population growth they have adopted family planning methods. Even the Muslim women have also gone for operation after two children.**
2. **It was found that a large majority (about 90%) of respondents of all the background were highly aware about the different aspects of child and maternity care and personal health and hygiene. Therefore, they are very particular about the immunisation of their children as well as the pregnant women of the slums. As a result, the IMR of the city (in slum area) has come down from 98 in the year 1991 to 56 in the year 1999 (per 1000). It was also found that they maintaining cleanliness in their houses as well as their locality, using mosquito net, drinking tube well water, using soap for cleanliness and checked their practice of keeping pig in their houses.**
3. **A great majority of respondents (about 90%) were found to have changed their attitude towards evils of alcohol, superstition, child marriage and dowry. They have become highly aware on these aspects in their day-to-day life. They have strongly opposed to child marriage and dowry and suggested for delayed marriage. They perceived dowry (both giving and taking) as crime. Further, their magico-religious beliefs have been controlled to a greater extent. Regarding evils of alcohol, they have very strongly opposed to drinking alcohol.**

They have also taken steps to control alcohol drinking and its business from their slums. As a result it has been checked in various slums.

4. It was found that a large majority of the respondents (more than 80%) from all backgrounds have developed a favourable attitude towards girls' education and the decision-making rights of the women in the family. They have shown a keen interest for the higher education of girls than the boys.
5. It was noticed that majority of them have become very much self-confident and were able to lead the women's group in different occasions. Grass-root level leadership among the slum women (including Muslim) have been tremendously developed in various slums.
6. Most of them (more than 80%) have developed positive attitudes towards the political participation of women. Many of then have joined different political groups and have been taking active part in decision-making process. It has become evident when a neo-literate slum women from Rourkela, contested for councilorship at last election and get elected by the people.
7. It was found that a majority (more than 80%) of the slum women from all the background have shown highly positive attitude towards raising voice against exploitation. It was also noticed that they have become assertive in their family, work field and even in the society whenever they get exploited or tortured.
8. It was found that more than half of the respondents (less than 60%) irrespective of their age, caste/community and earning status were found to have developed positive attitudes towards the helping of husbands in their household chores, property rights of women, different developmental schemes and some social functionaries. About half of the slum women have not yet developed favourable attitudes for the same.
9. It was found that almost all the slum women have developed a keen interest to become economically self-sufficient. Therefore, a great majority of them have undergone a variety of in generation and skill development training by RSS through Shramik Vidyapeeth.
10. It was found that a majority (more than 85%) respondents irrespective of their age, caste/ community and earning status have shown highly favourable attitudes towards communal harmony. They have shown their keen interest to take active part in social activities. It was found that they have played (a large group of neo-literate) a remarkable role as agents of socio-cultural integration during the communal flare-up during 1992-93 at Muslim dominated areas of Rourkela. Further, their contribution in the form of cash, kind and even personal service to the victims of Latur Earthquake (1993), Super Cyclone of Orissa (1999) and Kutch Earthquake (2001) were note-worthy.
11. It was noticed that almost all the neo-literate slum women from all the backgrounds were found to be aware about the education of their children. They were also highly aware about the school-going age of their children, their own responsibility to send their children to the school in time and about the NFE centres as alternative arrangement for poor children and child labourers of the slum.
12. Age, Caste/Community background didn't play any significant role in developing their level of awareness or attitudinal changes. There was some influence of occupational background of the respondents in developing very high level of awareness or attitudinal changes among the respondents.

13. It was found that the respondents of middle age group have shown relatively a better level of awareness and attitudinal changes than the younger and the older, and the ST, SC and Muslim have shown relatively better than the GC and OBC respondents in many aspects of life and concerning issues, and the earning respondents have shown relatively better than the non-earning category.

Causes for the Unsuccessfulness the Slum Women Who are not Successful

It was found from the case studies of the unsuccessful slum women that constant illness, over-protection of the illiterate and superstitious parents and lack of self-motivation and interest were the main causes for unsuccessfulness of case no.1. It was further found that irregularities of the immature school volunteers in the literacy centres have also de-motivated of the illing respondent. Therefore, the respondent who was of sixteen years old had not shown interest for learning and neglected her study. As a result she achieved neither the NLM expected proficiency level in learning skill, nor even developed desired level of awareness through the literacy programme.

For case no. 2, it was found that acute poverty, alcoholic parents and husband, tensed family environment, day long hard labour, non-co-operation from the family and unsuitable timing of learning were the main causes for the negligence of attending literacy classes and her unsuccessfulness. Therefore, she did not achieve the NLM expected proficiency level in literacy skills. She was not even able to develop the desired level of awareness.

Factors Responsible for the Outstanding Performance and Active Participation of the Slum Women

It was found that sincere and selfless efforts of the grass-root volunteers as well as RSS organisers, self-motivation and strong of the respondent, involvement and co-operation of the community people through Chetana Kendra were the responsible factors for the success of case no. 1. Therefore, despite her acute socio-economic and physical problems, she had shown highly satisfactory performance in literacy skill and level of awareness as well as unique success in life.

For case no. 2, immense will-power, inner-potential and self- interest, moral support and encouragement of her husband, internalising the acute problems of her slums and above all the efforts, scope, co-operation and various support extended by the RSS organisers in every step were the responsible factors for her literacy achievement and success as a neo-literate social worker.

Suggestions for Further Improvement of Literacy Programme of RSS

Suggestions derived from the study on the basis of the needs felt and problems overcome in the field by different types of literacy worker, functionaries slum women, and the experiences of the investigator herself are presented below for further development of slum women and future course of action of the RSS :

1. To retain the literacy skills of neo-literate slum women they should be kept motivated by RSS organisers and participate in the literacy and other activities of Chetana Kendra regularly. Continuity of programme through post-literacy and continuing education programme should, therefore, be given priority by RSS. Timings of the programme should also be fixed according to the suitability of the slum women. They should be encouraged to participate in different types of writing, reading and comprehension competitions, and numerical quiz and competitions etc. Pilot experiments on new ideas with regard to and other developmental aspects should be conducted in different slums.

2. The reading materials provided to the neo-literates should be need based, redesigned and modified. The regional language, local culture and tradition (tribal) should be reflected in those reading materials.
3. Chetana Kendras of the slums should function like community centres, where all sorts of teaching-learning, other development and entertainment programmes can be organised for the neo-literates. Library facilities should be made for the slum-dwellers.
4. Since accommodation problem is the greatest constraints in slum areas, some alternative arrangement should be made like construction of UBS Mahila Samiti room by Municipality in each slum, or the office of the smaller body like ward council can be used for the purpose of Chetana Kendra for TL and PL activities. Further, infrastructural support to the slum people through Chetana Kendra should be given. So that on the basis of the available infrastructure and by extending people's participation and assistance, Chetana Kendra can be build-up.
5. Frequent environment building through various activities including cultural programmes like, street plays, women Kala Yatha, different types of folk dances and dramas carrying the messages of post-literacy and continuing education should be organised. Special health camps for women and adolescent girls and children, plantation, sports, literacy melas (fairs) etc., should be organized in the slums and central level from time to time.
6. Initiative should be taken by RSS to provide financial and infrastructural support, loan and marketing facilities to the slum women, and in opening of women's co-operatives. RSS should therefore, co-ordinate and involve different types of organisations (Govt., Non-Govt., and voluntary) so as to extend their co-operation to providing infrastructure support to the slum women. Further, need based vocational and skill development, and income generation training should also be extensively given to the slum women in the Chetana Kendras.
7. Sincere and dedicated volunteers and activists should be well recognised and awareness various occasions. They should get the support and be encouraged for their women by the senior organisers and decision-makers of RSS. Remuneration or honorarium should be given to the unemployed and willing volunteers. Further, vocational and income generation training and loan facilities should also be provided to the selfless unemployed volunteers to fulfill their basic needs.
8. Involvement of more number of activists and volunteers should be made by RSS. For this sincere volunteers be identified and provision of their training should also be made accordingly. They should also be encouraged for middle level leadership in a positive direction, so as to handle the field situation, monitor the literacy and other activities and co-ordinate the work.
9. Regular training and orientation to the existing grass-root level volunteers, activists should be provided on literacy and other concerned aspects. They should also be given scope to participate in training programmes organised in and outside the city and even at the state and national level. The newly joined/involved volunteers should also be provided regular training by the experienced and senior activists. They should be given field training more intensively.
10. Scope should be given to the volunteers/activists to visit different successful literacy campaigns for the state as well as outside the state to gain experience. The neo-literate

slum women should also be given chance to visit successful campaign and interact with the learners and neo-literates of other campaigns which will motivate and encourage them for further learning and active participation in programme.

11. Sincere monitoring and interaction should be done by RSS for its Chetana Kendras and their activities. Provisions for some more vehicles should be made for this purpose. Experienced people from different sectors of life, even from political parties should be encouraged to join the RSS activities, specially for monitoring and interaction.
12. Fresh survey of the neo-literates, illiterates and dropout be made for the mopping-up operation. Internal as well as external evaluation of the activities of the programme should also be conducted.
13. The small amount of monthly contingency grant (Rs. 200/- only) given to each Chetana Kendra for their maintenance by RSS, should be increased.
14. Involvement of more number of women and members of Chetana Kendras with the decision-making process of RSS should be encouraged.
15. Fulfilment of basic requirements like drinking water, electricity, ration card, BPL Card, etc., of the slum women should be taken care of by the RSS Chairman-cum-ADM, Rourkela. He should co-ordinate the concerned. Departments and government for the protection of their basic civic rights.
16. Top level managers of RSP should be coordinated to extend their medical and education services to the non-RSP people of the slum areas specially to the women and children to avail healthcare facilities at nearly RSP healthcare facilities at nearly RSP health centres of slum areas, and educational facilities from the Primary Schools of RSP.
17. The organisers of "Mobile Medical Services" of "Sevasadan" should also be coordinated to extend their services in interior slum areas of Rourkela.
18. Political will should also be generated by involving the local representatives to the Govt. (local MPs, MLAs) in the RSS networking and interest among highly educated people should be created to demand for the developmental activities of Rourkela like opening of more primary schools in slum areas, implementation of different developmental schemes for urban poor specially the women, fulfilment of basic civic needs like ration card, water, electricity, etc., for the slum-dwellers.
19. The number of NFE centres should also be increased by the RSS organisers to meet the need of slum children. Hence, they should move to MHRD for the sanctioning of more NFE Centres. Further, special provision for the enrolment of children of the neo-literates be made in formal schools.
20. Family and legal counselling to the slum women should be organised in the Chetana Kendra very frequently. The neo-literate other slum women should be given properly guidance, counselling and information about various developmental programmes, legal rights, civic information etc.
21. Parents of the young girls should be counselled and encouraged to give freedom to their daughters in selecting their life-partners.
22. Male members of the society should be guided and counselled in a positive direction through RSS networking and encouraged to go for vasectomy.

23. Media services should be active in broadcasting, and telecasting the RSS activities. The press media should also be active and impartial in spreading over the message related to literacy development and neo-literates. Activities of the media services should be properly coordinated and taken care of by RSS Chairman and Secretary.
24. Legal support (both administrative and police) should be given to the slum women and grass-root level women volunteers while protesting against any criminal or anti-social activities of the slum areas.
25. Interference of the corrupt and harassing police officer in the developmental activities of the women group of Chetana Kendra should be checked.
26. Records regarding the activities of central as well as Chetana Kendra level of RSS should be properly maintained.
27. All the documents should be properly recorded on CD and other techniques. Photographs (album), video and audio records, etc., should also be kept with care for future information.
28. The neo-literate slum women should also be made conscious about the limitations of RSS in fulfilling their basic demands from the very beginning.

IMPLICATION OF THE STUDY

Ever since independence, India dreams for a literate nation various programmes promoting literacy have also been on the run accordingly after independence. Presently the total literacy programmes have been going on nation-wide since the successful total literacy experiment at Ernakulum. The findings of the present study proved that RSS has been able to develop the level of literacy skills and the level of awareness in the slum-dwellers, especially the women. It was also been able to change their attitudes in a positive direction as well as their living conditions, which indicate a healthy impact of the programme. It is important to mention here that National Literacy Mission sees the on-going literacy programme in the form of continuing education programme as an extension of TL and PL programme. It aims at a totally literate society as well as total enrolment of school-going age children and their retention in school. Therefore, there is essence of potentials in the ongoing literacy programmes to achieve the objectives of National Literacy Mission. The implication of the findings of the present study has the potential to contribute towards the growth of a literate society, and the educational development of its people especially the downtrodden and the children.

This study could also have conducted by following any quantitative method of research like experimental design of any other method. But, taking into the consideration of the context phenomenological approach has been mainly followed for this study.

However, for the growth of a literate society the following care should be taken.

(a) The changing interests, attitude, behaviour, and the experiences of the downtrodden in general and women in particular should be taken care of by the organisers of the literacy programmes of various campaigns. Further, their social and educational needs should be identified and need-based, and effective programmes and activities of TL, PL and continuing education programme should be well designed, planned and monitored for their further development.

(b) For acquisition of sustainable literacy, the literacy programme should look beyond their target achievement. Further, retention of literacy skills is as important as acquiring them.

Therefore, the planners and decision-makers of the literacy programme of NLM at national level need to give due importance to "What is learnt?" as much as to meeting the target.

(c) Various training programmes on literacy and its concerned aspects can be organised under the leadership of Mass Education Department, SRC for Adult and Continuing Education, different voluntary organisations like BGVS, Siksha Sandhan etc. in the State Level, and NLM, NCERT, NCTE, BGVS and other equivalent institutions at national level for the volunteers, resource persons, activists and organisers.

(d) Initiation can be made for innovation of teaching methods and techniques for the learners and neo-literates to retain their literacy skills and creation of zeal for further learning. Participatory group discussions, role plays, problem dramas in the form of dramatisation, field trips, intro-conversation, dialogue exchange, slum and centre exchange programme of learners and volunteers can also be organised at teaching centres. And case study, participatory observation, in depth discussion followed with brain storming techniques can also be adopted by the volunteers and resource persons to know further details about the interest, feelings and attitudes, etc., of the learners. Strategies and techniques can also be developed in an innovative form for effective monitoring and feedback mechanism and evaluation of the activities of TL, PL, and CE programmes of NLM. Apart from these, resource persons from government, non-government and voluntary organisations having the necessary experiences be invited and involved in the activities of the centres and share their experiences, expertise, and demonstrate and discuss various aspects related to literacy, awareness, and functional development of the learners.

(e) The findings of the study indicate that the neo-literate as well as the grass-root level volunteers and activists have potentials to work for a greater cause i.e. for a social cause. So their potentials can also be utilised and their experiences, technical skills can also be applied for nation building activities through various other programmes and activities of the voluntary organisations.

(f) The university department of Adult and Continuing Education, and the NSS Unit of the colleges can extend their educational activities for the illiterates and neo-literates with a live link to the literacy campaigns.

(g) The findings of the study indicate that most of the neo-literate slum women want to be economically self-sufficient. Thus they need to have infrastructural support in the form of loan or raw material from the government through literacy programmes to start their own income generation activities. Therefore, policy for different income generation schemes in the form of loan or co-operative can be made at the state and national level especially for the women and the downtrodden people irrespective of their geographical boundaries. The schemes can be implemented through the local administration in co-ordination with the literacy campaigns.

(h) The Ministry of Human Resource Development can strengthen the activities of NLM through its Total Literacy Campaigns by introducing community schools with the help of people's participation, sanction of NFE centres and establishment of primary schools specially in unauthorised slums, and other underdeveloped areas. Disbursement of grants for those schools can be made through the state government accordingly.

SUGGESTIONS FOR FURTHER RESEARCH

The present study was confined only to the impact of literacy programme on the slum women. Keeping in view the limitations of the study, more researches are required to substantiate the findings of the study for generalisations. Because every research study, while attempting to find answers to some questions, develops a number of other questions. These new questions guide further research. With this idea in mind the investigator has made some suggestions for further research. Research studies can be conducted in the following areas :

- People's participation in the literacy programme and its effect on educational growth of the downtrodden societies.
- By applying experimental designs to find out the impact of literacy programme in general.
- Human resource management of the literacy programme.
- Preparation of reading material, environment building and motivational activities based on the need and aspirations of the slum women as neo-literates.
- By applying the tools like case study, brain storming, participatory decision-making technique, participatory observation and intro-conversational method.
- On minimum level of learning required for the retention of literacy skills of the neo-literates.
- Development of strategies and innovative techniques for monitoring and evaluation of the literacy programmes both (total literacy and post-literacy).
- Case studies to be conducted on successful grass-root level women leaders.
- Techniques to be innovated so as to develop self-image of the downtrodden women for their empowerment.
- Influence of literacy programme on cent per cent enrolment and high retention of school children.
- Meta research in the field of literacy and adult education.

CONCLUSION

The overall impact of literacy programme in Rourkela on neo-literate slum women was found to be effective and remarkable. Over and above, the programme has been able to make a sea change in the life and living style of the people. It is revealed from the present study that impact of literacy programme is vital for the educational development of the neo-literates. It develops according to the expected levels of literacy skills, desired level of awareness and change of attitude in a positive direction. It gets affected when the level of literacy and awareness face barriers in their way of development. So the literacy activists, family members of the slum women, organisers of the programme, members of the community and the neo-literate slum women themselves should take care of it and take steps accordingly. Since the success of RSS was mainly possible due to the dedication and selfless contribution of a good number of volunteers and activists working at grass-root level, their level of motivation should be maintained and their devotion for such a great work must be recognised. Their expertise skills and knowledge, field experiences and suggestions should be analysed, internalised taken into the consideration for further improvement and extension of the programme. If effective training is imparted, their efforts and activities are recognised, constraints and problems are solved, and their voluntary spirit is properly respected, the impact of literacy programme would go a long way in the educational development of downtrodden people in the social system.

APPENDICES

RESEARCH TOOLS USED IN THE FIELD FOR INVESTIGATION

(TRANSLATED FROM ORIGINAL IN ORIYA)

APPENDIX - 1

Investigator
KISHORI DASH

INTERVIEW SCHEDULE FOR THE NEO-LITERATE SLUM WOMEN

Name :

Father/Husband's Name :

Married/Unmarried : Caste : /SC/ST :

Occupation : Income :

Name of the Slum : District :

1. When did you know about the Literacy Programme ?
   (a) After the launch of the programme
   (b) Many days after the launch of the programme
   (c) Only some time back
2. When did you join the literacy programme as learner ?
   (a) From the beginning *(b)* Only some time back
   (c) Many days after the launch of the programme
3. Who encouraged you to join this programme ?
   (a) Nobody *(b)* Members of the family
   (c) Ownself *(d)* Volunteer
   (e) Government or non-government employee or friends.
4. Who had come to your slum to encourage slum dwellers especially women to join the literacy programme ?
   (a) Nobody *(b)* Government employees
   (c) Volunteers of the non-government organisations
   (d) Literacy workers *(e)* School teacher and Students

5. What are the different media used in your slum to arouse interest among the people towards literacy programme ?

   (a) Television *(b)* Newspaper
   (c) Radio *(d)* Advertisement
   (e) Booklets *(f)* Wall Writings
   (g) Hoardings *(h)* Leaflet used on the vehicles
   (i) Cultural Programme

6. What are the cultural programmes utilised as medium/media to encourage the slum-dwellers especially women?

   (a) Different Folk Forms *(b)* Street-Plays
   (c) Women Kala Yatha

7. In which activities of literacy programme meant for people's awareness and awakening have you directly participated ?

   (a) Slum meetings
   (b) Procession on foot from one slum to another
   (c) Literacy convention *(d)* Literacy Fair
   (e) Marathan *(f)* Alpana (Rangoli) competition
   (g) Street Plays/Folk Forms/Songs, etc.
   (h) Procession for Motivation *(i)* Human Chain
   (j) Women Conventions *(k)* Cooking Competitions
   (l) Cycle Rallies(m) Debate Competitions
   (n) Mahila Jagruti Talim

8. What were the materials given to you for reading in the literacy center ?.

   (a) Ama Katha (1st Part) *(b)* Ama Katha (2nd Part)
   (c) Ama Katha (3rd Part) *(d)* Nothing was given

9. After completing the above mentioned three books what were the other books given to you for reading ?

   (a) Hita Katha *(b)* Bapa Maa Nka Payen
   (c) Saksharata Samachar *(d)* Other Library Books
   (e) Nothing *(f)* Naba Taranga

10. What was the material given to you for writing ?

    (a) Slate/Chalk *(b)* Note-book/pen/pencil
    (c) Nothing

11. How much in time was the reading and writing material provided to you ?

    (a) Provided in time *(b)* Provided in between with a little delay
    (c) Not at all provided

12. How was the reading writing material provided to you in accordance to your need ?

    (a) Inadequately provided *(b)* Not at all given
    (c) Provided according to the need

13. What are your improvements by using the reading and writing materials given to you ?
    (*a*) No improvement (*b*) To a certain extent
    (*c*) We are able to read and write.
14. What was your time of coming to the centre to learn ?
    (*a*) During the morning hour (*b*) During afternoon
    (*c*) During Evening (*d*) After 7 p.m.
15. What type of light was being used in your centre during the evening hours or in the night?
    (*a*) Lantern (*b*) Electricity (*c*) Gas Light
16. What type of light arrangement was made for your centre?
    (*a*) Lantern (*b*) Kerosene (*c*) Electric Bulb
    (*d*) Electric Wire (*e*) Gas light (*f*) No arrangement was made
17. What were the problems encountered in literacy programme due to lack of light facilities ?
    (*a*) Centre remains closed
    (*b*) In stead of night it was functioning during day time
    (*c*) The slum-dwellers arranged for the light through their own collection.
18. Since how long the volunteer has been teaching you in the centre ?
    (*a*) From the beginning (*b*) At the middle
    (*c*) Only sometime back
19. Does he teach regularly in the centre ?
    (*a*) He/she comes everyday (*b*) Comes in between
    (*c*) Not very often
20. What are the difficulties that occur in your study due to the absence of the volunteers?
    (*a*) Nothing happens (*b*) Interest of reading decreases
    (*c*) Despite his/her absent the centre functions
21. What are the other activities done by the volunteer in the centre other than teaching ?
    (*a*) No extra activities (*b*) Taking care of the slum-dwellers
    (*c*) After discussing with the area-coordinator, organises developmental work for the centre.
22. When does the area-coordinator come to your centre ?
    (*a*) Regularly (*b*) Not at all (*c*) Occasionally
23. What does the area-coordinator do in your centre ?
    (*a*) Checks the note-books etc. (*b*) Does nothing
    (*c*) Verifies about the teaching of the centre
    (*d*) Talks only to the volunteers
    (*e*) Discusses the various problems of the slum and the centre with the learners and slum-dwellers.
24. Besides the coordinator who are the people visiting your literacy centre ?
    (*a*) Government Officer (*b*) Leaders etc.
    (*c*) Monitoring team of the Saksharata Samiti (*d*) Nobody

25. **What does the monitoring team of Saksharata Samiti do in your centre ?**
    - *(a)* **Monitors the teaching-learning activities**
    - *(b)* **Inspects the work of the volunteer**
    - *(c)* **Just comes and goes**
    - *(d)* **Discusses issues related to the development of the centre**

26. **What are the works done in your centre other than teaching-learning ?**
    - *(a)* **Distribution of Library Book**
    - *(b)* **No other work is done**
    - *(c)* **Slum Meeting**
    - *(d)* **Discussions held among the learners and slum people with regard to the topics of Saksharata Samachar**
    - *(e)* **Discussions are made on different problems of the society**
    - *(f)* **Plan of action for the developmental work of the slum are made**

27. **Who organises the activities for slum through Chetana Kendra ?**
    - *(a)* **The volunteer himself** *(b)* **Only the slum-dwellers**
    - *(c)* **Only the learners**
    - *(d)* **By combined effort of the learners, volunteer and slum-dwellers**

28. **What are the difficulties you face by joining this programme ?**
    - *(a)* **Neglect to the family members**
    - *(b)* **Family members become dissatisfied**
    - *(c)* **Problem does not arise due to the extension of family co-operation.**

29. **What are the benefits you have got through your active participation in other programmes of literacy besides reading writing ?**
    - *(a)* **I was not benefited** *(b)* **Instead of getting benefit, beared the loss**
    - *(c)* **I came to know a little about the outside world.**
    - *(d)* **I came to know many things about my ownself, slum-dweller, and the people of the country as well as abroad.**

APPENDIX - 2

ACHIEVEMENT TEST
FOR THE NEO-LITERATE SLUM WOMEN OF ROURKELA

1. Name :

   Father/Husband's Name :

   Age : Caste : ST/ SC

   Occupation: Name of the slum :

   Name of the city : District :

   State :

   (Excellent, Very good, Good, Very Poor, Poor)

2. **Copy down the Stanza given below.**

   Whether be Oriya or Telugu
   Rajsthani or Gujurati ;
   From Kerala, Goa or Punjab may one be,
   India is our Janma Mati

   (Excellent, Very good, good, Poor, Very Poor)

3. **Dictation (Five Words)**

   (Excellent, Very Good, Good, Poor, Very Poor)

4. **Answer the questions given below in not less then ten lines.**

   What are the new things you have learnt, and applied in your family after being literate ?

   OR

   Write a letter to your friend about the work you do for your slum as a neo-literate women through Basti Chetana Samiti.

   (Excellent, Very Good, Good, Poor, Very Poor)

5. **Read a loud the passage given below**

   The sister tutor of Mahila Samiti teaches the women every evening. One day Neta narrated the story of her sufferings to her. Sister tutor asked "don't you know about the law made of the government ? Women do have an equal right like men. If you desire, you can have half of the share of your parental property. You can also get the proper wages by fighting against the contractor in the labour court."

   (Excellent, Very Good, Good, Poor, Very Poor)

6. **Read Properly and Answer**

Uncle said, "This soil, water, air, forest and mountain form our environment. We are destroying them. The human waste, affluent and sewage of the city are being poured into river and canals, and pollute the soil, water and air. Due to this people get affected by dangerous disease like jaundice, tuberculosis, tetanus, etc." Now Meeta understood that environment is our life. Without conservation of environment there is no way out of the human society.

(a) What does our environment consists of ?

(b) How does the water of river and canal gets polluted ?

(c) What are the various diseases affect people because of this pollution?

(d) What happens if the environment is not protected ?

(Excellent, Very Good, Good, Poor, Very Poor)

7. **Read the sentences after having seen the traffic signal given below and answer correctly to the question :**

- Road should not be crossed when there is red light in the traffic post.
- It is needed for getting ready to cross the road when there is orange light.
- Road should be crossed when there is green light in traffic post.

Answer the following :

(i) What happens when one crosses the road when the traffic signal is red ?

(ii) When one should cross the road ?

(Excellent, Very Good, Good, Poor, Very Poor)

8. **Add the following :**

(a)	*(b)*	*(c)*
52	70	24 Kilogram 350 grams
+ 69	+ 38	+15 Kilogram 250 grams

9. **Subtract the following.**

(a)	*(b)*	*(c)*
87	69	8 Meter 85 cm.
– 35	– 42	– 3 Meter 55 cm.

(d) Rs. 75.60 Paisa

–Rs. 44.80 Paisa

10. Multiply the following :

(a) 22 × 4

(b) 18 × 5

11. Divide the following :

(a) 85 ÷ 5 =

(b) **Pratibha saved Rs. 90 in the Mahila Bank with in 9 months. What was her monthly saving ?**

TO BE FILLED BY THE INVESTIGATOR

1. Name of the Neo-literate women :

2. Age:

3. SC/ST/Other Caste:

4. Name of the slum area:

5. Date of Evaluation:

6. Total Grade obtained:

Reading :

Writing :

Numeracy :

Total:

Signature of the Investigator

Date :

APPENDIX - 3

INTERVIEW SCHEDULE FOR THE NEO-LITERATE SLUM WOMEN OF ROURKELA TO KNOW THEIR LEVEL OF AWARENESS WITH REGARD TO THE DIFFERENT ASPECTS OF LITERACY

Name :

Father/Husband's Name :

Age : Caste : SC/Other Caste :

Occupation : Monthly Income :

Name of the Slum : Name of the City :

1. What happens when the size of a family increases ?
   (*a*) Income increases (*b*) Scarcity increases
   (*c*) Misery increases
2. What is the effect of population explosion on environment?
   (*a*) Environment remains clean
   (*b*) Environment becomes polluted
   (*c*) Nothing happens
3. On whom is the number of children in a family dependent?
   (*a*) Upon both father and mother (*b*) Upon father only
   (*c*) Upon mother only (*d*) Upon God.
4. Who is absolutely responsible for the birth of a female child ?
   (*a*) Mother (*b*) Father (*c*) Both father and mother
5. What happens when the parents are literate and aware ?
   (*a*) The family becomes large and unhappy
   (*b*) It makes no difference (*c*) The family becomes happy
6. What should be the number of children in a family ?
   (*a*) No limit should be there
   (*b*) One or two (*c*) More than two
7. What is the minimum age of marriage for girls ?
   (*a*) 25 years (*b*) 18 years (*c*) 15 years

8. **What happens when the mothers are literate and aware?**
   - *(a)* **There is an increase in disturbances in the family**
   - *(b)* **The possibilities of all round development of the family increase**
   - *(c)* **Only the education of the children gets faciliated**

9 **What do the family members think, when a baby girl is born?**
   - *(a)* **That she is a burden and curse to the family**
   - *(b)* **That she is a blessing to the family**
   - *(c)* **It makes no differences**

10. **What happens in the family when the married daughters and the daughter-in-laws go for learning ?**
    - *(a)* **Problems arise in the household chores**
    - *(b)* **Family is benefitted**
    - *(c)* **Problems do not arise in the house hold chores**

11. **What is the advantage of girl's education ?**
    - *(a)* **They become self-reliant and don't bother anybody**
    - *(b)* **They utilise the facilities meant for them**
    - *(c)* **They change the economic condition of the family by becoming self-dependent**

12. **What happens to the girls when they become literate and economically self-sufficient ?**
    - *(a)* **The need to give dowry ceases**
    - *(b)* **Their value in the society increases**
    - *(c)* **Prestige of the family gets hampered**

13. **What is the result of giving or taking dowry ?**
    - *(a)* **The social status of the person increases.**
    - *(b)* **Economic condition of the person improves**
    - *(c)* **It gives birth to crime**

14. **What are the legal provisions made for the women to get a share of parental property ?**
    - *(a)* **They have no right to a share in the parental property**
    - *(b)* **They can avails of equal property rights**
    - *(c)* **There is no specific law to get a share in the parental property**

15. **What happens when the husbands help their wives in household chores ?**
    - *(a)* **Family prestige is hampered**
    - *(b)* **Self-prestige of the males is affected**
    - *(c)* **The housewives get co-operation and family peace prevails in the family**

16. **What is the name of the special scheme introduced by Bank of India for Women to improve their financial condition by starting small scale business.**
    - *(a)* **Indira Vikas Yojana** *(b)* **Nehru Yojana**
    - *(c)* **Priyadarshini Yojana**

17. **What is the consequence of mothering at an early age ?**
    - *(a)* **The baby becomes healthy** *(b)* **The mother becomes weak and diseased**
    - (c) **The mother remains healthy**

18 What type of food is required for pregnant women ?

(a) Food rich in fats (b) Food rich in proteins
(c) Food without vitamins

19 When should the pregnant women medically registered ?

(a) Within 7/8 months of pregnancy
(b) Within 4/5 months of pregnancy
(c) Registration not required

20 When should the pregnant women be given tetanus toxite?

(a) No need of tetanus toxite
(b) Within 5/6 months of pregnancy
(c) Just before the delivery

21. How does breast-feeding affect the infant ?

(a) Mother becomes weak
(b) Infant becomes healthy by increasing immunative power
(c) It makes no difference to the health status of the mother and the infant

22. What are the possible dangerous diseases that are vulnerable to infants ?

(a) Cancer, Plegue, Jaundice, Diptheria
(b) Polio, Tetanus, Whooping Caugh
(c) Small Pox, Skin Disease, Cholera

23. What are the essential vaccines given to the child immediately after birth ?

(a) Measles vaccines (b) BCG and DPT
(c) Polio booster

24. When should the first dose of Polio drop be given to the child ?

(a) Immediately after birth (b) After six weeks of birth
(c) Just at completion six weeks of birth

25. When do the children need to be sent to school for primary education?

(a) At the age of three (b) At the age of five
(c) After six years of age

26. Where will the children of poor and labour class people learn, those who are unable to go to formal school ?

(a) In the Literacy Centres (b) In the NFE Centres
(c) There is no justification for their learning

27. Where will the child labourers learn, those who are unable to go to the school?

(a) In the Literacy Centres (b) In the NFE Centres
(c) No need of their education

28. It is whose main responsibility to send the children to school in time ?

(a) Only mother (b) Both father and mother
(c) Father

29. What is the evil of over growth of population in the country ?

(a) Increases the scarcity of agricultural land
(b) No harm on the increase of the scarcity of agricultural land
(c) Increases human resources

30. What should be done to control of over crowding in schools, colleges, roads and transport?

(a) By increasing more human resources
(b) By controlling population growth
(c) No need of doing anything

31. What should be the mechanism to protect environment ?

(a) Deforestation of the social forestry
(b) Huge plantation
(c) To establish a number of industries and factories

32 What should be done to get purified water from well ?

(a) Putting lime in the well
(b) Use of clean-bucket
(c) Not washing clothes near the well

33. What is the risk of attending nature's call in the field ?

(a) Getting disease by hook worm
(b) Environment becomes polluted
(c) Spreading diseases like cholera or diarrhoea.

34. How can cleanliness be maintained after attending the nature's call ?

(a) Nothing doing (b) Using soap to clean hands and feet
(c) Washing hands and feet with clay or ash.

35. What is the risk of eating fly infected food ?

(a) Spreads jaundice (b) Spreads cholera
(c) Nothing happens

36. What can be done to get rid of mosquitoes ?

(a) To spread smoke regularly in the house
(b) Using mosquito net
(c) Keeping the environment clean

37. What are the effects of alcohol and drug abuse ?

(a) The individual loses his sense
(b) Individual feels active
(c) Increases of social prestige
(d) Health of the individual improves
(e) Health of the individual deteriorates

38. Who should be consulted when affected by disease ?

(a) Consulting black magician (b) Leaving on fate
(c) Doctor (d) By worshipping Goddess

39. Where should the theft in a house or slum be reported ?

(a) Town services (b) Health department
(c) Town administration (d) Police department

40. Where should you apply to install a tube well for your slum ?

(a) Police Department (b) Health Department
(c) Local Administration (d) Town services

41. Whose education gets priority in your family ?

(a) Daughter (b) Son (c) Both

42. Why should the education of son be over-emphasised to that of daughter ?

(a) The family burden is borne by the son
(b) Since the girls leave for their in laws families after marriage, the amount spend for their education goes waste
(c) There is development in the girl and her family.

43. Reasons as to why women should not have the right to take decision like men

(a) From mental and physical point of view women are much weaker than the men
(b) They also manage all sorts of social responsibilities
(c) Family cannot run smoothly without women

44. Why should the daughters help their mothers in household chores and not sons?

(a) Since sons are more intelligent, they should study instead of engaging in household chores
(b) Son and daughter both should do the household activities
(c) Participation in household activities lowers the prestige of sons

45. What is evil of doing country liquor business in slums ?

(a) There is no harm of doing country liquor business
(b) It lures the people towards a wrong direction
(c) It helps to improve the economic condition of the country

46. Why should women take part in politics ?

(a) Their social status increases
(b) By entering politics their social prestige is hampered
(c) The country develops when they posses equality of political rights like men

47. How many letters do you write to your friends and relatives every month ?

(a) One or two (b) Not at all (c) Regularly

48. In which type of programme or training would you prefer to participate for the improvement of yourself and the women of your slum ?

(a) Mahila Jagruti Talim
(b) Training in Child and Maternity Care
(c) Training in Women and Law
(d) Income generation training

49. What should be done against women sufferings ?
    - *(a)* One should tolerate
    - *(b)* It should be reported to the local police
    - *(c)* After being self-aware and making others aware voice should be raised jointly

50. Why should everybody leave in harmony in the slum irrespective of castes, creeds and religions ?
    - *(a)* People of different castes and religions should live separately
    - *(b)* People of all religions should live together
    - *(c)* There is no harm in living, whoever may the person be wherever he wants to live

APPENDIX - 4

QUESTIONNAIRE FOR GRASS-ROOT LEVEL VOLUNTEERS/SENIOR ACTIVISTS

Dear Friends,

I would like to approach you with an assignment, which is a part of my research work entitled "A STUDY OF THE IMPACT OF LITERACY PROGRAMME ON EDUCATIONAL DEVELOPMENT OF THE SLUM WOMEN OF ROURKELA". For this purpose a set of questionnaire is attached. You are requested to respond to these questions according to what you feel and experience as a grass-root level volunteer/senior activist in your practical situation and not according to what you are supposed to believe or any biasness.

Your truthfulness in the questions statements would be valued and your co-operation is solicited for making the research a success. I would like to assure you that your responses shall in no case be used other than research and will be treated as confidential.

Thanking you for your co-operation.

Yours sincerely

(KISHORI DASH)

APPENDIX - 5

QUESTIONNAIRE FOR THE GRASS-ROOT LEVEL VOLUNTEER/AREA COORDINATORS

1. Name :
2. *(a)* Age : *(b)* Male/Female : *(c)* Married/Unmarried/Single:
3. *(a)* Caste : SC/ST/Other *(b)* Religion
4. Educational Qualification :
5. Occupation :

6. Monthly Income :
7. Correspondence Address :
8. Name of the area/slum where he/she works :
9. Your role in Literacy Programme :
10. When did you join the literacy programme ?
    (a) From the beginning
    (b) Few days after the launching of the programme
    (c) Middle of the Programme (d) Only some time back
11. Why did you join this programme ?
    (a) Interest in social work (b) To spend leisure hour
    (c) Could not avoid the request of slum-dwellers
    (d) Hope for future prospect due to unemployment
    (e) Any other
12. What kind of training were you given to join this programme?
    (a) Volunteer's training
    (b) Resource Person's Training
    (c) Key-Resource Person's Training
13. (If trained) In what aspects were you trained ?
    (a) Teaching technique to the learners
    (b) Methods of motivating to the people
    (c) Principles of field supervision (d) Any other
14. To what extent did your training help you in actual field of work ?
    (a) Not at all
    (b) It was sufficient to solve different types of problems related to literacy work
    (c) Helpful to some extent
    (d) Instead of helping, lead to trouble
15. What are the works you do directly in the Literacy Programme ?
    (a) Teaching
    (b) To involve the learners and slum-dwellers in the programme by motivating them
    (c) To organise different types of programme in the slum
    (d) To guide the learners and volunteers after field visit
    (e) Participating in cultural programmes like street plays etc.
16. To what extent did your training help you in teaching learners ?
    (a) Not at all (b) To some extent (c) To a great extent
17. How far is the training helpful in motivating the slum-dwellers and learners especially the women ?
    (a) To a great extent (b) Not at all (c) To some extent

18. **How did you start literacy work in the slum areas ?**
    - *(a)* **On the demand of the slum-dwellers**
    - *(b)* **Due to the spirit of social work**
    - *(c)* **By seeing the literacy work of other places**
    - *(d)* **Inspired by the organisers of Saksharata Samiti**
    - *(e)* **Any other reason**
19. **How did the slum-dwellers co-operate with you in organising different programmes in the slum ?**
    - *(a)* **In arranging place for literacy centre**
    - *(b)* **In identifying learners and motivating them to come to centre**
    - *(c)* **Remaining silent by non-cooperation**
    - *(d)* **Insteading of co-operating, creating trouble**
    - *(e)* **Helping in organising necessities like kerosene/electricity and mat for the centre**
    - *(f)* **Any other**
20. ***(i)* Did the slum-dwellers oppose you while starting the centre? Yes/No**

    ***(ii)* If Yes, How did you solve it ?**
    - *(a)* **By seeking the help of the previous committee**
    - *(b)* **By explaining it to the leaders of the slum**
    - *(c)* **By seeking the help of Saksharata Samiti**
    - *(d)* **By seeking the help of other government organisation.**
    - *(e)* **By arranging special meetings**
    - *(f)* **Any other**
21. ***(i)* Is there any committee prior to the literacy centre ? Yes/No**

    ***(ii)* If yes, how does it help you ?**
    - *(a)* **In identifying the illiterates**
    - *(b)* **In motivating the people to join the centre**
    - *(c)* **In making the programme successful**
    - *(d)* **In organising special meeting**
    - *(e)* **Any other**
22. **What were the public awakening and environment building activities organised by you in the slum before the start of the teaching-learning programme ?**
    - *(a)* **Slum meeting** *(b)* **Literacy Street Play**
    - *(c)* **Procession on foot from one slum to another**
    - *(d)* **Cycle Rally** *(e)* **Poster Writing Campaign**
    - *(f)* **Women convention** *(g)* **Literacy convention**
    - *(h)* **Human Chain** *(i)* **Any Other**
23. **How do you motivate people to join the literacy centre ?**
    - *(a)* **By trying to make them understand about different advantages of literacy**
    - *(b)* **By discussing about the development of their socio-economic condition and family welfare**
    - *(c)* **Door to door campaign**
    - *(d)* **By citing examples of the people who have become helpful by being literate**
    - *(e)* **Any other**

24. *(i)* Whether the women learners attend the centre regularly or not ? Yes/No

(ii) If not, the reason for their not coming :

(a) Teaching timing does not suit to them
(b) They feel tried after having worked hard through out the day
(c) Due to lack of motivation
(d) Dissatisfaction of the family members in their learning
(e) Due to ignorance about the advantages of literacy programme
(f) Because of the uninteresting syllabus and monotonous teaching
(g) Any other

25. *(i)* Did you face any problem while involving women in teaching-learning activities of your centre ? Yes/No

(ii) If yes, how did you overcome it ?

(a) By be-friending them and highlighting the advantages of the different aspects of literacy programme
(b) By discussing the advantages of literacy rogramme with their family members
(c) By requesting the senior and experienced women, and through them the learners were encouraged
(d) By giving examples of woman learners from other literacy centre

26. What is the age group of women in your cetnre ?

(a) 10 to 15 years *(b)* 16 to 35 years
(c) 36 to 45 years *(d)* 45 years and above

27. What are the steps you have taken to ensure regular attendance in the centre ?

(a) By showing friendly behaviour
(b) By discussing their problems and to guide them in finding solutions
(c) By changing the teaching timing of the centre to suit their convenience
(d) Any other

28. *(i)* Did you receive the teaching-learning material from saksharata Samiti in time ? Yes/No

(ii) If no, what measures you have taken to get them in time ?

(a) By writing to the Chairman/Secretary of the Samiti
(b) By requesting the zone co-ordinator
(c) By meeting the controller of the samiti personally
(d) Any other.

29. *(i)* Did you receive the teaching-learning material in adequate quantity ? Yes/No

(ii) If no, how did you manage ?

(a) Learners were asked to share the materials
(b) Learners were asked to borrow from other centre
(c) Any other

30. How was the teaching-learning materials provided to your centre ?

(a) By giving all the three primers at a time
(b) After completion of one primer another was given

31. How was the language of the primer for the learners ?

(a) Simple to read
(b) Simple to read and understand
(c) Simple to read and comprehensible to certain extent
(d) Simple to read but incomprehensible

32. Do the topics in the Primers reflect the way of slum life ?

(a) To some extent (b) To a great extent (c) Not at all

33. Do the pictures in the Primers reflect the life style of the slum-dwellers ?

(a) To some extent (b) Not at all (c) To a great extent

34. Do the content of the Primers match with the life style of the slum-dwellers ? Yes/No

35. (i) Do you come to the literacy centre regularly ? Yes/No

(ii) If not why don't you come regularly ?

(a) Feeling hope less due to lack of co-operation from the slum-dwellers.
(b) Feeling irritated due to irregular attendence of the learners
(c) Due to lack of time
(d) Feeling disgusted by working without renumeration
(e) Lack of motivation from the seniors of the Samiti
(f) By observing lack of interest among women learners
(g) Any other

36. How often does the monitoring team visit to your centre ?

(a) Once in a week (b) Twice in a month
(c) Once in a month (d) Occasionally
(e) Not at all (f) Frequently
(g) During the functions/programmes

37. (i) Do you discuss with the team about the problems of your centre and Chetana Kendra ? Yes/No

(ii) If yes, what do they do to solve these problems ?

(a) Listen to you carefully
(b) Avoid the discussion by introducing some irrelevant topics
(c) They guide to how to solve the problems of the centre
(d) Any other

38. (i) Do you receive any remuneration for this work from the Saksharata Samiti ? Yes/No

(ii) If yes, How much ?

(iii) If No, Why ?

39. How much does the Basti Chetana Samiti receive as monthly grant from Saksharata Samiti to meet its expenditure ?

40. How do the members of Basti Chetana Samiti spend this money ?

(a) By organising developmental programme for slum-dwellers

(b) By distributing it among the members of the Samiti.
(c) By purchasing necessary materials for the Chetana Kendra
(d) By arranging different types income generation training programme
(e) By spending towards the conveyance of the volunteers
(f) Any other

41. (i) Whether the monthly grant for Chetana Samiti is sufficient to meet the expenditure ? Yes/No

(ii) If not, how do the Samiti people manage ?

(a) Pay from their own pocket (b) Ask the learners to contribute
(c) Stop the functions of the centre (d) Arrange from the community
(e) Any other

42. What arrangement of drinking water has been made in the slum where you are working?

(a) Not at all (b) good (c) workable

43. If the arrangement of drinking water is not good, what measures do the neo-literate women and members of Chetana Samiti take for it ?

(a) By requesting to the political leaders
(b) By writing repeatedly to the town administrator and town services
(c) Digging well on their own
(d) By demonstrating before the office of the district administration and town services
(e) Without doing anything

44. How do you encourage women to maintain cleanliness in the slum ?

(a) Through cleaning campaign of the slum
(b) By organising special meetings and explaining to the people
(c) By doing cleaning work in the slum especially with the help of women and members of Chetana Samiti
(d) Any other

45. (i) Is there any medical facility in that areas ? Yes/No

(ii) If no, what steps do the members of Chetana Samiti take for it ?

(a) By writing to the district administration and health department time and again
(b) By requesting the political leaders repeatedly
(c) By availing of the mobile health services organised by other voluntary organisations on request
(d) Without doing anything.

46. Except literacy work of the Chetana Samiti, when do you visit to the slum again ?

(a) During the festivals celebrated in the slum
(b) To attend the family functions of the members of the Chetana Samiti and learners
(c) During the need of the slum-dwellers
(d) Whenever wishes (e) Not at all

47. How do you join the festivals of the slum ?

(a) On the invitation of the slum people

(*b*) As audience
(*c*) To co-operate with them after getting the message
(*d*) Spontaneously

48. (*i*) Did you mark any change among the neo-literate slum women before and after joining the literacy programme ? Yes/No.

(*ii*) If Yes, in which aspects the changes are marked ?

49. Did their economic condition improve through this programme ?

50. What are the attitudinal changes observed in them ?

51. What are the steps taken by slum women against alcohol and drug abuse ?

52. What are the steps taken against women's exploitation and dowry system ?

53. (*i*) Have they done anything for environmental protection ? Yes/No.
(*ii*) If yes, what they have done ?

54. What is the impact of this programme with regard to their health status ?

55. How far they have developed the power of decision-making in their family life through this programme ?

(*a*) Satisfactorily
(*b*) Not at all
(*c*) To some extent

56. What are the changes observed in the slum areas with regard to IMR through this programme.

(*a*) Decreased (*b*) Increased (*c*) As it is

57. What are the changes observed in their attitudes with regard to family planning?

(*a*) They have planned the family
(*b*) They have increased the size of the family
(*c*) They themselves have planned the family and encouraged others to do so
(*d*) Seniors have encouraged others for family planning.

58. What are the changes marked in them in their day to day life through this programme ?

59. What is the impact of this programme on political aspects of their life ?

(*a*) They have availed of their voting right properly
(*b*) They have joined politics directly
(*c*) They are away from politics

60. How do they join politics directly ?

61. How do the neo-literate women participate in various programmes of their slums ?

(*a*) Actively (*b*) Like leaders (*c*) Inactively
(*d*) Like silent spectator(e) Not at all come

62. ***(i)*** **Do you observe any special changes among the neo-literate women through the impact of literacy programme ? Yes/No**

(ii) **If yes, specify from your own experience.**

63. **Being a volunteer of Literacy Programme, to what extent do you derive satisfaction from your work ?**

(a)	**To a great extent**	***(b)***	**In expressible**
(c)	**Not at all**	***(d)***	**To some extent**

64. **How will the Literacy Programme for the slum women be effective for their development? Give your wise suggestions in this regard.**

Signature of the Volunteer

Date :

APPENDIX - 6

QUESTIONNAIRE FOR THE SENIOR ACTIVISTS, RESOURCE PERSONS AND ORGANISERS OF RSS

1. Name : Age :

   Male/Female : Married/Unmarried :

   Caste/SC/Others : Religion :

   Educational Qualification :

   Occupation : Monthly Income :

   Correspondence Address :

2. When did you join the literacy programme ?
3. Who inspired you to join this programme ?
   - *(a)* Collegues
   - *(b)* Organisers of District Administration
   - *(c)* By self-inspiration
   - *(d)* By seeing the involvement of others
   - *(e)* On official order
4. Were you given any special training to join this programme? Yes/No
5. (If trained) In which aspects were you trained ?
6. What is your role in literacy programme ?
7. What are the activities performed by you for this programme?
8. How do you manage the responsibilities given to you ?
   - *(a)* Without any difficulty
   - *(b)* With much difficulty
   - *(c)* To some extent *(d)* Not at all
9. If you are not able to manage properly, why ?
   - *(a)* Due to lack of co-operation from the organisers of the samiti
   - *(b)* Lack of necessary information about the programme from the volunteer
   - *(c)* By not giving sufficient time

(*d*) By not getting co-operation from the slum-dwellers
(*e*) Feeling irritated due to time long involvement with literacy activities

10. (*i*) Do you Supervise/Monitor the Chetana Kendras regularly ? Yes/No

(*ii*) If not-specify the reasons ?

11. What are the matters you take into consideraction while monitoring the Basti Chetana Samiti and Literacy Centre ?

12. How often do you monitor a Chetana Samiti/Literacy Centre in a month ?

(*a*) Once in a month (*b*) Once in a week
(*c*) Twice in a month (*d*) Frequently

13. How long have you been doing this work ?

(*a*) From the beginning of the programme
(*b*) From the middle of the programme
(*c*) Since some time back

14. (*i*) Did you notice any impact of your visit on Chetana Kendra on the neo-literates, especially women ?

(*ii*) If yes, what is the type of impact noticed ?

15. (*i*) Don't the slum-dwellers feel irritated by your frequent visits to them and supervision and monitoring to the Chetana Kendras ? Yes/No

(*ii*) If no, how did you know ?

(*a*) (*b*)

(*iii*) If yes, what remedial measures you do take ?

(*a*) (*b*)

16. How do you motivate to the neo-literate slum women to join in various developmental activities during your supervision/monitoring to Chetana Kendra ?

17. What is the imapct of your visit on the volunteers to the Chetana Kendra ?

18. How do you help to the volunteers to solve the problems of Basti Chetana Samiti ?

19. Do you have to give any field training for this ? Yes/No

20. What do you do, if a problem, is not solved both by you and the volunteer ?

(*a*) The problem is left as it is
(*b*) The solution is found after thorough discussion with the slum-dwellers and members of the Chetana Samiti.
(*c*) The solution is found by drawing the attention of the organisers viz. the Chairman, Secretary etc. of the Saksharata Samiti (*d*) Any other

21. (*i*) Do you receive any honorarium/remuneration from the Samiti for this work ? Yes/No

(*ii*) If yes, how much you receive ?

(iii) **If no, why don't you receive ?**

(a) Because of voluntary spirit
(b) As deputed from Government/Non-government, Organisation to the Samiti
(c) As Samiti is not in favour of giving any remuneration/honorarium
(d) Because of the non-receipt of others

22. When do you come to the slum other than literacy work ?

(a) During the marriage functions etc. of the learner's family
(b) During the Socio-cultural functions celebrated in the slum
(c) By getting message in the need of the slum
(d) Otherwise I don't come to the slum

23. How do you participate in these activities ?

(a) By getting invitation of the slum-dwellers
(b) On the request of the members of Chetana Samiti and the volunteers
(c) Spontaneously after getting message
(d) Any other

24. *(i)* Have you noticed any changes in the neo-literate slum women between today and prior to literacy programme ? Yes/No

***(ii)* If yes, in which aspects the changes are marked ?**

25. What are the changes which have taken place in their financial condition due to this programme ?

26. What are the changes in their mental layers ?

27. *(i)* Do they perform their social as well as family responsibilities properly by this programme?

***(ii)* If yes, how do they perform ?**

(a) By sending their children to the school in time
(b) By following small family norms
(c) By showing help and sempathy to the neighbours and slum-dwellers in their need
(d) By participating actively in family as well as social activities
(e) By co-operating the activities of Chetana Kendra for the unity and improvement of the slum
(f) By tolerating silently

28. How are they benefited through this programme with regard to health ?

29. *(i)* Did they try to possess their social and political rights by this ? Yes/No

***(ii)* If yes, how have they done ?**

(a) (b) (c)

30. What are the measures adopted by them against alcohol and drug abuses ?

31. *(i)* Are you aware of the steps they have taken against the cause of women suffering and dowry system ? Yes/No

***(ii)* If yes, what have they done ?**

32. How did you observe/record their participation in the social as well as developmental activities of the slum ?

(a) As a leader	**(b) As a Silent Spectator**
(c) As an active partner	**(d) As an organiser**
(e) As a director	**(f) They don't come at all**

33. *(i)* Did you notice any specific changes in their style/standard of living/activities in the slum?

***(ii)* If yes, what are those ?**

34. As a senior activists of RSS involved since long, to what extent did you derive satisfaction from your work ?

***(a)* To a great extent**	***(b)* To certain extent**
***(c)* In-expressible**	***(d)* Not at all**

35. How will the literacy programme be effective for slum women for their development ? Give your wise suggestions :

Signature of the Senior Literacy Activist/Organisers

Date :

BIBLIOGRAPHY

Adam, Curle, "Educational Strategies for Developing Societies", Tavistock Publication, London (1970).

Adam's Report on Female Education", ORISSA Administrative Records, 1881 82.

Adiseshiah, M., "Towards a Literate World", National Literacy Mission, DAE, Government of India, New Delhi, 1991.

Agnihotri A. & Sivaswamy G., "Total Literacy Campaign in the Sundargarh District of Orissa", A Documentation, NLM, DAE, Government of India, New Delhi, 1993.

Agrawal, S.P., Development of Education in India, Vol.5, Selected Documents - 1995-97, New Delhi, 1999.

Agrawal S.P., Women Education in India(1995–98), Present Status, Perspective - Plan, Statistical indicators with a Global View (Volume-Three), Concept Publishing Company, Delhi, 2001.

Agrawal, C.M., "Dimensions of Indian Womenhood", Srhi Almora Book Depot, Almora, 1993.

Agrawal, S., "Status of Women", Printwell Publication, Jaipur, 1988.

Agrawal, S.P., "Development of Education in India, Selected Documents", Vol.5, Concept Publishing Company, New Delhi,1997.

Ahmad, Karuna, "The Social Context of Women's Education in India - 1921–81, Tentative Formulations, Occasional Papers on History and Society," No. 6, 1982, Nehru Memorial Museum and Library, 1982.

Ahmad, N., "Managing Urban Literacy Programme" IJAE, Vol. 60, No. 2, April-June, 1999.

Ahmed Msushtq. "What is National Literacy Mission" ? IJAE, Vol.51, No.4, Oct.-Dec.,1990.

Aleen, Shamim (Ed.) "Women's Development : Problems and Prospects", APH Publishing Corporation, New Delhi, 1996.

Ambasht, N.K. "Adult, Continuing and Non-Formal Education : A Trend Report," Report of 6th Education Survey, NCERT, New Delhi, 1996.

Apte, J.S., "Education and Women's Empowerment" IJAE, Vol. 56, No. 3, July-Sept.,1995.

Ashok Kumar, "Women in Contemporary Indian Society" Vol-2, Anmol Publication, New Delhi, 1993.

Azim, Shaikh R., "A Study of Life Style of Slum Dwellers and its Relationship with Education", Ph.D. Thesis in Education, CASE, M.S.University, Baroda, 1983.

Baroda Municipal Corporation; "A Report on the Slums of Baroda", 1976.

Bastia, K.C., "A Study of the National Adult Education Programme in the Tribal Region of Orissa", Ph.D. Thesis in Education, CASE, M.S.University, Baroda, 1982.

Bataille, L., "A Turning Point for Literacy", Pergamon Press, New York, 1976

Bautista, Feny de Los Angeles; "The Filipina Girl : From Vulnerability to Resilience and Power", VENA JOURNAL, Vol. 6, No. 2, Dec.,1994.

Beers, Henk. Ven,, "The Girl Child : An Introduction", VENA JOURNAL, Vol. 6, No. 2, Dec.1994.

Behera, D.K. & Team, "Report of the External Evaluation Team on the Total Literacy Campaign of Rourkela City, ORISSA, P.G. Deptt. of Anthropology, Sambalpur University, ORISSA, 1993.

BGVS, New Delhi, "A Guide Book For a Mass Campaign for Total Literacy", 1990.

BGVS, Report on the "Samata" Jatha of BGVS 1993, at Jhanshi" BGVS, New Delhi,1994.

BGVS, Gyan Vigyan Varta March,1997, New Delhi, 1997.

Bharat Sevak Samaj, "Slums of Old Delhi-A Report of Socio - Economic Survey of Slums", Atma Ram and Sons, Delhi, 1958.

Bhangoo, Satwant Kaur., "Effectiveness of Selected Teaching Methods for Adult Rural Women Learners in Punjab", Ph.D. Thesis in Adult Education, Punjab University, Patiala, 1987.

Bhatt, S.C. (Ed.) "The Encyclopaedic District Gazetters of India", Eastern Zone (Vol. 9), Gyan Publishing House, New Delhi, 1997.

Bhowmik, K.L., "Urban Development", Inter India Publication, New Delhi, 1988.

Bijlani, H.U. & Pradipto Roy, "Slum Habitat", Vikas Publication, New Delhi, 1991.

Bijlani, H.U., "Urban Problems", Indian Institute of Public Administration, New Delhi, 1980.

Biswas, and Agrawal, A.S., "Indian Educational Document, Since Independence : Committee, Commissions, Conferences", The Academic Publishers, New Delhi, 1971.

Biswal, G.C., "Needs and Problems of Tribal Community in Orissa with Regards to Education: An In-depth Study", Ph.D. Thesis in Education, CASE, M.S.University, Baroda, 1991.

Black, Naomi & Cottrell, Ann-Baker, "Women and World Change: Equality Issues in Development", SAGE, Publications, London, 1981.

Bobby, J., "A Study on Neo-Literates With Special Reference to Lalam Block of Kerala", Indore School of Social Work, 1993.

Bordia, Anil, "Agenda for Adult Education Research : "A South Asian Perspective", Adult Education and Development, Vol. 45, 1995.

Bose, A., "India's Urban Population", 1991 Census Data, State, District, Cities & Towns, Wheeler Publishing, New Delhi, 1994.

Bose, A., "Supplement 1998: Demographic Diversity of India, State and Districts Level Data, 1991 Census", B.R. Publishing Corporation, Delhi, 1998.

Bose, A., "Population of India, 2001 Census Results and Methodology", B.R. Publishing Corporation, July, 2001.

Bryman, A., "Quality and Quantity in Social Research." Unwin Hyman Ltd., London, 1992.

Buch, M.B. (ed.), "Survey of Research in Education", CASE, Faculty of Education & Psychology, M.S.University, Baroda, First Edition, 1974.

Buch, M.B.(ed.), "Second Survey of Research in Education", Society for Educational Research and Development, Baroda, First Edition, 1979.

Buch, M.B.(ed.), Third Survey of Research in Education" (1978–83), NCERT, New Delhi,1987.

Buch, M.B. (ed.), "Fourth Survey of Research in Education, Vols. I & II,(1983–88), NCERT, New Delhi, 1991.

Bulmer, Martin (ed.),"Sociological Research Methods, An Introduction", Mc.Mill Press Ltd., 1977.

Burgess, G. Robert (ed.), "Field Research a Source Book and Field Manual", George Allen & Unwin Publishers Ltd., 1982.

Census, 1951, Government of India, New Delhi, 1951.

Census , 1971, Government of India, New Delhi, 1971.

Census of India, 1991, Series 1, India Paper 2 of 1992. Final Population Totals : Brief Analysis of Primary Census Abstract, New Delhi, 1993.

Census, 2001, Government of India, New Delhi, 2001.

Charles, Abraham, "Man's Struggle for Shelter in an Urbanizing World,", London, 1970.

Chaturvedi, V. and Brahma P., "Impact of Functional Literacy Programme in Rural Areas of New Delhi" IJAE, Vol. 44, No. 3, March,1983.

Chopra, Rita, "Adult Education", Himalaya Publishing House, Bombay, 1993.

Choudhary, D. Paul, "Women Welfare and Development, A Source Book" Inter India Publication, New Delhi, 1992.

Chaudhary, K., "Education for Slum Dwellers : The Ideological Dimension", New Frontiers in Education, Vol. XXVII, No. I Jan-March,1997.

Chugani, Rama, "A Study of Rural Functional Literacy Project in North Arcol District of Tamil Nadu", Ph.D. Thesis in Education, CASE, M.S.University, Baroda, 1987.

"Circulars of the Nizamat and Suddar Diwani Records": Board of Revenue Records - 1836–42 ORISSA, Vol.78, No. 2625.

Conant, James Briant., "Slums and Suburbs", New York ; Mc Graw, Hill Book Co., 1961.

Das, G. & Mahatab, H.K., "History of Freedom Movement in Orissa", Vol. IV, Cuttack, 1957.

Das, Rajani (ed.), "Rourkela Reporter (Special Issue)", Rourkela, 1995.

Dash, K. "A Comparative Study of the Attitudes of Tribal and Non-Tribal People of Sundargarh District (ORISSA) Towards Adult Education", M.Phil Dissertation, Punjab University, Chandigarh, 1987.

Deogaonkar and Deogankar, "The Tribal Girl," Edited in "Girl Child in India", (ed.) - Devasia, L. and Devasia, V.V., Ashish Publishing House, New Delhi, 1991.

Denzin, K. Norman & Lincoln, S. Yvonna (ed.), "Handbook of Qualitative Research", SAGE Publication, 1994.

Desai, N., "Born to Die", The Indian Post, October, 7, 1987.

Desai & Pillai (Ed.), "A Theory of Slum and Urbanization" Popular Prakashan, Bombay, 1971.

Devasia, L. & Devasia, V.V., "The Girl Child in India" , Ashish Publishing House, New Delhi, 1991.

Devasia, L. and Devasia, V. V. "Empowering Women for Sustainable Development", Ashish Publishing House, New Delhi, 1994.

Devi, S. "Nari Sikshya", Sambalpur Hiteisini, Debgarh, 7th August,1920.

Devi, S. "Narijatir Adhikar", Sambalpur Hiteisini, 8th July, Debgarh, 1922.

Dighe, A. & Patel, Ila, "Gender Equity in Literacy : Some Considerations" Back Ground Paper of National Institutes Adult Education, New Delhi, January, 1992.

Dighe, A. & Patel, I., "Gender Equity and Literacy in India : Some Issue Perspective in Education", Vol. 9, No. 1, January,1993.

Dighe, A. "Trends in Adult Education Research in Asia", Adult Education and Development, Institute for International Co-operation of the German Adult Education Association, Vol. 45, 1995.

D.P.I.(ORISSA), "Education in ORISSA", Bhubaneswar, Statistics and Information Cell, 1978.

Dubey, S.C., "Educating Weaker Sections", Times of India, Ahmedabad Ed., 15th July, 1981.

Dudly, S. "The Meaning of Development," International Development Review, December, 1969.

Dudly, S., "The New Meaning of Development", International Development Review, No. 3, 1977.

Dutta, S.C. (ed.) "From Literacy to Liberation", Indian Adult Education Association, New Delhi, 1986.

Dwivedi, S.N., "Smruti Sampark" Rourkela, 1996.

Everret, J.M., "Women and Social Change in India", Haritage Publishers, New Delhi, 1981.

Extract from the Proceedings of the Nisamat Adalat, Vol. 523, 21st May, 1819 (On Sutee Pratha) O.S.A., 1819.

Fager, Lind., Ingemar, and Shah, Lawrence, J., "Education and National Development", A Comparative Perspective - 2nd Edition, Pergamon Press, Oxford, 1989.

Flick, Uwe., "An Introduction to Qualitative Research", Saga Publication, New Delhi, 1998.

Freire, Paulo, "Cultural Action for Freedom", Harmonds Worth (England) Panguin, (1970/72), 1975.

Galtung, J.,"Theory and Methods of Social Research", George Allen & Unwin Publishers, 1970.

Gee, Wilson, "Social Science Research Method," Appleton Century Crofts Inc., New York, 1950.

George, Psacharopoulos. Maureen. Wood Hall, "Education for Development", An Analysis of Investment Choices - A Word Bank Publication, Oxford University Press, 1985.

Gilada, I.S., "Prostitution in India : Causes, Extent, Prevention and Rehabilitation". Published in "Social Problems and Welfare in India", Edited By, Shankar Jogan, Ashish Publishing House, New Delhi, 1992.

Gill, Rajesh, "Slums as Urban Village", Rawat Publications, Jaipur, New Delhi, 1994.

Gist, N.P. & Halbert, L.A., "Urban Society", New York, 1950.

Government of India, "All India Report of Social Education for 1947–51", Ministry of Education, New Delhi,1954.

Government of India, "Challanges of Education; A Policy Perspective", Ministry of Education, New Delhi, 1955.

Government of India, "Teacher's Handbook of Social Education", Ministry of Education, New Delhi, 1955.

Government of India, "Report of the Advisory Committees on Slum Clearance" Government of India, New Delhi, 1959.

Government of India, "The Constitution of India", Ministry of Law, New Delhi, 1967.

Government of India, "Towards Equality, Report of the Committee on the Status of Women in India", Department of Social Welfare, Ministry of Social Welfare, New Delhi, 1974.

Government of India, "Women in India" Country Paper, Ministry of Social and Women Welfare, New Delhi, 1985.

Government of India, "National Literacy Mission", MHRD, DOE, New Delhi, 1988.

Government of India, "National Perspective Plan for Women", 1988–2000, MHRD, New Delhi, 1988.

Government of India, "National Policy on Education; Programme of Action", MHRD, DOE, New Delhi, 1992.

Government of India, Planning Commission, "Mid Term Appraisal of 9th Year Plan (1997–2000), New Delhi, October-2000.

Government of India, "India, 2000 - A Reference", Annual Publication Division, Ministry of Information and Broadcasting, New Delhi, 2000.

Gore, M.S., "Women's Equality", University News, April 20, 1987.

Gore, M.S., Indian Education Structure and Process Article : Education for Women's Equality, Rawat Publication, Jaipur, 1994.

Graff, Harvey, J., "The Labyrinths of Literacy Reflection on Literacy Past and Present", The Falmer Press : London, New York and Philadelphia, 1987.

Gupta, Amit Ku. (Ed.) "Women and Society: The Developmental Perspective", Criterion Publications, New Delhi : 1986.

Halder, Saraswati, "National Policy for Women in India, 1996 : A Critique", Social Scientist, Vol. 25, No. 3–4, March-April, 1997.

Hanna Myer (Ch. ed.), "India 2001 Encyclopaedia", Ind. Mark Publishing, New Delhi, 1999.

Haptulla, Najama (ed.), "Reforms for Women; Future Options", New Delhi, Oxford and IBH Publishing Company, 1972.

Hara, Hiroko "Status of Women," in : ESCAP Population of Japan, Published the Abstracts in Women, Population and Development Abstract - Bibliography Series No.11, UNESCO Principal Regional Office for Asia & the PACIFIC, Bangkok, 1991.

Hate, C.A. (1969), "Changing Status of Women in Post Independence India", Allied Publishers, Bombay, 1969.

Heredero, J.M., "Education for Development", Manohar Book Services, New Delhi, 1989.

"Harijan", 5–6–1937, in the Collected Works of Mahatma Gandhi, New Delhi, The Publication Division, M.65, 1976.

Hug, Muhmmad Sahmsud, "Education, Man Power and Development in South East Asia", Stearling Publishers, Pvt. Ltd., New Delhi, 1975.

Hunter, N.N., ORISSA, Vol. II, 1872,

IIPAS (International Institute of Population Science) Bombay, "National Family Health Survey", ORISSA, Population Research Centre, Utkal Universtiy, Bhubaneswar, 1995.

"India, 2000 A Reference", Annual Publication Division, Ministry of Information and Broadcasting, Government of India, New Delhi, 2000.

I.U.A."Empower of Women" : Multidisciplinary Perspective. XXIII Annual Conference of Indian Universities Associations for Continuing Education, S.N.D.T. Women's University, Bombay (1989).

Jain Devaki (ed.) "Indian Women", Publication Division, Ministry of Information and Broadcasting, Government of India, New Delhi, 1975.

Jarvis, Peter, "Notion of Development and Their Implication for Adult Education", International Review of Education, UNESCO, Vol. 32, No.1, 1988.

Jena, V., "Literacy and Development", IJAE, Vol. 60, No. 2, April-June,1999.

Jogan, S. (Ed), "Social Problems and Welfare in India", Ashish Publishing House, New Delhi, 1992.

Kaur, N. "Research in Adult Education in the State of Punjab" IJAE, Vol. 61, No. 2, April-June, 2000.

Khandai, H.K. "Preparation of Manual for Developing Literature for Neo Literatures", Ph.D. Thesis in Education, Devi Ahalya University, Indore, 1993.

Kidd, J.R. and Timus C.J., "Adult Education: An Overview", in International Encyclopaedia of Education : Research and Studies, Vol. I, 1992.

Krishnaraj, M., "Women and Development", SNDT, Monograph on Sociology, Subhada Saraswati - Publication, Pune, 1988.

Kulandiswamny, V.C., "The Nature of Education" University News, Vol. 35, No. 19, May 12, 1997.

Kundu, C.L., "Adult Education Research: Future Direction", Kurukshetra, Kurukshetra University, 1987.

Laso, Biloris. Lyndem, "Women and Basic Education", SRC News, NEHU, Shillong, 1997.

Levine, Kenneth : "The Social Context of Literacy, Language, Education and Society," Rout Ledge & Kegal Paul Inc., London, 1986.

Lewis, Nonford, "The Slum and its Origin", Chapter-2,(Ed.) Desai & Pillai, Bombay, 1970.

Lind & John ston, "Adult Literacy in the Third World", Stockholm, Sida, 1990.

Mahanta Bhajan Chandra, "Mo Sangrami Jivan" P.P. Press, Rourkela, 1994.

Majumdar, Veena, "Education and Social Change," Simla, Indian Institute of Advanced Study, 1983.

Marshal, B. Clinard, "Slum and Community Development, Experiment in Self Help", Chapter-I, Toronto, 1966.

Mathew, K.M. (Ch. ed.), "Manorama Year Book", Malayala Manoroma Press, Kottayam, 1995.

Mathur M. B., "Adult Education and Social Change", Indian Publication, Ambala Cantt,1989.

MHRD, "National Literacy Mission: Action Plan, 1990-91", NLM, DOE, GOI, New Delhi, October,1990.

MHRD, "Evaluation of Literacy Campaigns in India: Report of Expert Group", NLM, DOE, New Delhi, 1994.

MHRD, "Status Report of Literacy and Post Literacy Campaign," NLM, DOE, New Delhi, July, 1994.

MHRD, Government of India, "Family Welfare Programme in India: Year Book 1996-97", Department of Family Welfare, New Delhi, 1997.

MHRD, Government of India, "Selected on School Education in India, As on 30th Sept.,1995", Planning, Monitoring and Statistical Division, New Delhi, 1997.

MHRD, Government of India, Department of Education, "Selected Educational Statistics" 1997-98, As on 30th Sept.,1997 Planning, Monitoring and Statistics, Division, New Delhi, 1999.

MHRD, Government of India, "Sarva Shiksha Abhiyan - A Discussion Document, Department of Elementary Education and Literacy", New Delhi, 2000.

Mittal, M. "Literacy for Women's Equality and Empowerment" - National Literacy Mission, Government of India, MHRD, New Delhi, 1996.

Millar, Harry, C.(Ed.) "Education for the Disadvantaged", New York, The Free Press, 1907.

Mishra, D.C.,"Development Activities, Literacy and Poverty", Journal of All India Association for Educational Research, Vol. II, No.1 and 2, March-June,1999.

Mishra, L.D., "Literacy as a Tool of Liberation and for Rural Development", Edited in the Seminar Report on "Adult Literacy and Development", India International Centre, IIC Monograph, Series No.16, New Delhi, 1981.

Mishra, Pandit, Godabarish, Godabarish Granthamala, (Autobiography), Cuttack, 1960.

Mody and Mhatre "Slum Women in Bombay" (Ed.), "Indian Women" By (ed.) Jain Devika, Publishing Division, Ministry of Information & Broadcasting, Government of India, New Delhi, 1975.

Mohanty, J. "Glimpses of Indian Women in the Freedom Struggle", Discovery Publishing House, New Delhi, 1996.

Munyakho, Dorothy, "Girls' Education in Kenya: Status, Obstacles and Challenges", Vena Journal, Vol. 6, No. 2, Dec., 1994.

Naik, S. "An Evaluation of the TLC of Betul District (Gharadongri Block) of Madhya Pradesh", Indore School of Social Work on behalf of MHRD, Government of India, New Delhi, 1994.

Nanda, S.K. "A critical Study of the Development of Adult Education in Punjab University, During the period from 1947 to 1972", Ph.D. Thesis in Education, Panjab University, Patiala, 1977.

National Commission for Women, New Delhi, "Development of Female Education among Tribal Communities" ; New Frontier in Education, Vol, XXVIII, No. 3, July-Sept.,1998.

"National Policy on Education-1986", MHRD, DOE, New Delhi, 1992.

"NPE (1968), National Policy on Education", Government of India, New Delhi, 1969.

"National Health Policy", Government of India, New Delhi, 1982.

Nayak, K. "Rourkela Darpan" Published by Arun & Tarun, Children's Literature Development Society, Rourkela, 1999.

Nayar, D.P." "Towards a National System of Education", Mittal Publication, New Delhi, 1997.

NCERT, "The Indian Year Book of Education", Second Year Book, Elementary Education, New Delhi, 1964.

NCERT, "Education and National Development; Report of the Education Commission, 1964-66", New Delhi, 1970.

NCERT, "Third All India Educational Survey", Vol.1, New Delhi, 1973.

NCERT, "Fifth All India Educational Survey, Selected Statistics", New Delhi, 1989.

NCERT, "Fifth All India Educational Survey", New Delhi, 1992.

NCERT, "Fifth Survey of Research in Education" (1988–1992), Vol.1, New Delhi, 1997.

NCERT, "Fifth Survey of Educational Research", 1988-92, Vol. II, New Delhi,2000.

NIEPA, "Education for All by 2000", Indian Perspective, New Delhi, March-1990.

NIEPA, "Sarva Shiksha Abhiyan, Report of the National Conference", New Delhi, 2000.

"NLM Report", Government of India, MHRD, New Delhi, 1988.

"NLM : Status Report-1994", MHRD, GOI, New Delhi, 1994.

"NLM, Evaluation of Literacy Campaigns; Summary Report", Vol. III, DOE, MHRD, Government of India, New Delhi, 1995.

NLM, "Concurrent Evaluation of TLC Districts", DOE, MHRD, Government of India, New Delhi, 1997.

NLM, "A People's Movement" DAE, MHRD, Government of India, New Delhi, 1997.

NLM, "Literacy: Fact at a Glance", Directorate of Adult Education, Government of India, New Delhi, 1997.

"NLM - Report (Annual), 1997-1998, Literacy Campaign in India", DAE, MHRD, Government of India, New Delhi, 1998.

NLM, "Literacy Campaigns in India, 1997-1998", DOE, MHRD, Government of India, New Delhi, 1999.

N.S.S.O. 53rd Round, Report, New Delhi, 1997.

Nuna, Sheel Chand, "Education and Development", NIEPA, New Delhi, 1987.

Nyerere, Julius, "Adult Education and Development", Journal of Adult Education and Development, German Adult Education Association, Department of International Co-operation, 1988.

O, Malley, L.S.S., "Bihar and Orissa District Gazetteer", Puri, Patna, 1812.

Palanithurai G.(ed), "Participation in the Development Process, Grass-root Experiences", Kanishka Publishers, New Delhi, 1996.

Pandey B. "Post Independence Educational Development Among Women in India", Occasional Paper No. 9, Centre for Women's Development Studies, New Delhi, 1987.

Panigrahi, S.C.," A Study of Educational Development of Tribals of KalaHandi District of Orissa", Ph.D. Thesis in Education, CASE, M.S.University, Baroda, 1992.

Parikh, G.O., "Evaluation of TLC of Amrali District", Gujarat SPIESR, Ahmedabad, 1994.

Parikh, G.O., "A Pilot Study on the TLC in Bhavnagar City, SPIESR, Ahmedabad, 1994.

Parikh, G.O., "Evaluation of TLC of Banaskantha District of Gujarat", SPIESR, Ahmedabad, 1995.

Parikh, G.O., "Evaluation of TLC of Baroda City", SPIESR, Ahmedabad,1995.

Parikh, G.O., "Evaluation of TLC in the District of Rajkot of Gujarat State", SPIESR, Ahmedabad, 1995.

Parmeshwaran, M.P., "A Participatory Democracy Seminar, New Delhi, No. 438, Feb.,1996.

Patel, Tara, "Development of Education Among Tribal Women", Mittal Publishing, Delhi, 1984.

Patel, Surabhi, "Educational Facilities for the Children of Urban Slums in Delhi", Ph.D. Thesis in Education, CASE, M.S.University, Baroda, 1978.

Patnaik, S., "Sambad Patrikaru Orissara Katha", 1856–1881, Cuttack, 1972.

Phillips, H.M., "Literacy and Development", Paris, UNESCO, 1970.

Prasad, Preeti, "TLC Campaign in Ernakulum District, An Evaluation", NCERT Journal, Vol. 20, No. 3, September,1994.

Premchand, "Statistical Debate for Literacy", Vol. II, Final Population and Literacy, 1991, National Institute of Adult Education, 1993.

Premchand, "Statistical Data Base For Literacy, Final Population and Literacy"- 1991, Vol. 2, National Institute of Adult Education, New Delhi, 1993.

Premi, Mahendra. K., "India's Population : Heading Towards a Billion; Analysis of 1991 Census, Provisional Reports", B.R. Publishing Corporation, Delhi, 1991.

"Proceedings: International Women's Conference - Women's Status : Vision & Reality", New Delhi, Feb., 27 - March 3, 2000.

Pushpanadham, K. "Sarva Shikha Abhiyan: A period of transition for Universalisation of Elementary Education," Seminar Paper Presented in the National Seminar on "Prespectives in School Education", 26-27, Feb., 2001, CASE, M.S.University, Baroda, 2001.

Ranjan, K.R., "Mass Literacy; The Ernakulum Experiment," The Ernakulum Distric Literacy Society, Ernakulum, 1991.

Rajan, T.S. Sundar, "NLM The Mission For All", Published by Deptt. of Education, MHRD, Government of India, New Delhi,1994.

Rajput, J.S., "Emerging Global Consciousness", Hindustan Times, March, 28, 1996.

Rangrej, Jahanara, : "A Study of the Schooling of Female Children in the Gayatri Nagar Slum Area of Baroda City," M.Ed Dissertation, CASE, M.S.University of Baroda, 1998.

Rao V.K.R.V. - "Education and Human Resource Development", Allied Publishers, New Delhi, 1966.

Rao, D.B., Pushpalata, D. & Harshik D., (Ed.) "Women as Educator" Discovery Publishing House, New Delhi, 2001.

Ray, J., "Problems of Girls Education in Dhenkanal District of ORISSA" Indian Educational Abstract, NCERT, New Delhi, Issue-3, July, 1997.

"Report of the Female Education, Bihar", Orissa Gazetter, Cuttack, Patna, Government Press, 1933.

"Report of the Education Commission 1964-66", Ministry of Education, Government of India, New Delhi, 1966.

"Report of the National Seminar on Qualitative and Quantitative approaches in Educational Research", CASE, M.S.University, Baroda, March 16-18, 1983.

"UGC Report, Report of the Review Committee", Appointed by University Grant Commission, New Delhi, UGC, 1987.

"Report of the National Seminar" at Bhubaneswar, ORISSA, March-1991, Tents of Women's Learning, Institute for Socio-economic Development, Bhubaneswar, March, 1991.

"Report of the Evaluation of TLC in Sundargarh District", 1993, Tribal & Harijan Research-cum-Training Institute, Bhubaneswar, 1993.

"Report on Literacy Development of the State", SRC, ORISSA, Bhubaneswar, 1995.

Rogers, Barbara, "The Domestication of Women Discrimination in Developing Societies", Tavistock Publication, London & New York, 1980.

Roy, Kum Kum, "Women in Early Indian Societies", Kumkum Roy (ed.), Manohar Publication, New Delhi,1999.

Ruskin, John : "Ruskin's Views of Social Justice", (Ed.) & Introduction by James Fuche, Vanguard Press, New York, 1926.

Thakur, L., "Socio economic Status of Slum Women", Social Change: Vol. 18, No. 3, September,1988.

Toynbee, O., "A Sketch of the History of Orissa" 1803–1828, Part-III, Reprinted in O.H.R.J., Vol. IX, No. 32.

Sachidananda, and Sinha, R.P., "Women's Rights : Myth and Reality", Jaipur, Print Well Publication,1983.

Sahu, N.K., "Buddism in Orissa", Published Ph.D. Thesis, approved by Utkal University, Orissa Mission Press, Cuttack, 1958.

Sabina, John, "Slum Children" with special reference to slums in Delhi, M.S.W. Dissertation, Indore School of Social Work, Indore, 1991.

Salvam, S., "Researches in Adult Education", IJAE, Vol. 44, No. 6, June,1983.

"Sambad Bahika", 15th Part, 17070, No. 29, Balasore, 1880.

Sapru, R.K., "Women and Development", Ashish Publishing House, New Delhi, 1989.

Seetharamu, A.S., "Education in Slums," Ashish Publishing House, New Delhi, 1983.

Seetharamu A.S., "Literacy Campaign in India", A.P.H. Publishing Corporation, Delhi, 1997.

Senapati, Fakirmohan, "Fakirmohan Granthabali", Radhanath Co-operative Press, Cuttack, 1927.

Senapati, N., "Orissa District - Gazatters, Bolangir, Koraput, Mayurbhanj", Cuttack , 1967.

Sengupta, P., "The story of Women in India", New Delhi, 1974.

Seth, P., "India A Traveller's Companion", Sterling Publishing, Private Limited, New Delhi, 1988.

Seth, M., "Development Sans Literacy: Unsustainable", IJAE, Vol. 58, No.1, Jan-March,1997.

Shah, A.. "A critical Study of the Programmes of Non-Formal Education in Baroda City and their Impact on the Community", Ph.D. Thesis, CASE, M.S.U., Baroda, 1978.

Shah, S.Y., "Indian Adult Education : A Historical Perspective", Directorate of Adult Education, MHRD, Government of India, New Delhi, 1995.

Shah, S.Y. (ed), "Encyclopaedia of Adult Education", NLM, MHRD, GOI, New Delhi, 1999.

Sharma, O.P., "Universal Literacy - A Distance Dream" Karkrupa Publishers, New Delhi, 1994.

Sharma U., & Sharma B.M. (Ed.), "Women Education in British India", Women and Development Series-4,Commonwealth Publishers, New Delhi, 1995.

Shirdhonkar, J., "Women's Participation in Urban Community Development" - with Special reference to Indore Habitate, M.S.W., Dissertation, Indore School of Social Work, Indore, 1992.

Sharama S., "Report of National Commission on Self-Employed Women and Women in the Informal Sector"- Ahmedabad, (SEWA), New Delhi, 1989.

Siddiqui, S. Sultana Hazarika, "Impact of Rural Functional Literacy Programme of Jorhat District of Assam"., Ph.D. in Extension Education, M.S.University of Baroda, Baroda, 1989.

Siddiqui, M.H., "Women Education : A Research Approach", Ashish Publishing House, New Delhi, 1993.

Singh, Andrea, Menefee Desouza Alfred, "The Urban Poor" Manohar Publication, New Delhi,1980.

Singh, Cheema, H.P. & Bawa, S.K., "Research in Adult Education " A review, Indian Journal of Psychometry and Education, Vol. 29, No. 2, July, 1998.

Singh, D. C., "A critical Study of Adult Education Programme in the State of U.P." Ph.D. Thesis in Education, CASE, M.S.University, Baroda, 1982.

Singh, M., "Impact of Adult Education Programme on Modernization," DAE, MHRD, New Delhi, 1997.

Singh, S., "History of Adult Education During British Period," IAWA, Delhi, 1957.

Singh, S., "Social Education: Concept and Method", Orient Longman, New Delhi, 1964.

Singh, T., "Literacy in Women's Development" IJAE, Vol. 57, No. 2, April-June,1996.

Sisodia, D.S. & Chauhan, V.L., "Female Literacy : Changing Attitudes", Asian Journal of Psychology and Education, Vol. 32, No. 7-8, Dec.,1999.

Sood, S. (ed)., "Violence - Against Women", Arihant Publishers, Jaipur, 1990.

Sounarapandian, M., "Women Entrepreneurship - Issues and Strategies", Kanishka Publishers, Distributors, New Delhi, 1999.

SRC for Adult Education, ORISSA, Bhubaneswar, "Women and Society", 1995.

Srivastava, N.K., and Ramshankar., "Impact of Adult Education on Scheduled Caste Women" : IJAE, Vol. 53, No. 2, April-June.

Srivastava, G., "Women's Higher Education in the 19th Century", Concept Publishing Company, New Delhi, 2000.

"Status Report of the Enrolment Figures of Students in Primary and Upper Primary Schools", Office of the D.I. of Schools, Rourkela, 1998-99.

"Status Report: Rourkela Total Literacy Campaign and Post Literacy Campaign", As on 30th Oct., 95 to 30th Nov., 96. Rourkela Saksharata Samiti, 1996.

Sudame, G.R., "Qualitative Research Methods- Some Issue": Published in "Research Methodology" by CASE, M.S.University, Baroda, 2000.

Sukla, S., "Literacy and Development: Retrospect and Trends", Perspective in Education, Vol.7, No. 3, 1991.

S.V.P., "Status Report of Shramik Vidyapith", Rourkela (Unpublished), 1998.

UNDP, "Human Development Report", Oxford University Press, 1981.

UNDP, "Human Development Report", Oxford University Press, 1993.

UNDP, "Human Development Report", New Delhi, Oxford University Press, 1994.

UNDP, "Human Development Report ", Oxford University Press,1995.

UNDP, "Human Development Report", Oxford University Press, New York,1996..

UNESCO ; "Progress of Literacy in Various Countries" : A Preliminary Statistical Study of Available Census Data Since - 1900, Paris, 1953.

UNESCO, "World Conference of Minister of Education on the Eradication of Illiteracy: Final Report", Paris, UNESCO, 1965.

UNESCO, "Teheran Congress: Speeches and Messages", Paris, 1966.

UNESCO, (1972–76), "Progress Achieved in Literacy Throughout the World–1980", Paris,1980.

UNESCO, "Adult Education in Asia and Pacific" Bankok, 1982.

UNESCO, "The Current Literacy Situation in the World", Paris, 1987.

UNESCO, "World Education Report", Oxford University, Paris, 1995.

Utkal Dipika, 4th Part, Cuttack, 20-2-1869.

Utkal Dipika., 8th Part, Cuttack, 28-3-1873.

Utkal Dipika, Vol. 65, Cuttack, 1930.

Utkal Sahitya, No. 1344-45, Utkal Sahitya Press, Cuttack, 1930.

Vaidyanathan, "Unicef Co-operation in Women's Development: Women's Development Problems and Prospects" (Ed.) Shamin, Aleem, APH Publishing Corporation, New Delhi, 1996.

Vanka, S., "Education for All: the Problem of Dropouts Among Women Learners in the Hyderabad District", IJAE, Vol. 56, No.4, Oct.-Dec.,1995.

Vena : Journal, "The Girl Child", Vol. 6, No. 2, December,1994.

Verma R., "Social Work in India", New Delhi, Sage, 1990.

Wagner, D., "The Future of Literacy in a Changing World," Pergamon Press, Oxford, 1987.

Webster, A. Merriam, "Webster's New Collegiate Dictionary", G & C Marriam Co., Publishers, Springfield, U.S.A., 1936.

Wood, Despatch, (Ed.) in J.A. Richeyt (Ed.) Selections from Educational Records 1840–1859, (Delhi, National Archieves of India, 1965), Vol. II, 1965.

World Bank, "India Reducing Poverty, Accelerating Development : A World Bank Country Study", Oxford, 2000.

"World Development Report", Oxford, 1988.

"World Development Report" , Oxford, 1991.

Yadav, S.K., "Education of Scheduled Caste," Commonwealth Publishers, New Delhi, 1999.

INDEX